Scott MacDonald

The Garden
in the Machine

A Field Guide to Independent Films about Place

UNIVERSITY OF CALIFORNIA PRESS

BERKELEY
LOS ANGELES
LONDON

University of California Press
Berkeley and Los Angeles, California

University of California Press, Ltd.
London, England

© 2001 by the Regents of the University of California

Earlier versions of several chapters, or portions of
chapters, have been published previously; the later
versions are reprinted here by permission: "The Garden in
the Machine," in *Prospects* 22 (1997): 239–62; "Voyages
of Life," in *Wide Angle* 18, no. 2 (April 1996): 101–26;
"Re-envisioning the American West," in *American Studies*
39, no. 1 (spring 1998): 115–46; "From the Sublime to the
Vernacular," in *Film Quarterly* 53, no. 1 (fall 1999): 12–25;
portions of the "The City as Motion Picture," in *Film
Quarterly* 51, no. 2 (winter 1997–98): 2–20, and in *Wide
Angle* 19, no. 4 (October 1997): 109–30; and "The Country
in the City," in *Journal of American Studies* 31, no. 3 (winter
1997): 337–60.

Library of Congress Cataloging-in-Publication Data

MacDonald, Scott, 1942–
    The Garden in the machine : a field guide to inde-
pendent films about place / Scott MacDonald.
        p.   cm.
    Includes bibliographical references and index.
    ISBN 0–520-22737-9 (cloth : alk. paper). —
    ISBN 0–520-22738-7 (pbk. : alk. paper)
    1. Experimental films — History and criticism.
2. Motion pictures — Setting and scenery.   I. Title.

PN1995.9.E96 M344   2001
791.43' — dc21   2001027877
                                                CIP

Manufactured in Canada
10   09   08   07   06   05   04   03   02   01
10   9   8   7   6   5   4   3   2   1

For Patricia Reichgott O'Connor—
lover, partner, family, advisor, witness—
this book begins and ends with you.

We have advanced by leaps to the Pacific, and left many a lesser Oregon and California unexplored behind us.

HENRY DAVID THOREAU, *THE MAINE WOODS*

Contents

Illustrations

Figures

Introduction

But there do come certain moments in the history of a community when people can look around and say, "Well, here we are. What's next?" We have arrived at such a pause for clarification and decision in Vermont. Our providential wilderness cannot be taken for granted today. Because for a century we stood outside America's economic mainstream, our region's nonhuman community enjoyed a rare opportunity to recover. But in this new era of telecommunications, when business is no longer so closely tied to major manufacturing centers, there will be no more security for beautiful backwaters. Unless we find the will to protect the North Mountains of our state— as terrain in which selective logging, human recreation, and wildlife can coexist— we could lose within just a few seasons the balance that has grown up here.

JOHN ELDER, *READING THE MOUNTAINS OF HOME*

The Garden in the Machine is the result of two explorations, one more obviously professional, the other more obviously personal; or to be more precise, the eleven essays that follow are the product of a decade-long intersection of these two explorations. Since the late 1970s, nearly all of my scholarly and critical energies, and a substantial portion of my pedagogical energy, have been devoted to what is variously termed "avant-garde film," "independent film," "experimental film" (in recent years, I have included "video art" as well): that immense world of alternative media that has developed generally outside the commercial histories of the movies and television and remains outside the awareness of both the mass audience and most teachers, critics, and scholars of media, the humanities, and cultural studies. I have found the many and varied achievements of this alternative media history endlessly stimulating and rewarding—and, in pedagogical contexts, remarkably invigorating. Indeed, one of contemporary academe's most stunning paradoxes is that, in an era when "media literacy" is so crucial and alternatives to conventional consumer culture so necessary, this unparalleled pedagogical resource is generally ignored.

The second exploration began as a personal response to my local circumstances, although in recent years it has become more fully a part of my serious research. Early in my forties, during the conventional midlife crisis, I came to realize not only that I had spent fifteen years in central New York—twelve more than I had expected or planned—but that I was likely to spend many more years here. Central New York was becoming "my place," seemingly without my conscious participation. I decided, of course, to "make the best of it" and did so by finding my way into the Adirondacks and Catskills, and into the cultural history of the region. The more I learned about upstate New York, the more interested I became not only in this place but in places in general, in all their specificity and interconnectedness. Inevitably, given my professional commitments, my developing interest in history and geography came to include—came to focus on—the history and geography of the *depiction* of place, in literature, painting (see fig. 1), and photography and especially in film and video.

Because many of the most inventive, evocative, and stimulating—even the most beautiful—twentieth-century depictions of place, particularly American place, are found in alternative films and videos and because nearly all these works remain unknown to most of those likely to find them interesting and useful, a book on some of the more remarkable and the issues they raise seemed called for. Further, because many of these works pose challenges to viewers, especially viewers coming upon them for the first time with expecta-

Figure 1. Frederic Edwin Church's *Sunset* (1856), oil on canvas, 24" × 36", one of the gems of the Proctor Collection at the Munson-Williams-Proctor Arts Institute, Museum of Art, Utica, New York.

tions developed by commercial media, some detailed contextualization and in-depth analysis seemed essential.

This book was written during a moment when the idea of interdisciplinary study has been increasingly exciting to a good many academics. My hope is that *The Garden in the Machine* will work across traditional academic boundaries: in other words, it should serve not only the field of film studies, but those many other sectors of academe involved with the idea and the depiction of place. Specifically, I have contextualized my discussions of particular films and videos in ways that, if I have chosen well, should demonstrate their relevance for American studies, for art history, and for environmental studies, most obviously—and with luck for other disciplines as well.

The order of the eleven essays, in addition to reflecting the progress of my thinking about the films and videos I discuss, has a certain rough trajectory. The first three chapters use developments in the visual arts during the nineteenth century, and earlier, as a context for films that engage the idea of original American nature and its depiction as wilderness or as pastoral. Chapters 4 and 5 focus on the exploration of the American West, in early and contemporary times. Chapters 6, 7, and 8 explore the development of the modern city and the city film, and ways of responding culturally and cinematically to the stresses of urban experience. Chapters 9 and 10 focus on critiques of romantic ideas about country and city. *The Garden in the Machine* concludes with a discussion of films that offer some sense of recovery from the lost innocence explored in "Expulsion from the Garden" (chap. 9) and "Satan's National Park" (chap. 10). I could not resist arranging the chapters "topographically": chapter 6, "The City as Motion Picture," focuses on urban spaces and is surrounded by chapters that focus on rural spaces or intersections of the rural and the urban.

The prose style of *The Garden in the Machine* is meant to be as accessible to students and general readers as to scholars and faculty, and to recognize several crucial practical realities, the most obvious of which is that most readers will be unfamiliar with most of the films and videos I discuss. This means that a certain amount of description of the works—both their physical nature (how they look and sound, their timing) and the viewing experience they create—is inevitable, although I have attempted to hold such description to a minimum and, where possible, to enhance the reader's sense of these works with visual imagery. The introductory mission of the book precludes anything like a thorough review of the critical histories of the films and videos I discuss— although, of course, I provide access to relevant sources for those in film studies and those in other fields interested in a more complex understanding of the critical history of these works. A detailed list of sources for the films and videos discussed is also included.

It will be obvious to my colleagues in film studies that my survey is anything but exhaustive. Certainly, I am aware of a good many films and videos that might have been included in my discussions; and no doubt, there are many relevant works I am not yet acquainted with. I have attempted to discuss a sufficient number of works to demonstrate the accomplishment and potential of the larger field my selections represent. If I have been successful, others will be drawn toward a more thorough exploration.

The obvious American bias of my discussions is certainly not meant to denigrate the accomplishments of those working in other areas of the world who have explored issues of place. For example, over the past generation a considerable body of film and video about landscape and cityscape has been produced in the United Kingdom. Clearly, Chris Welsby's films could sustain a lengthy discussion; and he is one of many. And Canadian filmmakers and videomakers have frequently explored issues I discuss. Michael Snow (*La région centrale* [1971], *Seated Figures* [1989]) and Joyce Wieland (*La raison avant la passion* [1969]) are particularly noteworthy instances.

Some readers may feel that my decision to focus on only a few American commercial films and even fewer documentaries is unfortunate. Why give several pages to *Twister* (1969) and only cursory mention to John Ford? Indeed, where is the whole history of the Western? Why not discuss Terence Malick's *Badlands* (1973) and *Days of Heaven* (1978)? What about all the documentary filmmakers who have represented American landscape and cityscape: Robert Flaherty, Willard Van Dyke, Pare Lorentz, Frederick Wiseman, Errol Morris, Sarah Elder/Leonard Kamerling . . . ? And those familiar with the history of video will wonder how I could include Ellen Spiro and George Kuchar but not Bill Viola and Mary Lucier. I can only hope that the discussions I *have* included in *The Garden in the Machine* are useful enough to justify the many obvious limits of my survey. That there *are* so many limits, of course, is inspiration for further explorations.

One thing, however, is already certain: whatever the extent or limitations in my coverage of independent cinema, my enterprise is constricted in another, far graver sense. Despite their remarkable visual and conceptual accomplishments and their virtually incomparable pedagogical value, the majority of the films explored in *The Garden in the Machine* (all those other than the commercial features and the documentaries) are instances of an endangered cinematic species. Because these films have been so consistently underutilized, their economic viability is seriously in jeopardy. When film rentals are not adequate, new 16mm prints cannot be struck, and the remaining prints suffer more and more damage. To cite one example of the extent of this problem: as this is written, so far as I know, only one good print of Larry Gottheim's *Horizons* (1973), the focus of chapter 2, remains available, and that print is showing signs of wear.

A related problem involves the increasing reliance of so many academic institutions on video and other new technologies and the atrophy of first-rate 16mm screening conditions. The overwhelming majority of the films I discuss were made in 16mm for exhibition in a public space where good 16mm projection is possible. Not only are these films generally unavailable in any format other than 16mm, but even if there were money for transfer from 16mm to video, laser disk, or DVD, so much of their visual subtlety might be lost that the transfer would be pointless (and, in any case, each new format seems to have a shorter life span than the one it replaces). Of course, the lure of the new technologies for academics is that once a new system is in place, the cost of buying or renting videos (or laser disks . . .) of films is far less than the cost of renting 16mm prints. The corollary is that those films available only in 16mm tend to be forgotten. The irony is that there is no necessity in this increasingly pervasive pattern. My experience as a teacher at a variety of academic institutions tells me that the resources for renting 16mm prints are nearly always available; I believe any dedicated teacher can raise the necessary rental money. And so long as prints are regularly rented, new prints can be struck, and the 16mm experience of the films can continue.

A central mission of *The Garden in the Machine* is to draw increased attention to that larger body of 16mm film represented by the films I discuss. If those academic disciplines that can profit from this body of work, and those creative exhibitors with the capability of presenting 16mm film effectively, can recognize that a major resource is currently being ignored—wasted—this remarkable cultural accomplishment may continue to invigorate lovers of the moving image for generations to come. If I can play a small role in this process, I will feel well rewarded.

In researching and writing *The Garden in the Machine,* I have had the assistance of a good many people.

Most obviously, the artists whose work is the subject of these essays have been entirely responsive to and supportive of my efforts, making their films and videos, their personal archives, and their time and energy available to me. I have also had consistent support from distributors of avant-garde film and video: most consistently, Canyon Cinema in San Francisco (Dominic Angerame and David Sherman assisted me at every turn) and the Filmmakers' Cooperative in New York (M. M. Serra was consistently patient and generous with me); but also Video Data Bank in Chicago (who shared its collection of George Kuchar tapes with me) and Women Make Movies (thanks to Debbie Zimmerman). Archivists at several major film archives made work available to me and assisted with illustrations: thanks especially to Robert Haller at Anthology Film Archives, to Rosemary C. Hanes at the Library of Congress, to Charles Silver at the Museum of Modern Art Film Study Center and Terry Geesken at the Film Stills Archive, and to Kathy Geritz and Steve Seid at the Pacific Film Archive.

I also had the good fortune to be able to attend two National Endowment for the Humanities Summer Institutes for College and University Faculty, both of them designed and hosted by H. Daniel Peck at Vassar College. The first, "Hudson River Valley Images and Texts: Constructing a National Culture in Nineteenth-Century America," was held during June–July 1993, while I was in the beginning stages of the project—it could not have come at a better time for me. This institute was a group process, and I am indebted to all those who contributed to the experience, though I was assisted in quite specific ways by Dan Peck, Charles Colbert, Wayne C. Franklin, Patrick McGreevy, Angela Miller, Bruce Richardson, and Don Scheese. The second institute, "The Environmental Imagination: Issues and Problems in American Nature Writing," came midway in my writing and helped energize me to complete *The Garden in the Machine.* This institute too was a group process (my thanks to all who participated), but I owe a particular debt, again, to Dan Peck and Wayne Franklin and to Ralph Black, Lawrence Buell, Douglas Burton-Christie, Karen Cole, Janice Simon, H. Lewis Ulman, Monica Weis, and Ning Yu.

During August 1996 I attended the Robert Flaherty Film Seminar, "Landscapes and Place," curated by Ruth Bradley, Kathy High, and Loretta Todd, and found it a valuable experience. Ruth Bradley, who has edited *Wide Angle* in recent years, also contributed to this project by providing me with the opportunity to edit "Movies Before Cinema," two special issues of *Wide Angle* (vol. 18, nos. 2, 3) devoted to forms of motion picture that predate the invention of cinema. I am grateful for her patience and support.

Several colleagues—Patricia R. O'Neill (at Hamilton College), Paul D. Schweizer (at the Munson-Williams-Proctor Arts Institute in Utica, New York), P. Adams Sitney (at Princeton University), and Patricia R. Zimmermann (at Ithaca College)—generously took time to provide valuable suggestions for revision. And other colleagues—Steve Anker (at the San Francisco Cinematheque), Mary Lea Bandy (at the Museum of Modern Art), Cindy Booth and Michael Schuyler (librarians at the Munson-Williams-Proctor Arts Institute), Frank Bergmann (at Utica College), Ed Dimendberg (at the University of Michigan), R. Bruce Jenkins (now at the Harvard Film Archive), Ann Martin (editor, *Film Quarterly*), Angela Miller (at Washington University, St. Louis), Marie Nesthus (at the Donnell Public Library in New York), Barbara Ras (at the University of Georgia Press), and Scott Slovic (editor, *Interdisciplinary Studies in Literature and Environment*)—as well as a number of my students at Utica College and Hamilton College (especially Joe Cintron, Ben Couch, Kyle Harris, Christian Tico, and Carl Wohnsen) and my neighbor, Terry Grimmer Krumbach, provided crucial forms of intellectual, moral, and practical support. My typist, Carol Fobes, worked tirelessly on revision after revision of chapter after chapter and never lost patience with me.

I have also had the support of family and friends, especially Ian MacDonald, Edward Burg and Annie la Salla Burg, Art Burg, LaMoss Messinger, and Larry Platt.

Earlier versions of several chapters, or portions of chapters, have been published previously, and these publications are listed on the copyright page. I am grateful for permission to reprint these essays.

chapter 1

The Garden in the Machine

Two American Avant-Garde Films and the
Nineteenth-Century Visual Arts

The image of the railroad on the shore of the pond figures an ambiguity at the heart of *Walden*. Man-made
power, the machine with its fire, smoke, and thunder,
is juxtaposed to the waters of Walden, remarkable for
their depth and purity and a matchless, indescribable
color—now light blue, now green, almost always pellu-
cid. The iron horse moves across the surface of the
earth; the pond invites the eye below the surface. The
contrast embodies both the hope and the fear aroused
by the impending climax of America's encounter with
wild nature.

LEO MARX, *THE MACHINE IN THE GARDEN*

I

One of the primary reasons I became interested in film studies was the seeming open-endedness of the field. Cinema was *new*, I reasoned, and would continue to be new, unlike other academic fields, particularly those devoted to historical periods: as a scholar and a teacher, I would face the future, endlessly enthralled and energized by the transformation of the potential into the actual. That my development as a film scholar-teacher increasingly involved me in "avant-garde film" seemed quite natural—a logical extension of the attraction of film studies in general: avant-garde film was the newest of the new, the sharpest edge of the present as it sliced into the promise of the future.[1] Scholars in some fields may empathize with the attitude I describe, but scholars in all fields will smile at its self-defeating implications. Of course, I can see now how "typically American" my assumptions were—as if one could maintain the excitement of youth merely by refusing to acknowledge the past! Obviously, film studies, like any other discipline, is only a field once its history takes, or is given, a recognizable shape.

My particular belated recognition of the obvious developed in a fashion that, I believe, has considerable utility for several academic fields that are usually thought of as roughly distinct from one another: film studies, American studies, environmental studies, and art history. Indeed, my fascination with avant-garde cinema has led me relentlessly into the past—and not simply into the past of film history, but back beyond the invention and development of modern cinema, into forms of image making that many film scholars, and other cultural historians, might consider peripheral to cinema, at best. I have become increasingly fascinated by a considerable number of modern American independent films that, by both accident and design, have invigorated traditions of thought and image-making generally thought to characterize the nineteenth century. While there are various topics that could be used to demonstrate how the "avant-garde" has become the "old-fashioned" and vice versa, the most fertile of these topics (if the reader can forgive the pun) is the American landscape.

The importance of the landscape in American cultural history hardly needs comment at this late date: landscape was a dominant issue in American painting and writing throughout the nineteenth century and, as a wealth of cultural commentary suggests, has remained crucial throughout this century, as the nineteenth-century fascination with "wilderness" and "nature" increasingly gave way, first, to a focus on cityscape and city life and, more recently, to a fascination with the forms of human signification that, in our postmodernist period, are the inevitable overlay of both countryside and city. What is often overlooked as this cultural trajectory is charted, however, is that earlier fascinations do not simply disappear; often they are taken so much for granted that, in effect, our consciousness of them becomes repressed: their very obviousness tends to render them invisible.

It may seem apparent that the nineteenth century's obsession with representing "wilderness" and the pastoral "middle state" had become anathema to most artists and art lovers by the early years of the twentieth century as modernism gathered momentum, but this certainly doesn't mean that the representation of wild and rural landscape disappeared from the arts. Any trip to a local art and craft show will reveal that landscape, in the most traditional senses, remains a central issue for many painters and photographers. And, more important for this discussion, any exposure to modern cinema makes clear that the American landscape—in both the broadest sense of the term and in the more particular and traditional sense of the depiction of wild and rural scenes—is virtually indispensable to film pleasure. This is especially obvious in the Western, of course, but is true of all commercial genres. These days, art lovers may be less likely to go to galleries and museums to see wild and rural scenes than art enthusiasts of earlier centuries, but they do see depictions of such scenes all the time.

Of course, that visions of landscape are crucial to many popular films doesn't mean that popular filmmakers are engaged with the complex, sophisticated discourse about landscape that developed in and around nineteenth-century American landscape painting and writing. That discourse may seem virtually defunct, except in the work of scholars, even if vestiges of the original forms are apparent in popular film. But here too a cultural repression is involved, though of a different sort. Many of the most intellectually interesting engagements with American landscape in modern American cinema have been occurring in the work of filmmakers who work independently of mainstream commercial cinema.

That late-twentieth-century independent filmmakers often share an interest in landscape with nineteenth-century artists and writers is less surprising than it may seem, once one considers the development of American independent film and the emergence of academic film studies during the 1960s and 1970s. For a good many filmmakers coming to maturity during those decades, a broad and penetrating cultural critique was essential. This critique was often directed at the commercialism of Hollywood, which was seen as a particularly visible index of the increasingly rampant materialism of capitalist culture. The arrival of commercial television as the preeminent national entertainment was causing the declining pop film industry to be at least as desperately commercial as it had ever been, and this desperation was reflected in an increasing tendency toward visual and auditory overload, the apparent assumption being that the only way to maintain the audience that still went to movie theaters, and to win back some of those who were no longer paying admission, was to provide consumers with more and more to consume: larger images and more of them per minute, more visceral violence, and more overt sexuality. For many filmmakers working outside the Industry and wanting to critique it, the fundamental question was how to develop a film practice that worked against the demands of the commercial and against this increasing tendency toward overload—and where to go for inspiration.

One set of answers developed along with, and in part because of, the academization of film studies. Inevitably, the development of cinema as a field of study catalyzed a new awareness of those whose "primitive" contributions to the rhetoric of cinema had been left behind as the industry developed the commercial feature as its most marketable form: the earliest filmmakers (Edison, the Lumière Brothers, Edwin S. Porter, George Méliès) and the motion photographers who preceded them, especially Eadweard Muybridge; and the tradition of image making and audience development that cinema's pioneers and original audiences inherited, including the "Great Pictures" of Frederic Church, Albert Bierstadt, and Thomas Moran, the landscape and sequential paintings of Thomas Cole (see plate 1; figs. 3–6), the still and moving panoramas of John Banvard and others, Louis Daguerre's Diorama, and Philippe Jacques de Loutherbourg's Eidophusikon.[2]

This new awareness of early cinema and precinema image making catalyzed a considerable body of work produced by filmmakers teaching or studying at academic institutions who were attempting to begin anticommercial filmmaking careers. Two instances of this body of work are Larry Gottheim's *Fog Line* (1970) and J. J. Murphy's *Sky Blue Water Light Sign* (1972). That neither of these films, or the names of their makers, will be familiar to most scholars and teachers outside film studies is, unfortunately, to be expected. While everyone understands the importance of the commercial cinema in the evolution of modern American culture, the remarkable contributions of the wide world of independent cinema (the extent of this history is suggested by the proliferation of names that have been used in connection with it: avant-garde film, underground film, abstract film, experimental film, the New American Cinema . . .) remains outside the awareness of most scholars and teachers—largely because of the general failure of film historians to bridge the gaps between the developing field of film studies and other academic disciplines. My decision to focus the following discussion on two, relatively brief films is a function not only of the perceptual impact and conceptual density of these particular films but also of their remarkable utility for teachers. Few films can create as much energy in a classroom as *Fog Line* and *Sky Blue Water Light Sign*, both of which are effective instigators of a wide-ranging discussion of the relationship between contemporary media practice and viewership and nineteenth- and twentieth-century cultural development. My hope is that my discussion will tempt some of those who teach and write American studies, environmental studies, and art history not only to try including these two films in their curricula and their scholarly deliberations, but to see an exploration of the full range of American independent cinema as vital to their, and their students', sense of American culture.

Gottheim made *Fog Line* soon after arriving at the State University of New York at Binghamton, having completed his Ph.D. in comparative literature at Yale; Murphy made *Sky Blue Water Light Sign* when he was a graduate student in cinema at the University of Iowa. Like the Lumière Brothers (and the Edison Studio), Gottheim and Murphy limited each of their earliest films to a single shot, made with the camera mounted on a tripod. For the Lumières, this procedure must have seemed quite obvious: having developed a successful business as manufacturers of still cameras before inventing their Cinématographe, they must have felt it sufficient to surprise the first Cinématographe audiences with photographs-in-motion. For Gottheim and Murphy, it seemed equally obvious to model their first steps toward a new film praxis on what they understood as their cinematic fathers' first steps. Of course, the seventy-five-year gap between the invention of cinema and these young academic filmmakers' entry into filmmaking is as obvious as their indebtedness to the Lumières. The early Lumière films were fifty seconds long (seventeen meters), long enough to reveal the subject-in-motion, but not so long as to bore the Cinématographe audience. The Lumières' goal was commercial: they needed to demonstrate the flexibility of the new technology. While their films were one shot long, even the earliest public Cinématographe shows in Paris included multiple films on a variety of topics, many of which, in 1895–96, would have been considered reasonably exciting, or amusing, or impressive: large groups of soldiers marching, a train arriving at a station, the demolition of a wall by construction workers (also presented in reverse) . . . And these single-shot views were presented one after the other without the intervention of the individual titles that were to become standard later, when the Lumière films were shown to film society and academic audiences. In other words, the early Cinématographe presentations were essentially advertisements, and their structure prefigures the barrage strategy of modern television commercials.

For Gottheim and Murphy, however, the salient fact was the simplicity and directness of the Lumière imagery; and from their position in the early 1970s, this simplicity and directness seemed a useful weapon in the service of an anticommercial aesthetic. They chose unusually "simple" subjects—a foggy, early-morning, rural landscape near Gottheim's home in Binghamton, New York, for *Fog Line;* and for *Sky Blue Water Light Sign,* the wilderness scene revealed by a light sign used to advertise Hamm's Beer in bars (the slogan for Hamm's was and is "from the land of sky blue waters"). And they extended the duration of their fixed-camera gaze on these subjects well beyond the early Lumière films: *Fog Line* lasts ten and a half minutes; *Sky Blue Water Light Sign,* eight and a half minutes.[3]

While the commercial industry can be said to have developed the visceral excitement of the first Cinématographe shows and their commercial purpose, Gottheim, Murphy, and others developed precisely those dimensions of the

Lumière films that, seventy-five years later, had come to seem least commercial and most primitive. Paradoxically, they became "avant-garde" filmmakers by accessing topics and themes that were more characteristic of the decades that preceded the invention of the Cinématographe than of their own time. Most obviously, *Fog Line* and *Sky Blue Water Light Sign* are "landscape films"; images of landscape are all we see in both films.

In the early 1970s the decision to focus on landscape alone for an extended duration—in both films there is a variety of evidence of human presence but no characters or human action—was distinctive, even radical; and, from my experience presenting the two films, it continues to feel at least as distinctive and radical for most viewers. In fact, as serene as both films can seem—once one allows that the filmmakers' minimalist tactics are legitimate—many viewers who see the films now are at least mildly annoyed, and some are angry: both filmmakers seem *not to mind* that their films are "boring."

That viewers have been trained, and have trained themselves, to feel that landscape is not a legitimate subject for even a ten-minute film experience provides us with a measure of how different our sensibilities are from those of art lovers of a previous century. Indeed, when I ask viewers immediately after a screening of *Fog Line* what they've just seen, a frequent response is a sardonic "Nothing!" Without overt human characterization and plot, contemporary film viewers are virtually blind to imagery and issues that fascinated artists and audiences alike during the nineteenth century, and they are blind regardless of the considerable visual subtlety and conceptual density of both films.

At this point, I must discuss *Fog Line* and *Sky Blue Water Light Sign* individually, for although they are similar in their makers' implicit defiance of late-twentieth-century taste and in their general affirmation of the nineteenth century's interest in landscape, the two films are worlds apart in their specifics—not only in the obvious sense that Gottheim's film presents a rural, cultivated landscape, a *pastoral* scene, and *Sky Blue Water Light Sign,* a *wild* scene, but in other senses as well.

Fog Line

While most audiences of *Fog Line* see, at most, only a foggy green landscape (*Fog Line* is silent)—what they define as "Nothing!"—the film offers a good bit more to the patient, discerning eye, both compositionally and as an experience in time. What one sees and can identify in *Fog Line* depends on the relative thickness of the fog, which gradually clears but does not disappear (see plates 2, 3). At the beginning of the film, the image is virtually abstract—a milky green rectangle—and this abstraction is emphasized by the fact that Gottheim provides no pre-image credits. During approximately the first third of *Fog Line,* the only motion is the very slight clearing of the fog, most noticeable in the center of the image where several shapes gradually become identifiable as trees. This tiny alteration is enough to reveal, after a minute or so, that the milky green space is in fact a landscape trisected horizontally by several high-tension wires (hence the separate word, "Line," in the title, which is not "Fogline" but suggests two separate categories of image). The viewer's gradual identification of the image as a landscape provides the film's easiest metaphor: as the fog clears in the image, enabling viewers to identify the scene, they are no longer "in a fog" about what they are seeing, at least on a literal level.[4]

Once this simple identification is made, however, most first-time viewers, assuming the cinematic riddle has been solved, "space out" and, as a result, do not see a variety of other minimal, but quite suggestive, developments. The most "dramatic" of these begins approximately a third of the way through the film and is confined to the lower third of the frame (between the bottom wires and the lower frame-line): two horses walk slowly through the image, entering from the lower right to graze their way across the field between the camera and the trees in the center of the composition, and exit the image on the left. In those instances when audiences have assured me that they've seen "Nothing!" during *Fog Line,* my follow-up question—"How many of you saw the horses?"—is generally greeted with disbelief and consternation. Because of the relatively low-light conditions in which Gottheim filmed the scene, the *Fog Line* imagery is rather grainy, and as a result the tiny, distant horses are just barely visible. Nevertheless, once the identification is made, the presence of the horses is perfectly obvious, as all viewers grudgingly admit during rescreenings of the film. The widespread failure to see the horses during the first screening reveals not only the viewers' inability to see anything of interest in a "landscape film" but also their further refusal to consider the filmmaker as the designer of the image. In fact, Gottheim's particular composition of *this* foggy space of countryside was determined by the regular movements of the horses through this space every morning: Gottheim had studied the scene for months, and filmed it more than once.

The process of identifying the image in *Fog Line* as a landscape and recognizing the horses is suggestive. For a few moments at the beginning of the film, viewers cannot be sure that the image they're looking at *is* a motion picture. Indeed, it is only once the fog has thinned enough for an identification of the image to be possible that we can recognize that something other than the movie projector—the fog itself—is moving. This first recognition is reminiscent of the development of photography during the early nineteenth century (indeed, the gradual appearance of the landscape image out of milky green abstraction is suggestive of the process of photographic development itself) and then, during the second half of the century, of motion photography: the two horses materializing out of the thinning fog suggest the fascination with the movement of horses that led to Eadweard Muybridge's earliest motion studies and his Zoopraxiscope, a forerunner of the motion picture projector.[5]

If the movement of the horses through the image defines the middle third of *Fog Line,* the continued, gradual clearing of the fog, especially in the space between the upper wires and the upper frame-line, defines the final third, which is punctuated by a bird flying through the image from left to right above the wires—a happy accident during the filming, as it echoes and balances the movement of the horses. Of course, those who have failed to see the horses are even less likely to notice the quick flight of the bird through the space.[6] As the fog in the upper third of the composition thins, a faint circular shape becomes more evident just above the upper wires, to the left of center. Some viewers assume it is the sun beginning to break through. *Fog Line* ends as abruptly as it begins, and no end credits are provided. [7]

Viewers attentive to the evolution of the *Fog Line* imagery are faced with at least three subtle conundrums. First, if Gottheim means to present a lovely rural scene—and the gradually evolving greens of the film are stunning and distinctive[8]—why not avoid the wires? Simply setting up the camera a few yards closer to the field would have made this possible. Second, we must account for the fact that if we do identify the horses, we can hardly fail to notice their diminutive size compared to the trees, which seem very large— not only larger than we may have at first assumed, but too large to be possible in this landscape. And finally, what *is* the circular shape just above the upper wires? By the end of the film we can feel reasonably certain it isn't the sun.

As the title suggests, the wires are central to Gottheim's thinking about the scene he depicts. Their compositional effect is to raise our consciousness of the upper and lower horizontal "lines" of the film frame, and of the frame's rigid rectangularity. While we usually tend to use the film frame as a window into a conventional illusion of a three-dimensional space, the lines within and around this image mitigate against our penetration of the space and draw our attention to the graphic makeup of the frame, which is emphasized by the flatness and graininess of the foggy image. The dispersal of the fog may be so gradual that one cannot be sure when changes are actually occurring in the image and when they're occurring in our consciousness, but the wires and frame-line combine to create a grid that rationalizes the natural process of the fog's lifting and allows us to measure the evolution of the image by spatially locating the subtler changes in relation to it—the way I've done in my preceding description of *Fog Line*'s tiny events.

The moment the linear elements of the image are recognized as indexes of the technological/aesthetic history that produced the motion picture camera and the illusion of Renaissance perspective that the motion picture camera is designed to mass produce (twenty-four images per second), we can recognize that *Fog Line* foregrounds not simply natural landscape, but the *intersection* of natural process and human technological development. And this recognition allows us to solve the other two conundrums. The perspectival impossibility of the *Fog Line* scene, evident in the comparative size of the horses and the trees, is a function of Gottheim's decision to film with a telephoto lens, a camera technology that allows for deeper penetration into space but at the cost of flattening perspective and fictionalizing the spatial relationships within the frame. To the extent that we do see and measure the scene before us in *Fog Line*, we realize that we are seeing not Nature but photography's transformation of it—a realization confirmed by the circular brownish dot, which indeed is not the sun but a smudge on the lens that Gottheim was fully aware of as he shot.

Gottheim's interest in the intersection of natural process and human technological development recalls one of the central themes of nineteenth-century American painting, a theme brilliantly dramatized in Thomas Cole's *The Oxbow* (1836) (the full title: *View from Mount Holyoke, Northampton, Massachusetts, after a Thunderstorm—The Oxbow* (see plate 1). For Cole, the cycles of nature on the left of *The Oxbow* represent a physical and spiritual opportunity that the cultivated fields of the Connecticut Valley, on the right side of the painting, do not—no matter how lovely and productive those fields might be and no matter how we honor those who labor in them. Cole, turned toward us in the foreground of the wilderness side of the image (a wilderness Cole is, at best, "remembering" rather than depicting, as by 1836 the view from the Mount Holyoke hills was a tourist attraction), seems to be using his position as artist to ask us to reconsider the process of change from wilderness to cultivation that is evident behind him, in the interest of our spiritual health and growth. To extend Leo Marx's famous phrase, the technological development of the Connecticut Valley, evident in the grid of farms in the distance, is the "Machine in the Garden" of the New World. As Angela Miller has argued, Cole recognizes that, as members of a democracy, the choice emblematic in the two halves of *The Oxbow* is ours, but even if we ally ourselves with Cole, we are, at best, near the edge of a momentous and deeply problematic historical change: the "drop into the distant agricultural prospect is precipitous rather than gradual," and by implication the potential of our falling away from God is considerable.[9]

Like Cole, Gottheim assumes a viewer who can recognize the complexities of our current situation vis-à-vis nature and technology. The ease with which a casual viewer might miss Cole's image of himself in *The Oxbow* parallels the tendency of contemporary viewers to see "Nothing!" in *Fog Line*—especially the subtle hand of Gottheim-as-filmmaker. But Gottheim's historical position with regard to the issue of nature/technology is fundamentally different from Cole's. When Cole painted *The Oxbow* a generation before the Civil War, much of North America was still undeveloped, at least in a European sense of "development." Certainly, in the Northeast—in Cole's Hudson Valley, in particular, and the Connecticut and other river valleys—the fast growth of trade and industry was doing considerable damage to "untouched" nature and even to the sense of pastoral harmony that some painters saw as the most logical accommodation between the Garden of North America and its exploitation by human society. But industrialization could still be seen as an inroad *into* a gigantic wilderness that continued to dominate America's sense of the continent. When Gottheim made *Fog Line* a century later, the reverse had become true. Industrial and agricultural development had put an end to "wilderness." What remained of the Garden that had defined North America for European Americans a century earlier had been enclosed within a system of national and state parks and forests that "protected" the enclosures from total commercial development. To put this another way, history had transformed the American scene from a garden housing a potentially dangerous machine into a continental machine in which vestiges of that garden, or really metaphors for it, are safely contained within grids of roads, fields, and power lines. For Gottheim, there was no question of declaring his resistance to industrialization and commercialization as Cole implicitly does in *The Oxbow*: the machine he was learning to control remained connected to the industrial revolution by a celluloid umbilical cord. But his access to the 16mm camera did provide an opportunity to critique his position within this history and, at least in one sense, to turn problematic aspects of this history against themselves.

As *Fog Line* makes clear, all that remains of an earlier concept of untouched wilderness and of the ideal, pastoral "middle state" is an illusion. "Nature," of course, is still *here*, but it functions entirely within those technological systems developed to exploit it, including the "system" of motion picture production (of which 16mm, "avant-garde" filmmaking is a "trickle down" development). Indeed, Leo Marx's original "machine," the increasingly ubiquitous locomotive, shares a particular technological heritage with the "machine" of cinema: the advances that brought the railroad track ultimately brought the image track and sound track as well; and when the Cinématographe arrived on the scene, it declared its technological kinship with its sibling technology in the Lumières' *L'Arrivée d'un train en gare de la Ciotat* (1895) and in what became a considerable tradition of cinematic trains, from Porter's *The Great Train Robbery* (1903) and Hale's Tours to Keaton's *The General* (1926) and Hitchcock's *North by Northwest* (1959).[10]

When nineteenth-century painters critiqued the ongoing exploitation of nature, they tended to share a set of attitudes toward "wilderness" and the "middle state" that were virtually part of their birthright. And they also shared a determination to use the traditions of painting as a means of attacking or coming to terms with the problematic elements of this exploitation. Their paintings were a means of improving on what they saw around them, a way of teaching a society in transformation a set of values that would mitigate in the direction of spiritual health. For Gottheim, the fundamental goal was the same, but he was functioning within a society already transformed, by nineteenth-century standards at least, although still faced with the issue of coming to terms with the combined advantages and dangers of technological "advance." The birthright of Gottheim's society—and especially of the post–

World War II generation—was the idea of the almost inevitable ameliorative impact of progress, defined as continued scientific breakthrough, technological development, economic advantage, and social mobility. Like his nineteenth-century predecessors in the visual arts, Gottheim inherited an image-making technology and tradition he was determined to use as a means of teaching the larger society where it was and where it should be going. But the historical transformations that had occurred between *The Oxbow* and *Fog Line* forced Gottheim to depict the lovely, meditative serenity of a particular intersection of natural process and technological development from the right side of *The Oxbow*, from within the changed world Cole was still able to detach himself from, at least in his paintings.

Of course, while we can exploit nature, we can never fully control it, a fact evident during any presentation of *Fog Line*. Because Gottheim's imagery is as minimal as it is and because the film is a single continuous shot, evidence of the material fragility of celluloid and emulsion and of the projection apparatus—scratches on the film, dust in the projector gate—is far more evident during *Fog Line* than during more conventional films. Because so little is happening, a wobbling scratch or a particle of dust inevitably catches the eye. While this might be considered a limitation of Gottheim's method, it is also an index of the fact that since film, like any mechanical technology, is constructed from nature and functions within a natural surround, natural process will inevitably make itself felt as friction and decay, relentlessly undercutting and recontextualizing our technological goals and our intellectual pretensions.

Sky Blue Water Light Sign

As was suggested earlier, *Sky Blue Water Light Sign* shares with *Fog Line* a "Lumièresque" commitment to the extended single shot. In other senses, however, Murphy's "landscape film" differs from Gottheim's, both in the particulars of its imagery and in its allusions to nineteenth-century image making. Most obviously, *Sky Blue Water Light Sign* does not document (and distort) a real scene; it records a fabrication of an imagined scene—and in a manner that disguises what is being recorded.[11] Specifically, during the filming, Murphy framed his shot so that the film frame coincides with the frame around the Hamm's light-sign imagery; the result is that viewers are unaware of the light-sign apparatus. Because we cannot see the superstructure within which the moving imagery is mounted, only the imagery itself, Murphy's framing magically transforms the reality of a strip of imagery moving leftward through the light-sign frame into the illusion of a continuous, smooth, rightward pan across the wilderness scene, filmed from a tripod mounted in the middle of the stream. This transformation of the sign creates an experience that, like *Fog Line,* is suggestive of early-nineteenth-century developments.

I have stressed the ideological connections between *Fog Line* and mid-nineteenth-century painting as represented by *The Oxbow,* but other connections between Gottheim's film and nineteenth-century image making are equally germane. There is, after all, a precedent for precisely the kind of experience Gottheim's film offers, in Louis Daguerre's Diorama shows of the 1820s and 1830s. A sensation from the beginning, the Diorama shows quickly adopted a particular structure: a spectator would see two fifteen-minute presentations, each of which provided a single view on a gradually evolving scene (after the first scene, the entire viewing room—in Paris it sat 350 spectators; in London, 300—swung around to reveal the second). Richard D. Altick's descriptions of characteristic Diorama scenes frequently reveal parallels to the experience Gottheim creates in *Fog Line:*

> [I]n Daguerre's *Interior of the Cloisters of St. Wandrill,* a portion of the desolate ruin was seen as lighted by the midday sun, while the rest was thrust into darkness. Outside, as fleecy clouds passed across the sun, the leaves of the shrubs that half-covered the decaying mullions rustled in the wind and their shadows were reflected in the adjoining columns. In the Rouen scene [Diorama shows frequently focused on the interiors of churches and cathedrals—Canterbury Cathedral, Chartres, Rouen—as well as on cloisters like St. Wandrill], following an early morning storm, a rainbow appeared and the roofs of the buildings shone as if recently wetted by the rain. The next season's picture of a ruined chapel began with a thick February fog enveloping everything beyond the wall; then gradually, as if dispersed by the wind, the fog lifted, the tops of the trees and the snow on the distant mountains became visible, and at the end the whole valley, with its variety of tints and shades, was revealed.[12]

If *Fog Line* is reminiscent of the Diorama, *Sky Blue Water Light Sign* provides an experience reminiscent of two related forms of nineteenth-century entertainment roughly contemporaneous with the Diorama: the still and motion forms of panoramic painting. Panoramic painting developed in England at the end of the eighteenth century largely as a result of the efforts of the Edinburgh painter Robert Barker, whose *La Nature á Coup d'Oeil* apparatus included specifications for creating 360-degree paintings that would be mounted in a circular building.[13] By the end of the century, a variety of panoramic entertainments had evolved and proliferated, making Leicester Square the center of London's popular entertainment industry. The public fascination with panoramic painting quickly spread through Europe, and to North America. The paintings themselves focused on 360-degree views of particular places—the city of London, for example—and on major historical events, especially important battles.

The limitation of the 360-degree panorama, especially on this continent, was that it required spectators to travel to particular buildings in big cities—something many Americans found impractical (although 360-degree panoramas were established in American cities, and have in some cases, remained popular: the "cyclorama" of Pickett's Charge completed by Paul Philippoteaux in 1884, for example, continues to be a Gettysburg attraction).[14] The solution to the problem of the relative immobility of 360-degree panoramic paintings was the "moving panorama," which evolved during the early decades of the nineteenth century in England and on the Continent, finally arriving in the United States in 1828, where the form—long strips of canvas were unrolled from a cylinder hidden from the audience, across a rectangular frame at the front of the theater, and onto a second cylinder—continued to develop. In its heyday, the moving panorama was a "feature-length" entertainment (that is, like modern feature films, about two hours long) that, characteristically, took viewers on a journey along a major river—in the United States, usually the Mississippi, the Ohio, or the Missouri. A series of scenes were represented in a sequence on the strip of canvas, each individual scene enhanced by in-person narration and other sound and visual effects. A self-taught St. Louis artist, John Banvard, became the leading painter-presenter of moving panoramas, claiming to have exhibited a Mississippi panorama to four hundred thousand customers during a nine-month tour from city to city. Indeed, for a time, St. Louis seems to have prefigured Hollywood: various studios vied to present audiences with the biggest, the longest, and the best moving panoramas.[15]

The "history" of most viewers' experiences with *Sky Blue Water Light Sign* echoes the historical development of moving panoramas out of the somewhat earlier still panoramic form. Indeed, once we understand how the original light sign and Murphy's film were constructed—either by being told the facts or by deducing them from the imagery itself—we recognize that the light sign is a modernized and miniaturized version of the moving-panorama experience,[16] with the obvious differences that the light-sign imagery is not painted on canvas but is printed on a celluloid strip and moves continually through the frame as long as the sign is turned on: the moving panoramas were unwound through the frame, a scene at a time, in one direction, and during each subsequent performance, back through the frame in the opposite direction.

While it alludes in this complex fashion to a particular precinematic motion picture evolution, however, *Sky Blue Water Light Sign* defies the overt goals and implicit ideology not only of the nineteenth-century panoramas but also of modern motion picture history, which can be understood to have evolved at least in part from these and related nineteenth-century technologies.[17] Like nineteenth-century panoramas, and contemporary industrial cinema, the light sign Murphy decided to film provides a moving-picture entertainment as a means to the end of making money, in this case, through beer sales. That the light sign pretends to portray a lovely wilderness scene is less a tribute to the traditional idea of nature as garden—though the pretense of the sign, of course, is that Hamm's Beer is as "natural" and healthy as the great outdoors—than still another instance of that very exploitation of wilderness that Cole was so deeply concerned about in *The Oxbow* and that the moving-panorama painters, like so many of their contemporaries, were interested in maintaining.[18] Like Gottheim, Murphy uses the technology of cinema to critique the very history and ideology that has placed this technology at his disposal, although he does so in somewhat different ways.

During the ten and a half minutes of *Fog Line,* we are offered the opportunity to see what we're looking at with greater precision. During the eight and a half minutes of *Sky Blue Water Light Sign,* we are continually presented with new imagery (at least until the very end when Murphy includes just enough overlap to convince us that we've returned to where we began), and, minute by minute, this new imagery revises our sense of what we've already seen and our sense of the experience as a whole. As the film begins, we are seeing—and apparently hearing—a broad stream as it winds its way through a forest of deciduous and evergreen trees, and the "pan" continues across a quiet backwater. In my experience teaching the film, most viewers assume, at least during these early moments, that they are seeing an actual scene. They may recognize that there's something unusual about the texture of this imagery, but

Figure 2. The campsite in J. J. Murphy's *Sky Blue Water Light Sign* (1972).

they tend to assume this is a result of some "artistic" manipulation of the original footage on Murphy's part. As the "pan" moves beyond the backwater and a campsite is revealed (see fig. 2), however, the original assumption that the footage was made plein air in some real wilderness location is thrown into crisis: it is obvious—especially from the impossible regularity of the campfire smoke and the way in which a canoe sits in the water—that *this* cannot be real. Indeed, for many viewers, the campsite is wryly humorous. To the right of the campsite is a large waterfall, almost as obviously unreal as the campsite, and after the waterfall, the pan continues back to the original view of the flowing stream. By the end of the film most viewers are left confused: many "know" the image is a fabrication of a wild scene but seem to believe the reality of the image anyway (Murphy's end credits—no credits introduce the film—are too brief to be read; and, as a result, his "Thanks to Hamm's Beer" is of no assistance in decoding the cinematic riddle he has provided). Of course, a moment's serious thought about the scene revealed by the "pan" makes obvious that the imagery is not "real" in the sense most viewers assume at the beginning of the film—the water of the stream, for example, flows toward the camera throughout the 360-degree pan![19]

There is no question but that the scene in *Sky Blue Water Light Sign* is indebted to nineteenth-century American landscape painting for its motifs, most obviously the waterfall. But it is also suggestive of the nineteenth century in other ways. As I've suggested, the Hamm's Beer light sign is a recent step in the continuous, still ongoing process of natural exploitation, already evident in the work of Thomas Cole. While Cole is usually understood to represent a resistance to this exploitation—a resistance predicated on his conservative attitude toward commercial-industrial development—the artists he inspired (among others, Durand, Church, Cropsey, Bierstadt) saw the transformation of "wilderness" into an American civilization as a divinely inspired Manifest Destiny, within which artists were—figuratively and sometimes literally—pathfinders. Indeed, master painters such as Church, Bierstadt, and Moran played direct roles in American commercial development not only by achieving record sales figures on both sides of the Atlantic for their own Great Pictures (and mass-market reproductions of them) but also by directly assisting in the industrial exploitation of the American West. Moran's images of the Yellowstone region were used by the Northern Pacific Railroad in its campaign to make Yellowstone a major tourist attraction (and our first national park) that would draw new customers to Northern Pacific rail travel.[20]

While Hudson River school painters, and others whose work is related to theirs, promoted western development by demonstrating the divinity of even the most distant and difficult terrains, the panorama painters in St. Louis and elsewhere used their technology of paintings-in-motion to promote and humanize the flow of commercial development along the rivers their paintings depicted. As Angela Miller has suggested, the moving panorama, even more fully than the Great Pictures, formalized the very *process* of wilderness transformation:

[P]anoramas abetted the imaginative colonization of the West. The exotic and unfamiliar elements depicted by the panoramas were confronted, enjoyed, and then passed by, in a symbolic enactment of their historical position within the rising commercial culture of the West.

In the process of appealing to the taste for the exotic and unknown, panoramas paradoxically familiarized their audiences with strange environments; they moderated the challenge of the new. . . . The cumulative effect of such devices [the panoramas' continuous narrative, the fictional voyage by steamboat, the friezelike composition] was to locate the threatening features of the West within a stable continuum of the known and familiar. By imposing eastern technology and its progressive time sense upon the landscape of the West, the panoramas demonstrated visually the historical process of settlement.[21]

While it is difficult to imagine that the Hamm's Beer organization—or even those who designed the light sign—had moving panoramas in mind, nevertheless, the sign can serve as a particularly poignant symbol of how fully domesticated the awesome landscapes of the American West have become in the century since the Great Pictures and the moving panoramas were painted. In the nineteenth century, the presumed accuracy of landscape paintings and moving panoramas was central to their cultural and commercial influence.[22] By the time Hamm's Beer had decided to image its slogan in the sign, however, the simple allusion to a (however distorted) natural scene was presumably enough to assist in convincing beer consumers that purer water was used in Hamm's than in other beers (in the past few years Coors has made an identical claim for its beer, using much the same imagery). And yet having said all this, the sign also reveals a poignant reality: even beer drinkers in an Iowa City bar long for the idea of wilderness strongly enough for the sign's approach to be effective. No doubt, for Murphy, sitting in that bar in 1972, this set of ironies was not only interesting and amusing but also an index of a larger set of issues he was wrestling with as a young filmmaker wanting to develop his own vision in defiance of commercial media (Murphy: "[M]ost people don't understand what they're seeing. Society is dominated by images used in the most manipulative way—by advertising, by politicians. To me it's important work to learn to see more critically").[23] And whether consciously or intuitively, Murphy recognized that one way of defying the commercialization implicit in the sign was to recontextualize it in a manner that might undercut its meanings.

This transformation is accomplished in three related ways. First, and most obviously, Murphy's framing transforms our understanding of the sign's motion. In a bar, the sign's endlessly revolving imagery would form part of the continuous commercial barrage of trademarks for beer and other products on sale. But seen in a movie theater, the sign is removed from its usual commercial context (this is true even in a cinematic sense: *Sky Blue Water Light Sign* was made for a noncommercial art or academic venue), and the motion of the original sign is redirected (again, literally as well as figuratively).

Second, the enlargement of the sign's imagery—an inevitable result of projection in a movie theater—not only removes the imagery from its originally enclosed, commercially domesticated environment, but magnifies the imagery so that viewers can examine it carefully: they can really *see* what they're seeing, distortions and all. Murphy's framing of the sign, and the projector's magnification of it, makes an everyday, throwaway experience into a cinematic mystery: it's a rare viewer who understands what Murphy is presenting, even though the film's title clearly identifies what it is (no title credit introduces the film, but the title is usually announced before the screening, by the presenter). The implicit function of the nineteenth-century moving panoramas was to domesticate the mysteries of the West, allowing viewers to feel more comfortable with the idea of commercial development. The implicit function of *Sky Blue Water Light Sign* is precisely the opposite: at the conclusion of the film, most viewers are left mystified—and their confusion is actually exacerbated by the brevity of Murphy's handwritten credits: not only does the film itself refuse us the information we need to understand and categorize the experience it provides, but the credits confirm that Murphy is refusing to solve the "problem" the film has created. Nothing could be more defiant of commercial film (and television) than this refusal to allay the spectator's confusion.

Murphy's decision to add the sound track to the image instigates a final recontextualization of the light sign. In the screening room, the auditory surround of the sound dramatically adds to the confusion caused by Murphy's visual recontextualizations, and, I suspect, has a good deal to do with the fact that a surprising number of viewers conclude that the scene before them is a film taken in an actual wilderness location, despite visual evidence to the contrary. But the sound also provides a clear index of Murphy's own process as filmmaker of *Sky Blue Water Light Sign:* it suggests that he himself has actually left the bar, found an actual stream, and recorded it plein air.[24] If the light sign itself pretends to bring the great outdoors into the bar, the ultimate act of commercial domestication, Murphy has used the sign as instigation to return, at least briefly, to the real outdoors. And by doing so, Murphy enacts that fundamental hunger for connection with the wilderness—or at least what is left of it—that is our contemporary vestige of the deep spiritual relationship that seems to have inspired Cole, Durand, Church, and their colleagues. Of course, in the nineteenth century, painters took considerable journeys to see the landscapes they wanted to honor. Murphy merely left the bar and drove to a local stream. But given the distance film history had come by the time Murphy picked up the camera, his decision to take viewers to *this* cinematic location, even for as short a time as eight and a half minutes, is a "long journey" conceptually, for him and for them.

I have not commented on the most frequent objection viewers make to my argument that *Fog Line* and *Sky Blue Water Light Sign* are worth watching and thinking seriously about: that the amount of energy and skill necessary to make the films was minimal, especially compared to what goes into "real" movies and "real" art—an effort *so* minimal, in fact, as to be nearly an insult. All Gottheim had to do to make his film was to buy (or borrow) a camera, walk outside his home, mount the camera on a tripod, compose the image, and turn the camera on and off; all Murphy had to do was take his camera to the local bar and make one shot, take his tape recorder to a local stream and record for a few minutes, and print sound and image together. If the filmmakers "studied" a particular landscape or a particular sign over a period of time, nevertheless, their procedures were neither labor intensive nor evidence of skills developed during a lifetime as professionals (as, say, Hudson River paintings are, and Hollywood cinematography). To put it simply, making *Fog Line* and *Sky Blue Water Light Sign* seems just too easy to justify demands on viewer energy and patience.

Even this virtually inevitable complaint, however, is relevant to this discussion. While nineteenth-century painters shared the concepts of wilderness and the pastoral middle state as their birthright, and used their hard-won abilities as master painters (the *technology* of painting) to demonstrate implicitly and explicitly the strength and complexity of their commitment to their ideals, the situations of Gottheim and Murphy on a transformed continent necessitated a very different deployment of artistic means. As the privileged beneficiaries of an already accomplished industrial revolution, Gottheim and Murphy automatically inherited access to the movie camera and its attendant apparatus and, therefore, the opportunity to make landscape imagery almost at will. What had come to be rare—as rare perhaps as the ability to paint well had been a century before—was the *concept* of meditating on nature with the patience and care demanded by *Fog Line* and *Sky Blue Water Light Sign,* especially in spaces normally used for popular entertainment and education. By maintaining viewers' attention on the "Garden" across the road and on the

"Garden" within a light sign in a bar, these filmmakers defy (even as they use) the historical processes of industrial exploitation and cinematic commercialization and offer viewers a metaphor for a spiritual state we often seem in danger of losing as a result of these processes. Gottheim and Murphy provide cinematic vistas that allow viewers to sample, if only for a long moment, something of that meditative sense of landscape that invigorates the painting of a previous century. Each filmmaker creates a "Garden" within the Machine of cinema and of contemporary society.[25]

chapter 2

Voyages of Life

The Voyage of Life as **Protocinema**

When I arrived in Utica, New York, in fall 1971 to teach film studies and
American literature at Utica College of Syracuse University, I brought with me
a set of aesthetic prejudices—common to my generation, I'm sure—that led
me to admire the twentieth-century art at Utica's Munson-Williams-Proctor
Institute (the collection includes paintings by Dalì, Picasso, Gris, Mondrian,
Sheeler, Hopper, Pollock, and Rothko) as fervently as I despised the highlight
of the institute's collection of nineteenth-century art: the 1840 version of
Thomas Cole's *The Voyage of Life* (see figs. 3–6).[1] Cole's four-part exposition of
the stages of human life—"Childhood," "Youth," "Manhood," "Old Age"—
seemed hopelessly old-fashioned, in its representationalism, in its theology,

Figure 3. Thomas Cole's *The Voyage of Life: Childhood* (1839–40), oil on canvas, 51¾" × 78"; Munson-Williams-Proctor Arts Institute, Museum of Art, Utica, New York, 55.105.

and in its assumption—an assumption obviously typical of most nineteenth-century art—that human life was the life of men ("Manhood," indeed!). During the following years, when I sent students to the institute and asked them to write essays about what they saw, I became accustomed to their admiration for Cole, whose accessibility they often used as a weapon in their attacks on the Institute's "obscure," "self-indulgent" modernist painters. As a teacher, I was simultaneously bored and excited by this response: that they inclined toward the easy, old-fashioned Cole paintings provided me with an opportunity to school them on the formal and ideological dimensions of the more challenging moderns.

Gradually, I came to realize that, regardless of its "old-fashioned" elements (and to some degree because of them), *The Voyage of Life* was "modern" in its own way: in particular, it had enough in common with cinema to be consid-

Figure 4. Thomas Cole's *The Voyage of Life: Youth* (1840), oil on canvas, 52 ½" × 78 ½"; Munson-Williams-Proctor Arts Institute, Museum of Art, Utica, New York, 55.106.

ered, if not precinematic, at least protocinematic. Most obviously, Cole's images had width-to-height dimensions not so different from the 16mm films I was presenting in my film classes; and like most commercial films, they focused on the development of a single character.[2] At first, it seemed a stretch to see Cole's paintings as cinematic in any but the most general sense, if only because his four compositions are presented in extreme "long shot" (a function of Cole's interest in seeing human development as part of nature's divinely instituted grand scheme), a far cry from the modern commercial cinema's usual articulation of long shots, medium shots, and close-ups. As I watched students engage *The Voyage of Life*, however, I realized that those willing to explore the individual images of the work and their relationships to each other inevitably developed an experiential process analogous to what modern film directors achieve through editing: that is, most viewers see each

Figure 5. Thomas Cole's *The Voyage of Life: Manhood* (1840), oil on canvas, 52" × 78"; Munson-Williams-Proctor Arts Institute, Museum of Art, Utica, New York, 55.107.

of the sections in an "establishing shot" and then move in to make their own "medium shots" and "close-ups."[3] Of course, what viewers discover as they explore the individual paintings is that Cole's articulations of the particular qualities that define each individual stage of human life make sense *only* in juxtaposition to the qualities defined in the other three paintings. As a result, many viewers move back and forth from one painting to another—creating their own intercutting between the four stages of life. Further, Cole's decision to use four successive paintings with considerable time gaps between the stages of life depicted is analogous to the way in which film editing condenses time as a means of generating storytelling energy.

The more I've examined *The Voyage of Life,* the more analogies to cinema I've discovered. For example, with benefit of twentieth-century hindsight, we can see that the four paintings are "edited" together in a manner that recalls a

Figure 6. Thomas Cole's *The Voyage of Life: Old Age* (1840), oil on canvas, 51¾" × 78½"; Munson-Williams-Proctor Arts Institute, Museum of Art, Utica, New York, 55.108.

major theoretical debate about film editing ("montage") that took place in the Soviet Union during the 1920s between filmmakers V. I. Pudovkin and Sergei Eisenstein. Eisenstein reviewed the debate in an often-quoted passage from "The Cinematographic Principle and the Ideogram":

> In front of me lies a crumpled yellowed sheet of paper. On it is a mysterious note:
> "Linkage—P" and "Collision—E."
> This is a substantial trace of a heated bout on the subject of montage between P (Pudovkin) and E (myself).
> This has become a habit. At regular intervals he visits me late at night and behind closed doors we wrangle over matters of principle. A graduate of the Kuleshov school, he loudly defends an understanding of montage as a *linkage* of pieces. Into a chain. Again, "bricks." Bricks arranged in series to expound an idea.
> I confronted him with my viewpoint on montage as a *collision*. A view that from the collision of two given factors *arises* a concept.[4]

Modern film editing can be understood, roughly, as a combination of the two approaches Eisenstein describes. A narrative is developed as related shots (Pudovkin's "bricks") follow one another, ensuring continuity of character and action; but this narrative continuity is periodically interrupted and energized by more heavily edited passages made up of more shots per minute with a greater disparity between the individual shots (i.e., in Eisenstein's terminology, by more, and more radical, "collisions").[5]

The Eisenstein-Pudovkin debate—and the synthesis of the Pudovkin and Eisenstein positions in modern cinema and television—is prefigured in *The Voyage of Life*. Certainly, the four paintings are "bricks" in a narrative development, and form a linkage with one another that is confirmed by the paintings' overall similarity in scale—the protagonist is virtually the same size in each painting, as are his golden boat and his guardian angel—and their individual titles: it is obvious that we are to assume we are watching a single "individual" (Everyman) during the various stages of his life, as these stages are dramatized by his changing appearance, by the changing appearance of the boat, by his relationship to the angel (she is in the boat with him in "Childhood," waves good-bye to him in "Youth," watches him from a distance in "Manhood," comforts and guides him in "Old Age"), and by the particulars of time and place: "Childhood" is set in the morning, in spring, at a place where a small stream leaves a cave to wind its way through flowers and small bushes and trees; "Youth" is set at midday, on a broader stream in the midst of the midsummer greenery of large trees; "Manhood" is set in autumn, judging from the red leaves on the blasted trees, in the evening just at the end of sunset, and depicts the river plunging through a dismal, rocky canyon; and "Old Age" is set at night on a calm sea into which the river has apparently delivered the boat, and where the angel directs the old man toward a heavenly light breaking through the darkness. Each painting builds on those previous to it, "brick" by "brick."

On the other hand, much of the energy in the experience of *The Voyage of Life* is a function of the "collisions" between each painting and the next, created by Cole's overall narrative and the formal design of the individual paintings. In Eisenstein's editing theory, the productive engagement of viewers in a film (and, by extension, in progressive, revolutionary action in real life, once the film is over) is a function of the size of the gaps between shots in a montage, that is, of the "violence" of the collisions created by the discrepancies in successive images. At least in theory, the harder viewers need to work to make sense of the discrepancies between shots, the more actively engaged they become in the narrative being developed. The temporal gap between each pair of paintings of *The Voyage of Life* is approximately fifteen years. These gaps in time, and the viewer activity they instigate, are made particularly dynamic by the formal collisions in the design of successive pairs of paintings.[6]

A brief examination of "Childhood" and "Youth" can suggest the nature of the collisions in the three successive pairings. In "Childhood" the boat is located to the lower left of the painting and is moving toward the foreground from left to right at a slightly downward angle; in "Youth" the boat is slightly to the right of center, moving slightly upward into the distance—that is, away from us, from right to left. In "Childhood" the angel is in the boat behind and to the left of the child; in "Youth" she's on the shore and to the right of the youth. The general background terrain of the two paintings confirms the dialectic opposition in the movement of the boat. The left two-thirds of "Childhood" is dominated by rocky, sometimes cloud-obscured cliffs that recede into the distance toward the misty mountains in the background of the right third of the painting; the left half of "Youth" is an open, airy space receding along misty mountains into the distance, while the right half is dominated by a thick growth of large trees behind which we glimpse distant rocky cliffs.

Further, in each of the paintings Cole develops an overall, dialectic sense of space that echoes the dialectic between the preceding and succeeding paintings. In "Childhood" the eye is drawn into the painting in two different directions: on the right, we look into the distant, bright vista that opens between the cliffs and the right side of the painting; and on the left, the eye is drawn toward the dark cave out of which the stream and the boat are coming. These two axes form an approximately 90-degree angle: the motion of the boat out of the cave, roughly toward us, "collides" with the eye's easy penetration of the space on the right. In "Youth" the eye penetrates the image in two directions also. I have mentioned the deep, bright vista on the left of the painting; but to the right of the painting, directly behind the angel, a gap in the foliage reveals distant cliffs through which the river continues its course: the youth (and, at least at first glance, the viewer) may assume his voyage will continue leftward and into the distance toward the castle-in-the-sky, but if we look carefully, we can see what the youth cannot, that the river makes an approximately 90-degree turn to the right somewhere downstream, a turn that may (and, of course, once we've examined "Manhood," we know it *will*) take him into more dangerous waters.

Finally, on a less literal level, "Childhood" and "Youth" juxtapose different symbolic elements central in defining the nature of these two stages of life's voyage. The cave in "Childhood" is an obvious reference to the birth canal, to the physical body of the mother (and Mother Nature). The open space to the left of "Youth," in contrast, is dominated by a white castle-in-the-air, a representation of the ideals of youth—or rather the foolish, immaterial fantasies of youth (this castle-in-the-air has none of the spiritual substantiality of either the angel or the heavenly light that offers the old man release in "Old Age").

The complex dialectic relationship between each successive pair of paintings endows the simple succession of images in *The Voyage of Life* with enough energy to engage contemporary viewers who express boredom with less dialectically organized landscape works. The viewer "voyaging" back and forth from one painting to another to examine the particulars of Cole's narrative is (literally) active. Of course, the viewer Cole constructs—a viewer exploring his spiritual relationship with God's world—could hardly be more different from the potential communist revolutionary Eisenstein and Pudovkin had in mind (a revolutionary committed to modern machinery, including the machinery of cinema, as a means to large-scale industrialization) or from the consumption-oriented commercial TV audience that has inherited the Soviet breakthroughs in editing, along with the material benefits, and problems, of the industrial revolution.[7]

Horizons as Landscape Film

During the years when I was personally coming to recognize the protocinematic dimensions of *The Voyage of Life*, I was simultaneously discovering that upstate New York had continued to produce visual artists fascinated with landscape and the human presence in it: specifically, a considerable number of film artists whose work betrayed the same resistance to commercial development as implied in Cole's vision of landscape in *The Voyage of Life*, *The Oxbow*, and other paintings. And I was particularly drawn to a film by Larry Gottheim—*Horizons* (1973)—because of what seemed to me fascinating parallels and suggestive distinctions between Gottheim's first feature and *The Voyage of Life*. These parallels are suggested by the way in which the film developed, by its structures, and by its explicit and implicit ideology.

Gottheim has described the origin of the *Horizons* project:

> I remember that I happened to be standing on a hill. . . . The hill was very green, and it was a very clear day, and there was a clear, cloudless blue sky, and I had this idea of making a film that would somehow involve shots in which the horizon would divide the frame into very clear areas of color. . . . It was a very vague idea, but on the basis of that idea I went out to film some horizons. Also, I decided there would have to be some very subtle movement within the shots—say, clouds moving or grass blowing in the wind. . . . I found myself being very, very selective. I would drive around for hours and not find anything, or I would find something that was somewhat close to what I had originally intended but that also had some element that was a departure. . . .
>
> I found myself being drawn to certain kinds of situations that weren't part of the original premise at all, and at first I rejected them. . . . Then I started to cheat a little bit. I might decide to use most of a roll for filming horizons, but if I happened to find something that interested me, that wasn't part of my original intention, I'd record it anyway. . . . I was finding myself more and more drawn into a process that was happening on its own. I decided . . . to trust that. . . . Originally my idea involved greens and blues, and I assumed my shooting would be completed in a fairly short time. But the process was extending into late summer, into autumn.[8]

The process Gottheim describes has much in common with the painterly tradition of sketching within the landscape, but it could hardly be more different from the conventional filmmaking process, where scripting and storyboarding provide an advance "map" of a film's structure (Hitchcock's famous attitude of being interested *only* in planning every detail of a film, and not at all in shooting the film, has often been taken as evidence of his particular seriousness as a director). Indeed, it was not until the middle of the winter that Gottheim began to have a clear sense of the structure of the film he was shooting (he continued to collect imagery through winter, spring, and summer 1972–73). And as this structure emerged, it confirmed the unconventional filming procedures that produced it. Using poetry (Virgil's *Georgics*) and music (Vivaldi's *The Four Seasons*) as models, Gottheim decided to organize *Horizons* seasonally and to develop an editing structure characteristic of each season: "[I]t was reading Dante, and the poetic form of the terza rima, that pushed me toward the idea of organizing the shots into some kind of rhyme scheme."[9] Gottheim finally decided to structure the film into four sections (see plate 4), each using material from one of the seasons and each having a different rhyme scheme: "I decided that the first section [summer] could be two shots that in some sense rhyme with each other; the second [fall] and third [winter] sections would still use this two-shot pattern, but would use two, two-shot groups in groups of four; the last [spring] section, which is the most complex, would use the terza rima." Specifically, summer "rhymes" *a a;* fall, *a b b a;* winter, *a b a b;* and spring, *b a b, c b c, d c d.* Actually, Gottheim's spring rhyme is not classic terza rima, in which the sound that ends the middle line of one stanza becomes the rhyme in the first and third lines of the following stanza—that is, *a b a, b c b, c d c,* and so on —but, given his particular topic, his modification of terza rima was both practical and expressive, as will be evident later.

The process of determining the complex system of rhymes for the 596 images Gottheim decided to use was as time-consuming as the shooting itself—and confirms the rough parallels between Gottheim's procedure and the process of designing nineteenth-century landscape paintings, even as it further distinguishes this procedure from conventional filmmaking. Gottheim drew and listed every particular of every shot on note cards, which he then began to place in juxtaposition to one another in the hope of discovering interesting rhymes, that is, particular visual details that several shots had in common. Ultimately, Gottheim "designed" four composite seasons—"composite" because within each season he was willing to ignore the literal chronological order established by his shooting, in order to develop a set of rhymes that nevertheless remained true to the essence of each season and to the typical temporal shifts that define the transitions from season to season, a procedure reminiscent of the tendency of nineteenth-century landscape painters to make composite landscapes out of typical elements: Asher B. Durand's *Kindred Spirits* (1849), Frederic Edwin Church's *New England Scenery* (1851), and Albert Bierstadt's *The Rocky Mountains, Lander's Peak* (1863) can serve as examples. To continue the analogy of poetry, each season in *Horizons* is composed of a set of stanzas, each set off from the next by one second of colored film leader (green for summer, red for fall, blue for winter, and yellow for spring), and organized according to the seasonal rhyme scheme.

A review of the particular rhymes in the opening stanza of each season will provide some sense of the internal structure of each type of stanza Gottheim employs. The opening stanza of summer is composed of two brief shots (four and eight seconds, respectively) of the same small tree or bush at the top of a low hill that creates a horizon line through the image. At first glance, the images seem quite different. The first shot is dominated by a deep green cornfield, and the horizon line is in the upper third of the frame, descending slightly toward the right; the tree is seen in long shot. The second shot is dominated by a red-gold quality of light created by the afternoon sun; the horizon line is at the lower middle of the image and is almost horizontal (it descends very slightly toward the left), and the tree is much closer. Indeed, the discrepancies between the two images are so considerable that few viewers would recognize on first viewing that they are looking at the same tree, especially since new pairs of imagery follow very quickly. In a sense, the brief summer section of *Horizons* (summer lasts approximately 12 minutes and includes 94 shots; fall, 13 minutes and 108 shots; winter, 30 minutes and 208 shots; spring, 22 minutes and 186 shots) is preparation for the more complex rhyme schemes of the other seasons.

In any case, once viewers have become accustomed to scanning juxtaposed images for visual correlatives, Gottheim provides a new challenge: to recognize the rhymes in any particular four-shot fall stanza, we must remember the first image in each stanza *through* the pair of rhymed images that follow and be ready to recognize the rhyming elements of the fourth shot (see figs. 7a–d). In the opening stanza of fall, Gottheim makes this relatively easy: the first and fourth images are of laundry hanging outside on a line in front of a background of autumn yellows and reds; and each of the middle pair of images is relatively minimal: a clear horizon line bisects the image into two uniform spaces of color. Of course, there are differences within these rhymed pairs (the all-white laundry in image 1 [fig. 7a] is farther from us than the multicolored laundry in image 4 [fig. 7d]; the horizon line in image 2 [fig. 7b] is made by a macadam road at the crest of a hill—an automobile is descending on the far side as the shot begins; and the horizon line in image 3 [fig. 7c] divides a green field from a clear blue sky); nevertheless, the rhymes declare themselves.

The winter section provides the most consistent challenges in terms of our distinguishing Gottheim's rhyme scheme. The choice of *a b a b* not only suggests the feeling of getting nowhere so characteristic of long central New York winters, it forces the viewer—or at least that viewer committed to deciphering the film's internal structure—to hold each of the first two images in mind

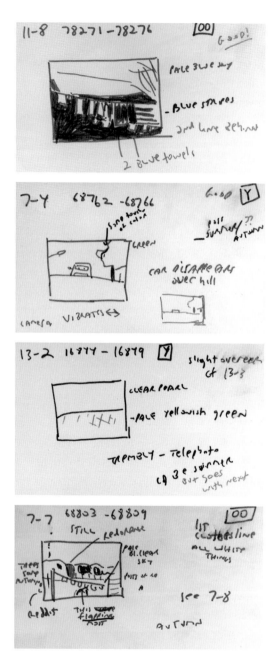

Figures 7a–d. Set of four index cards Larry Gottheim used in arranging the rhymes in *Horizons* (1973). Courtesy Larry Gottheim.

through a subsequent image that does not rhyme with it. Again, however, in the first stanza of the season Gottheim makes the rhymes relatively easy to recognize. In shots 1 and 3, landscapes—the first with a low horizon and a dark red sunset sky, the third with a horizon more toward the middle of the image dividing a white sky from a brown field—are punctuated by plants that interrupt the otherwise straight horizon line: both plants—a bit of a tree in black silhouette in image 1, a bleached-out tree in image 3—are at the lower left of their respective images. Both image 2 and image 4 are filmed from cars moving to the left: in the distance we see blue mountains (the lower Catskills along U.S. Route 17 in New York State), and in the foreground the leftward movement is punctuated by a telephone pole (in image 2) and several trees (in image 4) moving to the right through the image; in both images a hexagonal reflection on the lens is visible at approximately the same position in the frame.

The modified terza rima of spring extends the demands on viewer memory a final step. Not only must we discover the rhyme in images 1 and 3 of each triad, but we must remember that rhyme through both the one second of yellow leader that divides successive triads and image 1 of the following triad, even as we scan this second image 1 in preparation for recognizing the next rhyme! It was precisely these difficulties that led Gottheim to modify terza rima for *Horizons*. To have used Dante's system would have prevented the viewer from having any idea of what detail to "hold onto" until the following stanza—and, as a result, little recognition of the rhymes would be possible. In Gottheim's modification, the identification of the rhyme in shots 1 and 3 of the previous stanza provides the viewer with a sense of what the rhyme might be, though, of course, viewers must wait until the following stanza to be sure.

For the introductory rhyme in the spring section, Gottheim uses images that, by this time in *Horizons*, have become recognizable motifs. In image 1, the camera is looking through a thick woods at distant light that, from time to time, creates lovely reflections on the camera lens; in image 3, reflections on the lens are created as the sun shines through laundry hanging on a line. These reflections are echoed in image 2 of the following triad by sunlight breaking through thick clouds (in the same left-to-right direction as the reflections on the lens in image 3 of the first triad). Image 2 of the first triad (a brief, 27-frame image filmed from a car coming out of a highway overpass) echoes the final image of winter (of a car moving into a highway tunnel).

Images 1 and 3 of the second triad (of distant tree-covered hillsides) are echoed by image 2 of the third triad of spring.

In general, Gottheim's seasonal system creates viewer experiences that are analogous to the real experience of the seasonal cycle in central New York. For most of us living here, summer passes much too quickly (an experience reflected in the brevity of Gottheim's two-shot stanza); winter seems to last "forever" (as does the long, long winter section of *Horizons*); and when spring finally arrives, it never seems to develop more quickly than "two steps forward, one step back." And these analogies between central New York seasons and Gottheim's rhyme schemes are confirmed by the percentage of shots in which the camera is in motion. In addition to the fact that all the shots in *Horizons* were hand-held (Gottheim: "I wanted to be sure the shots would have at least the movement imparted by my own ways of holding the camera"), in 30 percent of the summer shots, the camera is panning or tracking (in an automobile), as compared with 45 percent of the fall shots, 26 percent of the winter shots, and 46 percent of the spring shots. That is, the seasons traditionally considered the most changeable are filmed with the most camera movement.[10]

While the process of discovering the rhymes in each stanza of *Horizons* is roughly analogous to the process of discovering the particular changes that occur during the successive paintings of *The Voyage of Life*, there are, of course, obvious differences. Most obviously, the complex system of rhymes in *Horizons* is presented in a form that virtually defies most viewers' ability to fully see this system, whereas those who go to see *The Voyage of Life* can take their time investigating the details of the paintings. If Cole means to develop, or confirm, a contemplative sensibility in his viewers, Gottheim's hundreds of rhymes appear to be a vestige of the frenzy of modern life, even if his choice of imagery and pacing seems nearly the opposite of the commercial media that reflect and create this frenzy.

Another way of understanding the differences in the two works has to do with the kinds of "movement" they instigate. To understand *The Voyage of Life*, viewers need to move from "long shot" to "medium shot" to "close-up" and back and forth from one painting to the others—a metaphor, perhaps, for Cole's preferred form of motion for experiencing nature, walking. To thoroughly experience *Horizons*, the viewer does not need to move in the physical sense (and is not "moved" in a conventional Hollywood sense) but must scan a series of rapidly changing images for details relevant to the rhymes—an implicit parallel to the painstaking exploration that produced the imagery for *Horizons* and that was necessary for editing the finished film. Of course, in another sense, both works seem meant to be seen, again and again, over long periods. My personal relationship with *The Voyage of Life* changed when I realized, as I revisited Cole's painting over a period of twenty years, that, for all my reservations, I had begun to see myself as more fully represented by "Manhood" than by "Youth." In the case of *Horizons*, repeated viewings are essential, if one is to have the several experiences Gottheim's film offers (at presentations of *Horizons*, Gottheim makes clear that viewers may want to sit back and simply enjoy the sense of the seasonal cycle the film creates before beginning to look for the patterns of rhyme).

On other levels, however, the experiences provided by Cole and Gottheim are not so terribly different. While the commercial film industry continues to assume that, except for a few film buffs and scholars, moviegoers will rarely pay to see a film more than once in a theater (i.e., that filmgoing is essentially a process of visual consumption aptly reflected by—and, insofar as theater owners are concerned, financially maintained by—moviegoers' consumption of food and drink), Gottheim made a very different assumption in *Horizons*, an assumption more characteristic of painters: he assumed an ideal viewer not only with sufficient patience to investigate the film's particulars but also with access to the leisure and the technology necessary for a sustained investigation of a work of film art. That such a viewer was a rarity in 1973 would have been no surprise to Gottheim: like so many other independent filmmakers of that era, Gottheim made the film he wanted to make, hoping *Horizons* would help to develop the sort of audience it required—just as a century earlier Cole's work was seminal in developing an expanded American audience for landscape painting. That such an expanded audience would be virtually defined by economic and educational privilege may be a limitation of *Horizons*, but it is a limitation shared by most serious works of art during most of recent history. Of course, my writing this essay and your reading it are proof that *we* have managed at least the necessary leisure and, perhaps, the technology for just such an exploration as Gottheim had in mind (even if, unfortunately, the development of the home-video, laser disk, and DVD market has as yet not included Gottheim and related filmmakers in any substantial and effective way).

The Voyage of Life and Horizons

A careful examination of *Horizons* also reveals parallels to the vision embodied in *The Voyage of Life,* as well as a set of differences that distinguished the two artists' centuries even as they connect them. The parallels are evident both on the level of editing and on the level of composition. Even the most thorough investigation of the many obvious and subtle differences among Cole's four paintings will not subtract from the cumulative effect of the paintings as a set: they chart *a* voyage with several particular tacks. A thorough understanding of this voyage demands a detailed comparison of each painting with all the others; and this comparison requires attention to both the voyager and the larger context within which we see him. If the voyager is the central focus of each painting, the meaning of his particular position is largely determined by Cole's rendering of the landscape that surrounds him. Indeed, the diminutive size of the voyager in a large painting ("Childhood" is $51\,\tfrac{3}{4}$" × 78"; "Youth," $52\,\tfrac{1}{2}$" × $78\,\tfrac{1}{2}$"; "Manhood," 52" × 78"; "Old Age," $51\,\tfrac{3}{4}$" × $78\,\tfrac{1}{2}$") results in different kinds of "focus": Cole's large-scale rendering of imaginative natural scenes draws us to the voyager's particular experience; and this experience, in turn, redefines our understanding of these natural scenes.[11] Similarly, Gottheim's painstaking division of *Horizons* into seasons and each season into stanzas is a strategy that has the cumulative effect of charting a single journey through a single representative year, a paradox evident on virtually every level of the film. For viewers who have committed themselves to the identification of Gottheim's complex rhyme scheme, the result is a new form of cinema seeing: while most shots in a commercial film have a particular "point," a single, obvious part to play in the progress of the developing narrative, *Horizons* challenges viewers to scan each image thoroughly in order to be conversant with *all* dimensions of the image. Indeed, to understand the elements of any given pair of shots that *do* rhyme, viewers must be fully conscious of all those elements in both shots that do *not* rhyme. There is no foreground/background in *Horizons,* at least not in the conventional filmic sense: any generality or detail anywhere within the frame might be part of a rhyme about to declare itself, and if it is not, it provides the context within which the rhyming can be identified. Or, to put this another way, Gottheim's aesthetic tactic of asking us to distinguish particular rhyming details within each pair of images has the long-range goal of expanding our seeing so that we are challenged to become aware of *every* dimension of *every* image.

This paradox is encapsulated in the film's central metaphor, the horizon line: that linear division between sky and land that exists nowhere except as a conceptual projection that helps us to locate ourselves in the world. As *Horizons* develops, Gottheim provides myriad instances of horizon lines within his landscapes, including some that challenge the definition of the term (the aforementioned shot of sunlight seen through dense woods, for example), and he presents these literal horizons within a cinematic structure that continually draws attention to the process of his editing; that is, to the "horizon line" of the splice that divides each image from the next, and each stanza from the colored leader that precedes and succeeds it, and each season from the others. Indeed, *Horizons* was, strictly speaking, the first film in which Gottheim used editing: that is, in 1972–73, editing was the "horizon" that challenged Gottheim on his journey as filmmaker. The six earliest films Gottheim distributes are all one-shot films that focus on composition rather than editing (editing is a factor in these films only in the sense that Gottheim refuses to use it), and for his first longer film, *Barn Rushes* (1971), he simply spliced together eight unedited tracking shots of a barn: that is, he presents the unedited "rushes" as his finished film. Paradoxically, in *Horizons* Gottheim's hundreds of cuts provide viewers with the opportunity to see past his editing not only to the continuities within paired shots (the rhymes), but, ultimately, to the overall continuity of the seasonal cycle itself.

In the final image of *Horizons,* viewers are once again looking through a thick woods toward the sunlight, but in this instance, the reflections created on the lens by the intermittent light are particularly dramatic: they create an exquisite, mandala shape within which four smaller circular shapes revolve— a perfect metaphor for the central continuity within which all the seasonal changes have a place. That the subject and motion of this final image is the action of light itself not only suggests the filmmaker's capturing of light with his camera, it implies a recognition of a higher source of energy that is the source of the seasonal mutability *Horizons* documents so painstakingly. This reference to a higher energy, a higher power, suggests a further analogy to *The Voyage of Life*. After all, one of the implications of Cole's use of the daily and seasonal cycle as the background of Everyman's "Voyage of Life" is that, at base, this life isn't simply a single passage from childhood to old age but one instance of an ongoing cycle. Is it too much to suggest that when the old man leaves the darkness of old age and moves toward the light-filled opening in the clouds, his spirit is preparing to enter a new world in a new form, to become, once again, that child in "Childhood," leaving the dark cave and returning to the light? Such a reading is sustained by the fact that the child's movement out of the cave is along virtually the same axis as the old man's gaze toward Heaven, as if the life of the soul were an endless coming and going.

While *The Voyage of Life* and *Horizons* have much in common, literally and philosophically, they are, simultaneously, quite distinct, and in ways that can be said to emblematize the two artists' different eras and the evolution of the concept of landscape during the gap between these two eras. Both painter and filmmaker were similarly "conservative" in their resistance to modern technology. In most of his paintings Cole idealizes a nostalgic vision of landscape that is predicated on a refusal to allow the technologies that were already transforming the American scene the privilege of being represented: if he couldn't keep disruption by the railroad out of the real landscape, he could at least keep it out of the painted landscapes he did control or transform this disruption into an element harmonious with the painted landscape.[12] Even when technological transformation was the overt subject of a picture, as it is in *The Oxbow*, the danger is represented at most as a pastoral scene.[13] While Cole's fears of what economic development was doing to the Hudson River valley and to the promise of the New World may have fueled his activity as an artist, this particular issue is in no way directly specified in *The Voyage of Life*, even in "Manhood" where an indirect reference to this particular aspect of the "rough rapids" of Cole's middle age might have been relevant. Like Cole, Gottheim avoids representing the more spectacular evidence of contemporary change, preferring to emphasize a pastoral vision quite close to what Cole depicts in *The Oxbow*. And even in those rare instances when Gottheim does include an image that reveals evidence of more dramatic technological developments (during two "winter" shots, the Manhattan skyline is just barely visible in the extreme distance), few viewers would be likely to notice: the forested northern New Jersey hills dominate the foreground and middle ground of the two shots. Like Cole, Gottheim tends to show us the world the way it *was*, or to be more precise, the way more of it once was, at least in our current imagining of it.

Though their general attitudes may be analogous, however, the gap between their two historical moments is enough to render the analogies almost ironic. Cole was able to remember a land before development, and could still travel beyond the frontier of development without too much difficulty. For Gottheim, no such memories and no such escape were possible: whatever natural scene Gottheim is able to envision in *Horizons* must be seen through the technological "grid" that development has superimposed on natural process. Every image in *Horizons* is shot from roadways (often, from vehicles moving along the roadways), and most shots depict farms or the activities of farming families: plowed fields, fields enclosed by fences, wash drying on clotheslines . . . Even when a forested hillside is seen, it is contextualized by cultivated fields and by the road Gottheim films from. In short, the rural, close-to-nature impact *Horizons* has on most viewers is a function of the fact that virtually all of us live in or near cities and suburbs. The world Gottheim shows us includes more of those vestiges of the world untouched by development we have learned—to some extent from Cole and those he inspired—to long for than we may see in our day-to-day lives (including our lives as film and television viewers), but by 1973 Gottheim was quite well aware that the "natural world" was visible at most through the interstices of the layers of technology within which we live.[14]

Of course, the most fundamental element of Gottheim's techno-pastoral vision is the motion picture camera itself. Some of the power of Cole's nostalgic vision of the American scene is a function of his working in the tradition of an aesthetic technology (painting, landscape painting) that was widely understood as a form of resistance to many forms of industrial development. But the vision of *Horizons* is created *with* a machine; it is quite literally a function not only of an industry, but of the fact that by 1973 the motion picture industry had existed for so long and so successfully that it had produced a tradition of critiques possible only because of "trickle-down" technologies, smaller film gauges (16mm, 8mm, Super-8mm, etc.). This industrial fact of the camera is evident throughout *Horizons*. Indeed, Gottheim is at pains to remind us of it. I have discussed the film's unusually "visible" editing strategy, which continually calls attention to the process of producing the film, and the persistent motif of reflections on the lens. But Gottheim's awareness of the cinematic apparatus is evident in other ways as well.

Horizons is full of visual motifs that refer to the technology of cinema—or, really, to the fact that this particular technology is one of many instances of a pervasive cultural pattern. Indeed, recognizing the "cinematic" aspect implicit in virtually all the film's motifs can be as engrossing as discovering the particulars of Gottheim's rhymes. For example, the motif of the light seen through

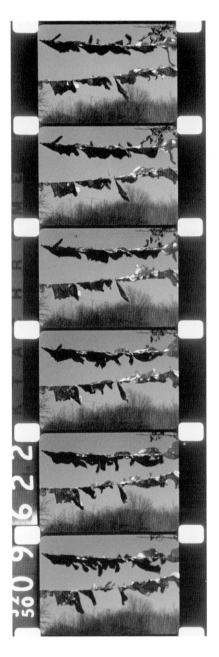

Figure 8. Wash on the line, one of many metaphors for shots (and frames) on the filmstrip, in Larry Gottheim's *Horizons* (1973). Courtesy Larry Gottheim.

the trees in the woods is an analogy for the light being allowed into the box of the camera between the intermittent moments of darkness created by the shutter. Indeed, the mandala shape described earlier is, in fact, the spinning shutter of the camera caught on the celluloid as a result of the intermittent action of the sunlight through the trees. And this analogy of light seen through trees and through the regular interruption of the camera's shutter is implicitly confirmed by the fact that these trees are planted in regular rows: this is neither an original forest nor a second growth but a technologically managed tree farm maintained for the production of paper—and presumably of imagery of various kinds. Similarly, the laundry-on-the-line motif (fig. 8) is an analogy to Gottheim's stringing individual items—shots, bits of colored leader—on the celluloid "line" of the film, an analogy confirmed by the frequent rectangularity of the laundry items. The repeated view through the panes of a window at the field outside parallels our view of the seasons through the regularly organized shots in each stanza of the film (that the summer section uses two-shot stanzas, i.e., fewer "panes," is fitting, as summer is the season when windows are more frequently open). The film's consistent focus on small-scale farming is both a documentation of life in central New York State and a metaphor: for Gottheim, the *Horizons* project was a form of cinematic farming; he "grew" imagery in celluloid furrows—and, in the process, became more fully a part of the rural world that surrounded him. That Gottheim's filmmaking was—and remains—small gauge (16mm) and low budget provides an analogy to the generally small-scale dairy farming that continues to characterize central New York State.

In the end, *Horizons* is more an act of hope than of loss. If Cole turned away from the commercial and industrial development that would, in the generations following his death, use the love of landscape he helped to inspire as a means toward its further exploitation,[15] Gottheim's decision to move away from his academic training and embrace a newly accessible industrial technology became his means of demonstrating that even a medium synonymous with exploitation of the crassest sort could itself be exploited to put viewers back in touch—at least for an extended moment—with the nineteenth century's faith in the natural world's utility in helping us achieve a spiritual connection with a higher power and with the world around us.

chapter 3

Avant-Gardens

Yes, the sowing of a seed seems a very simple matter, but I always feel as if it were a sacred thing among the mysteries of God. Standing by that space of blank and motionless ground, I think of all it holds for me of beauty and delight, and I am filled with joy at the thought that I may be the magician to whom power is given to summon so sweet a pageant from the silent and passive soul. I bring a mat from the house and kneel by the smooth bed of mellow brown earth, lay a narrow strip of board across it a few inches from one end, draw a furrow firmly and evenly in the ground along the edge of the board, repeating this until the whole bed is grooved at equal distances across its entire length.

CELIA THAXTER, *AN ISLAND GARDEN*

In both of the creation stories in Genesis, the Garden of Eden is created separately from humankind. Actually, in the earlier creation story, no garden is mentioned: God creates the heavens and the earth in six days and places man and woman in charge of the creation. In the second creation story, God first breathes life into man, who he has formed from the dust; then He plants a garden in Eden and places man there, to till it and keep it, and finally creates Eve from Adam's rib so that he'll have company. When the serpent beguiles Eve, and she offers Adam the fruit of the tree of knowledge of good and evil, their fall from grace is demonstrated in their expulsion from the garden. While in both stories God makes clear that man and woman should be fruitful together and multiply (Gen. 1:28) and that they are to become "one flesh" (Gen. 2:23), love—in the conventional, modern sense of the word—is not mentioned. In Christian myth, romantic love seems a relatively minor issue, and the crucial meaning of the fall of Adam and Eve is in Christ's redemption of humankind: the consciousness of good and evil that resulted from the original sin becomes a means for transcending humankind's fallen state through the mediation of Christ whose life on earth transforms the original shame into a Fortunate Fall.

In modern American, middle-class thinking—at least insofar as commercial movies reflect this thinking—the meaning of the garden and of Adam and Eve has been radically transformed. Indeed, the garden has become a "garden," the psychic state of true love. Man and woman weren't created to till a garden but rather were made for each other; and the Fortunate Fall has become boy meets girl, boy loses girl, boy wins girl—or a variation on this pattern—and they live happily ever after in a middle-class Eden, characterized not by the biodiversity evident in the biblical Eden but by adequate material goods. If the modern Adam and Eve are fruitful and multiply, this is a by-product, not the goal of the love they share.

American alternative cinema, which has generally set itself up as a critique of commercial media and conventional thinking, has reacted against the mainstream by rarely privileging heterosexual romantic love. Indeed, when romantic love has been conjured up, at least implicitly, the focus has tended to be the demise of romance. Maya Deren and Alexander Hammid's *Meshes of the Afternoon* (1943) can easily be read as a psychodramatization of Deren's resistance to conventional marriage and domesticity; and in Hollis Frampton's *Critical Mass* (1971) the breakup of a couple is reflected in the increasing separation of image and sound: Frampton's implicit rejection of Hollywood's privileging of synchronization, his embracing other forms of sound-image relationship, is a reflection of, and is imaged by, the increasing psychic distance between his two protagonists.

There is, however, a tradition in avant-garde film of using the idea of the Garden as a means for critiquing Hollywood romantic conventions, for re-thinking the ways in which the commercial cinema has revised the biblical sense of the Garden. The discussion that follows focuses on several films, each of which provides a different sense of the Garden and a different critique. That the majority of the films are by women may be a vestige of the tendency, so evident in nineteenth-century America, for women to be involved in nature as gardeners while men were surveying vast landscapes, either literally or as part of the tradition of landscape painting. This chapter is much indebted to John Dixon Hunt's *Gardens and the Picturesque* and the evolution of landscape architecture Hunt charts.[1]

Kenneth Anger: *Eaux d'artifice*

Eaux d'artifice (1953) is the third earliest Kenneth Anger film currently available for public exhibition (it was preceded by *Fireworks* [1947] and *Puce Moment* [1949]); its first distributor was Cinema 16, the New York film society. Anger's original catalog description for the film calls it "[a]n evocation of a Fairbank [P. Adams Sitney explains that Anger is referring to author Ronald Firbank][2] heroine, lost in a baroque labyrinth, in pursuit of . . . a night moth. Fountains, cascades, a fan, and . . . a transmogrification." For thirteen minutes, the woman Anger has identified as the "Water Witch" (a midget in drag played by the Italian Carmillo Salvatorelli) is seen walking and at times running through the gardens of the Villa d'Este, Tivoli. These spectacular gardens, twenty miles east of Rome, distinguished in particular by their complex system of fountains, were commissioned by Ippolito II d'Este, cardinal of Ferrara, and designed and built by Pirro Ligorio.[3] The film's seventy-five shots were recorded on "Ferrania Infra-Red film and printed on Ektachrome through a Cyan filter,"[4] resulting in a consistent deep blue tonality, interrupted momentarily by the blue-green, hand-colored fan unfolded by the Water Witch during the second half of the film (see plate 5). The visuals are accompanied by and deftly coordinated to passages from Vivaldi's *Four Seasons*. Salvatorelli, dressed in an elaborate gown with a fountainesque headdress, moves through the gardens in a stately way during much of the film, then—after the unfolding of the fan—is seen running, until she/he fades into a fountain, disappears, and is then seen, seemingly in an underground bower, continuing on her/his stately way.

Few avant-garde films are as sure to please a general audience as *Eaux d'artifice*. While ignoring virtually every commercial cinematic "rule," Anger's short film has a powerful, sensual impact: the combination of the spectacular gardens, the Vivaldi music, and Anger's exquisite compositions and editing rhythms create an experience most viewers identify as "beautiful," in a most traditional sense: the film seems to represent the very idea of classic Art in a space usually devoted to pop entertainment. That there are a number of deeper levels to *Eaux d'artifice*, however, including levels that might shock the very audiences the film so powerfully moves, is suggested by Anger's dedication of the film to the painter Pavel Tchelitchew, whose famous *Hide-and-Seek* (1940–42; see fig. 9) is referred to in another catalog note provided by Anger: "Hide and Seek in a nighttime labyrinth of levels, cascades, balustrades, grottoes, and ever gushing, leaping fountains. . . ."[5] Tchelitchew's eerie, powerful, surrealistic painting envisions a child entrapped in a psychic web of terrifying influences. The painting's design and coloring remind a filmgoer of creepy transformations in such horror–sci fi films as *Alien* (1979), *Aliens* (1986), and John Carpenter's remake of *The Thing* (1982). Even if we see *Eaux d'artifice* as a good bit more lighthearted than *Hide-and-Seek*, which it certainly *is*, Anger's evocation of Tchelitchew's painting is a hint that more is involved in his film than first meets the eye and ear.

Figure 9. Pavel Tchelitchew's *Hide-and-Seek (Cache-cache)* (1940–42), oil on canvas, 78½" × 84¾". The Museum of Modern Art, New York. Mrs. Simon Guggenheim Fund. Photograph © 2000 The Museum of Modern Art, New York.

In *Gardens and the Picturesque,* Hunt charts the transformation of the English garden from the "emblematic garden" to the "expressive garden," that is, *from* gardens which were designed to be read, in quite specific ways, as emblems of their owners' ideas and political-moral commitments, *to* gardens that were expressive of more generalized contemplative moods. The English emblematic garden was a function of the neoclassic era's determination to see England as a modern culture carrying on the classic traditions that had evolved in Greece and Rome. Gardens were designed so as to include references to classic mythology and history, readable to any sophisticated visitor; or to put it in terms relevant to this discussion, these English gardens were attempts to emulate classic gardens such as the one at the Villa d'Este. Certainly, for the culturally sophisticated visitor, the gardens at Tivoli were "readable": "the garden at Tivoli through its fountains and sculpture expressed a very complicated iconographical program devised by Ligorio, perhaps with the assistance of the cardinal's court humanist, the Frenchman Marc-Antionie Muret, to honor the cardinal."[6] So far as I am aware, Anger did not have the time or the interest to align his film with Ligorio's particular iconography. Indeed, the fountains themselves, and the particular figures we see in close-up, are presented as classical architecture in a state of decay (beautiful decay, to be sure) that relates closely to the romantic era's fascination with the ruin (see figs. 10–11). That is, Anger's film transforms an originally emblematic garden into something closer to an expressive garden, creating a pleasure as close to what has come to be known as the "picturesque" as to the kinds of intellectual pleasure the garden at Tivoli might originally have offered.[7]

However, in *Eaux d'artifice* the garden (which is not identified in any way in the film itself) does imply an iconography of the director's own devising, an iconography available to those familiar with Anger's earlier, and subsequent, filmmaking. In particular, Anger's earlier film, *Fireworks*, was, and remains, a landmark of what has come to be known as "psychodrama," a genre of American avant-garde film in which the filmmakers dramatize disturbed states of consciousness: key instances include Deren and Hammid's *Meshes of the Afternoon*, Sidney Peterson's *The Lead Shoes* (1949), and Stan Brakhage's *Reflections on Black* (1955).[8] *Fireworks* may also be the first openly gay film by an American filmmaker: the particular disturbed state of consciousness dramatized in the film is the simultaneous sensual excitement and psychological terror felt by a young gay man coming of age in an American society where gay desire was, to say the least, dangerous. The film takes the form of a dream during which the dreamer (played by Anger himself) imagines going to a bar frequented by sailors, where the dreamer is aroused, then attacked by the sailors. The sensual excitement of gay desire is implicit throughout the film. Early on, we see the protagonist with what looks to be a huge erection (it turns out to be an African statue the awakened dreamer is holding under the covers); and near the end of *Fireworks*, following the attack by the sailors, cream is poured over the dreamer's face and body, and he subsequently opens his fly to reveal a roman candle sticking out like an erection and, once lit, exploding in a

Figures 10–11. Fountains in the gardens of the Villa d'Este in Kenneth Anger's *Eaux d'artifice* (1953). Courtesy Anthology Film Archives.

firecracker orgasm. While *Fireworks* reveals the vulnerability of the young man, it is—as may be obvious from my description—full of a courageous, whistling-in-the-dark humor that is evident even in the gruesome scene of the attack: when the sailors use a broken bottle to cut into the dreamer's chest, we discover, instead of a heart, a mechanical "ticker."

Fireworks is a perfect emblem for the situation of gays in postwar America. Certainly there was an underground network where gays could meet each other; but in general, being gay was fraught with danger: at any moment, desire could lead to disaster. For Anger, gay desire was not a matter of choice; and even if the desire were repressed, it would find expression. In a voiceover prologue to *Fireworks* that is no longer part of the film, Anger explained, "In *Fireworks* I released all the explosive pyrotechnics of a dream. Inflammable desires dampened by day under the cold water of consciousness are ignited that night by the libertarian matches of sleep, and burst forth in showers of shimmering incandescence. These imaginary displays provide a temporary relief."[9] If *Fireworks* represents the impossibility of denying gay desire, even in a repressive, antigay society, *Eaux d'artifice* is an emblem of the release of repressed desire in societies less hostile to the full range of human sensuality. In 1951 Anger moved to Paris, where he worked at getting various film projects into production, including the one that was to become *Eaux d'artifice*, though at first Anger called it "Waterworks," presumably to indicate a connection with the earlier film: "I also have an idea for a 15-minute poetic study transpiring in the fantastic gardens of the Villa d'Este at Tivoli, to be called 'WATERWORKS.' "[10] Perhaps the change in title was a means of emphasizing the *European*-ness of the film, while implicitly connecting it to *Fireworks*.[11] That the gardens at Tivoli had originally been part of a monastery—which Anger may well have known—might have made their sensual beauty all the more poignant for him. Even Anger's dedication of the film to the painter Tchelitchew seems relevant here, as the Russian surrealist was not only gay, but openly, even flamboyantly so, both in his life and in his painting, where homoerotic sexual longing is frequently obvious.[12]

If we approach *Eaux d'artifice* from the standpoint of gay desire expressed, the exuberant arcing water of the fountains takes on an erotic suggestiveness, the precise opposite of the cold water that dampens Anger's inflammable desire in his prologue to *Fireworks*. Certainly Anger's frequent slow-motion shots of arcing water are as suggestive of male orgasm as are the flying sparks from the roman candle in *Fireworks*—and this seems particularly evident in the wake of American hard-core pornography in which the "cum shot" was frequently presented in arcing slow motion. Whether one wants to go further and see the fountains as emblematic of what is sometimes referred to as "water sports," that is, forms of erotic interaction involving urine and feces as well as semen, I'll leave up to the reader—although this idea has been suggested to me more than once and is given support by Bill Landis in his unauthorized and unreliable biography of Anger: Landis claims Anger wanted to make a film about a teenage descendant of the d'Este family, who—Landis quotes Anger as saying—"liked being pissed on, by goats, men, women, I don't know—whoever's capable of pissing. So the whole garden is actually a private dirty joke. It has ten thousand fountains and everything is pissing on everything else."[13] Landis exaggerates the degree to which *Eaux d'artifice* needs to be seen as a film about eroticism, and especially forms of eroticism widely considered perverse. But the film does suggest erotic release, and indeed, if the reader can forgive a somewhat ham-handed reading, the figure of the woman loose in this garden may be Anger's way of suggesting that Europe had allowed Anger to release the "woman" inside himself, within homosexual erotic and romantic encounters.

In his *Un chant d'amour* (1952), Jean Genet suggests the paradox that in prison gay men are freer to reveal their gay desire than they are in "normal" life. For an Americanist, *Eaux d'artifice* reveals a related paradox. The idea of the North American continent as the New Eden—whether we interpret the New Eden as God's original creation, as Thomas Cole did; or as God's gift to the worthy, who as Second Creators will develop a new, superior society on the basis of its resources—must always have been ironic for gay men. America may be "the land of the free" for many people, but it has never been as free as much of the European continent for gays. If heterosexuals have moved westward with the translation of empire from Greece, to Rome, to England and France, and across America, homosexuals have often needed to move eastward to achieve anything like a comparable level of freedom. And if we think of the Hollywood movie industry as the ideological spearhead of American empire, at least in this century, Hollywood's fundamental commitment to the maintenance of the heterosexual couple confirms the pattern. Anger was born in Santa Monica and grew up in Hollywood; indeed, he has supported himself with his series of written histories of Hollywood scandal: *Hollywood Babylon*

(1975) and *Kenneth Anger's Hollywood Babylon 2* (1984)—he is currently writing *Hollywood Babylon 3*. However, as an individualistic *filmmaker* interested in exploring and expressing his own psyche and his own experience, Anger was forced to move against the grain of Hollywood, to move East, first to New York, then to Europe, and precisely away from the "normalcy" marketed (so hypocritically, it would seem from Anger's *Hollywood Babylon* books) by the industry. Paradoxically, it was in a sixteenth-century Italian garden, built by a high-ranking official of the Roman Catholic Church, that Anger was first able to cinematically celebrate his own life, liberty, and pursuit of happiness.

Marie Menken: *Glimpse of the Garden*

> There was a very lyrical soul behind that huge and very often sad bulk of a woman, and she put all that soul into her work. The bits of songs that we used to sing together were about the flower garden, about a young girl tending her flower garden. Marie's films were her flower garden. Whenever she was in her garden, she opened her soul, with all her secret wishes and dreams. They are all very colorful and sweet and perfect, and not too bulky, all made and tended with love, her little movies. —JONAS MEKAS'S *VILLAGE VOICE* OBITUARY FOR MENKEN AND WILLARD MAAS, JANUARY 14, 1971[14]

> Yet, Marie and Willard had their own bed, over which hung one of Marie's sand paintings, with an actual rattlesnake skin implanted in it, which she had titled "The Garden of Eden." —STAN BRAKHAGE, *FILM AT WIT'S END*[15]

As of 1999 probably no woman who has had as significant an impact on American cinema as Marie Menken remains as little celebrated. Except for several of her colleagues of the 1950s and 1960s—Stan Brakhage, Jonas Mekas, and P. Adams Sitney—virtually no one has been interested in assessing her films and their impact on others; and only Brakhage has written as much as a chapter on Menken. Indeed, Sitney's "greatest regret" as chronicler of American avant-garde filmmaking of the post–World War II era is that he did not include Menken's work in his *Visionary Film*.[16] Menken was not a prolific filmmaker. Eighteen films are currently in distribution, nearly all of them quite short, including most of the films that established and maintained her reputation at least among avant-garde filmmakers of her era: *Visual Variations on Noguchi* (1945), *Hurry! Hurry!* (1957), *Glimpse of the Garden* (1957), *Arabesque for*

Kenneth Anger (1961), *Eye Music in Red Major* (1961), *Bagatelle for Willard Maas* (1961), *Notebook* (in various versions, from 1961), *Go! Go! Go!* (1962–64)—the last two are compilation pieces made up of several mini-films.[17] Only her portrait of Warhol, *Andy Warhol* (1965), is more than fifteen minutes.

Menken's contributions to film history are twofold: several of her films repay careful engagement as complex, finished works; and Menken's *approach* to filmmaking was a pivotal influence on filmmakers who themselves have had considerable impact on modern avant-garde film history. Of her earliest films, *Glimpse of the Garden* may be the best for revealing both dimensions of this impact. *Glimpse of the Garden* is a response to the Long Island garden of Dwight Ripley, an ex-lover of Menken's husband, Willard Maas. According to Brakhage, Ripley "was an alcoholic who . . . had become very dependent on Marie. She came to love him deeply, long after Willard was through with him and they were great friends. Dwight was a painter, and, as well, was passionately involved in gardening."[18] Ripley's extensive garden was full of rare imported plants; it included outdoor expanses of plantings and a greenhouse. As her title suggests, Menken's little film creates a counterpoint to Ripley's garden, both in scope and, implicitly, in the style with which Menken engages the garden spaces. While Ripley's garden reflects the organization and regular maintenance necessary for keeping a wide variety of plants alive, Menken's film feels offhand, free form, nearly spontaneous.

Not that *Glimpse* is disorganized. Menken edited the film's sixty-odd shots into rhythmic clusters that play off one another in a variety of formal ways,[19] within an overall structure punctuated by two brief shots of Ripley's greenhouse reflected in his pond (filmed with the camera upside down so that the reflection of the greenhouse is seen right side up): the first approximately two minutes into the film; the second, near the end. The various clusters of imagery seem to enact a catalog of ways in which a camera can "glimpse." Early in the film, for example, two rightward pans with mounted camera across the pond and nearby rock gardens lead into a series of brief images of particular plants, which are followed by two clockwise pans from a tripod and then by a long, hand-held traveling shot along a line of bushes, ending as the camera pans up a tree and back down to the garden where a series of very brief shots moves us successively closer to a bush with orange flowers—possibly a Roxana (*Potentilla nepalensis*). Each of these visual strategies is echoed during the second half of the film. The middle of the film explores the greenhouse, beginning with a continuous hand-held pan that moves to the right across potted plants; then after an ambiguous, relatively still image of a yellow plant, a second pan moves to the left, echoing the first. Menken's visual imagery is accompanied by a sound track of birdsong from a phonograph record. No attempt is made to synchronize sound and image. At most, one might conjecture that Menken hoped some of her more free-form camera movements might evoke the birds that must have flitted around the garden. Indeed, the obviously prerecorded bird sounds (sometimes distorted by the transfer to optical sound) seem a wry comment on the idea of nature, roughly in keeping with the implicit self-reflexivity of Menken's moving camera.

Despite the evident care in Menken's editing, however, and despite her topic—which offered her the possibility of a conventionally beautiful film—Menken's response to the Ripley garden is at least quirky and often abrasive. If her friends and colleagues recognized the quality of *Glimpse of the Garden,* most viewers then and now would, I'm sure, be skeptical of Menken's film. An audience ready for a film about a beautiful garden, or about nature, would be likely to find *Glimpse* lacking not only the smooth, generally predictable rhythms normally associated with the idea of filmically rendering a beautiful space but also the quality cinematography one expects of the competent nature photographer. Indeed, by the time the viewer reaches the final section of *Glimpses* and several conventionally beautiful shots of flowers, these images seem surprising: most viewers would wonder why Menken didn't work harder to create *consistently* well-photographed, beautiful images and would assume the answer was either laziness or incompetence. That several of the earliest shots in the film reveal that the camera gate had not been cleaned—bits of dirt are clearly visible at the upper left edge of the frame—seems to confirm such a conclusion.

Menken would be quick to point out that her films are not aimed at a general audience, or at an audience interested in conventionally capable depictions of nature; like Gertrude Stein, Menken made film for herself and a few friends. When asked in 1963, "Who is your audience?" she responded, "Mostly people I love, for it is to them I address myself. Sometimes the audience becomes more than I looked for, but in sympathy they must be my friends. There is no choice, for in making a work of art one holds in spirit those who are receptive, and if they are, they must be one's friends."[20]

If we respond to *Glimpse of the Garden* as Menken's friends—and if one has seen *Go! Go! Go!* and *Notebook,* one is inclined to give her the benefit of the doubt—we can use the very abrasions of Menken's little film as an opening into the complex sensibility that informs it. No one who knew Menken and Maas doubted they were serious artists; indeed, by the 1950s Maas's *Geography of the Body* (1943), for which Menken did much of the camera work (she also appears in the film), was justifiably recognized as a landmark avant-garde film. And they were artists at the center of the New York scene of that era: visitors to their apartment included such notables as Marilyn Monroe and Edward Albee (Menken recalled later, "Albee used to come here every time to eat and just sit and sit and listen while Willard and I argued. Then he wrote *Who's Afraid of Virginia Woolf*. That's supposed to be me and Willard arguing about my miscarriage"),[21] and many major contributors to independent film, including Norman McLaren, Kenneth Anger, Stan Brakhage, and Andy Warhol (Menken would have a starring role as an addict in Warhol's 1966 film, *Chelsea Girls*; see fig. 12).

Even if Menken was not a first-rate cinematographer by professional standards, she surely knew the difference between a beautiful image and an underexposed one, and fully understood the implications for viewers of her compositions ("As a painter of some experience, I can frame immediately with

Figure 12. Marie Menken *(left)* with Gerard Malanga, in Andy Warhol's *Chelsea Girls* (1966).

no deliberation of arrangement").[22] The logical conclusion is that in *Glimpse* Menken was exploring an aesthetic somewhere *between* a commitment to conventional forms of beauty (exemplified, of course, by the flowers in Ripley's garden and by the garden itself) and what Patricia R. Zimmermann describes as "reinvented amateurism" ("Since the 1950s . . . the American avant-garde has appropriated home-movie style as a formal manifestation of a spontaneous, untampered form of filmmaking").[23] Near the end, *Glimpse* provides a series of quite beautiful close-ups of flowers—enough to place the less-than-beautiful images into relief as another *option,* or set of options, for rendering the scenes offered by the garden: that is, she provides conventionally beautiful images, but *not too many.*

In fact, Menken's film seems to hover between a variety of possibilities, each of which, pursued too enthusiastically, might have rendered the result less fully a work of art that she and her friends could respect. On one hand, the film seems childlike (the bold, painted credits evoke children's art); on another, sophisticated (the witty irony of her use of canned bird sounds with the garden, itself a kind of "canned" reality). Some shots seem dedicated to a reasonably realistic rendering of the Ripley garden; and yet, at certain moments, Menken's freewheeling camera moves her imagery in the direction of abstraction—evoking the gestural dripping or brushwork of Pollock and de Kooning.[24] Her decision to accept imagery in which dirt from the camera gate is visible seems the epitome of artistic nonchalance, even laziness; and yet *Glimpse of the Garden* is quite heavily edited and in a manner that makes this heavy editing obvious. Finally, *Glimpse,* like other Menken films, is a response to another person's work (in *Visual Variations on Noguchi,* Menken responds to the sculptures she saw in Isamu Noguchi's studio; in *Arabesque for Kenneth Anger* [see fig. 13], she responds to Anger's *Eaux d'artifice*)[25] but is neither an imitation of the Ripley garden nor an homage. *Glimpse* is a self-expressive engagement with Dwight Ripley's garden—a kind of after-the-fact collaboration. It is *her* film as fully as it's *his* garden.

To put it simply, Menken's work, *Glimpse* in particular, is the result of her attempt to be a serious artist without being pretentious (or self-effacing), and a working-class woman without being anti-intellectual or disdainful of aesthetics. In *Glimpse of the Garden* Menken seems to reveal a filmmaking process and practice that are innocent of the corruptions of capitalism—her film is a defiantly little film, of virtually no commercial value—*and* of the class sensi-

Figure 13. Marie Menken (right)—with Kenneth Anger?—
shooting her *Arabesque for Kenneth Anger* (1961): the fountain
imagery in Menken's film is an homage to Anger's *Eaux
d'artifice*. Courtesy Anthology Film Archives.

bilities of communism: she may be a working-class filmmaker, but *Glimpse* is
defiantly individual; it is aimed at a coterie audience; and it luxuriates in a
wealthy friend's hobby. I'm reminded of comments by Jonas Mekas, Menken's
friend and admirer and fellow Lithuanian, in his *Lost Lost Lost* (1976): "Oh let
my camera record the desperation of the small countries. Oh how I hate you,
the big nations . . . you always think that you are the only ones, and others . . .
should only be part of you and speak your language. Oh come, come, the dic-
tatorship of the small countries."[26] Menken's aesthetic seems a version of this
sensibility: just as Mekas could (in the 1970s) see the "small countries" as
innocent of the immense crimes of the "major nations," Menken's film creates a cinematic Edenic space—a psychic garden, as well as a literal one—not
compromised or colonized by the "big countries" of cinema history. In this
garden, as Mekas would suggest in his obituary, Menken was able to grow a
variety of "flowers," some more impressive than others.

Further, Menken's way of being a filmmaker became puissant for the filmmakers who knew her and her films, which were clearly the seeds for filmmaking projects far more ambitious than her own. Among the filmmakers for whom Menken's work was pivotal are Brakhage and Mekas, two of the most powerful forces in the modern evolution of independent film. For these men, Menken was important for her general approach to making art. Brakhage called Menken "a 'natural,' her world the world of openings. . . . It is the ideology, if you can call it that, of Marie's working processes which have influenced my work. She made me aware that I was freer than I knew, that those chains were daisy-chains, those locks free flowing hair, etc."[27] Mekas's enthusiastic embracing of Menken's approach seems to have instigated an expansion of the notebook form Menken was exploring in *Notebook* and *Go! Go! Go!* first in his *Film Magazine of the Arts* (1963) and subsequently in the epic film "diary" originally known as *Diaries, Notes and Sketches (also known as Walden)*—now, simply *Walden*—filmed in 1964–68, edited in 1968–69, and the many diaries that have followed.[28]

More specifically, both Brakhage and Mekas (and no doubt others) were formally influenced by Menken's free-form camera work, the stylistic embodiment of her general attitude and approach, first in *Visual Variations on Noguchi* and subsequently in *Glimpse of the Garden.*

BRAKHAGE: "Visual Variations on Noguchi" liberated a lot of independent filmmakers from the idea that had been so powerful up to then, that we have to imitate the Hollywood dolly shot, without dollies—that the smooth pan and dolly was the only acceptable thing. Marie's free, swinging, swooping hand-held pans changed all that, for me and for the whole independent filmmaking world.[29]

MEKAS: . . . Brakhage and Menken represent the spearhead of . . . a film poetry free of obvious symbolism and artistic or literary influences, a poetry where the filmic syntax achieves a spontaneous fluidity. . . . The structure of Menken's filmic sentences, her movement, and her rhythms are those of poetry.[30]

In fact, Brakhage and Mekas were so committed to Menken's work that when Amos Vogel refused to show or distribute Brakhage's *Anticipation of the Night* (1958) and Menken's *Glimpse of the Garden* at Cinema 16, Brakhage refused to let Vogel show his other work, an incident that seems to have been pivotal in Mekas's subsequent formation of the New American Cinema Group and the Film-makers' Cooperative.[31]

If Menken's films are not currently in the forefront of the critical discourse about independent cinema, the influence of her early work remains pervasive. The "little film" she did so much to legitimize remains one of the options for avant-garde filmmakers from Brakhage to Jennifer Reeves. And 16mm, 8mm, Super-8mm, and video cameras, having been loosed from their Hollywood moorings, gesture from within the work of many film- and video-makers, and even from commercial film and television. Menken's individual films may have flowered only briefly, from the late 1940s through the mid-1960s; but her approach remains a perennial, if underrecognized, influence on contemporary media making. She seems sure to reemerge, however, not simply because of the accomplishments of her films and their considerable influence, but because the story of the life Menken and Maas shared—a heterosexual woman married to a sexually active, uncloseted gay man (whose response to Menken's accomplishments was at best ambiguous)—and the psychic toll it took seems to beg for a biographer. Indeed, in the context of this complex relationship, Menken's discovery of a mode of film practice that allowed her moments of psychic release from the traumas of the everyday and opportunities to have her own relationships with her husband's lovers—in the case of *Glimpse of the Garden,* to spend some moments merging Dwight Ripley's Eden with her own Edenic practice—is all the more poignant.

Carolee Schneemann: *Fuses*

At some point in the late 1950s, soon after I got my driver's license—it must have been the summer of 1958 or 1959—I went to the Cahokia Drive-in Theater (just across the road from the Cahokia Mounds near East St. Louis) to see *The Garden of Eden* (1956, directed by Max Nosseck). I do not remember who I went with or, for that matter, anything about the film itself—except that it did not simply tell the story of Adam and Eve, which in that age of the biblical epic, I had expected. I knew only one thing about the film, and that had been enough to get me to the Cahokia Drive-in: there was nudity. Indeed, I remember thinking that it would be impossible for a film about the Garden of Eden *not* to have nudity. Ironically, I don't even remember what nudity there was (although I do remember it had nothing to do with the "real" Adam and Eve)[32]—all I remember is my excitement at the prospect.

At the start of the new millennium, it's difficult to imagine that nudity could ever have been as important as it seemed to us then (although obviously it remains a central element in media marketing). We were the generation that grew up in the era of the Hollywood Code and of the conservatism of the postwar years, when Lucy and Ricky slept in separate beds, when the only images of naked women available were in the new, funky-smelling girlie magazines we'd have to steal from the one local store that carried them (since no one would sell them to kids, and since we wouldn't have had the nerve to be seen buying them anyway). These magazines were of limited educational value: for example, pubic hair was routinely airbrushed out of the photographs, which resulted in my receiving one of the shocks of my adolescent erotic life during an early heavy petting session with a real girl.

For that economically lucky, emotionally and sexually confused generation, Eden *was* Edenic because Adam and Eve were naked there "and were not ashamed." That the biblical Eve and Adam didn't actually have sex in the Garden (Adam doesn't "know" Eve until Genesis 4:1, after the Expulsion) didn't matter: if they were nude together and were not ashamed, they clearly lived in a sexualized state we could only dream of, a state of sensual freedom that was only alluded to in commercial film romances like *A Summer Place* (1959, directed by Delmer Daves), in which sex, at least between young people, was at best furtive and dangerous to one's name and future. Indeed, it was not for the better part of the decade that film history would produce a film that matched our sense of what Eden ought to be like, and that suggested that a man and woman, living in the real world now, could experience, on a day-to-day basis, the central fantasy of our adolescence. The film, Carolee Schneemann's *Fuses* (1967), has become one of the quintessential sixties films— though it was controversial then and has remained controversial, for a variety of different reasons, ever since.[33]

For *Fuses,* Schneemann and her partner, the composer James Tenney, recorded their sexual activity over a period of months; and Schneemann, who realized early on that the simple filming of sexuality did little to capture her/their psychic experience during sex, worked the resulting imagery in a wide variety of ways: she painted the filmstrip; etched into the emulsion with a razor blade, a toothbrush; bleached portions of it; baked it . . . Indeed, she became so involved in layering imagery on the filmstrip that "[i]t was a horrible shock, one of the worst" after three years of work, "to be told by the film lab that *Fuses* in its collaged layers was too thick to run through the printer!"[34] The finished film is, as several commentators have recognized, a remarkably textural experience, which reveals sex as at least as fully an experience of touch as of visual spectacularity (see fig. 14).[35] And, to return to the idea of sexuality *as* Garden of Eden, the sex depicted in *Fuses* is not seen as a series of acts that takes place within the confines of a physical garden; rather, the lovers' sexual intimacy *is* an Edenic state from which the world around them acquires new meaning and is transformed.

Within Schneemann's abstract-expressionist design, a variety of imagery in addition to the sex itself is visible. There are frequent shots of Schneemann's cat, Kitch, who is this film's spirit of place. Kitch is alert to her surroundings but in an entirely nonjudgmental way: sex is something that, of course, is going on in her world. And there are frequent images of a window (often Kitch is sitting in the window) that simultaneously allows light into the room and allows us to see out, although we see only the leaves of nearby trees and, in winter, a bit of snow-covered field.[36] If it is clear that this lovemaking has a

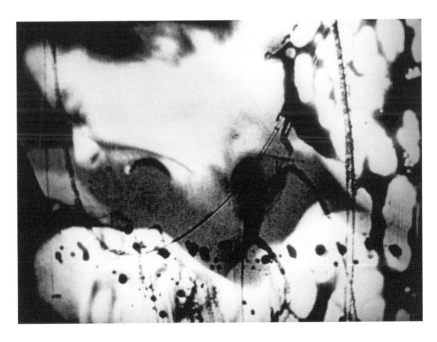

Figure 14. Carolee Schneemann and James Tenney in the throes of sexual abandon, in *Fuses* (1967). The filmstrip combines photographed imagery and painting-on-film. Courtesy Anthology Film Archives.

life that spans the seasonal cycle, it is also obvious that the life of the lovemaking proceeds regardless of what the season is. While we do see a few images of life away from sexuality—several shots of Tenney driving; one brief passage of crossing the George Washington Bridge into Manhattan; and, at the end, images of Schneemann running on a beach—most of them confirm the rural surround implicit outside the window (since 1964 Schneemann has lived in an eighteenth-century Dutch farmhouse in the Hudson Valley, on the west side of the river in the shadow of the Shawangunk Mountains, and a few miles from John Burroughs's retreat at Slabsides). In many instances, Schneemann develops explicit comparisons between the nature outside the window and the "nature" inside. At one point a close-up of Tenney's scrotum and testicles is followed by a close-up of a cluster of grapes hanging from a vine; and Schneemann says, "[T]here's a close-up of my [Schneemann's] 'bush.' Then the clouds over a silhouetted bush—the sun setting behind the shrub. I loved discovering those associations."[37]

The connection between the nature outside the window and the sexual intimacy inside is confirmed, first, by the fact that Schneemann provides little sense of the indoor space she and Tenney are living in: we see that they are often on a bed; at Christmas time we see a decorated tree (just before we see the lovers' bodies decorated with Christmas lights); but we are generally more fully aware of the natural surround outside the home than we are of the indoor spaces: cinematically, the lovers are juxtaposed with nature, not with the conventional accoutrements of domesticity. Second, in addition to the several means of working the surface of the filmstrip, Schneemann often experimented with more direct, visceral means: at times, she hung strips of film outside during rain- and electrical storms to see how such natural events might affect the filmstrip; she even put strips of film in a bucket of her own urine. And throughout her work on the film, she says, "I was working in a very dusty space. Every day another bunch of spiders had crawled over the table there. The cat was in my lap. . . . [G]iven the physical conditions I worked in and my own temperament, what I made could never be pristine. . . . I felt that all my images had to be available to the natural kinds of damages that would occur in my working situation."[38]

However, while *Fuses* does evoke the tradition of the garden, Schneemann's Eden defies the biblical Eden in a variety of ways and counters the pervasive American tradition of visualizing New World nature, in Annette Kolodny's words, as "a maternal 'garden,' receiving and nurturing human children."[39] If Western sexual politics has depended on the second creation story, where Eve is created after Adam as a helper, in Schneemann's Eden the woman and the man are sexual equals (as Adam and Eve are in Genesis 1), *partners* in sexual pleasure; and this equality is expressed visually in a variety of ways. Schneemann and Tenney do not enact a frieze of sexually and politically charged "positions," and even when one or the other is "on top" (what would often during the 1970s and 1980s be understood as an index of the politics of male domination), Schneemann prints the image both right side up and upside down: in a sexually political sense, there is no "up" or "down" in this interaction; both man and woman give and take pleasure. Even when Schneemann alludes to the artistic tradition of the nude, as she does, for example, in a slow pan of herself in a reclining position, this relatively conventional image is balanced with images where the camera pans Tenney's body in the same way: *both* bodies are at times objects of an erotic gaze on the part of the viewer, of the camera, and, implicitly, of Schneemann and Tenney; and neither body is frozen by this gaze: "I had to get that nude off the canvas" and away from "art history's conjunction of perceptual erotica and immobilizing social position."[40] While an immobilizing, scopophilic gaze has been as fully a part of film history as of art history, Schneemann's combined activity as both sexual partner and filmmaker was, and remains, a feminist response.[41]

If the sexual equality of the man and woman in Schneemann's Eden conforms more fully to the Eden of Genesis 1, however, *this* Eve defies the Creator in Genesis in a most crucial way: God's first demand of the newly created man and woman is to be fruitful and multiply, but Schneemann's Eden is clearly childless. In fact, Schneemann claims that Stan Brakhage's *Window Water Baby Moving* (1959) instigated her decision to make *Fuses;* her mixed feelings about Brakhage's birth film led Schneemann to balance Brakhage's paean to motherhood with a film in which sexuality/eroticism was definitely *not* a means to the end of fruitfulness/multiplication.[42] In this sense, *Fuses* is a reimagining of the Genesis Eden, from Eve's point of view. Both creation stories suggest that at least the primary, perhaps the only, creativity available to woman is the creation of children; but *Fuses* argues that if "God created man in his own image, in the image of God he created him; male and female he created them,"[43] then women, like men, should be honored, not simply for the creation of children, but as God-like creative beings in general, capable of original creation as well as of the replication of the species. In Genesis 2 and 3, the serpent is condemned for beguiling Eve by appealing to her desire for wisdom. As *Fuses* makes clear, however, Schneemann is committed to the wisdom of women, not just about childbirth and child rearing, but also—and despite the norms of fifties and early sixties America—about all aspects of life, including sexuality. If the serpent has often been read as a stand-in for the phallus, Schneemann is not only not "beguiled" by this "serpent," she accepts him into herself: one of the earliest recognizable sexual images in *Fuses* is Schneemann putting her mouth over Tenney's penis (see also fig. 15).

Fuses reverses the trajectory of the Eden story. Adam and Eve are driven from the garden as a result of their desire for knowledge and freedom, into the drudgery of toiling in the earth and the pain of childbirth, and, in Christian mythology, cannot reattain Paradise except through a second dispensation—a sacrificing of the things of this world in the name of Christ. By means of their love, Schneemann and Tenney are able to transform their everyday world back into an Eden, a place where love—as expressed not through self-sacrifice but through physical unification—exists unendingly between the lovers, and the seasons outside their window fly by, as if the lovers exist in a timeless world. Schneemann does not till a literal garden in *Fuses:* we do not see her gardening in the imagery; and although she did, in at least one instance, use the filmstrip as a garden "bed" in which to grow mold (*Vietflakes,* 1965), she doesn't do that here.[44] But her reworking of the filmstrip *was* an attempt to move a technological medium, a quintessential product of the industrial revolution, in the direction of the organic.

As a young painter, Schneemann struggled with the question of how to represent the complex experience of sitting in a landscape, simultaneously trying to see its structure and to be a living part of it. In *Fuses* Schneemann uses the filmstrip as a space in which she can represent the fusion of her physical and psychic life during lovemaking; but, more fundamentally, where she can attempt a fusion of the traditionally gender-distinct realms of technology and biology. By painting and etching over and across the precise, individual spaces of the frames, Schneemann fuses the preordained, technological regularity of the filmstrip with expressive gestures that develop from her biological rhythms, dramatized *in* the film by both the sexual rhythms of the lovemaking and by the imagery of Schneemann running on the beach.[45] Like the ocean and like other women, Schneemann is on a lunar cycle of ebbs and flows that

Figure 15. Carolee Schneemann and boa constrictor, in *Boa Constrictor*, photographed in London in 1970 by Alexander Agor. Courtesy Carolee Schneemann.

endlessly resists the assembly line structures of modern history, structures that seem dedicated to the suppression of the erotic and the organic in the interests of producing endless forms of redirected desire and multiplying industrial products dedicated to the momentary illusion of relief from our fallen state.

Stan Brakhage: *The Garden of Earthly Delights*

While Schneemann was using *Fuses* to reimagine Eden for a generation raised on a diet of delayed gratification, during the same era Stan Brakhage was manifesting a new cinematic vision that assumed that each of us is born into Eden, although the process of acculturation, especially our entry into language, quickly destroys the early beauty (and terror) of perceptual innocence. In the famous paragraph that opens his *Metaphors on Vision,* Brakhage describes this state of innocence.

> Imagine an eye unruled by man-made laws of perspective, an eye unprejudiced by compositional logic, an eye that does not respond to the name of everything, but which must know each object encountered in life through an adventure of perception. How many colors are there in a field of grass to the crawling baby unaware of "Green"? How many rainbows can light create for the untutored eye? How aware of variations in heat waves can that eye be? Imagine a world alive with incomprehensible gradations of color. Imagine a world before the "beginning was the word."[46]

During the past fifty years, Brakhage has dedicated himself to the use of the technology of cinema, a technology designed to market modern society's assumptions about itself, to conceptualize primal vision, and to provide visual evocations of it. And, not surprisingly, the idea of the Garden has always been important to Brakhage: his titles include *The Animals of Eden and After* (1970), *The Machine of Eden* (1970), *Star Garden* (1974), and *A Child's Garden and the Serious Sea* (1991).

But Brakhage's half century of using cinema as a perceptual adventure poses a virtually unique problem for the commentator. Brakhage has become so prolific (the new Canyon Cinema catalog lists nearly three hundred films) that a scholar trying to comprehend Brakhage's work can feel like a modern version of Tristram Shandy, who discovers—in Lawrence Sterne's *Tristram Shandy* (1767)—that he is living 365 times faster than he can explain his life to us: Brakhage seems to complete new films faster than even those devoted to his work can see and digest them.[47] This is not simply an issue of productivity, however; Brakhage's films are subtle and complex; they do not declare simple, clear meanings even to a viewer watching intently, but usually require a sustained engagement. One solution is to focus on a microcosm of Brakhage's work, as a beginning toward understanding the macrocosm. If I choose that approach out of self-defense, I do so recognizing that, in fact, it is particularly appropriate to Brakhage's vision: the perceptually innocent child's visual adventuring is often evoked by Brakhage's comparatively sustained engagement with individual, "tiny" facets of experience.

The Garden of Earthly Delights (1981) is a brief film (two and a half minutes), and as is true of most of Brakhage's films, silent.[48] Like the earlier, better-known Mothlight (1963), which remains Brakhage's most frequently rented film, The Garden of Earthly Delights was produced by using what Brakhage felt, at the time when he was making Mothlight, "was a whole new film technique."[49] Having collected bits of natural detritus—seeds, tiny flowers, leaves, blades of grass—Brakhage arranged them as a collage along a 35mm filmstrip (actually, the materials were sandwiched between two 35mm filmstrips) and had the results printed so that the finished film could be projected (see plates 6, 7).[50] The experience of The Garden of Earthly Delights is as unusual as the technique that produced it: the viewer's eye/mind is barraged with myriad particular images that often declare themselves to be what they are—imprints of seeds, flowers, leaves—in a flickering kaleidoscope that, if it is difficult to grasp in any particularity, does reveal a general overall shape: the experience begins and ends with darker, more densely textured imagery, which frames a central section of the film that, while also fast moving, reveals particular bits of seed, flower, leaf more clearly and with more light and a wider range of color. This general shape suggests the daily cycle, from darkness to day and back to darkness, and perhaps the seasonal cycle as well.

Because Brakhage's films must be apprehended as in-theater experiences, rather than as texts—the only possible notation for The Garden of Earthly Delights might be a frame-by-frame reproduction of the entire film, but this would be only a "score" for the reality of the projected work's rapid-fire motion—they have received less critical assessment than films that can be more easily notated in screenplays or other forms of verbal text. But if Brakhage's films resist easy verbal codification, they are immensely evocative, in ways that do connect them with major strands of cultural discourse. The *experience* of *The Garden of Earthly Delights* evokes a complex, multileveled set of implied comparisons between Brakhage's filmmaking and gardening. The most obvious level of comparison is suggested by Malcolm LeGrice's insight into *Mothlight:* "The physical problem of making a printable collage, which also allowed the passage of light through the surface, determined that the objects used should be thin or translucent. This makes them a metaphor for the nature of the celluloid on which they are supported."[51] This comparison works both ways (both in *Mothlight* and in *The Garden*): that is, Brakhage's filmstrip is equally a metaphor for the moth wings in *Mothlight* and the leaves and flowers in *The Garden of Earthly Delights* (there are also leaves and flowers in *Mothlight*—though the two films emphasize different elements).

Just as the seeds, flowers, and leaves we see in *The Garden* are a residue of natural processes going on in Brakhage's backyard as he was making this film, the strip of film we see projected is a residue of the creative process that produced it. Brakhage has always spoken of his films as having been "given to him" to make, as if he, like the plants he sees growing, is simply another instance of natural process. Plants naturally develop from seeds, putting out leaves and flowers; Brakhage has a "seed" of an idea for a film, from which it develops and flowers.[52] Indeed, cellulose, the main constituent of all plant tissues and fibers, is also the source of celluloid. Green plants live and grow through the process of photosynthesis, the action of light on chlorophyll-containing cells; Brakhage's filmic garden comes to fruition from the action of light—first of the printer, then of the projector—on the "cells," the frames of his filmstrip. Brakhage's "garden" is one technological step removed from the "garden" that produced the detritus he recycles; but the shape of his creative process echoes the shape of the more fundamental creative process his film honors.

A second level of evocation is implicit in the overall experiential shape of *The Garden of Earthly Delights*. The very brevity of the film—and the dense, ever-changing experience that is created in less than three minutes—evokes the more specific form of a household garden: a particular, often small, carefully defined space of ground that is tilled, planted, weeded, until the flowers or fruits are mature and can be enjoyed and harvested. Brakhage uses the filmstrip as a furrow; he plants seeds, arranges "beds" of particular flowers, until his garden, *The Garden,* can be harvested (printed/projected) and enjoyed

Plate 1. Thomas Cole's *View from Mount Holyoke, Northampton, Massachusetts, after a Thunderstorm — The Oxbow* (1836). Oil on canvas, 51½" × 76". The Metropolitan Museum of Art, Gift of Mrs. Russell Sage, 1908 (08.228). Photograph (1995): The Metropolitan Museum of Art.

Plates 2 – 3. The fog slowly clears in Larry Gottheim's *Fog Line* (1970).

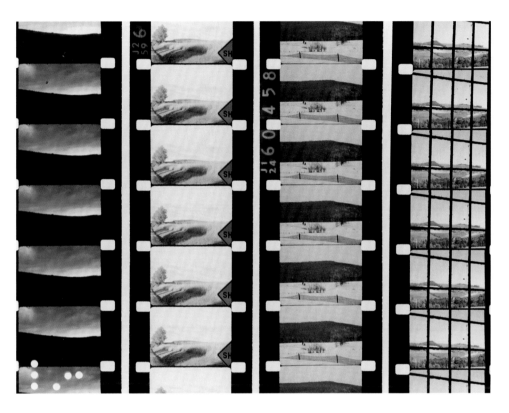

Plate 4. Four filmstrips from Larry Gottheim's *Horizons* (1973).

Plate 5. The water spirit unfolds her fan, in Kenneth Anger's *Eaux d'artifice* (1953). Courtesy Anthology Film Archives.

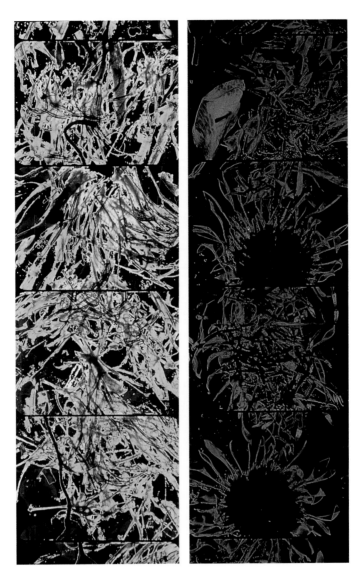

Plates 6–7. Filmstrips from Stan Brakhage's *The Garden of Earthly Delights* (1983). Courtesy Anthology Film Archives.

Plates 8–9. Filmstrips from Rose Lowder's *Bouquets 1–10:* *(left)* from *Bouquet 9* (1995); *(right)* from *Bouquet 10* (1995). The imagery on the left was recorded along the Route de Signes; the imagery on the right, in the Alps (the bottom frame of this filmstrip depicts an artificial lake created by the Serre-Ponçon Dam on the Durance River). Courtesy Rose Lowder.

Plates 10–11. Mono Lake *(above)* and a mountain scene *(below)*, from Babette Mangolte's *The Sky on Location* (1984). Courtesy Babette Mangolte.

(viewed/consumed) by himself and others. The wild effusion of imagery in the completed film evokes a gardener's fascination with the continual series of tiny changes that are inevitable as a garden is developing. And the overall shape of the film—the dense, often multilayered imagery of the opening and closing sections—may suggest the edges of a garden plot, where the gardener must continually contend with plant (and animal) life that might endanger the healthy development of the chosen crops.

A final level of "gardening" in *The Garden of Earthly Delights* occurs on an entirely different level. If we remember that Brakhage's quest is for an innocence of vision/Vision, for a "Garden of the Eye," the particular nature of the visual experience created in this film makes additional sense. Whereas conventional motion picture imagery creates the illusion of motion from a succession of slightly different images that strike the rods and cones of the retina and are processed by the brain, the motion in *The Garden of Earthly Delights* is created by series of frames of imagery that are in general quite different from one another, so different that, instead of resolving into the conventional illusion of motion, they create what is sometimes called "retinal collage": images seem to pile onto the retinas, creating evanescent collages.[53] The "retinal collage" may not have a sure scientific foundation (there is continuing debate on the status of the "retinal image"),[54] but *wherever* motion picture imagery is assembled for/in the brain becomes—for Brakhage in *The Garden of Earthly Delights*—a "garden space." In this space Brakhage "grows" exotic plants, or to be more exact, plants seeds and layers dead leaves and flowers (compost?) so that through the addition of light (of the printer and projector) they are endowed with at least a momentary facsimile of life within the eye/mind of the viewer, who in this instance is as much host (in the biological sense) as viewer.

That Brakhage does not exactly create the imagery we see in *The Garden of Earthly Delights* (he can know that the disparate frames of image will pile up, but he cannot know for sure how they'll look when the viewer sees them, until he prints and projects the filmstrip), that he merely implants various visual elements onto the filmstrip for subsequent replanting on the retina, in a sense frees the viewer's eye and mind to explore this visual garden in whatever way seems comfortable. Certainly our exploration discovers a variety of "exotica," as parts of different plants combine into impossible new organisms. But speaking for myself, I cannot watch *The Garden of Earthly Delights* without at times blinking to see how my interrupting the pile-up of images affects the experience: I am free to wander in this garden.

Of course, the exotic combination of separate plants into synthetic visual organisms can be seen as an allusion to the Bosch painting that gives Brakhage's film its title: Brakhage's Canyon Cinema catalog note indicates that the film is "an homage to (but also an argument with) Hieronymous Bosch." In the Bosch *Garden of Earthly Delights,* parts of human beings and animals are combined into impossible beings, presumably distorted by their hungers and sins. At the same time, Brakhage's garden seems less a warning to viewers than a direct attempt to return them to at least one kind of visual innocence: that is, he doesn't frighten with the sensual spectacle of sin, he conjures a new form of sensual spectacle that does not exploit human failings but sings both the spiritual excitement of working with the things of the earth (even if we're not clear about the details of how *The Garden of Earthly Delights* was produced, we are clear that Brakhage has painstakingly arranged details of his environment on the filmstrip) and the sensual enjoyment these simple, natural details of Brakhage's landscape can create, even in a medium usually devoted to the exhibition of sensual excess.[55]

Brakhage's *argument* with Bosch involves the gap between Bosch's tortured humans and what Brakhage calls Bosch's "puffy, sweet, idealized plant life." Through in-close exploration of the vegetation in his backyard, Brakhage came to feel that "these tiny plants were engaged in their tortured struggles too; they reach for a space in the soil and among the competing vegetation where they can find purchase—and they hunger for light."[56]

That Brakhage made a point of specifying in his catalog note for the film that he used only montane-zone vegetation for *The Garden of Earthly Delights* locates this project within the ongoing debate about which region of the United States is most quintessentially "American," a debate that in recent decades has often taken the form of the westerner's frustration with the cultural hegemony of northeastern landscape—the Hudson and Connecticut Valleys, the Catskills, the Adirondacks, the White Mountains, Niagara Falls— in American thinking. Brakhage was born in Denver and has lived most of his life in the Denver/Boulder area, including a good many years in the cabin in the woods at nine thousand feet in the Rockies above Boulder where *The Garden of Earthly Delights* was made. While he claims no specific biological knowledge of his region, for *The Garden* he used only leaves, flowers, seeds that he knew well (in an unscientific sense) from regular, close-up explorations of his yard. Of course, not only Brakhage's collage procedure but film projection itself automatically transforms what the camera records; as a result, it is virtually impossible even for a trained biologist to identify the vegetation we are seeing.

If Brakhage implicitly identifies himself as a westerner, distancing himself from eastern concepts of the Garden—both the landscape of the Northeast as the "garden" of the New World and the Eden story as understood by the European Christian churches that have emigrated west to America—he has distanced himself equally from the most visible elements of the New West, and especially from the marketing of the spectacle of sensual decadence (in both the personal and the environmental senses) so characteristic of Hollywood and Las Vegas. Of course, neither eastern nor western influences can be avoided in Denver, Boulder, or, really, even in the Rockies: Brakhage's act of respect for the Rocky Mountain ecosystem, after all, is produced by and for machines invented by Europeans and easterners and developed in Hollywood. Nevertheless, the concept of the Garden does continue to exist amid the machinery of cultural development; and Brakhage's *Garden of Earthly Delights* allows us to share an evocation of (visual) innocence with him, at least for a moment.

Marjorie Keller: *The Answering Furrow*

Marjorie Keller's *The Answering Furrow* (1985) seems as fully indebted to Marie Menken, and perhaps to *Glimpse of the Garden,* as any Mekas or Brakhage film. I know of no place where Keller makes a specific connection between her garden film and Menken's, but she does make a historical claim for Menken's cinematic style: "Menken opened a [William Carlos] Williams-like poetic dailiness to film. Williams's attention to detail—poetry as a series of close-ups—is analogous to Menken's cinematic style, which Brakhage has radically extended."[57] In *The Answering Furrow,* and in her other films, Keller has extended it as well.

In *The Answering Furrow* Keller uses her father's vegetable garden in Yorktown Heights, New York, as an emblem of her connection—as daughter and as filmmaker—with European spiritual and aesthetic traditions thousands of years old. The four sections of *The Answering Furrow* overtly echo

Virgil's *Georgics;* each section begins with a text (as is true in Virgil's paean to pastoral life) that describes the imagery the viewer is about to see:

> *Georgic I*—The annual produce first seen in spring—The furrowed earth ready for planting—The distribution, support, and protection of young plants—The implements of the garden.
>
> *Georgic II*—The life of Virgil is recapitulated in summer, with a digression on the sacred—The sheep of Arcadia—The handling of bees—The pagan lion of Kéa.
>
> *Georgic III*—The skill and industry of the old man in autumn—Ancient custom and modern method—The use of implements of the garden.
>
> *Georgic IV*—The compost is prepared at season's end—The filmmaker completes THE ANSWERING FURROW with the inclusion of her own image.

Keller's attitude toward the literary father of this film, like her attitude toward her physical father (and toward *The Answering Furrow* itself), is one of deep respect, qualified with a wry good humor, evident even in her use of these descriptions to introduce sections of a relatively brief (27 minutes), 16mm film.

As is clear in Keller's introductory texts, *The Answering Furrow* is organized seasonally, from spring through summer into fall, though there are other organizational trajectories as well. "Georgic I" (4 minutes, 39 seconds, including the text and the pause before the imagery of the garden) is organized into clusters of hand-held shots, accompanied by environmental sounds, first of birds and then of distant church bells, that feel in synch with the visuals though they were recorded separately. These clusters of shots—of the plowed garden; of deep green plants growing in furrows and along a fence; and, later in the season, guarded by strips of aluminum foil, cat masks, and pinwheels to frighten away birds and rabbits—begin in low-light conditions, making the imagery grainy, although by the end of the section, as summer nears, the imagery is brighter and clearer. That the individual clusters are separated from one another by moments of darkness suggests that, for Keller as for Brakhage, the filmstrip is a metaphor for the gardening furrow. As the seeds germinate in darkness as a result of the action of sunlight, the "furrow" of Keller's filmstrip in spring reveals a series of isolated images—also created by the action of light—that fill out the cinematic furrow by summertime.[58]

Near the conclusion of "Georgic I," we see a blue-headed rake; a small, yellow, gas-driven tiller; and a red wheelbarrow (perhaps an allusion to the famous William Carlos Williams poem "The Red Wheelbarrow")—the "implements of the garden." On one level, these modern tools seem to clash with the serious tone of this georgic, which is maintained by the tolling of the bells, although, like the quirkiness of this gardener's means of dissuading birds and rabbits from eating the seeds and young plants, the bright-colored modern implements evoke humor in the American tradition epitomized by Washington Irving's "Rip Van Winkle" and "The Legend of Sleepy Hollow." Irving's interest in creating a mythic past for the young American nation by inventing obviously tall tales and claiming considerable historical evidence for their factuality was a way of simultaneously admitting that great cultures must have traditional mythic tales while recognizing that, *whenever* these stories are created, they are fabrications by real people. If Irving cannot supply his American mythic tales with sufficient age to render them classic, he can offer his unpretentious good humor as a replacement. Similarly, Keller knows she is not likely to match the remarkable, classic accomplishments of Virgil; but the bright colors of her father's garden implements add a good-humored American exuberance to her classic theme: bright primary-colored plastic and metal may seem the opposite of the pastoral, but in fact they are the American means for maintaining the Virgilian tradition, and judging from the success of this garden, they work reasonably well.

"Georgic II" is the longest section of *The Answering Furrow,* though Keller's textual description develops the slightly mock-heroic quality subtly evident in "Georgic I." "Georgic II" certainly cannot "recapitulate" the life of Virgil, but it does provide a multilayered evocation not only of the great Roman poet's life and work but also of the Greco-Roman classic tradition in general. "Georgic II" reviews a trip Keller took that included France (St. Remy en Province), Italy (Mantua, Rome, Brindisi), and Greece (Arcadia, the island of Kéa); a further, implicit location is evident on the sound track of "Georgic II," a recording of "Ambrosian Chant" by Capella Musicale del Duomo di Milano. These locations do, very roughly, suggest the life of the Roman poet who was born in Mantua, was educated in Milan and Rome, used Arcadia as the mythic location for his earliest poems, the *Ecologues,* and died in Brindisi after setting out to visit Greece (on the voyage he caught the fever that killed him) presumably to research Greek locations for a final revision of the *Aeneid.* Keller's imagery of sheep certainly recalls Virgil's dedication to the pastoral; and a stunning, golden, slow-motion passage of a beekeeper and his bees is an allusion to a well-known passage in Virgil's *Georgics* on beekeeping, not only in its subject matter, but in the beauty of Keller's imagery as well. These evocations of Virgil are humorously confirmed by a glowing, golden image of a pat of Virgilio Burro (Virgil-brand butter).

On another level, Keller's trip—especially in the larger context of her Georgics I, II, and IV—suggests an American odyssey: Keller leaves her father's garden in Westchester County (north of New York City), travels the Mediterranean, and, in the end, finds her way back home. If she doesn't undergo the trials and tribulations of Greek or Roman heroes, she presumably does hear a "siren's song" (the chant) and feel its (monastic) allure; and while she confronts no Cyclops, she does see the (stone) pagan lion of Kéa. While Keller's imagery of Europe is often lovely, the farther east and into the classical past she goes, the less fruitful the landscape seems: the mountainous terrain in Greece is particularly dry and inhospitable (this is emphasized by what appears to be a vertical band of overexposure on the film). As a result, when the filmmaker returns to her father's New York garden in "Georgic III," its lovely autumnal colors and obvious productivity are all the more obvious. Keller reminds us of a paradox familiar to nineteenth-century American writers: this American garden may be part of a very young nation, but in its simplicity and unpretentious engagement with the earth, in its very youth (which is confirmed by the appearance of a young girl child in the garden), it declares its kinship with the pastoral origins of the great classic cultures.[59]

A parallel relationship is evident on the sound track of "Georgic III," which begins with the tolling of the bells and with the sounds of chirping insects and continues with a passage from Charles Ives's "Sonata for Violin and Piano #4 (Children's Day at the Camp Meeting)." Heard first during the textual introduction of "Georgic I," the Ives piece represents a distinctive contribution to American music—indeed, according to some commentators, Ives was "the first important distinctively American composer" whose work "anticipated some of the most radical developments of twentieth century music (dissonance, polytonality, polyrhythm, and experimental form)."[60] The obvious dissonance of the violin in the repeated Ives passage, which is heard a third time in Keller's brief fourth georgic (1 minute, 59 seconds), is a key to her own aesthetic as it is embodied in this film.

"Georgic IV" begins with Keller tending to the garden in late fall, flashes back briefly to imagery from her European trip (as if she is remembering it while she works), then concludes with her preparing the compost at season's end. On the most literal level, she is carrying on her father's work, maintaining the fertility of the garden he has established. At the same time, since this activity also "completes THE ANSWERING FURROW," clearly Keller means for us to see gardening as a metaphor, not just for filmmaking, but for a particular tradition of filmmaking that may have begun in Europe but has flowered in America: what is generally called avant-garde filmmaking.[61] Throughout her tragically short life (she died in 1994 at the age of forty-four), Keller was devoted to this history in virtually every way possible: in addition to her filmmaking, she was a writer, an editor, a teacher, and a programmer.[62] *The Answering Furrow* suggests that she saw her position in regard to the commercial film industry as analogous to the way Virgil positioned himself in relation to larger cultural developments.

Coming of age in the generation after Augustus had ended the Roman civil wars, Virgil argued, especially in the *Georgics,* for a return to traditional agriculture and a movement out of the overly crowded urban centers of power. By 1985 Keller—like many of us—may have seen herself moving out of what had been a volatile period of American cultural "civil wars" and interested in reaccessing the possibility of fruitful domesticity and spiritual connection. And just as small-gauge (16mm and Super-8mm) filmmaking had allowed Keller in the 1970s to mount her own critique of the American gender politics marketed in mainstream media, it now allowed her to argue, at least implicitly, for the necessity of familial connection and for a simpler, more deeply considered life. While those whose understanding of cinema is determined by mass-market cinema/TV are sure to find *The Answering Furrow* too informal, "unprofessional"—in a *dissonant* relationship to the smooth, marketable continuities of the mainstream—the film's unpretentious, handcrafted subtlety speaks with considerable elegance, with *poetry,* to those willing to cultivate a more complex, broad-ranging cinematic sensibility.

Anne Charlotte Robertson: *Melon Patches, Or Reasons to Go on Living*

Like Menken, Schneemann, Brakhage, and Keller, Anne Robertson uses the particulars of her domestic surround as the raw material for her films; but in her case, the relationship between life and filmmaking is both more consuming and, in at least one sense, more intense. The crucial fact of Robertson's personal life, and of her epic *Five Year Diary,* which has been growing for nearly twenty-five years, is the bipolar syndrome with which Robertson has been struggling, both at home and in mental hospitals, throughout her adult life. Making her film diary and reworking it into individual reels of diary film—to use the distinction David James developed for his discussion of Jonas Mekas, one of Robertson's cinematic mentors[63]— has been not only the central activity of her life, but one of her most effective means for managing the ravages of her disability: filming, editing, and showing her films has become a celluloid lifeline, providing coherence and continuity amid the demands of the sometimes self-destructive voices she hears. Working in Super-8mm, the quintessential domestic film gauge of the 1970s and 1980s, Robertson documents her own recoveries and relapses, both visually and vocally; her bipolar rhythm is expressed directly in her commentary and, indirectly, in her depiction of her own experience and the life around her. The only periods of Robertson's life not documented in *Five Year Diary* are her hospitalizations: for legal reasons, of course, cameras are not allowed in mental hospitals.

In recent years, the advent of video, combined with the precariousness of Super-8mm (fewer and fewer exhibition sites are willing and able to show Super-8 film; Kodak no longer manufactures Super-8 sound film stock—though, like other Super-8 devotees, Robertson stockpiled film stock before Kodak ceased manufacture), has led Robertson to release portions of the *Diary* on VHS. Several reels of *Five Year Diary* are available on video,[64] along with two cassettes of shorter films, including the subject of this discussion: *Melon Patches, Or Reasons to Go on Living* (1994). While Robertson does not consider *Melon Patches* part of *Five Year Diary,* it is closely related to the *Diary,* not only because it uses many of the same sorts of imagery, but also because its meaning and impact are to a considerable degree a function of its relationship to Robertson's ongoing project.

Each reel of *Five Year Diary* is introduced by the same opening credit and contains a variety of visual and vocal gestures that have remained motifs throughout the project,[65] including two auditory tracks (on one Robertson comments on what we're seeing, the way many of us "narrate" our home movies when we show them to friends and family; the other presents the more troubled voice of Robertson's disorder as she records it on tape or in sound Super-8);[66] time-lapse imagery of Robertson in her apartment; visual and/or auditory references to *Dr. Who*, the British sci-fi series starring Tom Baker, with whom Robertson has been romantically obsessed since the seventies; imagery of the backyard of her family home in Framingham, Massachusetts, just outside of Boston, where her mother lives (in more recent years Robertson has lived there, too), and in particular of a gazebo where Robertson has always dreamed of being married; imagery of the obsessive eating, drinking, and smoking with which Robertson struggles; her related obsession with her weight . . . ; and documentation of two gardens: one a community garden where Robertson has regularly grown her own organic produce; the other, behind the Framingham house.

Gardening is a special activity for Robertson—one that often provides a gauge of her current sense of her life. Early in Reel 23, her tenuous hold on psychic stability is reflected in her desire to liberate the root vegetables in her refrigerator by replanting them in the community garden. Reel 76 begins with the line "it was the end of the gardening season"—a fitting preview to the disillusionment with Tom Baker that occurs when she travels to Chicago to attend a Tom Baker conference. And Robertson's agony at the shocking loss of her three-year-old niece, Emily (in Reel 80), is reflected by her use of garden flowers to represent, on the one hand, the fact that Emily was "the flower in our lives" and, on the other, the impossible paradox of the loss of the child in the spring, and in the flower of her youth.

The films that reveal Robertson at her happiest are also much involved with gardening. The most obvious instance is *Melon Patches*, in which gardening becomes a metaphor for sanity and connection with family. While *Melon Patches* is (at 28 minutes, 10 seconds) approximately the same length as the individual *Diary* reels, it has its own structure and, at least overtly, reveals little of the psychic struggle dramatized in the *Diary*. With a single exception, there is no explicit representation of breakdowns or bipolar syndrome; the focus is consistently on Robertson's pleasure in growing melon seedlings from seeds, planting the little seedlings in the two gardens, frequently looking in on the growing melons (often, she reveals them to us as if they were a secret treasure shared with intimate friends), and finally harvesting and eating the melons with her mother. About halfway through *Melon Patches* Robertson begins the whole process a second time—in black-and-white we see her, again, growing seedlings from seeds, planting the seedlings, looking in on the melons: the implication seems to be that this is an annual process, a yearly ritual. At the end of the second season, the melons are shared not only with her mother, but with members of her extended family, including several nieces and nephews. The imagery was recorded during the successive years 1990 and 1991.

The sound track of *Melon Patches* is much simpler and less troubling than the sound tracks of the reels of *Five Year Diary*. During the first part of the film, we hear a baby playing nearby and at times apparently with the tape recorder microphone during what seems a quiet morning; later, we hear baby sounds with traffic in the background and the sound of the parents talking with the baby—"Tape recorder," says the mother. "It's a machine." During the second half of the film, and the second growing season, we hear an older child—or the same child, a year older—talking with her mother and father as they read a book and sing "Teddy Bear Picnic."[67] At the very end, there are just the sounds of nearby sparrows and distant traffic. The auditory pervasiveness of children throughout the film suggests, of course, that the melon seedlings and growing melons are Robertson's children. As she says in Reel 80 of *Five Year Diary*, "I had no children; all I had was a garden"; but near the end, the round faces of the babies of Robertson's siblings come to seem a different sort of melon crop; and family life itself—particularly the years with young children—is envisioned as an Edenic moment. Judging from *Five Year Diary* in general, it is virtually the only Edenic moment in Robertson's experience.

For those familiar with *Five Year Diary,* and for Robertson herself, *Melon Patches* is all the more poignant because of its subtle references to the troubled life documented in the *Diary* reels. These references include several passages of time-lapse imagery of Robertson smoking (typically, the pixilation gives her smoking a somewhat hysterical edge) and one shot of her taking some pills. There is also the frequent appearance of the gazebo in her mother's backyard: Robertson's dream of her own marriage and family increasingly seems (she was forty-two when she finished *Melon Patches*) a nostalgic, impossible fantasy, as Robertson is well aware. The only solutions seem to be frustration and anger, which move her toward further hospitalization and those forms of creativity that are available to her: gardening and filmmaking. Gardening is clearly a pleasure in itself and a metaphor for the ongoing, yearly "growth cycle" of *Five Year Diary*. In *Melon Patches* Robertson takes this metaphor one step further: the lovely developing spheres of the melons are a metaphor for this Edenic film and the psychic and familial wholeness it represents for Robertson.

She may never find an Adam with whom she can have children, but the little Edens she cultivates do matter. It is obvious in *Melon Patches* that Robertson's gardening contributes to the experience of her extended family—we see them enjoying the melons—and the gardens also seem to attract her nieces and nephews, whom she films amid the plants. Robertson's filmmaking also adds to the experience of her extended family, the way home movies, and more recently home video, have always added to the sense of family; and further, because Robertson's filmmaking is a bridge to a world beyond the domestic (*Five Year Diary* documents trips to New York City for shows at Anthology Film Archives and the New York Film Festival, to San Francisco, and to other screening venues), one can only infer that the family recognizes that *Five Year Diary* and its satellite shorter films embed them in a larger cultural arena.

During the 1950s and 1960s, at least in the United States, amateur film became virtually synonymous with home movies—not surprising during an era when the nuclear family was seen as "the only social structure available for the expression of common shared experiences that could shore one up against alienation and isolation."[68] Robertson's "home movies" are powerful because they simultaneously confirm and critique home-movie conventions. Robertson may idealize the nuclear family as fully as any home-movie maker, but she does so from a position to the side of that institution. She idealizes what she cannot achieve, and the poignancy of her films is a function of the fact that the longer she films, the more fully the combination of aging (with all the difficulties aging still brings women in our youth-oriented, image-obsessed society) and bipolar syndrome places this ideal beyond her grasp.

Or to put this in terms provided by *Melon Patches* itself, we need only be alert to the film's opening sequence—and the single exception, mentioned at the beginning of this discussion, where Robertson refers directly to her disability. Immediately following the credits, we see—as if in the first person—Robertson's closed hands held out in front of the camera. The hands open to reveal pills: specifically, the Trilafon she uses to control her bipolar swings. The hands close, and when they reopen they reveal cantaloupe and watermelon seeds. The gesture is evocative of traditional magic tricks—and, of course, the incorporation of magic into cinema—but within Robertson's film, and within her epic chronicling of her adult struggle to achieve something like a "normal" happy life, the transformation of pills into seeds is an act of hope and a fitting opening to *Melon Patches*' lovely reprieve—one of the very few in the many hours of Robertson's filmmaking—from the relentless unending fall from innocence chronicled in her work.

Rose Lowder: Toward an Ecological Cinema

By the time Rose Lowder bought her own 16mm camera, she had spent years working with loops of 16mm film, trying to determine whether the smallest unit of film structure was the single frame—as the Austrian Peter Kubelka had theorized[69]—concluding finally that "that's not the case at all," that in fact "pieces from different frames can make up what you're seeing on the screen."[70] Lowder's researches into the microcosmic units of cinema continued after 1977, once she was shooting her own imagery (for those early experiments she had used various film leaders and had worked directly on strips of clear celluloid: punching holes through frames, scratching or drawing lines along the filmstrip). While some of her earliest films use relatively long, continuous shots, others involved a painstaking process of recording imagery a single frame at a time, refocusing from one focus point to another in a single framed space, according to precisely organized "scores." This approach came to fruition in a triad of films, each of which focuses on a different kind of garden.

For *Rue des teinturiers* (1979), Lowder set up her camera to look out the balcony window of the second story of her house in Avignon, through her tiny balcony garden, at the Rue des Teinturiers across the way.[71] Over a period of months, she recorded this space, using a range of focus points so that, in some instances, elements of the street are in focus through the blur of nearby leaves, while at others, the leaves are clear and the distant street is a blur (see fig. 16). Of course, because the focus point changes in virtually every frame, the resulting experience creates a continual retinal collage that suggests the perceptual immensity of even the tiniest space and the myriad intersections between Lowder's cinematic plan, the activities on an Avignon street, and the various changes in light, breeze, color—some of them predictable, others out-

Figure 16. Four consecutive frames from Rose Lowder's *Rue des teinturiers* (1976): Lowder has refocused after each frame. Courtesy Rose Lowder.

side of Lowder's control—occurring in the balcony garden. In a sense, the little garden and Lowder's camera provide an analogy: each becomes a medium between Lowder's inner world (her domestic space, her plan for the film) and the space of the world outside: just as Lowder organized the garden to provide a tiny but effective "screen" between the busy street and her private space, the finished film is meant to screen out (if the reader can forgive the pun), at least for a moment, the usual commerce of film narrative and conventional exploitation of space.

Much the same procedure was used to make *Retour d'un repère* (Recurrence, 1979), in which Lowder explores a portion of a public park in Avignon; and for *Champ provençal* (Provençal Field, 1979), for which she filmed a peach tree in a Provençal orchard on three separate occasions (April 1, April 16, and June 24). In all three instances, Lowder uses her painstaking, even obsessive, procedure to expand what for most filmmakers—and especially commercial directors—would be a minimal bit of setting into a substantial film experience.[72] Beginning with *Les tournesols* (The Sunflowers, 1982), however, Lowder began to shift her tactics. *Les tournesols* is a brief (3 minutes) film of a field of sunflowers, photographed from a wide variety of focus points within the camera's field of vision. While the film certainly maintains its gaze on a single scene for far longer than any commercial film would, Lowder's single framing of the field seems to energize the field, condensing the subtle movements of the sunflowers that occurred during a period of hours into a comparatively brief cinematic moment. That the film's energizing of the field seems particularly reminiscent of van Gogh's sunflower paintings, which were painted in nearby Arles, was not Lowder's conscious intent: "I didn't go out to make a Van Gogh film, and never imagined that I had, because the brush strokes of Van Gogh . . . are so far removed from the kind of work I had to do to make the film."[73]

In the years after *Les tournesols*, Lowder's "minimalism" became less and less an attempt to reveal the complexity of tiny local spaces by expanding them cinematically and more and more an attempt to explore what might be accomplished by condensing events that took place over the period of a day into a single, limited duration of film. Whereas the early films often explore the deep space of a single composition, recent films explore time more fully than space. In *Impromptu* (1989) Lowder focuses on three trees and a field of poppies, each location filmed on a different day in a different way and strung together to make the finished film: "In the case of the first tree in *Impromptu* [a tree in a courtyard in Avignon], I just exposed one frame, left the next one black, exposed the next, left the next one black. Then I wound the film back, to exactly the same place . . . and then . . . exposed the second, fourth, sixth frames."[74] In the resulting imagery of the tree, the space remains constant, but the time is reconstructed so that during any one second we see twelve frames filmed during one sustained moment during the day, interspersed with twelve frames filmed at a later time during the same day; and because various natural factors—the light, the breeze, the shadows—are continuously undergoing more or less dramatic changes of their own, the resulting intensification of time within the space of the frame causes the tree to shimmer and quiver; it is as if the time-condensed imagery of the tree reveals the remarkable but normally invisible energy of photosynthesis. When Lowder concludes this first roll with a few seconds of normal motion, the normal motion looks as mysterious and surprising as the intensely worked passage that precedes it. Subsequent passages of *Impromptu* focus on a peach tree in an orchard near Avignon, a field of red poppies, and a peach orchard; in each instance, Lowder energizes a limited space by condensing and reorganizing the hours it took to make the imagery into the brief, seemingly continuous durations of the finished film.

Lowder's urge to explore the spaces and times of life in and around Avignon, and especially to condense experience into minimal cinematic durations, culminated in *Bouquets 1–10,* ten one-minute mini-films, made during 1994 and 1995 (see plates 8, 9). Even more than the earlier films, the *Bouquets* are meant to provide a cinematic model for ecological awareness: for Lowder, the relationship between her filmmaking and commercial filmmaking is analogous to that between organic farming and industrial farming:

MACDONALD: But do you see your concentration in your films as a kind of cine-politics? You eat organically; you don't own a refrigerator. Is your decision to work frame by frame a kind of environmental statement?

LOWDER: In opposition to big budget TV or cinema footage, yes. A developed society doesn't have to be a wasteful society. Take the example of organic farming. To survive today in France, an organic farmer has to be much more technically knowledgeable than an industrial scale farmer. The traditional farmer will be comparatively uneducated on the whole and will have technological sales representatives come along and tell him what to do, and when to do it. To reduce the number of people working on a farm, you need a tremendous amount of heavy equipment. You depopulate the countryside; you do very little manual work; and you produce a tremendous amount of food—too much, so much you have to throw some of it away (the government pays you to throw it away so that the prices stay up). Now if you look at the organic farmer, besides having to have more education, he or she will have to do more manual work. The field will need to be dug up by hand, or by more gentle machines, three or four times. The organic system requires that people are brought back to work on the land. Actually, in organic farming, there are more pieces of machinery, but smaller, more precise, and designed to accomplish particular tasks.

As an artist—to come back to your question—it's the same choice. You can work in a very precise way and make very particular decisions about everything you do. When I worked in the Industry, we sometimes had a sixty-to-one shooting ratio. I worked in one television company where I was throwing away sacks and sacks of stuff every day. In the Industry, the only things that count are the ones you sell. . . .

I don't propose that things change all at once—that would be unecological—but hopefully things could change in an ecological direction by gradually moving toward a world that is more in the interests of everyone.[75]

The idea of digging up a field by hand, more than once, describes Lowder's procedure in a variety of her films, especially in *Impromptu* and in sections of *Bouquets 1–10,* where our field of vision is created by Lowder's planting—on our retinas—images made by moving along the furrow of the film and exposing individual frames to light, several times. The unusually high energy of the landscapes in *Impromptu* is analogous to the high energy achieved by an organic diet.

Like Lowder's earlier films, *Bouquets* is arranged formally, like a carefully planned formal garden. Each *Bouquet* is exactly one minute long, and is separated from the *Bouquet* that follows by six seconds of dark leader punctuated by a single frame of a single flower in close-up.[76] Each *Bouquet* begins with the title, spelled out one letter at a time, and ends with "Rose Lowder" and a completion date, spelled out a single letter or number at a time. In any particular *Bouquet,* Lowder explores a range of visual possibilities of working one frame at a time, sometimes creating effects familiar from *Impromptu, Les tournesols,* and other earlier films, sometimes creating powerful, strobelike flicker effects. Whereas earlier Lowder films tend to arrange successive frames that have a clear compositional relationship to one another, gaps between successive frames in *Bouquets* are often so considerable that viewers tend to be seeing several kinds of spaces simultaneously: one triad of successive frames in *Bouquet 10* (1995), for example, reveals a close-up of a yellow *Lactuca perennis,* followed by a long shot of the artificial lake near the French Alps created by the Serre-Ponçon dam on the Durance River (completed in 1960, the dam flooded two villages, leaving only a hilltop church—in the center of the frame—above water level), followed by a close-up of a yellow hieracium. Another triad (in *Bouquet 7*) reveals a Provençal skyscape, a close-up of a tiny waterfall, and a tree in a courtyard. Lowder's consistent interplay among multiple spaces has the opposite effect of her articulation of multiple focus points in *Rue des teinturiers:* the earlier film expands a minimal physical space into an expanded cinematic space; each *Bouquet* condenses a considerable number of small, medium, and large spaces into a single, tiny, multilayered cinematic experience.

Not only do particular moments in individual *Bouquets* sometimes create "retinal bouquets"—more literally, when successive frames reveal a succession of different flowers, and always figuratively, since Lowder is almost always gathering the "flowers" of the physically beautiful region in which she lives—but the series of mini-films, as the title suggests, is conceived as a bouquet: a bouquet of *Bouquets.* Like a conventional bouquet of flowers, this one is designed not just for a single look but to be savored over a period of time. Certainly the visual density and the distinctive visual design of each individual *Bouquet* (*Bouquets 1–10* is silent) demands multiple viewings—the way an individual flower can sustain attention to its particulars. And the cluster of films involves so many different images of so many different places, presented in so many ways, that few viewers can summon the energy necessary to see the entirety of what Lowder has done during any single viewing. Fortunately, this cinematic bouquet has a life span considerably longer than a real bouquet—although, as Lowder's title also implies, each *Bouquet* she has presented us with is fragile, not only in the obvious sense that our eyes and memories can't hold onto its complex imagery for long, but also in the sense that like all objects in the material world, any particular film (and especially every color film) is subject to decay the moment it leaves its creator's hands. *Bouquets 1–10* requires that we gather our (cinematic) rosebuds while we may.

chapter 4

Re-envisioning the American West

In *Discoverers, Explorers, Settlers: The Diligent Writers of Early America,* Wayne Franklin defines three forms of narrative that developed during the first centuries of European expansion into North America, as a means of "domesticating the strangeness" of the vast new continent Europeans were in the process of "discovering," exploring, and settling. In the "discovery narrative," the writer stands in rapt wonder at the magnificent vista before him (the earliest writers were all, so far as I know, men), astonished at the immensity and the beauty of the reward God has provided at the end of his long ocean voyage. His prose is simple, overflowing with delight—sometimes merely a listing of the wonders he is faced with.[1] In the "exploratory narrative," the explorer longs to harness New World nature, "to transform its details into human objects or artifacts." Fittingly, the explorer's narrative prose style is grammatically more complex than the prose of the discoverer: "The invention of true sentences, by which things are subordinated to human will, provides a concise model of colonialization."[2] Finally, in the "settlement narrative," the settler-writer is faced with the problem of adjusting the discoverer's wonder at God's ideal creation, in light of the difficult facts of life that settlement in the now-explored territory has revealed: "The feat of writing becomes . . . an attempt to recognize the shape of recalcitrant truths and to name them by their proper names."[3]

Franklin's model developed from his analysis of sixteenth-, seventeenth-, and eighteenth-century literary texts, but it is suggestive for twentieth-century cinematic texts as well—despite the fact that the nature of the terrain to be discov-

Figure 17. No one did more to provide a cinematic vision of the American West than John Ford, beginning with *Stagecoach* (1939). Courtesy Museum of Modern Art.

ered, explored, and settled has changed dramatically, precisely as a historical result of the work of those whose lives are documented in the texts Franklin discusses. America is a terrain so thoroughly discovered, explored, and settled that we must struggle to find even the illusion of a distinctive, personal place for ourselves (see fig. 17). Commercial media makers have tended to distract us from any concern with coming to terms with the specifics of our real geography, often by implicitly arguing that our "place" is simply to consume whatever modern commerce makes available (including whatever geographic locales film directors and television pretend are the locations for particular on-screen activities). Many independent film- and videomakers, however, have attempted to use cinema as a means of reviving our sense of place in all its complexity—that is, for evoking something of the original discoverers' wonder at where we are, something of the original explorers' excitement in transforming the possible into the actual, and something of the original settlers' understanding of the practical failures of their surround—while at the same time recognizing the problematic moral, environmental, and political implications of five centuries of European involvement in the Western Hemisphere.

I have chosen three films and one videotape—Babette Mangolte's *The Sky on Location* (1983), James Benning's *North on Evers* (1991), Oliver Stone's *Natural Born Killers* (1994), and Ellen Spiro's *Roam Sweet Home* (1996)—to stand for that considerable body of independent, experimental narrative that fruitfully engages the issue of place, and, in particular, the American West, as a paradigm of the American experience.

The Sky on Location as Rediscovery Narrative

By the time Babette Mangolte made *The Sky on Location,* she had spent a decade in New York City and had established herself as one of the foremost independent cinematographers working in America. Having come to New York in 1970 to see films by the avant-garde filmmakers Stan Brakhage and Michael Snow, she stayed because of the excitement of the New York art scene and supported herself by working as a still photographer, specializing in the documentation of performance art and dance. Soon she was also doing cinematography for a series of landmark feminist films: Yvonne Rainer's *Lives of Performers* (1972) and *Film about a Woman Who . . .* (1974), Chantal Akerman's *Jeanne Dielman, 23 quai du commerce, 1080 Bruxelles* (1975), Anthony McCall,

Claire Pajaczkowska, Andrew Tyndall, and Jane Weinstock's *Sigmund Freud's Dora* (1979), and Sally Potter's *The Gold Diggers* (1983). By the mid-1970s she was also making her own films, only one of which, *What Maisie Knew* (1975), an evocation of the Henry James novel, received anything like support from reviewers and audiences of independent cinema.[4]

In the case of *The Sky on Location,* the gap between accomplishment and recognition was particularly wide, probably because in 1983 Mangolte's decision to reexplore the American West could hardly have seemed less attuned to the American independent filmmaking scene, which seemed focused on gender, ethnic, and sexual cine-liberation. As was true for many of the early settlers, Mangolte's decision to go west involved an escape from the doctrinaire conventions of her moment. And it offered Mangolte a topic commensurate with her considerable gifts as a cinematographer.

During 1980–81 Mangolte traveled (with one assistant), making imagery, for a little over eleven weeks (there were five separate automobile trips), during all four seasons: "Altogether I drove close to 20,000 miles. I was always trying to make sure I would take a road that would lead me to something interesting, even though I couldn't be sure: I was always taking the road for the first time."[5] In *The Sky on Location* Mangolte's focus is on western landscapes that show no obvious indication of human interference[6]—filmed with the kind of solemn respect evident in the paintings of Thomas Moran and Albert Bierstadt and in the photographs of William Henry Jackson, A. J. Russell, Carleton Watkins, and Ansel Adams (see fig. 18). All Mangolte's carefully composed images are made with a 16mm camera mounted on a tripod, although there are frequent pans, some of them evocative of the panoramic paintings and photographs of the nineteenth century (and of still and moving panoramas), others expressive of Mangolte's own excitement at being in these remarkable landscapes (see plates 10, 11).

The first of Mangolte's journeys begins in midsummer (July 27, 1980) in the Togwotee Pass near Grand Teton National Park and moves through Yellowstone and up to Glacier National Park. A second begins in Silverton, Colorado, jumps to Wyoming's South Pass and moves west across Nevada to Death Valley. Next, we're in the Rio Grande Valley and circle up through Utah's Kodachrome Basin to Bryce Canyon, Monument Valley, Zion Canyon, then into Arizona to the Grand Canyon, Canyon de Chelly, and the Hopi reservation. A brief moment in the Sonoran Desert is followed by a trip from

Figure 18. Fog lingering in the Tetons, from Babette Mangolte's *The Sky on Location* (1983).

Yosemite Valley, across the Sierra Nevadas to Mono Lake and into Nevada to Pyramid Lake, Carson Sink Pass, Humboldt Sink, and Dry Lake. Then the film returns to Utah—to Cedar Breaks and Zion; then, again, to Death Valley. Another journey begins in the San Juan Mountains in southern Colorado, moves north through Silverton along the Great Divide to the Great Divide Basin in Wyoming, to the Green River Flaming Gorge, back to South Pass and Fremont Lake. Next, we're back in the Tetons, moving north into Yellowstone. *The Sky on Location* jumps north and west to the Cascade Range, beginning at Mount Hood and Mount Saint Helens (after the eruption) and then moving south to Crater Lake and the Klamath area and into the redwood forests of northern California. A final journey returns us to Kodachrome Basin, Bryce Canyon, Canyon de Chelly, and the Painted Desert; and the film concludes in late spring with brief visits to Mono Lake, to the Sonoran and Mojave Deserts, and to Yosemite.

Mangolte explains at the beginning that she wanted to see what it was like to be in "unknown territory"; and while the locations through which she travels are hardly unknown except insofar as her personal experience is concerned—in many cases, they are the standard tourist destinations of the West—the seeming disorganization of the film's sequences is for most viewers "unknown territory," at least given the standard sensibility, common both to touring and to filmgoing, of knowing precisely which route and which stops will be "covered" in a particular, limited time. Well into *The Sky on Location*, during Mangolte's second visit to Death Valley, she provides a close-up of several bird and insect tracks and a snake track and wonders, "What happened here? We follow the tracks of the snake. Are they [the insects, bird, snakes] all gone? We look as the story progresses." The tiny mystery of these wanderings can be read as a metaphor for Mangolte's unusual, even somewhat "mysterious" route. Indeed, even the one clear trajectory in Mangolte's travels—the seasonal cycle—is a fabrication. Though she traveled for only eleven weeks, *The Sky on Location* creates the sense that we are gradually moving through the seasons, from midsummer through fall and winter (temporal "unknown territories" for tourists who flood the popular western sites during midsummer) into spring.

The sound track of *The Sky on Location* contextualizes the film's visual imagery in a variety of ways. It includes a complex narration, the sounds of the areas where Mangolte filmed, and intermittent music. While Mangolte is the film's primary narrator (we hear her first and most often), she is not alone: two other voices—one female (Honora Ferguson), one male (Bruce Boston)—comment on the imagery and provide quotations about the West (the sources are often not indicated) and other sorts of information. Mangolte's narration feels intimate, almost diaristic, and its accent clearly defines her as French. The other voices, recorded after Mangolte's journeys were completed, seem comparatively detached from the imagery and from the feeling for the imagery that is evident in Mangolte's narration—in large measure because they were obviously recorded in a studio.[7] Generally, in fact, these studio voices are abrasive. As Mangolte has explained, "You [the viewer] struggle with the information addressing itself to your intellect at the same time that you are seduced by the visuals. . . . [T]he dynamism of the film lies in that disjunction between the studio aspect of the voices commenting after the fact (even when they actually speak very literally of what is in the frame) and the presence of the actual landscape itself."[8] All in all, the impact of Mangolte's dispersal of narrative identity is to force us to see these ideal landscapes through two separate, though related, histories: the history of the American West itself and the history of the representation of this region.

The narration includes references to the ancient civilizations of the West, to early European explorers and missionaries, to the emigrants trekking westward along the major trails, to the 1871 geological survey and the establishment of Yellowstone National Park, and to the early-twentieth-century tourist regime at the Old Faithful Inn, the emptying of Mono Lake (see plate 11) and of the surrounding water table during the development of modern California cities, and Ronald Reagan's interest in dismantling land-protection laws. The second history, of the imaging of the West, is evident in the narrators' references to ancient petroglyphs, to Thomas Moran and William Henry Jackson (whose paintings and photographs of the Yellowstone region and the Grand Canyon were instrumental both in causing the U.S. Congress to protect these areas and in helping the railroads to entice potential tourists to travel west),[9] to the films of John Ford (Mangolte: "Like most Europeans, the first images of the West I saw were in John Ford's movies"),[10] and to the naming of a region of Utah after a film stock (Kodachrome). Another aspect of this second history—the history of scholarly responses to the depictions of the West—is suggested not only by the somewhat pedantic voices on the sound track but also during Mangolte's closing credits: "The filmmaker wishes to acknowledge her indebtedness to Barbara Novak's remarkable book, *Nature and Culture*."[11] The history of painting Novak charts in her book, and in her other work, is frequently referred to in *The Sky on Location*.

While the visuals are arranged so as to suggest Mangolte's free-form wanderings within the seasonal cycle, the sound track is organized poetically. The comments of the narrators "move the viewer around" historically in a more or less random fashion analogous to Mangolte's free-form geographic wanderings; but as *The Sky on Location* evolves, Mangolte provides various echoes and other auditory structuring devices. At times, each narrator speaks separately of some place or issue; often, the three speakers collaborate on a particular issue; but in two instances, each of the three speakers successively makes the same statement (during the second visit to Yellowstone, each narrator says, "You see deer tracks everywhere"; and in southern Oregon near the end of the film, each narrator says, "Spring is here; there are signs of melting everywhere").

Mangolte herself tells us during her first visit to Mono Lake that she is looking "west again. And south. And east" (each direction is accompanied by a different shot), and later (during her second visit to the Tetons) that "we look at the world below, north, west, and west again, and south." The similarity of the two passages is confirmed in the rhythms of the editing. The entire film is framed by a passage of music (except for excerpts from "Onward Christian Soldiers," "My Darling Clementine," Brahms's "German Requiem," and Strauss's "Last Song," the intermittent music was supplied by Ann Hankinson) and a pan of clouds in a blue sky that we see/hear with the brief opening and closing credits, although the exact same musical passage plays just before the narrators announce the arrival of spring, signaling the closing movement of the film.

Early in *The Sky on Location,* Mangolte is looking at a southwestern sky, at the pattern of clouds moving over the patterned land, and remarks, "You pride yourself in thinking you were maybe the only ones ever to see that . . . junction of two distinctive patterns sliding one on top of another." While she herself recognizes the naïveté of her conjecture, the image it creates provides a way of thinking about the structure of her film: the relatively free-form pattern of the sound track "slides" over the different free-form pattern of the imagery, allowing us to meditate on the relationships between being in a place and thinking about a place, between geography and history, between nature and culture.

The original "discoverers" of the New World saw its magnificence as God's reward for the arduous voyage they needed to endure to reach this continent. They were able to process this awesome natural immensity (and the cultural potential implicit in it) by deploying a comparatively rudimentary version of their native language to describe it. That is, the size of their "discovery" tended to render them linguistic children, with some control of vocabulary but limited ability with syntax.[12] For Mangolte, a contemporary, European rediscoverer of the New World, no grueling ocean voyage was necessary for experiencing America's awesome landscapes. And yet, on one level, her "voyage" had its own difficulties: in order to see the West with the eyes of a (cinematic) child— that is, in one self-contained composition after another, shot from a camera mounted on a tripod, developing virtually no complex narrative sequence or syntax: the approach used by the Lumière Brothers at the dawn of cinema history—Mangolte needed to overcome the distractions of history, including nearly a century of film history that has conventionally been seen as teleologically in service of the development of complex storytelling. Mangolte's remarkable imagery does evoke the childlike awe of the New World that seems so clear in early discovery narratives and in the words and images of those first European Americans who explored the Far West. The paradox of *The Sky on Location* is Mangolte's use of photography (an epitome of Western technological advance, surveillance, and control) and especially motion picture photography (the source of the West's most visible industry, an industry virtually dedicated to the maintenance of European-American heritage) to return us for a (cinematic) moment to a visual innocence—or, really, an illusion of innocence—quickly left behind by North American exploration and settlement.[13]

North on Evers as Reexploratory Narrative

Whereas *The Sky on Location* was Mangolte's first attempt to explore landscape as the focus of a film, James Benning's *North on Evers* is a distinguished addition to a series of films dealing with landscape and cityscape. Indeed, by the time he finished *North on Evers,* Benning's reputation, which had been established by his distinctive depiction of midwestern locales during the mid-1970s—especially in *8 ½ × 11* (1974), *11 × 14* (1976), and *One Way Boogie Woogie* (1977)—had moved into eclipse. Benning's 1970s films made their mark on audiences (and on other filmmakers) in large measure because they seemed to prove that, despite the seeming hegemonies of New York and San Francisco in the history of independent cinema, the "fly-over zone" of the Midwest was, in fact, making its own contribution. Benning's move to New York City in 1981 and to California in 1988 (he has taught at the California Institute of the Arts since 1989) may have had the effect of compromising his influence as a regionalist, but the quality of his work has remained reasonably consistent. *American Dreams* (1984), *Landscape Suicide* (1986), *North on Evers,* and the recent series of "Westerns" (discussed in chapter 10) stand with the very best of his work, and with the most interesting (and academically useful) independent cinema of recent years.

A number of Benning's early films focus on very particular locales (*One Way Boogie Woogie,* for example, provides sixty one-minute shots of the industrial south side of Benning's native Milwaukee—shots often infused with nostalgia for the romantic awe that factory landscapes could produce in those of us born during World War II), but other films record journeys across considerable portions of the American landscape. For example, *The United States of America* (made with Bette Gordon in 1975) records a trip from the Brooklyn Bridge to the Pacific Ocean near Los Angeles: Benning and Gordon mounted a camera in the back of their car and at more or less regular intervals during their journey turned it on; the automobile windshield becomes a movie screen on which the filmmakers' wanderings are played out (the sound track—environmental sounds, music and commentary on the radio—was tape-recorded in the car). *North on Evers,* however, records Benning's most geographically extensive journey—or, really, journeys—for a film.[14]

Using an organization familiar from his *American Dreams,* Benning divides the viewer's attention between two different, but related, experiences, each of which presents a journey across the United States. One of the two journeys is recorded visually (environmental sound was postsynched); the other is presented verbally—in a handwritten text that scrolls across the bottom of the film frame from right to left (see fig. 19). The production of *North on Evers* began in 1989, when Benning set off on a motorcycle trip from his home in Val Verde, California, and crossed the country along a southern route through Arizona, New Mexico, and Texas and through the South via Mississippi (Benning visits Fayette and Jackson, looking for the place where Medgar Evers—the "Evers" in his title—was murdered) and Nashville, to Washington, D.C., and New York City, returning to California by a northern route through central New York, Chicago (where he documents the U.S. Steel works in Gary in a manner reminiscent of *One Way Boogie Woogie*), and Milwaukee, then across the upper Midwest to a motorcycle rally in Sturges, South Dakota, to Yellowstone and the Tetons, to the Great Salt Lake, Hoover Dam, the Salton Sea, Death Valley, and back to Val Verde. During this first trip, Benning recorded no imagery or sound, but on his return to California, he made notes on his experiences, which became the basis for the scrolling text.

As Benning explains in the text—midway through the film and his journey, just as he is arriving in New York City—"A year later I made the same trip again. I searched for the same people and places. I had a purpose. I looked both outside and in. I filmed landscapes and portraits. I recorded sound."

While *North on Evers* shares a number of western locales with *The Sky on Location* (the Grand Canyon, Monument Valley, Yellowstone, the Tetons, Death Valley, and the Mojave Desert), it is, as even a basic description suggests, a

Figure 19. James Benning's motorcycle, with scrolling text, from *North on Evers* (1991). Courtesy James Benning.

very different film. Whereas Mangolte suppresses her personal history (even the personal history taking place during the production of her film) in the interest of focusing on the landscape itself within a general context of its social and aesthetic history, Benning is, from the beginning, frankly personal: his opening comments in the rolling text about Val Verde end, "I like living here, but I decided to leave for the summer. I had been feeling anxious and thought travel might help." And as his journeys unfold, this personal motivation remains central: Benning's route is determined not by the many rural and urban landmarks he records but—even during his first trip—by the locations of friends and family members. And, of course, during the second trip, he carefully revisits not only these same friends and family members but also, insofar as possible, those new acquaintances he met on the original trip. Even during what, by conventional movie standards, is probably the most dramatic event described in *North on Evers,* Benning's personal experience is more fully his focus than the landscape itself.

On his way east, he mentions, "I met a Navajo woman at a rest stop on I-40. She asked me for a ride. In the morning we drove to the Grand Canyon. Two days later I dropped her off in Monument Valley." Later, staying in Oshkosh, Wisconsin, with friends, Benning fills in some of the details of those two days:

I was just about to put down my sleeping bag when a woman appeared. At first I thought she was Mexican, but she turned out to be Navajo. She asked me for a ride.

I told her I was on a motorcycle. She said she knew. I said I only had one seat. She said she could sit on my sleeping bag, that she had to get back to her child. I said I could give her a ride, but first I had to get some sleep. She said she'd wait. I got in my sleeping bag and she lay down on a blanket next to me. When I woke up she was still sleeping. I walked to the other end of the rest stop. Two men in dark suits asked me if I had seen an Indian girl. For some reason I said no.

I waited for them to leave. They drove off in a yellow station wagon. When I got back she was gone. I found her standing in the doorway of a vacant shack. She said she was running from fear. We drove on back roads to the Grand Canyon. We climbed to the bottom and slept near the Colorado River. The next day we headed for Monument Valley. I was going sixty and she said to go faster. I accelerated to ninety. She yelled that last night when I was asleep, she thought about cutting my throat.

Later that day I dropped her off in Monument Valley. She never told me her name. I watched her walk across the desert to a house trailer and disappear through a red door. She never looked back.

While Benning's approach is much more personal than Mangolte's, he too uses a more general social and aesthetic history of the places we see as a context for the imagery and the events he depicts and recalls; that is, as in *The Sky on Location*, Benning's travels are both geographic and historical—and in Benning's case, representative of a certain generation of Americans. Benning has never quite recovered from the sixties and from the knot of political events and aesthetic issues that came to dominate the decade: especially the struggle for racial equality, integration, and political-economic power and the small-scale and large-scale violence (including, of course, the Vietnam War) that was transforming the American social landscape in those years. *North on Evers* is full of obvious and subtle references to these events.

That Benning lives in a mixed-race town and that the very first textual information he provides is that Val Verde "was a Black resort town in the Thirties, separate but equal. Lots of jazz musicians came here to party" confirms the theme of race implicit in the title, which is developed during the body of the film by the aforementioned incident with the Navajo woman; by Benning's attending an all-black rodeo in Dallas on Juneteenth (the day when Texas slaves were freed); by his visit to the white separatist, "Christian," New Holy

Land in Eureka Springs, Arkansas; by his visit to the all-black Arkansas town, Cotton Plant; by his personal research into Medgar Evers in Mississippi; by his troubled meeting with an angry drunk in a black bar in Montgomery; by his visits to the artist Mose T and the Reverend Howard Finster; and by racist comments by whites in Montgomery, by Klan members at the motorcycle rally in South Dakota, and (in a textual flashback to his youth) by his mother. As Benning crosses America, he is never far from the issue of race or from his lifelong consciousness of race as a central personal and political concern. If Benning has "travelled further" into the issue than many white Americans (and certainly further than most white filmmakers), he is under no illusions about the state of American race relations or even about his own effectiveness in dealing with the issue as it confronts him in his personal life: on several occasions he says nothing to racist comments by others. Race, which has always been the sociopolitical frontier for Americans, remains the personal frontier for Benning.[15]

Wayne Franklin distinguishes between the discovery narrative and the exploratory narrative both on the basis of what is noticed by discoverer or explorer—what is *there* versus what *is happening*—and on the basis of the organization used in communicating the different visions: "much as the explorer bequeathed his sense of timeless awe, and his innocent eye, to those who followed him" so the "pattern of narrative" is the "explorer's central gift to national language": "In exploratory texts . . . experience is filtered through the grid of initial design. . . . As the discoverer attempts to control the given world of American space by describing an ideal passage through it, the explorer tries to organize New World experience—whether actual or in prospect—by subordinating possibly corrosive events to the ideal pattern of plot."[16] If we see *North on Evers* as a reexploratory narrative in the sense that *The Sky on Location* is a rediscovery narrative, Franklin provides a way of distinguishing between the viewer's experience of Mangolte's film and the very different experience of Benning's. While *The Sky on Location* asks only that we observe and meditate on characteristic western spaces, *North on Evers* requires sustained activity on the part of viewers; while Mangolte asks us to consider one image and one idea at a time, Benning requires us to distinguish different times and spaces *and* to continually synthesize them within the overall design of his film.

My description of *North on Evers* makes clear that its fundamental organizing principle is Benning's simultaneous presentation of two journeys across America, one presented in the rolling text, the other in the imagery and sound. And while this unusual structure requires an unusual kind and amount of activity on the part of viewers (or, really, viewers-readers), a general description of the film tends to oversimplify the experience Benning has created, in several different senses. The most obvious—or at least, the *first* obvious—oversimplification involves the viewer's difficulty in comprehending Benning's twofold presentation. Of course, at any given moment during *North on Evers,* the viewer must choose between the text and the other imagery: we cannot read and scan the frame simultaneously. But, whichever choice we make at any given moment, we are continually tempted by the other alternative. No matter how compelling the imagery, the rolling text draws the eye (as the filmmaker Hollis Frampton, one of Benning's mentors, once remarked, "Once we can read, and a word is put before us, we cannot not read it");[17] and no matter how compelling a particular textual story is, the movements within Benning's compositions, and his editing, interrupt the ease of our comprehension of the text.

As if this weren't enough, Benning includes other forms of distraction as well. At times the scene behind the rolling text is dark enough or complex enough that words, phrases, even whole sentences are rendered invisible, and viewers must imagine what they missed on the basis of what preceded and succeeded it. Further, in filming *North on Evers,* Benning consistently used a hand-held camera (for the first time in his career), and the result is that the visuals are often jittery and—especially for viewers accustomed only to conventional film and television—disconcerting.

The perceptual activity required of Benning's viewers instigates our awareness of the film's complex narrative, which asks of us other forms of activity. Assuming we do follow Benning's journeys in both text and image, we are inevitably thrust into the continuing evolution of the relationship *between* text and image. This relationship has at least two distinct levels. First, the temporal relationship between what we're reading and what we're seeing is continually undergoing gradual changes. At the beginning of *North on Evers,* Benning's text moves the reader from Val Verde through Boron, California, to the Grand Canyon and Monument Valley, and through New Mexico into West Texas while the visuals are still documenting the Borax factory in Boron. The visuals remain consistently behind the text throughout much of the first half of the film—though as Benning rides north to Washington, D.C., the text and visuals converge, until we see the Vietnam Memorial *before* we read Benning's text about it. During his trip from Washington to New York, the text and imagery are roughly parallel, but at the end of the New York visit, the text again moves ahead of the visuals and in general remains ahead of the visuals by various amounts of time during Benning's trip west. Text and image converge once again as Benning reaches the Great Salt Lake and searches for the remains of Robert Smithson's *Spiral Jetty* (1970; see fig. 20). From the moment when we look down at the water of the Great Salt Lake and read, "I suppose in a way my trip ended there at the end of the spiral," until Benning is back in Val Verde, the imagery precedes the text.

That the textual journey precedes the photographic journey through so much of *North on Evers* is, of course, a reminder that the journey that was the basis for the text preceded the journey during which Benning recorded imagery and sound; but it also creates a temporal gap that develops an

Figure 20. Robert Smithson's *Spiral Jetty,* April 1970, Great Salt Lake, Utah, black rock, salt crystals, earth, red water, algae, 3½" × 15" × 1,500". Photographed by Gianfranco Gorgoni. Estate of Robert Smithson. Courtesy James Cohan Gallery, New York. Collection: DIA Center for the Arts, New York. Art – Estate of Robert Smithson/Licensed by VAGA, New York, N.Y. All photographic rights VAGA, New York.

unusual form of suspense: as we read about people and places, we cannot help but wonder how they will look, and subsequently, as we see various places and people, we cannot help but make as many of the relevant identifications as possible.

Second, once we have engaged both the textual and the visual imagery, we become aware of changes that have occurred during the year's gap between the two journeys. When Benning first arrives in San Antonio (that is, during the rolling-text journey), he is looking forward to seeing an old friend, his wife, and their child, only to learn "that his wife had moved out. He was very upset." A few minutes later when we see the father and daughter, we not only make the relevant identification, we realize we are seeing them a year after the breakup, and perhaps we can read a year's worth of adjustment on their faces. When Benning visits old friends in central New York (film- and videomaker John Knecht and artist Lynn Schwarzer), he tells us, "My friends live in the country on a small road. Cattle graze in the nearby fields. I was happy to see them again. They were expecting their first child soon." Moments later when Benning presents a portrait of these friends, we see them with the child.[18]

The exploratory narratives Franklin analyzes have as their goal the exploitation of what for the discoverer is the awesome potential of the New World terrain. Benning's reexploratory narrative (reexploratory on several levels: in the imagery we generally resee what we've already read about, just as Benning was revisiting people and places on his second journey; and the two journeys together review Benning's psychic return to the places and people of his past and of the past of his generation) represents a modern version of this exploitation. Of course, the practical function of the original explorers' grueling travels west—first across the Atlantic and then across the continent—was to open routes that could be used for the transportation of agricultural and industrial products back East: the exploitation of the New was a means to the reconfirmation of the wealth and power of the Old. The remarkable long-term success of these ventures is evident throughout *North on Evers*, in the many images of industrial production (most obviously in Boron, near New York, and in Gary, Indiana) and of the generation of power itself (the film is full of images of power lines, and near the end, we see Hoover Dam, shining "brightly in the afternoon sun").

Indeed, the industrial exploitation of North America has been so massive that, as is clear in Benning's imagery, we have entered a period of industrial decline: generally, the factories we see seem in a state of decay (the first person Benning meets in his travels, a worker who has recently been laid off at the mine in Boron, tells Benning that Boron is a one-horse town and that the horse is wounded), and even the technological wonder of Hoover Dam, which in 1932 "symbolized hope for the future," now seems to Benning "one of the last technologies to be trusted": it may shine in the sun, but it's the *afternoon* sun. If the original explorers' journeys West, then back East, symbolized hope and the coming industrial might of the new nation, Benning's journeys East, then back West, reflect not only his personal anxieties (halfway through his circular journey, Benning tells us that his drifting is perhaps "a desperate attempt to outdistance my anxiety or deny the murmur of advancing age") but also a more general American anxiety about the future, now that our "best" industrial days seem behind us.

But *North on Evers* is not simply a tale of despair and of the entropy symbolized by Smithson's *Spiral Jetty*.[19] And even if Benning tells us that, in some sense, his journey around America finishes at the end of Smithson's spiral (an end that seems confirmed by subsequent visits to the abandoned Bombay Beach Site on the Salton Sea and to Death Valley), in fact, his journey did *not* end there but in his return home. Indeed, the journey chronicled in Benning's text catalyzed the *second* journey, documented in the imagery. And together, these two journeys became the raw material for what was then Benning's newest film, and one of his most compelling—that Benning frequently tours with his films (such touring is a tradition among American avant-garde filmmakers) has continued to extend the films' original journeys.

Benning's nostalgic look at America from the other side of a level of industrial development the original discoverers and explorers could not even have fantasized is itself a new, creative form of exploitation, not so much of the natural resources of the nation, but of the history this exploitation has produced. The last person Benning describes to us on his travels is a woman in the bar of a motel in central Utah: "She was well into her seventies. She wore tight red pants and black high heels. She looked as if she had been fused together at the waist with a twenty year old." She asks Benning to dance; he stays at the bar until closing. This woman—half-old, half-young—is the muse of *North on Evers*. She energizes Benning and counters the film's motifs of industrial decay and continued social compromise (in the struggles of Native Americans, of African Americans, of women . . .) with two equally pervasive motifs: the energy of young people and of artists bent on transforming frustration, anxiety, and limitation into art.

North on Evers is full of children, and in virtually every instance—and regardless of the struggles these children are dealing with—Benning is struck with the child's energy and by his own feeling of connection with this energy. In Albuquerque, when Benning leaves the New Age chapel where his old friend is a member, the friend's daughter follows him out: "We talked for an hour. I felt closer to this young runaway than to her father." In San Antonio, he is struck by his friends' four-year-old daughter: "I like kids that age. They want to learn so bad." This theme of the energy of the young culminates when Benning visits his own daughter, Sadie, who is "seventeen and full of life": "We drove in the rain. I said I was glad we weren't on my motorcycle. I told her that rain really hurts. She rolled the window down and stuck her head out and said it felt just like getting a tattoo." That a substantial portion of Benning's audience will know that by age sixteen Sadie Benning was an accomplished video artist (indeed, by the time of *North on Evers* her reputation had eclipsed her father's) adds a poignant power to Benning's faith in the young—a faith that frames the film. *North on Evers* opens as a Val Verde school bus picks up children and closes when the bus leaves them off at the end of the day.

The motif of art making confirms the motif of youthful energy. Again and again, Benning visits creative people who have found ways of transforming deprivation into productivity: the eighty-two-year-old widower in San Antonio who used to make sewer pipes but now makes objects out of cement that look like they're made from trees, for example; and Mose T, the black folk artist from Alabama whose work is widely known (Benning buys a painting for his daughter—"She likes him too"—which we see in her room a year later). In other instances, the people Benning records have made valuable contributions to American independent film and video: director Richard Linklater (*Slacker,* 1991); filmmaker Bette Gordon (*Variety,* 1983); actor Willem Dafoe (*Platoon,* 1986; *The Last Temptation of Christ,* 1988); video artist Les LeVeque . . .

Of course, the most obvious instance of this process of transforming loss into creative work is *North on Evers* itself, which—as has been true throughout his career—Benning found a way to complete on a budget so small that it could hardly fund a single scene of a film from industrial Hollywood (Benning estimates that *North on Evers* cost $20,000, including the $5,000 he spent for three months of travel). *North on Evers* is still another independent, narrative film that reveals the constricted thinking of the popular cinema and demonstrates that even after a productive century of Hollywood filmmaking, a single cinematic explorer, working alone, can find a new way of surveying the American history that the original discoverers and explorers made possible, including the film history that America's most influential western industry has produced. Indeed, when from time to time during *North on Evers* Benning's leftward-moving text is superimposed over an image of a leftward-moving plane or freight train, the unusual optical effect conflates two related industrial developments, reminding us of Hollis Frampton's argument that "cinema is the last machine."[20] If this Machine—the American industrial Machine, including the Machine of commercial cinema—is nearing the end of its life span, *North on Evers* makes clear that for some filmmakers and some audiences cinema remains full of energy—especially in those instances when the maker and the audience have the courage to explore the possibilities of exploiting decay itself and transforming limitation into possibility.

Natural Born Killers as Resettlement Narrative (#1)

Wayne Franklin's chapter on settlement narratives begins with an excerpt from a 1713 report by Antoine de la Mothe, Cadillac, the founder of Detroit, to Pontchartrain, the newly appointed governor of the Louisiana colony. Cadillac describes a supposed New World paradise:

> I have also seen a garden on Dauphine Island which had been described to me as a bit of terrestrial paradise. It is true that there are a dozen fig-trees that are very fine and that produce black figs. I saw there three pear-trees of wild stock, three apple-trees of the same sort, a little plum-tree about three feet in height that had seven poor plums on it, about thirty feet of grape-vines with nine clusters of grapes in all, some of rotten or dry grapes and the rest somewhat ripe, about forty feet of French melons, a few pumpkins: that is the "terrestrial paradise" of Mr. Artaguette and of several others, the "Pomona" of Mr. De Remonville and the "Fortunate Isles" of Mr. De Madeville and of Mr. Phillippe; their memoranda and their relations are pure fables. They have spoken about what they have not seen at all and they have too readily believed what was told them.[21]

Cadillac's realistic reassessment of the Dauphine Island garden—his measure of New World myth against what he knows from experience—is the quintessential settler's stance, a stance that can transform the discoverer's and explorer's wonder and hope into bitterness;[22] and it provides a useful context for Oliver Stone's *Natural Born Killers,* which can function here as an instance of a "resettlement narrative."

That Oliver Stone, one of the most successful commercial filmmakers of the 1980s and 1990s, has had a very different kind of career from Mangolte or Benning is obvious—although in Stone's case popular assumptions about who he is as a director have blinded even some of his admirers to what he accomplished in *Natural Born Killers.* And, in fact, in many ways *Natural Born Killers* is formally and historically closer to independent, experimental narratives such as *The Sky on Location* and *North on Evers* than it is to the films that established Stone's reputation. Jane Hamsher, one of the film's producers, sees it as "the biggest experimental film . . . ever made . . . because we could put all these resources into experimenting."[23] Indeed, all three films, and all three filmmakers, were nourished by the same vibrant cinema culture of the 1960s and early 1970s. If most young filmmakers with a desire for Hollywood success begin with experiments and evolve in more cinematically conventional directions, Stone seems to have decided, at least by 1994, to use the

Figure 21. Mickey (Woody Harrelson) and Mallory (Juliette Lewis), in Oliver Stone's *Natural Born Killers* (1994).

freedom and economic leverage his commercial success had brought him to sustain his interest in evolving in the opposite direction, that is, in making highly experimental narratives that challenge the very viewers his more conventional features have attracted.

Like Mangolte and Benning—and like the long history of film and literary narrative, and of painting—Stone uses the American West as a symbol of American ideals and, in particular, of freedom of movement and of action. We first meet the protagonists of *Natural Born Killers,* Mickey (Woody Harrelson) and Mallory (Juliette Lewis), as they are rampaging across the Southwest celebrating their freedom from their pasts (we learn in flashbacks that both were brutalized as children) and their passion for each other—by killing men and women virtually at random (see fig. 21). Like Mangolte and Benning, Stone locates his action (at least during the first half of the film, until Mickey and Mallory are apprehended) in an identifiable western geography: the first image in the film is of Shiprock, in the northwest corner of New Mexico, and the following action takes Mickey and Mallory along U.S. Route 666 between Cortez, Colorado, and Gallup, New Mexico, and (for their self-performed wedding ceremony) to the Rio Grande Gorge Bridge near Taos, New Mexico. Once captured they are held in a prison (supposedly out West, the prison scenes were actually filmed at the federal prison at Joliet, Illinois).[24]

While Mangolte is at pains to present visual imagery that does not reveal the economic exploitation that has transformed nearly all of the West and while Benning reveals a West that is poised between pristine beauty and industrial decay, for Stone, the idealized West has become little more than a figment of his delusional protagonists' imaginations. Whatever hopes and dreams earlier generations of explorers brought west with them have been destroyed by the social institutions that came west along the routes established by their journeys—in particular, three institutions that seem crucial in contemporary American society: the nuclear family, the criminal justice system, and the mass media. For Stone, the failures of these institutions are closely related. Even if Mickey does see himself as a "natural born killer" in the sense that he—like other animals—is a predator, Stone portrays the extent and thoughtlessness of his and Mallory's violence as a product of the sexism and violence endemic to the real American family.

Mallory's home life is dramatized at some length: her physically repulsive father (Rodney Dangerfield) brutalizes her mother (Edie McClurg) and has raped Mallory, with her mother's knowledge, since childhood. Judging from the flashbacks Stone provides, Mickey's home life is as grotesque as Mallory's: his mother seems to have had sexual relationships with both Mickey's father and his grandfather, and as a child, Mickey witnesses his father's suicide. The internalized damage of the institution of the family is clearly the background for Mickey and Mallory's violence toward others; and this familial violence is reconfirmed by the equally corrupt criminal justice system set up to punish them: the investigator Jack Scagnetti (Tom Sizemore), who captures the pair, is violent toward women in exactly the way Mallory's father is, and like Mallory's father, the warden at Batongaville Prison (Tommy Lee Jones) is infuriated by any resistance to his self-serving plans. And, of course, the mass media exploits the ongoing failures of family and law enforcement for its own purposes, just as the family and the law enforcement system exploit both the mass media and those entrusted to their care (Scagnetti is marketing a book; the warden has brought media coverage into the prison; Mallory's father is usually found in front of the TV).

Born a century after the twilight of the American frontier, and coming of age in the 1960s, Stone has always explored the collision between American ideals developed during the century of American expansion across the continent and the practical fallout that has resulted from a misapplication of these ideals to the complexities of life in the modern world: the Vietnam War, most obviously. In *Natural Born Killers,* Stone again stands with one foot in the present and one in the past, but if more traditional literary and cinematic narratives have tended to contrast the corrupt complexity of modern city life with the simpler, freer, purer lives of American frontier heroes (or in some recent instances, have contrasted the corruption of European America with the "innocence" of indigenous tribal life), Stone is well aware that such conflicts are nostalgic fantasies and that he must deal not with conflict itself but with the endless representations of American conflicts that flood our movie and television screens. That is, at least in *Natural Born Killers,* the "Good Guys" are *representations* of American history and contemporary life that are honest about social realities and respectful of the pain they cause; the "Bad Guys" are *representations* whose *only* function is exploitation, representations that reveal no respect either for ideals or for the pain of those sacrificed to them.

Like so many American artists, writers, and filmmakers concerned about where the ongoing commercial development of the New World is taking us,

Stone does turn to the past for guidelines in understanding the confusions of the present, but in *Natural Born Killers,* this past is the *media* past he became aware of as a Vietnam veteran while he was studying for his M.F.A. at New York University (Stone attended NYU from 1969 to 1971). Or, to put it more precisely, *Natural Born Killers* is Stone's reflection on two related aspects of media history. The more obvious of these is the two-decade lap dissolve from the movie screen to the television set as the nation's primary source of narrative entertainment and visual information—a development that culminated in the late 1960s by nearly destroying the film industry altogether. On one level, *Natural Born Killers* is a rough, contemptuous satire of commercial televison.

Stone's satire of TV has two dimensions. During the first half of *Natural Born Killers,* the focus of his attack is the family sitcom, which he burlesques during two sequences: Mickey and Mallory's flashback to Mallory's home life and Mickey's return to Mallory after his escape from prison to free Mallory from her parents. By presenting a highly exaggerated version of a sitcom (modeled specifically, I assume, on *All in the Family* but implicitly referencing many instances of the form), Stone seems to suggest that the conventional TV sitcom's happy placidity is a means of repressing the ugliness of so much of the real family life of the time in order to maintain and develop product marketing. During the second half of the film, Stone uses the Wayne Gayle (Robert Downey, Jr.) character to satirize the talk show and TV news in general. Gayle's show is modeled on *Geraldo* (Gayle's interview with Mickey is based on Geraldo's interview with Charles Manson) but again references many particular shows. It represents the new commercial television, where problems and pain are not repressed but revealed and transformed into entertainment.

Near the end of their violent cross-country spree, Mickey and Mallory are invited into a Native American dwelling by its owner, a shaman who sees words on Mickey's and Mallory's chests: first, "demon"; then, "too much TV." For Stone, both the rampage Mickey and Mallory have caused and the institutional sicknesses of American society that have made this rampage seem a logical response to their acculturation (at least to its two perpetrators) are confirmed by the one-two punch of TV's repression/exploitation of human agony, and of the degree to which the experience of watching TV has replaced constructive, public activity.

Stone's own response to the victory of commercial TV over the hearts and minds of most Americans is defiantly cinematic: from Stone's point of view, cinema—with all its own compromises and limitations—was, and remains, a healthier medium than television (and healthier, ironically, at least to some degree, *because* of television's onslaught). Both narratively and formally, *Natural Born Killers* sings the comparative diversity and democracy of the older medium by alluding to the explosion of alternative cinematic practices during the 1960s: the older medium's multifront "last stand" against the pervasiveness of TV and its homogenization and infantilization of American life.

Perhaps the earliest of these cinematic responses to TV to affect Stone was the arrival in the United States of "foreign film" in general and the French New Wave in particular. Both in its basic plot and in the freedom of Stone's style, *Natural Born Killers* echoes Jean-Luc Godard's *Breathless* (a Stone favorite) and François Truffaut's *Shoot the Piano Player*.[25] Stone's focus on visceral violence also suggests films from the American New Wave of the 1960s: Arthur Penn's *Bonnie and Clyde* (1967); Sam Peckinpah's *The Wild Bunch* (1969; a clip from *The Wild Bunch* is included in the film); and George Roy Hill's *Butch Cassidy and the Sundance Kid* (1969), big-budget commercial films in which outlaw buddies die, upholding an innocent acceptance of honest violence in the face of the violence of gradual social decadence. Probably Stone's most obvious commercial reference is to Stanley Kubrick's *A Clockwork Orange* (1971), which, like *Natural Born Killers,* divides into two halves: an earlier section focusing on young people on a violent rampage and a later section focusing on violence toward the individual at the hands of the criminal justice system. Indeed, Stone's use of the Joliet prison, with its panopticon design (see note 24), may be an allusion to Kubrick's use of a prison with a panopticon design in *A Clockwork Orange.* That *Bonnie and Clyde, The Wild Bunch,* and *A Clockwork Orange* frightened the audiences of their time with what seemed extreme levels of violence makes them of particular relevance for Stone's film, which caused considerable consternation—especially for TV movie reviewers—because of the "excessive" violence of its protagonists (whose final victim is TV announcer Gayle) and Stone's seeming approval of it.

A second set of references is to the small-budget, independent narrative features that were proliferating during the late 1960s: Roger Corman's films, and *Easy Rider* (directed by Dennis Hopper, 1969); and the films of Paul Morrissey (*Trash,* 1970, for example); and especially those of John Waters, whose trash melodramas of the time (*Mondo Trasho*, 1969; *Multiple Maniacs*, 1970; *Pink Flamingos*, 1972; and *Female Trouble*, 1974) seem the obvious source for Stone's disgusting sitcom of Mallory's home life and especially of Mallory's father. Also, Waters's recognition that serial murderers inevitably become media heroes in a society devoted to the spectacle of brutality and agony—the central idea of *Female Trouble*, in particular—is closely related to Stone's stance toward television in *Natural Born Killers*.

Still another set of references (perhaps "echoes" is a better term here) is to what was called "Underground Film" in the 1960s and before and since has more frequently been termed "avant-garde" or "experimental" film. What makes *Natural Born Killers* distinctive and watchable is neither its plot, which is one of the clichés of American film—albeit a still-fertile cliché, as *Natural Born Killers*, *Thelma and Louise* (1991), and *True Romance* (1993) make clear— nor its over-the-top acting (though both Harrelson and Lewis are memorable) but the remarkable visual experience of the film, which seems an evocation of a range of avant-garde filmmakers who arrived on the scene, or at least came to prominence, during the 1960s.

Perhaps the most obvious visual gesture in *Natural Born Killers* is Stone's continual shifting between color and black-and-white, both throughout the film and in individual sequences. Of course, the shift from black-and-white to color has a long history in American film, as a means of distinguishing "reality" from "fantasy" and the past from the present. But Stone's relentless intercut- ting from black-and-white to color has no particular relationship to narrative event; it has more to do with exploring the options film provides: indeed, there are many kinds of color and of black-and-white in *Natural Born Killers*, each of which recontextualizes the others. The precedent for Stone's energetic explo- ration of color and black-and-white is the history of such exploration in avant- garde film: in Stan Brakhage's *Dog Star Man* (1962–64) and Andy Warhol's *Chelsea Girls* (1966), for example, and Bruce Baillie's *Quixote* (1965) and *Castro Street* (1966), Michael Snow's *Wavelength* (1967), Paul Sharits's *Peace Mandala/End War* (1966), Robert Nelson's *Bleu Shut* (1970), Yvonne Rainer's *Kristina Talking Pictures* (1976) . . .

Another of Stone's strategies that is closely related to avant-garde filmmak- ing is his recycling of material from earlier films of all kinds into his own work. Indeed, "recycled cinema" (or "found footage film") has been a central avant-garde strategy in the United States since Joseph Cornell developed his version of the approach in the 1940s and Bruce Conner popularized it in the 1960s (in *A Movie*, 1959; *Cosmic Ray*, 1962; and *Report*, in various versions, 1963–67). Not only does Stone combine material from a wide range of films in a manner reminiscent of Conner; in some instances he uses—that is, reuses—shots from educational films, a typical Bruce Conner gesture. (This connection with Conner is particularly clear in *Burn*, the Nine Inch Nails music video in which imagery from *Natural Born Killers* is edited into a complex montage; this video is included in the Director's Cut video of Stone's film—see note 23.)

Natural Born Killers is also evocative, at particular moments, of a wide range of other avant-garde filmmakers. Particular compositions and uses of color, for example, are reminiscent of Kenneth Anger (especially his *Inauguration of the Pleasure Dome*, 1954; and *Scorpio Rising*, 1963). The motif of using the windows in the motel rooms where Mickey and Mallory stay as frames for motion picture imagery that implicitly externalize the characters' psychic goings-on is reminiscent of Richard Myers's use of the same procedure in such films as *Akran* (1969) and *37–73* (1974). And in several instances, Stone uses an image in which the viewer looks down a cone of smoke—an image familiar to anyone who has experienced Anthony McCall's *Line Describing a Cone* (1973).

Regardless of what particular borrowings, thefts, evocations, and homages one can trace in *Natural Born Killers,* however, the point is that the stunning visual phantasmagoria of Stone's film sings the remarkable range of options available to the filmmaker by the early 1970s.[26] And it is precisely this remarkable cultural resource that, from Stone's point of view, commercial television ignores (except to rip off for an effect here and there) in its mindless, soulless embrace of a simplistic, homogeneous fantasy of American life and of a degraded American Dream based on continual exploitation, acquisition, and consumption. The true potentials of American film culture were being realized precisely at the moment when television was supplanting cinema; and in the decades that have followed, this trajectory of cultural evolution has not changed: the traditions evoked in Stone's phantasmagoric visuals are even more fully endangered than they were thirty years ago, and television's transformation of both the cinema culture it inherited and the mass audience continues. If Mickey's and Mallory's destructive spree is a metaphor for Stone's decision to escape conventional, commercial, often-TV-inspired film approaches and live free for a time,[27] their capture and incarceration suggests the degree to which even Stone's own film career—like virtually all American commercial film careers—is a prisoner not merely of television but of one of the same TV genres Stone so violently disapproves of in *Natural Born Killers:* the TV talk show, where most big-budget films are marketed.

Nevertheless, *Natural Born Killers* ends with Mickey and Mallory escaping, not only from prison, but—by killing Wayne Gayle (whose camera runs out of power just before he's shot)—from commercial television as well. Unlike the pantheon of television victims and perpetrators Stone reviews in the moments after Mickey and Mallory shoot Gayle—the Menendez brothers, Rodney King, Tonya Harding, O. J. Simpson, and the Branch Davidians at Waco—Stone's protagonists are allowed to escape back into domestic life: we see them, with their kids, traveling American back roads in their camper, as part of the film's final, exuberant montage.[28] If the fantasy of the original settlers was the transformation of their natural surround into a productive domesticity and a better future for themselves and their descendants, the 1990s fantasy of Stone and his protagonists is an escape from the institutional brutalities and confinements of modern mediated society to an imagined past in which personal and cinematic freedom were still conceivable.

We are face-to-face with a set of paradoxes. New World settlement narratives are about the failures of the settlement experience to live up to the dreams of the discoverers and the hopes of the explorers; and yet, in the end, the New World was to become far more economically productive than even the most sanguine early chroniclers could have imagined. But for Stone the very accomplishment of New World settlement has left no safe place for a healthy American individual. In the end, he resettles Mickey and Mallory within the fantasy of a sixties-style domesticity; and, by making *Natural Born Killers,* he himself "settles" for at least the illusion of a momentary cinematic escape—an "escape" that, ironically, seems to most viewers merely another instance of the very status quo Stone finds so repulsive. If American settlers hoped to create for themselves a more liberated future, only to discover that, in most instances, they were re-creating the past, Stone tries to escape into the past only to discover that for many viewers he seems to promote the horrifying future he seems to deplore.

Roam Sweet Home as Resettlement Narrative (#2)

In *The Sky on Location* Mangolte does her best to ignore the industrial and social developments that have transformed North America, at least in the visual imagery she records. Of course, these developments are implicit in the film technology Mangolte is using and in the system of roadways that allows her to "explore" much of the West in only eleven weeks and explicit in the histories sketched on the sound track. Nevertheless, her quest is to reimagine the vistas of the West as they might have looked to those original explorers with a sensitivity to landscape; Mangolte wants to *feel* like an explorer in unfamiliar territory. In *North on Evers,* on the other hand, Benning surveys the signs not only of industrial and social development but also of industrial decay and social compromise and failure, although his frequently arresting imagery of American vistas provides a regular series of creative surprises amid the entropy he sees everywhere, just as his new film develops out of the entropy he feels within himself. And in *Natural Born Killers* Stone laments the loss not so much of the landscape itself (the most spectacular space recorded in the film—the chasm of the Rio Grande near Taos—is spanned by a bridge from which Mickey and Mallory throw pieces of apparel into the gorge: neither they nor Stone seem

Figure 22. Ellen Spiro and Sam on the road during the shooting of *Roam Sweet Home* (1996). Courtesy Ellen Spiro.

concerned with pristine nature), but of the freedom and individualism this landscape has come to represent in American myth. For Stone, the psychic space of Americans is so clogged by the institutions that dominate American society that the most one can hope for is a spree—a momentary defiance. In *Roam Sweet Home,* however, Ellen Spiro takes a different tack: she transforms our sense of the West, neither by ignoring development, nor by surveying (and artistically overcoming) its results, nor by lamenting the effects of the institutional products of this development—but rather by accepting the aging of the West and transforming our sense of how to come to terms with the aging process. Spiro finds a liberating new way of, in Franklin's words, recognizing the recalcitrant truths of settlement and naming them by their proper names.

In *Roam Sweet Home* Spiro embraces age, both as a historical and geographic reality and as personal experience. Like Mangolte, Benning, and the protagonists of *Natural Born Killers,* Spiro and her traveling partner, her dog, Sam (a small, aging mongrel who provides a poetic narration to the video; he describes himself as "pure-blooded American road-dog"), wander the West—in particular, the Southwest, from the Texas panhandle across New Mexico and Arizona to the southern California desert (see fig. 22). Ignoring most of what would today be considered the tourist attractions of the region, Spiro seems drawn to our touristic recent past. The first extended stop in the videotape—after an introductory sequence and the title credit, Spiro flashes back to leaving Manhattan for the West—is at an Airstream trailer rally (actually, this rally took place in Canada, though Spiro edits it into the tape so that we assume it takes place in Texas) where the focus is on those aficionados who are committed to Wally Byam's original design of the Airstream. *Roam Sweet Home* is full of old trailers, and old motels, restaurants, tourist sites, and roads (the final sequences of the tape focus on old Route 66). Spiro and Sam stop for a time at Quartzsite, Arizona, "the Flea-Market Capital of the World," and at Slab City, a trailer village established in a now-defunct marine base in southern California, near the Salton Sea (like Benning, Spiro includes imagery of the now-flooded town of Bombay Beach; as Benning explains in *North on Evers,* "In 1905 the Colorado River broke its levee and created the Salton Sea. Over the past ten years increased irrigation run-off has caused flooding. The town of Bombay Beach was drowned and discarded"). Even what might be considered a relatively recent tourist site—the media-collective Ant Farm's *Cadillac Ranch* (1974), near Amarillo, Texas—has been "redesigned" by graffiti artists and vandals. Like Mangolte, Spiro avoids major sites of industrial decay, though she focuses on places and things recently "left behind" by what is generally considered progress.

Like *North on Evers,* Spiro's tape seems instigated by the personal aging process, but whereas Benning runs *from* the reality of aging, Spiro runs *toward* it: the exclusive human focus of her travels is aging women and men, in particular, women and men who see life, and growing old, not as loss but as opportunity. As one older, single woman tells Spiro early in the film, "You want to experience everything there is, and being old is just one of the parts of life." During *Roam Sweet Home,* Spiro meets and talks with dozens of older people, whose lives seem as varied as the lives of any comparable group—and often a good bit freer. While some of these people are wanderers (the introductory sequence includes two comments, one by a man: "I have the same kind of brains as a bird. I fly south in the winter and north in the summer"; the other by a woman: "I've been a wanderer as long as I've been free to wander"), others seem to have settled, at least for a time, in small, simple desert communities where they feel, and to a considerable degree *are,* free of societal restriction. Some women seem to live happily alone; others enjoy having boyfriends (sometimes several at one time); and others live in groups, some presumably lesbian-defined, others not.[29] All seem to agree with one woman, who gave up marriage, established a temporary-help agency, and saved enough money to live unfettered: "I thank God every day I don't need a man to take care of me. I take care of myself." The men, too, seem happy to have escaped most of the economic, political, and social developments that dominate the media and see their lives as acts of political defiance. In Truth or Consequences, Gypsy George explains, "We just can understand how the system works and we're side-stepping the system." In Slab City, Charles (who lives in a trailer with a poodle and two llamas—the poodle, he explains, demanded they get the llamas) says, "You have control of your life here, and that's something that most of these people did not have for most of their life."

Of the many older people Spiro visits with, two seem the quintessential instances of aging as opportunity rather than as accumulation of loss: Leonard Knight, a folk artist who arrived in Slab City with the idea of a brief stopover but has remained to paint the side of a small mountain; and Margie McCauley, a sixty-six-year-old woman who is walking Route 66 with her dog, Lollie, as a response to the Gulf War. Knight has apparently remained in Slab City

Figure 23. Margie McCauley, at sixty-six years old, filmed walking Route 66, in Ellen Spiro's *Roam Sweet Home* (1996). Courtesy Ellen Spiro.

because of the nature of the community it offers. "I'm proud of the people of Slab City," he explains to Spiro, "I think that they're the 1994 pioneers of this country." And he sees his environmental painting as a monument to this particular pioneering spirit (one Slab City resident explains that outsiders are sometimes interested in "improving" Slab City with an array of services that would kill freedom by destroying opportunities for imagination).[30] Margie McCauley, who explains, "When you're dead, honey, you're dead a long time, and so you better get busy and do what you're gonna do," is seen walking along Route 66 with a glorified pushcart (see fig. 23). Bob Waldmire, who introduces her to us, explains that while he attempts to live an environmentally moral life (he drives his trailer at a speed that's "sub-lethal" for butterflies), he doesn't have the nerve to do what *she* is doing—walking and camping along the old road full-time as a protest against the nation's dependence on petroleum products and as a legacy for her grandchildren. Margie McCauley is the last person Spiro meets on her journey.

In *Roam Sweet Home* age is not only livable and enjoyable (even politically committed), it's an improvement. One woman tells Spiro, "The more wrinkles, the better," and (by this point, well into the videotape) the discovery that she's talking about her dog, a sharpei, is virtually a punch line. In addition to painting the mountain, Knight shows us his method of dealing with cracks in the surface of his trailer: he uses window putty, which causes the repaired cracks to look like vines and flowers—"The more cracks in it, the better it looks!" The discovery of the creative energy in what society calls "decay" is the central theme of *Roam Sweet Home,* and in general the most effective means for exploiting this discovery involve a reversal of conventional consumer patterns. Whereas industrial society develops by convincing people that a good life means expanded accumulation of ever-better products, the people Spiro meets are minimalists; for them, less really *is* more—more time, more freedom, more peace, more happiness. If Oliver Stone is nostalgic about the idea of living on the frontier, Spiro's acquaintances have defined age *as* the frontier, and are content to explore it, using the simple technologies they can carry with them. For these people, improving the quality of life involves getting more out of what they have and what they know. Early in the film, during her visit inside Spiro's trailer, a woman explains that Spiro's trailer stove isn't broken, she just doesn't know how to turn it on: "You need *experience!*" And in general, the magic of the trailers Spiro visits is a function of their owners having found ways, over time, to modify those simple living spaces using the most frugal means, until they are comfortable for and expressive of those who live in them.

That Spiro is fascinated with these people, and that they are at home with her fascination, is also, implicitly, a function of a transformed sense of economics. For Oliver Stone, television is a monster in danger of consuming/destroying its own parent; it is the quintessential, materialistic New destroying the spiritually essential Old. In general, the people Spiro meets seem unusually detached from television: we don't see them watching it (we don't even see TV sets) and they rarely talk about it. Virtually all the activities Spiro records are outdoor activities.

Further, the camcorder she carries and especially its economic accessibility and one-person portability are historical functions of the aging of the

Hollywood film industry, of its being "past its prime." Of course, Hollywood continues to deploy ever-larger budgets—budgets big enough to finance even more extravagant directors than Oliver Stone; but on the byways of media production, independent filmmakers and videomakers, using the technological spin-offs and trickle-downs of the industry and very limited budgets, continue to produce a various and vital alternative media history that provides its audience with exhilarating visions of reality and possibility. Spiro and her camcorder are a media version of Margie McCauley and her pushcart.

Roam Sweet Home's other crucial theme—the relationships of humans and animals, especially dogs—may appear unrelated to the idea of age *as* frontier; but, in fact, it is an intrinsic dimension of this idea. As is made clear in Sam's narration (written by Allan Gurganus, spoken by Sam Raymond), Sam is more than Spiro's property or pet (Sam's introduction of himself and Spiro: "It's me, Sam. Experienced, if gettin' up in years. And Ellen, a pup who sometimes slips and calls herself my owner"). He *is* her companion—as the many dogs Ellen and Sam meet on their travels are companions to those they travel with—but he (and implicitly his colleagues in *Roam Sweet Home*) is a particular kind of companion: a teacher, a guru. As Sam explains, "You guard them [humans] whenever possible . . . but you're really training *them* to guard *you*. It's a service occupation really. When you die, what you've left them is the skill of noticing others." The perceptual alertness of Sam, and of dogs in general, is a model for Spiro's videomaking. As Sam says early in the tape, "Her strange need to shoot everything matches my strange need to smell it." One of the central motifs of *Roam Sweet Home* is Spiro filming Sam as he leans out the passenger's-side window.[31] We see him sometimes from the driver's side, sometimes reflected in the side mirror; and appropriately, it is in these shots that we most regularly see Spiro herself—in the double-lensed side mirror. Sam is not only Spiro's subject; he is her model: she is learning to smell the roses, and everything else, from her aging dog.

That virtually all those Spiro spends time with in *Roam Sweet Home* live and travel with a dog or dogs functions as a sign of their creative stance toward aging. In Hemingway's "Big Two-Hearted River," Nick Adams's war experience—his having come close to death and having experienced the violent deaths of others—has made him more perceptually alert. What Nick has learned from the sudden violence of war the free spirits of *Roam Sweet Home* have learned from the long lives they have lived and witnessed; and the result is a Zen-like ease with the everyday that's reflected in Spiro's camera work. Spiro frequently uses extreme close-ups of Sam as he watches the world go by, and she regularly provides "dog's-eye view" imagery: a beetle crossing a roadway, for example. Of course, it is precisely *because* of the history of the close-up as dramatic emphasis in the violence of industry melodrama that Spiro's gentle, in-close observation is arresting and amusing.

Unlike *North on Evers* and *Natural Born Killers,* and less openly than *The Sky on Location, Roam Sweet Home* creates a scrambled geography. Many of the places Spiro passes through and stops to see are identified; but no attention at all is given to providing anything like a coherent trajectory through the Southwest. Even in the opening sequences we are everywhere at once, including, in one instance, in a location quite distinct from the Southwest: one of the earliest images is of an old northern California trailer park entered by a tunnel cut into a redwood tree. Basically, this is a reflection of the lives Spiro documents: for these people, location may be important (the Slab City residents love Slab City) but trajectory is not; they have learned to enjoy life wherever they are. In fact, Slab City's close proximity to a bombing range seems ironic and amusing to its residents. Most of those with whom Spiro talks may agree with Sam's mantra, "Elsewhere is better; elsewhere better *be*," but their wanderings are a means not for getting anywhere in particular but for keeping the spirit occupied and at peace. Even Margie McCauley's plan to walk Route 66 to Chicago is open-ended; she reserves the right to change direction whenever the spirit moves her.

There is also no seasonal organization in the tape. The only temporal emphasis Spiro provides is a focus on sunset—not as a metaphor for conclusion and loss, but as one of life's great beauties and rewards. Just after Margie tells Spiro that life is "more magical than anything we can begin to think about," we see, amid shots of sunset, circular reflections created by the light of the setting sun striking the camcorder lens—it is essentially the same mandala shape that Larry Gottheim uses to conclude his exploration of the seasonal cycle in *Horizons* (see chap. 2). For Spiro, and for those she meets during *Roam Sweet Home*, the beauty of life is precisely in the *completion* of *all* its phases, the entire cycle, and the recognition not only that each phase offers its own rewards but also that the particular pleasures of age are *only* possible for those who have recognized the limitations of "progress" and "success."

For Spiro, the settler's—or *resettler's*—vision need not take the form of the jaundiced nostalgic cynicism evident in *Natural Born Killers* (and in so much of the history of the American Western since World War II); if originally *settlement* was a process of facing the real problems and difficulties of cultural development, *resettlement* can be a process of confronting reality and using this confrontation as a means of moving beyond the apparent limitations of an often-corrupt history. In the case of *Roam Sweet Home,* "reality" is not, as in *The Sky on Location,* a (however beautiful) nostalgia for the "depopulated," wilderness West as it was envisioned by nineteenth-century European-American painters; or, as in *North on Evers,* the disconcerting reality of the filmmaker's (and America's) being past middle age; or, as in *Natural Born Killers,* the "reality" that the ideals of the past have been thoroughly corrupted (except, perhaps, in the production process of Stone's defiant film). In Spiro's tape, reality is the fact that real people, many of them economically lower class, can and do create lives that are meaningful to them and exemplary for us—and that personal, low-budget media-making can be an accessible, progressive emulation of this creativity.

The "Jericho gypsies" in *Roam Sweet Home* and *Roam Sweet Home* itself can serve as metaphors and models for a revived sense of national (and media) history. Though we may often feel ethically immobilized as a result of the corrupt compromises of generation after generation of European Americans—with Native America and with our own more vigorous and rigorous ancestors—history has placed us at a moment of remarkable opportunity: so much remains to be done! In the time we have left, we can surprise ourselves and the world by learning from the lessons of the past and moving into a more capable future, one more respectful of human and environmental development and variety. And as lovers of culture, we can recognize the emptiness of so much of commercial media and the breadth, diversity, and relevance of so much of independent/avant-garde film and video; and in the time cinema has left, we can make sure that at least some of the accomplishments in all the economic "classes" of film history are passed on to the next generation. We can work to be sure that the best of alternative media making inspires a morally, aesthetically, and culturally respectable media future.

chapter 5

From the Sublime
to the Vernacular

The older I grow and the longer I look at landscapes and seek to understand them, the more convinced I am that their beauty is not simply an aspect but their very essence and that that beauty derives from the human presence. For far too long we have told ourselves that the beauty of a landscape was the expression of some transcendent law: the conformity to certain universal esthetic principles or the conformity to certain biological or ecological laws. But this is true only of formal or planned political landscapes. The beauty that we see in the vernacular landscape is the image of our common humanity: hard work, stubborn hope, and mutual forbearance striving to be love. I believe that a landscape which makes these qualities manifest is one that can be called beautiful.

JOHN BRINCKERHOFF JACKSON,
DISCOVERING THE VERNACULAR LANDSCAPE

Twister

It is difficult to imagine a more typically American film than *Twister* (1996). The focus, of course, is the tornadoes that rip through the American Midwest—particularly Oklahoma, North Texas, and Kansas—during the spring, annually pelting the region with hailstones the size of quarters, golf balls, or baseballs and tearing the roofs off of houses and, in some cases, the houses themselves off the land. If *The Wizard of Oz* (1939, directed by Victor Fleming) remains the best-known filmic rendering of a tornado, the advent of the Weather Channel has brought to the regular attention of millions of TV watchers spectacular imagery of tornadoes swirling across vast midwestern spaces. In spring 1996 Jan DeBont was able to turn this new media awareness of tornadoes into gold. As a result of the film's impressive special effects and the casting coup of signing Helen Hunt to play the female lead (and perhaps the timing of the film's release, which allowed it to profit simultaneously from the usual May–June excitement of moviegoers ready for an industry blockbuster and the particular consciousness of violent weather, at least in substantial areas of the United States, during the late spring and early summer), *Twister* became one of the leading moneymakers of the year.

The central character of *Twister* is Bill (Bill Paxton), a scientific researcher turned weatherman, who is in the process of leaving the adrenaline rush of storm chasing for the more secure space of the television studio.[1] His momentary choice of an adventureless maturity over an exciting youth is reflected by the two women in his life: Professor Jo Harding (Helen Hunt), his former collaborator in storm chasing and the passion of his youth; and Dr. Melissa Reeves (Jami Gertz), a reproductive therapist who loves him but comes to recognize that she cannot compete with the more energetic, active Harding. That the male hero is rewarded with two beautiful lovers, both of whom are true only to him; that these lovers are capable, professional women who, despite their accomplishments, remain incomplete without a man; that the ultimately victorious lover is a blond while the rejected lover is darker, "more ethnic" looking; and that the energetic Jo Harding is seen in juxtaposition to the land and the elements while Melissa Reeves is depicted as a city person ministering to the psychic ills of city folk are instances of patterns endemic to American pop film and television. As a result, the reuniting of the original couple is as inevitable as the counterclockwise spinning of the tornadoes that periodically interrupt the plot and, for an hour and a half, conveniently (and often spectacularly) forestall the inevitable.

At least as quintessentially American as the film's heartland of America location and its central characters and plot is the way its midwestern spaces are filmed. Few films have made more dramatic use of the helicopter shot. As the storm chasers follow the twisters from one town to the next, their speeding cars and vans are, again and again, filmed from helicopters that track their movements from considerable distances and heights. These helicopter shots express the characters' excitement about the adventure they're on (and the fear this excitement creates for Melissa) and in some instances provide a storm's-eye view of the land reminiscent of the shark's-eye view of swimmers in *Jaws* (1975, directed by Stephen Spielberg).

More fundamentally, the helicopter shots in *Twister,* as in so many other Hollywood films, reveal a typically American cinematic attitude toward moving through space. During the 1960s, as I was becoming familiar with the European features that were making their way into American art houses, I was regularly struck (as I'm sure many others were) with a difference between the way the European films and American films of the era depicted automobile travel: in the European films, travel in an automobile was filmed either from inside the vehicle or from directly in front of the windshield, creating (at least for Americans) a sense of claustrophobia. In the American films, automobile travel was filmed from outside the vehicle, often from above and moving along with it, creating a sense of exhilaration and freedom. The "wide open spaces" of the American frontier, first depicted by such painters as Frederic Church, Albert Bierstadt, and Thomas Moran in the nineteenth century[2] and marketed so effectively by American automobile manufacturers after World War II, have

Figure 24. Bill (Bill Paxton) and Jo (Helen Hunt) run from tornado in *Twister* (1996). Photo by Ron Batzdorff.

remained central to American thinking about automobile travel—and about freedom, which for many Americans is less a question of the ability to choose between political or even economic options than an emotion connected with the opportunity to take off in a car and, at least for a brief moment, escape from the claustrophobic demands of family, community, and society.

Of course, as is typical of American action-adventure films, the vortex of *Twister* is not character development and the evolution of plot but the special effects wizardry that creates the remarkably realistic illusions of monster tornadoes (in this instance, done at Industrial Light and Magic in San Francisco). Indeed, the characters and plot are, for all practical purposes, excuses for these special effects—a flimsy observation platform from which we can admire the "storms" created in the film studio, storms that look remarkably like the twisters seen on television in the marketing of videos made with footage recorded by real storm chasers (see fig. 24). The privileging of special effects over character development and plot, and even over research into the phenomenon of tornadoes—despite the fact that the "Good Guys" are weather researchers, we learn remarkably little about tornadoes from this feature—is obvious throughout *Twister*. Even as we watch the film we recognize that, implicitly, the real heroes are not the storm chasers—who are merely types, rather than complex, puzzling individuals—but the filmmakers themselves who have "done the impossible" by creating a believable, large-scale facsimile of a reality with which television has made us familiar. Indeed, *Twister* periodically alludes to the tradition of the special effects film of which it is a part: the device the storm chasers mean to place in the path of a tornado so that the winds can lift it into the funnel (the computer device will allow for the more sophisticated study of tornadoes and more accurate predictions about their paths) is called "Dorothy" after the *Wizard of Oz* character, and when a house rolls across the road during a chase late in the film, it is difficult not to think of Keaton's tornado in *Steamboat Bill, Jr.* (1927). Indeed, *Twister* was marketed as a landmark in special effects history: "From the Producers of 'JURASSIC PARK' and the Director of 'SPEED,'" the *Twister* poster tells us.

Still another typically American dimension of *Twister,* and one of the most fundamental, is the paradox at the heart of the film. As usual in an American action-adventure film, *Twister*'s plot has two basic elements: first, there's a romance between a man and a woman (at first they don't get along, but slowly they come to love each other—in *Twister,* the gap between the man and woman is unusually small); and second, there's a competition between the Good Guys and the Bad Guys. In this instance, the Good Guys are the storm chasers who developed Dorothy out of a love of pure science and a commitment to saving lives (a commitment originally instigated by a tornado's carrying away Jo's father, before her eyes, during her childhood, which we see in a period-piece flashback at the beginning of the film). The Bad Guys are a less capable but better financed rival group who have stolen Bill and Jo's ideas and plan to market the data their version of Dorothy collects, for personal gain and media prestige and for the profit of their corporate sponsor. It is quite clear in the film that the Bad Guys have no concern for human life; they refuse to stop to help the Good Guys even when it appears someone is injured, unlike the Good Guys, whose respect for human life fuels both their research and their practical acts. The Bad Guys' corruption is reconfirmed when Bill, who has fallen from innocence to become a weatherman, realizes he cannot live with the Bad Guys' desecration of his principles and leaves his corporate media career to return to his immersion in the natural world, outdoors with his Eve.

In other words, the producers of *Twister* sing the praises of a set of attitudes and a course of action precisely the opposite of their own. The men and women at Industrial Light and Magic who labored to produce the realistic illusions of tornadoes at the center of the film were hardly outdoor workers; they confined themselves to their studio facilities as fully as TV weathermen are confined to the TV studio. And, of course, the goal of their work was media prestige (i.e., the public recognition of their special effects efforts) and, in the end, the financial success of the film and those who invested in it. In *Twister* the Good Guys are simply a means to the achievement of the Bad Guys' aims; and romance and the idea of innocence are a means of distracting the audience from recognizing that, by buying tickets to *Twister,* we're supporting Bad Guys in order to have the opportunity to root for and identify with Good Guys.

This paradox is, of course, a contemporary version of a pattern that has informed the history of the American visual arts for more than a century (as well as, Simon Schama has shown in *Landscape and Memory,* a good many of the cultures emigrants to America in the nineteenth century brought with them).[3] Albert Boime has defined this pattern in *The Magisterial Gaze:*

> Hence the losing game played by Americans [during the nineteenth century]: on the one hand, their conditions for success depended on the razing of the wilderness and the cultivation of a splendid civilization, while with each inch of cultivated soil a little piece of their innocence disappeared. There was no way not to glorify the material development as progress, and there was no way to avoid condemning its results. The realization of the American dream implied the total corruption of the dreamer.[4]

Boime's focus is landscape painting, but the loss of innocence he describes is played out in *Twister,* both in the narrative and on the production level of the film. At the end of *Twister* the Good Guys are, of course, successful: Dorothy is deployed, thousands of individual sensors are carried into the funnel of the F-5 tornado,[5] and the storm chasers' computers are flooded with new information about this tornado, and, implicitly, all tornadoes—so much information that Bill and Jo are already arguing about who will be in charge of which of the facilities they'll need to build to process it. Implicitly, the sublimity of the tornado—the real, uncontrollable power that is communicated by the Weather Channel imagery of tornadoes and by the special effects of *Twister*—is destroyed; the "wilderness" at the center of the funnel is rendered understandable and, if not harmless, at least predictable, that is, soon to be no longer a danger to the population of Oklahoma; and the more intensive tornado research now in the offing surely promises new industries and new products.

On the production level of the film this same pattern is played out, although at an even more complete level of control. While the Good Guys have begun to develop a new database for the study of the elements at their most sublime, the special effects people at Industrial Light and Magic are in the business of manufacturing the illusion of sublimity itself.[6] Whether their special effects are based on a thorough knowledge of tornadoes or simply on a body of special effects research with only a tenuous connection to meteorological realities, they have found a way to duplicate the visual experience originally provided by real storm chasers in the field, without putting themselves in any physical danger. That is, the adventurousness that seems to have inspired *Twister* has become, at most, a technical and financial challenge not very different from the many other challenges the history of special effects has overcome.

During the final credits of *Twister* (the final, and only, credits: no credits open the film—presumably a way of carrying viewers into the adventure), DeBont provides a poignant visual coda, both to the film and to the history of visualizing the sublime that implicitly informs his film. For the most part abjuring studio-produced special effects (and even the flashy helicopter shots that energize the body of *Twister*), DeBont provides a montage of shots of skyscapes, impressive both because of their subject matter and because we so rarely see the 35mm, wide-screen image devoted to showing weather. Compared with the frenetic action during the film, these shots provide an obvious denouement, a calm *after* the storm, that allows those willing to stay

Figure 25. Martin Johnson Heade's *Thunder Storm on Narra-gansett Bay* (1868), oil on canvas, 32⅛" × 54½". Amon Carter Museum, Fort Worth, Texas (1977.17).

in the theater the opportunity to see a series of lovely but impressive images reminiscent of the tradition of storm representation in nineteenth-century American painting: Thomas Cole's *View from Mount Holyoke, Northampton, Massachusetts—The Oxbow* (1836; see plate 1), *Tornado* (1831), and *Catskill Mountain House: The Four Elements* (1843–44); Bierstadt's *Storm in the Rocky Mountains, Mt. Rosalie* (1866), and *Buffalo Trail: The Impending Storm* (1869); and Martin Johnson Heade's *Approaching Storm: Beach Near Newport* (ca. 1860) and *Thunder Storm on Narragansett Bay* (1868)—a tradition periodically revived in the twentieth century, for example, by the Wisconsin regionalist John Steuart Curry in *Tornado over Kansas* (1929) and *Line Storm* (1934). (See figs. 25, 26.) And yet, a century after a generation of painters provided oppor-tunities to meditate on the divinely informed storms that shape the North

Figure 26. John Steuart Curry's *Tornado Over Kansas* (1929), oil on canvas, 46¼" × 60½". Reprinted by permission of the Hackley Picture Fund, Muskegon Museum of Art, Muskegon, Michigan.

American environment, DeBont's faith in viewers' ability to enjoy even a fleeting glance at what, a century ago, was the mainstream of what was considered sublime is so tenuous that his montage is, literally, an afterthought. Indeed, just as the tornadoes we see in *Twister* are studio facsimiles of twisters seen on television—that is, many levels removed from the reality of the elements—even these final images of sky, storm, and land must be seen "through" the rolling credits listing the film's dozens of special effects workers.

Weather Diary 1

By the time he made *A Town Called Tempest* (1963), George Kuchar had been making films (in collaboration with his twin brother, Mike) for six years.

Using the most inexpensive film equipment available—silent, 8mm, "home-movie" equipment—the boys had begun, at fifteen, by enlisting their friends, family, and neighbors and using whatever money, costumes, and props they could scrounge. They produced a series of bizarre melodramas, based on the commercial films they loved but (because of their limited resources) so distant from Hollywood as to seem like send-ups of the industry—and so distinctive as to influence many of the filmmakers and prospective filmmakers who saw the Kuchar brothers' films in New York City at screening venues devoted to what was then called "Underground Film."[7]

A Town Called Tempest was one of the most elaborate of the brothers' 8mm melodramas. For it, they developed a preposterous, risqué plot about an adolescent midwestern boy whose parents don't appreciate him. He decides to build a storm cellar, but his shallow parents worry that he's a bit demented. To "make him a man," his father gives the boy five dollars to go to a brothel. On his way to the brothel the boy meets a girl who asks him to go to Mass, but he does as his father has ordered and proceeds to the brothel, where he meets a middle-aged prostitute. Before the boy can discover sex, the threat of a tornado sends him running home and into his storm cellar. He survives the tornado and joins the other survivors in a parade through the destroyed town. Once again, he meets the young girl who wanted him to go to Mass and confesses to her that he kept his parents out of the storm cellar on purpose (the girl is shocked, leaves, and turns to drugs). The procession ends at the brothel, the only house still standing. The prostitute the boy had met earlier has survived the tornado and has decided to go straight. When the boy arrives, she grenades him, then the brothel.

While it is tempting now to read *A Town Called Tempest* as a parable of the filmmakers' own adolescence—and perhaps of their filmmaking as a place of safety within what they felt was an inhospitable environment—viewers at the time were entertained by the humorous absurdity not only of the plot but also of the presentation of the story: the awkward acting, the ridiculous costumes, the "incompetent" continuity (for the parade of survivors, the Kuchars filmed a real church parade of some sort held in an obviously different location from their action), and the amusing juxtaposition of the Kuchars' makeshift visuals with passages of music lifted from commercial melodramas. But what was, and remains, most impressive about *A Town Called Tempest* is the tornado itself. Using toys, drawings, whatever they could make or find, the Kuchars created a storm that is impressive despite (or because of) the obviousness of its fabrication. It is a special effects sequence that disobeys the most fundamental rule of commercial special effects: in *A Town Called Tempest* all the seams show, and we can see exactly how the effects were produced. And yet the sheer dedication of the young filmmakers, obvious in the elaborateness of the sequence, gives the climax of the film a bizarre dignity based more on our recognition of their creative desire (and of their obvious awareness of how real Hollywood effects are, in fact, accomplished) than on the film's ability to fool us into believing what we know is not true.[8]

By the mid-1960s the Kuchar twins were working separately, and both had begun to work in 16mm. Many of George Kuchar's early 16mm films are melodramas that have much in common with the collaborative 8mm films, especially in their frankness and personal openness—but with an increasingly remarkable visual sense that is already evident in his second 16mm film, *Hold Me While I'm Naked* (1966), a portrait of Kuchar himself as a filmmaker using his power as director to compensate for his erotic frustrations.[9] In addition to melodramas, however, Kuchar was also, from time to time, making personal documentaries: including a diary of his relationship with the visual artists Red Grooms and Mimi Gross (*Encyclopedia of the Blessed,* 1968), a documentation of George Segal at work (*House of the White People,* 1968), and *Wild Night in El Reno* (1977), a short evocation of a stormy night Kuchar spent in El Reno, Oklahoma (thirty miles due west from Oklahoma City and one hundred miles due south of Wakita, Oklahoma, a crucial location in *Twister*). *Wild Night in El Reno* was to become the seed for a series of videotapes Kuchar would call "the Weather Diaries."[10]

Wild Night in El Reno is an exquisite, carefully composed and edited, overtly diaristic, six-minute short, which begins with several postcard images of Oklahoma countryside (these are shot from projected slides; Kuchar pulls aside a curtain to reveal the images) and the opening title: "Wild Night in El Reno/Photographed at the FRONTIER MOTEL 2215 Sunset Drive." During the body of the film, Kuchar first presents a sequence of beautiful shots of grass blowing in the wind, filmed behind the motel and through the window of his room; then (after a posed snapshot, filmed from a projected slide, of himself standing near a wall with the graffiti "Jimmy Rush is a pussy") we see shots of a storm. The storm intensifies into the night, and at its height Kuchar intercuts between impressive shots of lightning and of a woman running to an outdoor phone booth through torrential rain. In the morning there is a gorgeous golden rainbow; and Kuchar concludes with more shots of the grass in the breeze near the motel and with the title, "by GEORGE KUCHAR May 1977 Canadian County Oklahoma." Like the early melodramas, *Wild Night in El Reno* has a sound track constructed of passages lifted from commercial movies: bits of music, a clock ticking, bells that toll as the storm grows violent, the sound of a door closing. But *Wild Night in El Reno* reverses the ratio of trashy humor and sensual beauty that characterizes the melodramas (with the exception of John Waters, few of Kuchar's imitators seem to have realized that it is this combination—not just the trashiness and the humor—that makes George Kuchar's films so distinctive). The title seems to suggest an experience akin to the melodramas, but with the exception of bits of humor supplied by the juxtaposition of sound and image and the "trashiness" of the graffiti, *Wild Night in El Reno* is a film dedicated to the everyday natural beauty, and sublimity, the filmmaker experiences in a particular place and time.

Kuchar remained a productive filmmaker well into the 1980s, working alternately on his own and with his students at the San Francisco Art Institute; but for reasons of cost and facility, he was also beginning to work in video and during the 1990s has become a prolific and widely known independent video artist (the Video Data Bank in Chicago publishes a separate catalog for Kuchar's videos).[11] The inexpensiveness of shooting video seems to have freed Kuchar's diaristic impulse and has led to a series of Weather Diaries—fourteen as of 1998, at least one a year. For me, the most interesting of these remains *Weather Diary 1* (1986). But a good case can be made for *Weather Diary 2* (1987), *Scenes from a Vacation* (*Weather Diary 6,* 1990), *Sunbelt Serenade* (*Weather Diary 9,* 1993), and *Season of Sorrow* (*Weather Diary 12,* 1996).

The relative accessibility of contemporary video technology (combined with Kuchar's resources at the San Francisco Art Institute) resulted in his redefinition of video production—just as his limited resources in the early 1960s resulted in a redefinition of cinematic melodrama. But while Kuchar was and is equally "himself" as a film artist and as a video artist—there is no mistaking a Kuchar film or video—the Weather Diaries are unconventional in quite a different sense than the early 8mm melodramas: whereas the Kuchar brothers' melodramas condense a considerable awareness of Hollywood filmmaking into shorts (most of the early films are from twelve to twenty minutes long), the Weather Diaries—especially the first few—are unconventional in their expansion of what, at least at first glance, seems a minimal amount of experience into generally longer works: *Weather Diary 1* is 81 minutes; *Weather Diary 2* is 70 minutes; *Weather Diary 3* (1988) is only 24 minutes; *Weather Diary 4* (1988), a second section of *Weather Diary 3*, which was made "to apologize for the lack of good weather" in the latter, is 47 minutes.[12]

Like *Wild Night in El Reno*, *Weather Diary 1* and the other Weather Diaries (except for the fourth) were made in the same neighborhood in El Reno. This time, Kuchar is staying at the Motel Reno, but the nearby Frontier Motel is visible in a number of shots. While *Wild Night in El Reno* focuses on the natural surround of the motel before, during, and after one stormy night, *Weather Diary 1* embeds its depiction of the rural surround of the Motel Reno during a month's worth of weather within a series of intimately personal observations and reflections—personal in the most literal sense: the first shot of Kuchar's motel room is a pan from the toilet in the bathroom to the unmade bed; and during the videotape we learn about all the details of his stay, from his bathroom habits (at one point, Kuchar documents his own feces!) to his personal hygiene (we see him washing his underwear, drying his socks).

Although to a contemporary sensibility Kuchar's diary would seem virtually the opposite of anything that could be called classic American literature, *Weather Diary 1* has so much in common with Thoreau's *Walden* that it can be considered a contemporary version of it. It's true that Kuchar is not in the woods, and his Bronx accent (an accent he continues to maintain, despite living more than twenty years in California) seems a far cry from Thoreau's educated literary style. But similarities between Kuchar and Thoreau are more fundamental and more suggestive. Thoreau's epic personal essay is a record of a "Life in the Woods"; Kuchar records a life in "the sticks." Like Kuchar's, Thoreau's idiom was defiantly personal, for his time. If he uses an educated literary address to the reader of *Walden*, Thoreau nevertheless was unusual in referring to himself in the first person ("In most books, the *I*, or first person, is omitted; in this it will be retained . . .").[13] In other words, even if we see Kuchar's video as a mock heroic version of *Walden* (just as it's possible to read *Walden* as a mock heroic version of the travel journals and wilderness writing so popular in the nineteenth century), Kuchar's mock-heroism is more fully an attempt to live an experience akin to the one Thoreau describes than to critique it.[14]

I like to think of this connection with Thoreau as confirmed by Kuchar's first vocal address to the viewer: as we look out the motel room window at the pouring rain, Kuchar says, "Sometimes there are so many pools of water outside this motel that it's like lakeside property. I think the animals love it, like the birds and the dogs. Certainly there's a lot of birds and dogs around." Like Thoreau in "Economy," the opening chapter of *Walden,* Kuchar makes clear the details of his place, revealing the simple wardrobe he's brought with him (a couple pairs of socks and underwear, one pair of tennis shoes . . .) and the simple food he's stocked in the motel room's refrigerator (a jar of jelly, a few cans of this and that): it is obvious that, like Thoreau, Kuchar has come to El Reno precisely to avoid a more "sophisticated," complex life and to see if he cannot learn, as Thoreau puts it, "sometimes to be content with less"[15]—and, of course, to use this opportunity to study developments taking place in the natural world around him.

Kuchar's imagery of the storms and skyscapes around El Reno is extensive and beautiful in the most traditional sense. *Weather Diary 1* is full of the kind of imagery we see through the rolling credits at the end of *Twister;* and even if the good video projection *Weather Diary 1* needs is less impressive than good 35mm film projection, Kuchar's composition and timing give his images of Tornado Alley's big skies, impressive cloud formations, and exquisite color considerable power (see figs. 27a–c). These images are arresting enough to recontextualize the rest of what Kuchar shows us. To put this another way, if conventional television seems to miniaturize and marginalize natural vistas, generally using such imagery as part of heavily edited news clips or ads, Kuchar reorients video technology with regard to his natural surround: while even the most impressive tornadoes shown by the Weather Channel on Kuchar's TV set are contained by the box itself, and by the structures of media language, Kuchar's unusual personalization of video production causes him— and to a degree us—to feel surrounded by the meteorological developments occurring outside the motel. The effect is to enlarge the storms, including a tornado that blows past El Reno during the month Kuchar is there—or, to put this in art-historical terms, to reinvest this particular landscape with the feeling of the sublime. While the Weather Channel and the local weather reports Kuchar listens to are involved in processing the storms they cover—and use imagery recorded by storm chasers to energize the viewer's interest in these storms—Kuchar's *Weather Diary 1* makes quite clear that those staying at the Motel Reno and those living in several trailers nearby have no storm cellar to

Figures 27a – c. Developing storm, from George Kuchar's *Weather Diary 1* (1986).

use should a tornado come their way. Kuchar jokes about the danger with a Native American woman who lives in one of the trailers, but it is clear that, as the storms develop, he (and she) are in some danger. The frightening power of nature is obvious both in Kuchar's imagery of the storm clouds and the storms themselves and in his narration: at one point during the storm he comments, "That Indian lady in her trailer must be shittin' in her underwear!" After a pause, he adds, "I soiled *mine* earlier."

As was true even in his earliest films, the power of Kuchar's work in video is his combination of the beautiful and the sublime with the mundane and, in some instances, with the disgusting. Indeed, for Kuchar, these very different kinds of experience define each other and, in their interface, characterize human experience. Early in *Weather Diary 1,* Kuchar includes a close-up of an empty, flushing toilet as a metaphor for the funneling air of the tornadoes he's come to El Reno to be near, and, of course, these spiraling motions are two versions of the same gravitational pull. For Kuchar, the connection is quite intimate: too much spiraling in the world outside his motel room tends to produce internal "storms" that require his more frequent use of the toilet. Late in the videotape, Kuchar mentions that the nearby tornado in Edmond, Oklahoma, "also caused . . . ," followed by a shot of vomit hitting the toilet. The viewer's disgust parallels Kuchar's personal turmoil during the storm. It's a while before he cleans up the bathroom, just as the cleanup in Edmond takes a while. In a general sense, Kuchar's tape develops a parallel between the damage tornadoes cause when they touch down and the "damage" Kuchar's tape can cause an unwitting viewer: when I've shown *Weather Diary 1* in classes, some students have been angered by Kuchar's candidness and take time to recover from his confrontation of their sensibilities; and at the 1996 Robert Flaherty Seminar, Kuchar's presentation of the tape resulted in the most volatile exchange of the seminar week.[16]

Kuchar's general awareness of nature's sublime power also has a very different effect. In *Twister,* the pressure of the danger of chasing tornadoes creates camaraderie among the storm chasers; in *Weather Diary 1,* such pressure intensifies perception. Like Nick Adams recovering from "shell-shock" by hiking to the Big Two-Hearted River in Hemingway's story, Kuchar's fear and excitement at being in Tornado Alley—and being there alone, for what feels an extended period of time—results in an alertness about natural phenomena, not only the beautiful skyscape and landscape vistas mentioned earlier, but also the more intimate natural events that happen within these vistas. As is clear in Kuchar's first comments in the video, he is particularly attuned to animals. His friendship with an apparent stray he calls "Runt" is a motif throughout the tape, and even a tiny spider he finds crawling on his ceiling lamp fixture is filmed in exquisite detail. In *Weather Diary 1,* Kuchar uses video technology to free himself and us from the usual distractions of media, in the interest of alerting us to a more engaged experience of the macrocosmic and microcosmic dimensions of nature.

During the century that passed between Thoreau's writing *Walden* and Kuchar's making *Weather Diary 1,* the relationship between Americans and their natural surround changed dramatically. If Thoreau is able to move toward what seems like the edge of the industrialized world by means of a short hike out of Concord (even he doesn't move *beyond* that world: local railroad tracks cut across one edge of Walden Pond's boundaries), Kuchar's journey to El Reno takes him from one developed region to another (indeed, the cheap motels he stays in during the Weather Diaries suggest that he has arrived in El Reno *after* development in the region has peaked: these motels have seen better days).[17] For those nineteenth-century Americans interested in experiencing the sublime, an escape from the mundane seemed essential, whether it meant traveling into the Maine woods from Concord or traveling long distances to see Niagara or Yosemite. Indeed, for some theorizers of the psychic and physical benefits of a periodic experience of the sublime, this exit from mundane reality was essential. As Frederick Law Olmsted put it in his preliminary report for the Yosemite Commission in 1865,

> It is a scientific fact that the occasional contemplation of natural scenes of an impressive character, particularly if this contemplation occurs in connection with relief from ordinary cares, change of air and change of habits, is favorable to the health and vigor of men and especially to the health and vigor of their intellect beyond any other conditions which can be offered them, that it not only gives pleasure for the time being but increases the subsequent capacity for happiness and the means of securing happiness.

And for Olmsted, full appreciation of this invigorating experience required that it be, as completely as possible, unalloyed:

> The first point to be kept in mind then is the preservation and maintenance as exactly as is possible of the natural scenery; the restriction, that is to say, within the narrowest limits consistent with the necessary accommodation of visitors, of all artificial constructions and the prevention of all constructions markedly inharmonious with the scenery or which would unnecessarily obscure, distort or detract from the dignity of the scenery.[18]

So far as Olmsted can understand, the deepest enjoyment of natural landscape can only be accomplished if nature's dignity is separated from the mundane, framed off from the industrializing surround.

In our time, the "frames" between the natural/sublime and the industrialized/mundane have become so permeable that there is virtually nowhere we can go to escape the sorts of distractions Olmsted means to avoid in Yosemite.[19] And yet, as Kuchar demonstrates in *Weather Diary 1,* even in our mediated, postmodern world, the beauty and even the sublimity of nature—as

Figure 28. One of George Kuchar's signature shots, from *Weather Diary 1* (1986).

well as the experience of escaping to rediscover them—remain available. After all, nothing helps Kuchar and the viewer recognize the awesome power of the tornado that rips by El Reno in May 1986 more fully than the presence of those flimsy trailers across the way. It may be that, as Olmsted suggests, we need to exit from our day-to-day lives and our usual terrain to reawaken our ability to perceive the loveliness of nature and to feel its awesome power, but *Weather Diary 1* suggests that wherever we go, we can find this experience, so long as we learn to use the inevitable, pervasive mundane to provide a psychic "frame" for an immersion within the awesome power of nature.

When Kuchar packs up to leave the Motel Reno, he seems ready to rejoin his workaday life, and he is also clear that his experience in El Reno has been valuable enough, for him as a person and as a videomaker, to return to: his last words, to Runt (and implicitly to the viewer) are, "Take care of yourself. Maybe I'll see you next year." That Kuchar's experiences did in fact reenergize him is explicit in the fact that he continued to travel to Oklahoma to produce an annual weather diary and implicit in the consistent self-reflexivity of each Weather Diary. *Weather Diary 1,* for example, is self-reflexive from its opening moments. Kuchar begins with a shot of the front of the Motel Reno in heavy rain, which is interrupted three times: first, by the painted title, "Weather Diary 1"; then by a shot of a nearby trailer and tree, followed by the pan from bathroom to bed; and finally by Kuchar's opening comment to the audience and a synch-sound extreme close-up of his face, filmed from below (see fig 28). This is a signature Kuchar camera angle that, ever since its use in *Hold Me While I'm Naked,* has been amusing not only because Kuchar's face is precisely *not* a face we expect to see in an extreme close-up but also because it is obvious that Kuchar is holding the camera himself. Kuchar fans share a camp awareness that the pensive look on Kuchar's face, his "candid" gaze into the distance, is being performed for the camera *he* is holding—and that he's holding the camera to mimic the kind of industry tracking shot he can't afford to make. A return to the opening shot of the motel leads into the videotape's first use of local coverage of tornado damage. As an expression of the narrative, this bit of intercutting (especially noticeable *because* we keep returning to the same shot) reflects the character's slight anxiety about the storm—subsequently substantiated by the news coverage of the tornado. But it is also Kuchar-the-director's immediate declaration that while we will see his personal experiences, we'll be seeing them as they were performed for the camera and fabricated into a work of video art.

Kuchar's self-reflexivity is an ongoing motif throughout the Weather Diary series. Indeed, each new Weather Diary implies a comparison with the previous ones that keeps viewers focused on Kuchar-as-director. Each change in approach, each evolution of the Kuchar persona becomes part of the meta-narrative that develops diary after diary. Indeed, my earlier comparison between Kuchar and Thoreau seems confirmed by Kuchar's regular return to El Reno. While the original one-month stay in El Reno for *Weather Diary 1* was too brief to be more than a metaphor for the two years Thoreau lived at Walden Pond, Kuchar's regular return to Oklahoma has resulted in his living in El Reno for nearly a year of Mays.

The most obvious relationship between the successive Weather Diaries is Kuchar's annual return to El Reno in May and his focus on weather. But there are many particular filmic gestures that become motifs in the Weather Diary series: the "signature shot," described earlier, for example; and the "shit shot" of Kuchar's feces—seeing turds in *Weather Diary 1, 2,* and *3* prepares us for *Weather Diary 4,* where we only *hear* Kuchar defecating; for *Weather Diary 5,* where Kuchar sits down on the toilet and we *don't* get a "shit shot"; and for *Weather Diary 6*, where an *animated* turd flies into the toilet.[20] In more recent Weather Diaries, Kuchar has developed another "signature shot," equally self-reflexive as his hand-held close-up: from the video camera on the ground, we see Kuchar from below, walking over the camera and into the distance. His pretense that he is just out for a walk and unaware of the camera is amusing—and an implicit comment on similar gestures in Hollywood movies (one thinks of John Ford's stagecoaches and wagons driving over cameras during skirmishes with Indians).

The meta-narrative of the Weather Diary series also charts Kuchar's increasing openness about his autoeroticism. He mentions that he "beats his meat" in *Weather Diary 1*, but in subsequent diaries he's more open about masturbating (in *Weather Diary 3*, we see him masturbating in the shower) and about his homoerotic desire (in *Weather Diary 4* and *Weather Diary 5*, his desire for young men is obvious; and in *Weather Diary 6*, Kuchar is visited by a young man who may be a male lover). There are also formal evolutions within the series (for instance, after using synch sound for *Weather Diary 1* through *5*, in *Weather Diary 6*, Kuchar returns to a nonsynch approach reminiscent of *Wild Night in El Reno*) and formal jokes on these evolutions: *Weather Diary 8: Interior Vacuum* (1992) begins as a tour of San Francisco homes that seems to have nothing to do with the weather or the Weather Diaries, but during a birthday celebration at the second home, Kuchar's gift is his new Weather Diary, which we subsequently see.

In the end, Kuchar's self-reflexive documentation of a performance of the personal can be read as a parallel to an aspect of *Walden* and of Olmsted's Yosemite report. Thoreau may have gone to the woods "because [he] wished to live deliberately"—"to front only the essential facts of life, and see if I could not learn what it had to teach, and not, when I came to die, discover that I had not lived"—but his stay at Walden Pond was *also* research for the book on which his reputation rests most firmly: Thoreau may have been literally earning his living "by the labor of my hands only," but he was storing up experiences that he would subsequently craft—"by hand," in a different sense—into a literary work.[21] Similarly, Olmsted may have believed that sites like Yosemite might be of inestimable value in reenergizing the psyches of those who visited because, unlike workaday life (which is devoted to what *will* happen), an experience of nature "is for itself and at the moment it is enjoyed.

The attention is aroused and the mind occupied without purpose, without . . . relating the present action . . . to some future end."[22] But his own exploration of Yosemite was part of *his* work, a means both to a larger end in general and to a government report in particular. Both Thoreau and Olmsted used the idea of escape from their parts in the process of industrialization, of "civilization," as a means of energizing their careers. Similarly, it is clear in the first of the Weather Diaries, and is confirmed by those that have followed, that when Kuchar travels to El Reno he is going into video production: Kuchar comes to El Reno to experience the sublimity of the weather *and* to produce a video about his experience. Indeed, *Weather Diary 1* was shot entirely in-camera: Kuchar fabricated his continuity as he shot, and when he left El Reno, the video was complete.[23]

Kuchar has found a way to use Thoreau's and Olmsted's insights (and something of their praxis) within a thoroughly developed, mediated world, reinvigorating the idea of the beautiful and the sublime without needing to eliminate, or to pretend to eliminate, the vernacular world. Kuchar's is a sublimity J. B. Jackson might appreciate.

Which brings us back around to *Twister*. In the context of the modern discourse on the issue of what "America" *is*, both *Twister* and Kuchar's Weather Diaries can be seen as quintessentially American, but in two different senses, which, however, contextualize each other. *Twister* is "American," even in addition to its reiteration of the rhetoric of the American action-adventure genre and its romanticization of both the sublimity of nature *and* the sublimity of technology. The characters' romance with Dorothy is reflected by the filmmakers' romance with special effects, and, of course, both levels of this romance with technology come together at the climax of *Twister,* by means of the most prevalent romantic technology of the 1990s, the computer: *Twister*'s computer-generated effects create the F-5 tornado that sucks Dorothy into the funnel and produces a world of new data on the storm chasers' computer system. On both levels, technology is in the process of supplanting nature's sublimity: Dorothy will render tornadoes less dangerous to people; and Industrial Light and Magic's twister technology not only produces imagery as convincing as live recording, it can generate mega-twisters at will and send them wherever the filmmakers decide they should go.

In the Weather Diaries, Kuchar is equally "American," in the particular nature of his *resistance* to technological development. Unlike the storm chasers in *Twister* and the special effects masters at Industrial Light and Magic, Kuchar's goal is not total control but a reinvigoration of the beautiful and the sublime within his everyday experience and the various benefits this reinvigoration can produce. That Kuchar is making a videotape is clear evidence that he is not antitechnology. But whereas the direction of technological development in and of *Twister* is centripetal (like the movement of air in a tornado), focusing increased power and money in the hands of a few people, the technological development represented by Kuchar is centrifugal: it argues for a dispersion of media power, a more media-democratic consciousness, and a far broader sensitivity to the particular natural realities within which we live. At personal appearances Kuchar explains that the production cost of *Weather Diary 1* was eleven dollars (the cost of the videotape itself), and even if we argue that the cost of living in El Reno should also be included, Kuchar's expenses were minimal: the Reno motel room rented for sixty dollars a week! In recent years, Kuchar has traveled the country, training would-be videomakers in "Very Low Budget Video Production" (to quote a 1996 Southeastern Media Institute brochure). Kuchar is a magician but in a very different sense from Hollywood special effects people: they spend millions producing realistic illusions of what we know isn't true, both literally and metaphorically (in recent generations we've certainly learned that technological advances alone won't save us), whereas Kuchar uses media to reconnect us with everyday realities that we know are the stuff of our lives as individuals and as Americans and to model the production of personal video responses to our experiences that we can share with one another. Like many independent film and video artists, Kuchar means to provide democratic balance to viewers swept up in the whirlwind of technological development, by using new technology to work against the winds of change and especially the centripetal accumulation of media power.

chapter 6

The City as Motion Picture

I've long recognized that, whatever pretensions I have about being an individual, for the most part my experiences are typical of large numbers of people; and, therefore, if I say that in my lifetime I am aware of three distinct attitudes toward the American city, I do not mean to privilege my personal experience but to recognize it as an index to the experiences of at least a portion of a particular generation. As I was growing up in Easton, Pennsylvania, during the 1940s and 1950s (I was born in 1942), New York City was for me "The City" and our family trips into The City were the most exciting moments of my life. While I was thoroughly bored by what my family called "beautiful scenery" (expansive vistas of the mixture of farms and low Appalachian mountains characteristic of Pennsylvania and Virginia), I was fascinated by cityscapes—the more industrial, the better. The drive from Easton across New Jersey on Route 22 was foreplay leading to two climactic moments: the incredible industrial vista that opened between Newark, Elizabeth, and Jersey City; and the sight of Manhattan from the Pulaski Skyway. For me, and for my father, New York City and its industrial surround were a human creation beyond art, and whatever pollution and environmental devastation we were vaguely aware of seemed not only inevitable but romantic as well. For my father, whose hopes of a college education vanished the year he graduated from high school, when the Great Depression hit, the distant, wavering flames burning off petroleum fumes in Elizabeth were candles lit in honor of America's postwar industrial boom and the smoke that darkened the sky was incense—even the horrific stockyard smell near Secaucus (if we were entering Manhattan via the Lincoln Tunnel) was humorous: "P.U. Se*cau*cus," we'd laugh. Of course, the conclusion of our journey and the greatest product of America's industrialization was New York City itself. It was the largest and, we assumed, the most dynamic city in the world. That seemed obvious from the panorama we could see from the top of the Empire State Building and from the awesome golden cavern of Radio City Music Hall, two of the inevitable goals of these trips.

This consciousness of New York City as the great American product of successful, democratic industrialization remained with me through my adolescence and into my twenties, when history and my personal circumstances revealed a new sense of the American city. During my six years living in Gainesville as a graduate student at the University of Florida, I couldn't help but wonder what Gainesville residents did for a living. Except for the university itself, there didn't seem to be any substantial employers, no big factories—and yet every year I was there, Gainesville grew by a considerable percentage. It wasn't until much later that I realized the obvious: Gainesville's "industry" was the building of Gainesville itself (when I arrived in 1960 the population was less than 30,000; as of 1990 the city had tripled in size and Alachua County had passed 180,000). Increasingly, my sense of the city as a product—epitomized by Manhattan—gave way to a new sense of the American city-in-process, growing larger and suburbanizing, so that increasingly it made sense to rank cities in terms of the population of the metropolitan areas of which they were a part. If I remained snobbishly loyal to the idea of New York as the best an American city could be, I couldn't help but recognize that the expanding metro areas in Florida, Texas, Arizona, and, especially, California were where the real city-building energy was, and as the metropolitan area of Los Angeles surpassed that of Chicago, I was forced to realize that it might be only a matter of time before the New York area was no longer the biggest urban space, even in the United States.

In recent years a third sense of the modern city has come to dominate our attention. More and more, city building transforms not merely the landscapes within city limits and immediately surrounding them, but landscapes geographically distant from city centers. The expansion of San Francisco, for example, necessitated the building of the Hetch Hetchy Dam, the only large dam ever built within a national park (Yosemite). This pattern has grown increasingly obvious in the American Far West and Southwest, where debates about where to get water for an expanding population and how to allocate it are ongoing. That the development of the modern cityscape seems to require the transformation, even the destruction, of rural and wilderness landscapes long distances away is a problem that increasingly confronts all thinking people who love both the dynamism of the city experience and the serenity of the traditional experience of nature. How can we achieve a sensible balance between the two?

Because the evolution of those technologies that made the twentieth-century city possible also made possible the modern motion picture and because the developments of the modern city and the cinema have been not only simultaneous but also interlocked—without concentrations of urbanites, there could have been no film industry—it is hardly surprising that film history has produced a history of depictions of urban life. In this country, the modern city has been crucial to two major strands of film history. Certainly, Hollywood has used cities as environments for melodrama in a wide variety of ways, from Harold Lloyd's stunt comedies to the long history of film noir. The modern city has also been a frequent subject of films identified with and often claimed by two traditions of independent cinema: documentary film and avant-garde film. In a general sense, the specific films that are the focus of this chapter—the New York "city symphonies," the panoramas of San Francisco life, and the films that mean to rethink the tradition of depicting the twentieth-century city from a position near the conclusion of the century—reflect the three stages in the development of my attitude toward the city, though sometimes in complex ways.

The New York City Symphony

During the decade or so after Robert Flaherty's *Nanook of the North* (1921; see fig. 29) established the nonfiction film as an aesthetic and commercial force, two apparently distinct, but closely related, approaches to the use of cinema as a means of documenting reality were most attractive to filmmakers—and to some extent, to audiences as well. Some filmmakers dedicated themselves to the depiction of distant, "exotic" cultures. Flaherty collaborated with the Inuit on *Nanook* and later with the Samoan Islanders on *Moana* (1926) to dramatize aspects of their traditional ways of life. In *Grass* (1925) Merian C. Cooper and Ernest P. Schoedsack documented the migration of the Bakhtiari people from Turkey to Persia in search of grass for their herds; and later, in *Chang* (1927), they recorded the lives of natives in the Siamese jungle. Of course, this fascination with the exotic was nothing new. The nineteenth century had produced a plethora of written and photographic records of "exotic" peoples now made accessible by the development of faster, easier, less expensive means of transportation;[1] and, of course, from the very beginning of the commercial cinema, the Edison Studio and the Lumière Brothers recognized a potential market for motion pictures of the exotic.

From our perspective, it is clear that the real subject of Flaherty's films and the Cooper-Schoedsack collaborations is the interface of modern industrialized society (as represented by the apparatus of cinema) and those preindustrial ways of life "left behind" by the industrial revolution. The romance of the exotic was (as usual) a function of its precariousness: in Flaherty, the traditional Inuit and Samoan ways of life had been largely supplanted by the time Flaherty arrived to film them; in *Grass,* the nomadic life of the Bakhtiari seems to "modern" eyes as bizarre and impossible as the existence of a giant ape called Kong accepting sacrifices of young women on Skull Island—Cooper-Schoedsack's later fictional version of their travels in search of the exotic. If Flaherty pays the Inuit more respect (by effacing his process and focusing on Nanook and his family, by filming in-close so that we are able to recognize individuals, by using an admiring intertitle narration) than Cooper and Schoedsack show the Bakhtiari, nevertheless, both the Flaherty and the Cooper-Schoedsack films implicitly provide a final look at what the filmmakers assume will inevitably be lost as a result of the spread of the modern, mechanized technologies centered in the world's major cities.

Figure 29. Nanook warms his son Allee's hands, in Robert Flaherty's *Nanook of the North* (1921). Courtesy International Film Seminars, New York.

The other major subject for early nonfiction filmmakers was the modern, mechanized city.[2] Indeed, the fascination of filmmakers with imagery of city life, evident in many of the earliest Edison and Lumière actualities and in Paul Strand and Charles Sheeler's *Manhatta* (1921), as well as in a series of European "city symphonies" of the 1920s, is the obverse of the contemporary fascination with "exotic" cultures: if Flaherty and Cooper-Schoedsack familiarized viewers with the exotic, the city films exoticized the familiar.[3] What has come to be called the "city symphony"—a film that provides a general sense of life in a specific metropolis, by revealing characteristic dimensions of city life from the morning into the evening of a composite day—matured during the mid-1920s. The general critical consensus is that Alberto Cavalcanti's *Rien que les heures* (Nothing but the Hours, 1926), Walther Ruttmann's *Berlin, die Sinfonie einer Grosstadt* (Berlin: Symphony of a Big City, 1927; see fig. 30), and Dziga Vertov's *The Man with a Movie Camera* (1929) remain the exemplary instances of the form, although Ruttmann's evocation of Berlin not only named the city symphony, but provided a most typical instance of it.[4] Ruttmann's titling his film a "symphony" is, of course, suggestive. Few forms encode the ideals of European thinking and cultural evolution more thoroughly than the symphony and the symphony orchestra. And for a filmmaker who wanted to honor Berlin as the quintessential modern European metropolis, the use of symphony structure as analogous to the structure of city life may have been virtually inevitable. In an orchestra dozens of musicians play instruments that have evolved over history to produce a multipartite but unified and coherent performance within which the individualities of the contributing musicians are subsumed; in the city the individual contributions of millions of people (working with technologies that have developed over centuries) are subsumed within the metropolis's mega-partite movement through the day, a movement that reveals several predictable highs and lows.[5] At the end of *Berlin: Symphony of a Big City*, symbolic fireworks celebrate the conclusion of the metropolis's productive daily and weekly cycle and of a visual masterwork of independent cinema.[6]

Each of the 1920s city symphonies can be seen as representing not only a particular modern metropolis but also at least one filmmaker's vision of the

Figure 30. Berlin intersection in Walther Ruttmann's *Berlin, die Sinfonie einer Grosstadt* (Berlin: Symphony of a Big City, 1927). Courtesy Museum of Modern Art.

nation this metropolis itself epitomizes; and the distinctions among these films reconfirm or polemicize national distinctions between the peoples they document.[7] If *Berlin: Symphony of a Big City* reflects Germany's postwar hunger for social order, *The Man with a Movie Camera* reflects the new communist Russia's excitement about the Revolution and the advent of modern industrialization; and *Nothing but the Hours* epitomizes the poverty, the cynical realism, and the aesthetic freedom for which France in the twenties has become famous.

If the 1920s and 1930s produced no American city symphony as accomplished as those by Cavalcanti, Ruttmann, and Vertov, the period did see the formation of a history of attempts to represent New York. William Uricchio discusses an early triad of New York City films—Jay Leyda's *A Bronx Morning* (1931), Irving Browning's *City of Contrasts* (1931), and Herman G. Weinberg's *Autumn Fire* (1933)—all of which are indebted to the European city symphonies.[8] Uricchio sees these films, correctly, as less interesting in their own right than as experiments: "Reworking continental developments through the American vernacular, these films continued the process of invigorating documentary with a new language of rhythm and evocation, while infusing avant-garde practice with a dose of reality and a capacity for social criticism."[9] More impressive than the early 1930s New York City films—though not a city symphony (it does not present a coherent vision of a specific city or a sense of city life during a composite day)—is the Ralph Steiner–Willard Van Dyke collaboration, *The City*, produced by the American Institute of Planners for the 1939 New York World's Fair (see fig. 31). Van Dyke and Steiner directed and photographed different sections of the film. Van Dyke was in charge of the opening and closing sections (an introductory paean to New England village life and a long closing essay outlining the ideal modern city envisioned by the American Institute of Planners); Steiner, of the three central sections: the first one depicting the effects of the Pittsburgh steel industry on the everyday lives of steelworkers; the second, the oppressive nature of big city life, focusing on Manhattan; and the third, traffic jams. The high-quality cinematography throughout, Aaron Copland's fine score (his first for a film: "*The City* started me as a film composer"), and Steiner's wit, especially in the Manhattan and traffic jam sequences, made *The City* a popular and critical success: like the more recent *Koyaanisqatsi* (1984), *The City* attracted a sizable audience to a

Figure 31. Industrial landscape from Ralph Steiner and Willard Van Dyke's *The City* (1939). Courtesy Museum of Modern Art.

long film (*The City* runs forty-three minutes) that does not rely on plot and character.[10]

Since World War II, filmmakers working in New York have produced an impressive series of city symphonies. While many of these are reminiscent of the European masterworks, they often provide progressive, democratic revisions of the form as it evolved in Europe—and are premonitions of the greatest American city symphony to date: Spike Lee's *Do the Right Thing* (1989), a film that has not been generally recognized as a city symphony at all.

Rudy Burckhardt

It is unlikely that any American filmmaker spent more time documenting New York City than Swiss-born Rudy Burckhardt, who arrived in New York in 1935 and lived there until his death in 1999. As soon as he arrived, Burckhardt began extensive photodocumentation of the city and by 1937 was showing his first New York City film imagery.[11] In a trilogy of short, black-and-white films—*Up and Down the Waterfront* (1946), *The Climate of New York* (1948), and *Under the Brooklyn Bridge* (1953)—the approach Burckhardt was to use in so many of his films about New York (and other locales) is already evident. Burckhardt did not see his documentation of New York City as a polemic for national identity; indeed, his fascination with New York was originally, and remained, that of a visitor taken with how the city looks and feels. Further, Burckhardt's films are less involved in attempting to capture the quintessential realities of the modern city than in observing specific aspects of New York that Burckhardt is repeatedly drawn to: particular architectural achievements—the Flatiron Building, the Empire State Building, the Brooklyn Bridge—and areas where a wide variety of people congregate—Central Park and Fourteenth Street, most frequently. These sites are presented as synecdochic representations of New York's immensity and social complexity.

If Burckhardt's New York films are less ambitious, and less pretentious, than the European city films of the 1920s, they nevertheless owe their overall structure to the city symphony form established by the Europeans. *Up and Down the Waterfront* begins with an early-morning pan from the Manhattan end of the Brooklyn Bridge down to the busy market along the East River. Accompanied by piano music by Willie "the Lion" Smith, Burckhardt's images document trucks arriving with produce for the downtown markets; men unloading boxes and barrels; tugboats on the river; men hanging out, resting (presumably after the morning's work); kids playing; men outside and inside local bars after work, then leaving to go home; and finally a man hosing down the street at the end of the day, followed by a pan of the bridge and Lower Manhattan in the evening.

The Climate of New York is more elaborate than *Up and Down the Waterfront*: it divides into five distinct sections, each separated from the next by a moment of darkness, and each focusing on a particular aspect of the city. (See fig. 32.) Except for the opening and closing sequences, each is preceded by a title taken from a poem by Edwin Denby. The opening section (2 minutes, 36 seconds long) surveys the Lower Manhattan skyline and various intersections (in general, Burckhardt intersperses "catalogs" of particular dimensions of the city—building fronts, water towers on roofs, architectural details—with more extended panoramic shots), accompanied by piano music

Figure 32. Times Square in Rudy Burckhardt's *The Climate of New York* (1948). Courtesy Rudy Burckhardt.

by William Flanagan, as are all sections of the film but one. The second section ("In Public, in Private," 5 minutes, 12 seconds) records on-the-street activities on a busy day: people come out of subways onto the street, walk, talk, interact, make phone calls . . . The emphasis is on the ethnic and personal variety of people engaged in similar activities. "Sunday in Astoria and Other Open Places" (3 minutes, 58 seconds) is a carefully choreographed sequence of open lots, comparatively empty streets, and the quiet Sunday activities of a Queens neighborhood—the Manhattan skyline is often visible in the distance. In "Evening" (part 1: 1 minute, 22 seconds), Burckhardt films the "canyons" of Manhattan streets, looking west in the dimming evening light (the imagery becomes increasingly abstract and graphically two-dimensional). This is followed by the film's first color sequence (part 2 of "Evening": 3 minutes, 5 seconds), of the lights of theater marquees and tavern signs in the Times Square area. "For a Dime Extending Peculiar Space" (3 minutes, 23 seconds; this sequence incorporates the sound of subways) docu-

Figure 33. The Brooklyn Bridge in Rudy Burckhardt's *Under the Brooklyn Bridge* (1953). Courtesy Rudy Burckhardt.

ments people going into subways and riding them. *The Climate of New York* ends with a fifty-one-second conclusion: three shots of the Brooklyn Bridge and the Lower Manhattan skyline.

Under the Brooklyn Bridge is structurally reminiscent of *Up and Down the Waterfront,* although it documents activities on the opposite end of the bridge, beginning with a carefully designed sequence (reminiscent of the editing in Ruttmann's *Berlin*) of doorways and windows in and around the Brooklyn approach to the bridge and ending with panoramic shots of the bridge itself (see fig. 33). A second sequence, which begins with a BUILDING COMING DOWN sign, documents the demolition of a building near the bridge, ending with several shots of falling walls (reminiscent of the Lumières Brothers' *The Falling Wall* [Démolition d'un mur, 1896]). The demolition sequence is followed by a sequence of the workers on lunch break, eating on the street and in a restaurant near the bridge. A fourth sequence focuses on a group of young boys swimming in the East River; this is followed by a sequence of men and women leaving work and walking home. *Under the Brooklyn Bridge* concludes with several shots of empty streets in early evening and with images of the bridge with the Lower Manhattan skyline in the background, filmed at dusk.[12]

Compared with the European city symphonies, the Burckhardt films seem, at least at first, to have no polemical agenda. They seem strictly observational. And Burckhardt's editing decisions seem almost entirely involved with organizing his imagery so that it can be enjoyed simply for itself. Of course, even the most apolitical film can accrue meaning as the years pass, by offering a context for our contemporary sense of ourselves. As the filmmaker Peter Hutton has noted in relation to the photographer Eugène Atget: "Atget recorded the details of the architecture, the atmosphere, the ambience of the streets of Paris in his time with loving care. At first, those images didn't seem to have any great value—they were familiar—but as time has gone on, they've become miniature museums."[13] Burckhardt's films are able to function this way, in some measure because his imagery is *not* chosen or edited with a polemical intent. The sequence of the young boys swimming in the East River in *Under the Brooklyn Bridge*, for example, is not only a pleasant evocation of an aspect of city childhood, it has come to reveal what I suspect is a change in the way American boys relate to the movie camera. Most of the boys in the swimming sequence are nude, and they betray no particular consciousness of their naked bodies before the camera. It is difficult to imagine a group of contemporary boys so at ease with themselves or with being filmed under these circumstances. In the intervening half century, Americans—even American young people (perhaps in the era of *America's Funniest Home Videos, especially* young people)—have become well aware of the power and potential personal danger of the motion picture camera and are automatically suspicious of the motivations of those using it.

On another level, despite their lack of any overt polemical edge, Burckhardt's films do provide an implicit politics. In the early trilogy of New York City symphonies and in his many depictions of New York in more recent years—most impressively, perhaps, in *Doldrums* (1972) and *Zipper* (1987)—Burckhardt's love of New York seems a function of its size and of the diversity of people this size accommodates.[14] As a Swiss émigré who had seen the devastation brought on by the ideology of nationalism and by the German, Italian, and Japanese obsessions with ethnic purity and superiority, Burckhardt's sensibility was a particularly democratic form of live and let live. While his films present many images of the city in long shot and panorama, images that sing the immensity of New York and the "accomplishment" of its architecture, equally characteristic is Burckhardt's documentation of people on the street, generally filmed from within the crowd, often eye to eye.

Burckhardt's filming stance toward those he records is one of equality, and if a contemporary documentary sensibility might complain about his intrusiveness and exploitation—some of those he films seem less than thrilled to be on camera—Burckhardt joins his subjects, filming them in situations in which he must feel, if not in danger, perfectly capable of being confronted if he goes too far: in working-class bars, for example, and at neighborhood events where his ethnicity must stand out. Burckhardt's films reveal him as a person who feels more at home in a variety of New York neighborhoods than most native-born Americans do. As a filmmaker, Burckhardt attempts to function as a Citizen of the World, both in his ongoing activity of filming New York City—not as the quintessential focus of a particular national identity but as a nexus of internationality and multiethnicity—and in his combination of distinct locales, filmed during different eras, in the lovely anthology *Around the World in Thirty Years* (1983), which presents material shot in Manhattan in 1966; in Port-au-Prince, Haiti, in 1976; in Naples, Italy, in 1951; in Peru, in 1975; in Tokyo, in 1982; and in rural Maine, in 1981. Each of the seven sections of the film is distinct from the others, but the same sensibility, the same democratic ease with the day-to-day lives of individuals of various classes, ethnicities, and geographies, is evident throughout.

Weegee's New York; N.Y., N.Y.; Go! Go! Go!; and *Organism*

While Rudy Burckhardt may have been the most regular producer of New York City films during the decades following World War II, other filmmakers also found New York City a compelling subject. Their films, like Burckhardt's, are much involved with the idea of individuality but often in a quite different—and sometimes paradoxical—sense. Burckhardt's New York City films focus on the distinctiveness of the myriad diverse individuals who live together in the city. While he sees himself as one of these people, literally on the same level as the New Yorkers who pass by his camera, his own personality is generally effaced: at most, he is a generic on-the-street cameraman. During the 1950s and 1960s, many filmmakers were more interested in *self-*

expression than in documenting the individualities of others.[15] Indeed, this growing interest in self-expression became the heart of what Jonas Mekas named the "New American Cinema," a movement that became synonymous with the development of new, more self-consciously expressive visual styles. Ironically, while this increasing commitment to self-expression resulted in a set of interesting New York City symphonies and new cinematic experiences of city life, the filmmakers' self-involvement tends to create gaps that limit these visions in one of two ways: either the filmmakers are not able to integrate their personal experience of the city with the experiences of its myriad citizens, or their fascination with technique tends to subtly conflict with ideas they mean to communicate.

Like Rudy Burckhardt, Weegee (Arthur Fellig) was a still photographer, and he was able to bring to much of the imagery included in *Weegee's New York* (1952?) the clear-eyed observation and the fascination with individual peculiarity that made his New York street photography famous. However, while Burckhardt's trilogy of New York City symphonies reveals not only his sensitivity to the individual image, but his concern about the ways in which these motion photographs might be effectively organized into a larger structure, Weegee does not seem to have concerned himself with the issue of film editing—at least insofar as *Weegee's New York* is concerned. The opening credits of *Weegee's New York* provide clues to the unusual origin of the film: "Cinema 16 Presents Weegee's New York," the titles indicate, followed by "A Travelogue with a HEART"/"Photographed by WEEGEE."

In the years before Mekas called the New American Cinema Group together, his "Sunday church," his "university," was the film society Cinema 16, which was founded by Amos and Marcia Vogel in 1947 and until 1963 presented a very wide range of independent films—including, on two occasions (June 1952, October 1955) *Weegee's New York*.[16] As director of Cinema 16, Amos Vogel saw his mission as broadening American film awareness in every way possible. While monthly screenings were the mainstay of Cinema 16 throughout its existence, Vogel also became the first American distributor to specialize in avant-garde films; and in a few instances, Vogel worked with filmmakers to be sure particular films were completed and shown to public audiences. The most popular and influential of these films was *Weegee's New York*.

Weegee's photography was well known to the Cinema 16 membership, and Weegee himself was a member; so when Vogel discovered that Weegee had been recording film imagery, he was enthusiastic about presenting Weegee's motion pictures at Cinema 16.[17] As Vogel remembers, Weegee had no sense of how to edit the considerable body of motion picture imagery he had produced, and no interest in learning. Not to be denied the pleasure of presenting Weegee-as-filmmaker, Vogel edited the footage himself, supplied the opening credits as well as the titles of the two subsections of the finished film, "New York Fantasy" and "Coney Island," and saw to the production of the music track that accompanies the film. The result is one of the most underrecognized independent films of the 1950s (underrecognized *now*, I mean; the film was popular not only at Cinema 16 but also within the network of film societies Cinema 16 inspired) and a work that simultaneously expresses Weegee's vision of New York City and Vogel's vision of himself as a cultural missionary for independent cinema.

The "New York Fantasy" section of *Weegee's New York* (7 minutes, 28 seconds) begins at dawn—"at five in the morning," an intertitle tells us—with a forty-second color passage of the New York City skyline seen from across the Hudson River, filmed from a mounted camera at successive moments during the early-morning hours. This is followed by a stunning time-lapse shot of the Empire State Building at dawn. These introductory images are followed by a sequence of harbor scenes filmed with a lens that blurs the imagery and adds a red-yellow-blue rainbow to the sometimes time-lapsed, sometimes normal-motion shots (this and the next sequence are accompanied by symphonic music). The intertitle, "The Empire State Building," is followed by a two-minute, forty-second sequence of street scenes (some with the Empire State Building), filmed in a highly expressionistic manner, focusing on reflections and subtle qualities of light and texture, and then by a two-minute, thirty-second evocation of Times Square at night, filmed in gorgeous color and, at the end of the sequence, with time-lapse imagery of streets and intersections. This section of the film concludes with an image of a man being shot out of a cannon and with a closing "The End."

The longer (13 minutes, 23 seconds) "Coney Island" section begins after a six-second pause, with the intertitle "A million people on the beach of a Sunday afternoon, is normal." The following sequences are Weegee at his witty and sometimes photographically invasive best. Color imagery of sun-bathers, lovers, walkers, swimmers negotiating the crowded beach is accom-panied by a series of popular songs that infuse the visual imagery with a vari-ety of generally upbeat moods (Kenneth Anger's 1963 film, *Scorpio Rising*, is often credited as the first film to use a series of previously recorded popular recordings as a sound track; *Weegee's New York* uses music in virtually the same way).[18] Like Burckhardt's films, the "Coney Island" section of *Weegee's New York* (and several of his more famous photographs; see fig. 34), celebrates the wild diversity of individuals and ethnic heritages that have come together on the beach to enjoy themselves. And even more fully than the skinny-dip-ping sequence in *Under the Brooklyn Bridge,* Weegee's Coney Island reveals a population seemingly at ease with its bodies, even under the persistent gaze of the movie camera. It is as if Americans of the 1950s understood what most of

Figure 34. *Coney Island, 22ⁿᵈ of July 1940, 4 o'clock in the after-noon* (1940), photograph by Weegee (Arthur Fellig). Courtesy A L L Photographs/Liason Agency.

us have forgotten—that a holiday should not only be freedom from work, but from the necessity of maintaining socially constructed models of correct physical appearance. As economically and morally uptight as we imagine the generation of the 1950s to have been, Weegee reveals and celebrates a society that comes to life precisely when it is not being "productive"—a people who seem to have no interest at all in what others think of them.

"Coney Island," and *Weegee's New York,* end in the evening, as the beach empties and the setting sun creates gorgeous reflections on the lens and in the water—natural "fireworks" that provide an appropriate conclusion for Weegee's celebration of New York, first, as a complex, phantasmagoric architectural space, and then, as an immense, wildly diverse community in unselfconscious celebration of itself. Vogel's structuring of *Weegee's New York* is a celebration of a different sort: by combining Weegee's straightforward, observational documentation of the crowd on the Coney Island beach with the more self-expressive, worked imagery of a fantasy Manhattan, Vogel epitomized—and provided a memorable cine-monument for—his commitment as Cinema 16's director to two general modes of independent cinema: the documentary exploration of the physical world and the avant-garde expression of inner realties.

Probably the most widely seen New York City symphony of the postwar era was Francis Thompson's *N.Y., N.Y.* (1957) (*N.Y., N.Y.* was also shown at Cinema 16, on January 21, 1958, as part of the annual Creative Film Awards hosted by the film society). In *N.Y., N.Y.,* Thompson ignores individual New Yorkers entirely and, instead, provides visual interest by means of an ingenious and witty exploration of lenses and reflective surfaces, some of which may have been indebted to the first section of *Weegee's New York.* Beginning with early-morning evocations of buildings and bridges, Thompson reveals, as the film's subtitle indicates, "A Day in New York" ("New York" meaning Manhattan), beginning with an alarm clock waking a city dweller by shattering itself into a cubist image reminiscent of the work of Juan Gris. The film moves chronologically through the day and evening, creating that set of emphases typical of city symphonies—waking and commuting, the busy morning, lunch and a quiet moment afterward, the busy afternoon, the trip home from work, and nightlife—using a variety of often-ingenious visual techniques and accompanied by Gene Farrell's capable score, a pastiche of musics that, like the sound track of *Weegee's New*

York, effectively suggests the city's varied moods.[19] At times Thompson's visual effects are quite beautiful; at other times (as when he uses a highly reflective surface to bend imagery into surreal shapes reminiscent of the imagery in funhouse mirrors), witty and amusing (see figs. 35a–b).[20]

As enjoyable as it is to watch, however, *N.Y., N.Y.* is as detached from particular lives as Ruttmann's *Berlin.* Indeed, Thompson uses several lenses that shatter the action he records into a graphic space suggestive of a beehive. Basically, *N.Y., N.Y.* is less an attempt to analyze or critique the modern city than to express Thompson's personal excitement about living in New York and about being an independent filmmaker. Even the word "Doom" in a headline seen within one of Thompson's cubist compositions comes across more as humor than as warning. That *N.Y., N.Y.* remains perhaps the most broadly accessible city symphony is a tribute to Thompson's success in providing a memorable sense of an emotion many of us have felt during our earliest trips to New York. Thompson expresses a sense of the city as a sublime, romantic environment, full of color, upbeat energy, and architectural beauty.[21]

N.Y., N.Y. seems infused with a sense of New York's then-rising importance in art history: the film is full of high-spirited evocations of such landmarks as the Brooklyn Bridge and of apparent allusions to American artists, such as Charles Sheeler and Lionel Feininger, who have celebrated the modern American city. Most of all, Thompson's obvious pleasure in the effects he is able to produce with techniques far more overtly "experimental" than those in the commercial cinema of the time, and his implicit confidence in the audience's ability to enjoy these techniques, not only reflects his own enjoyment at being part of an exciting art scene, it evokes our parents' excitement in taking us to New York to show us something far beyond our usual childhood environment. The New York City of *N.Y., N.Y.* renders viewers visual children. It may well be that the city also needs to be analyzed for its sociopolitical role in modern society, but from Thompson's point of view, we might just as well admit—and enjoy—the fact that, whatever its limitations and extravagances, New York is *also,* for many of us, a wonderful place to visit and to live.

One of the pivotal developments in the evolution of more personally self-expressive filmmaking during the 1960s was the increasing commitment on the part of filmmakers to "gestural camera work," that is, to hand-held camera work that consciously incorporates the filmmaker's personal gestures into the

Figures 35a–b. New York bridges; New York skyscrapers; both from Francis Thompson's *N.Y., N.Y.* (1957). Courtesy Museum of Modern Art.

imagery recorded (Stan Brakhage and Jonas Mekas are the best-known figures in this development). The primary influences here were probably abstract expressionist painting, with its unabashedly gestural brushwork, and related developments in jazz and pop music; and Marie Menken's combination of a hand-held camera and a free-form approach to making film (see the discussion of Menken in chap. 3). Menken's *Go! Go! Go!* (final version, 1964) is a particularly endearing city symphony (in the eleven and a half minute, silent, color film, the title is simply *"Go!"* though Menken interrupts our focus on this title, which is handwritten on reflective glass, by waving her arm—presumably an attempt to suggest the repetition of the word).

Go! Go! Go! is the result of Menken's excursions in and around New York City from 1962 to 1964, and whether or not Menken conceived it as a city symphony, the form provided a loose structure within which she could present a range of observations. Menken begins with a walk across the Brooklyn Bridge and around Lower Manhattan; the following sequences record New York harbor; the pedestrian and vehicular traffic at various intersections in and around office buildings; a body-building contest; a May Day celebration by women in fancy dresses; people arriving for a wedding; Willard Maas (Menken's husband) working at a typewriter on the porch of their apartment in Brooklyn Heights, the Lower Manhattan skyline visible behind him; a day at Coney Island (including beach scenes reminiscent of those in *Weegee's New York*); and more Manhattan street and New York harbor scenes. *Go! Go! Go!* concludes—in a typical city symphony manner—with shots of late afternoon across New York harbor and with sunset.

The most obvious implication of Menken's title is spelled out in her own description of the film: "the busy man's engrossment in his busyness make [sic] up the major part of the film."[22] Another implication of the title relates to Menken's use of time-lapsing for nearly the entire film. This technique, of course, has the effect of speeding up whatever is filmed; with it, Menken creates a variety of kinetic effects. What may have been several hours of walking around downtown Manhattan is reduced to a few seconds, causing single-frame images of different people and places to pile up into "retinal collages";[23] her stunning time-lapse imagery of New York harbor causes the tugboats, ferries, and barges to scoot across the water like water bugs (this particular effect may have been suggested by the time-lapsed ferries in *Weegee's New York*, which Menken probably saw at Cinema 16); and her time-lapsing of a college graduation ceremony sometimes creates effects reminiscent of *N.Y., N.Y.,* without the use of special lenses.

Menken's distinctive hand-held camera and time-lapsing (along with her choice of composition) have the further effect of seeming to miniaturize big events and normally awesome aspects of city life. Her record of the body-building competition transforms the competitors' attempts to impress their audience into high-speed humor; in one instance Menken's camera points vertically down, reducing a construction site to an anthill; and her time-lapsing of an ocean liner making its way across the harbor suggests "The Little Engine That Could": Menken frames the ship so that it looks particularly small, next to the waves in the foreground, and so that in one instance it seems to be struggling to sail uphill (Menken interrupts the movement of the liner, repositioning it within her frame, so that she seems to control it).

By the time Menken made *Go! Go! Go!* the awesome complexity of the modern city, documented over and over, had come to seem so self-evident that Menken's playful, personal approach has the effect of reinventing New York, and the city symphony form, by critiquing the very seriousness of the tradition she inherited. Ironically, while Menken may have felt she was conveying a serious message through *Go! Go! Go!* the impact of her film has more to do with her stylistic playfulness and her implicit defiance of conventional seriousness about the city and modern man. For Menken, as for Thompson, the city is a wonderful location for personal cinematic exploration.

If time-lapse has come to seem the cliché of the city film, the recent popular fascination with time-lapse imagery (in recent years it has been used frequently in television commercials and music videos) came at the end of a period that saw a good bit of exploration of the device by independent filmmakers. *Go! Go! Go!* seems to have inspired Jonas Mekas's similar use of time-lapse in his lovely *Cassis* (1966), a portrait of a French port on the Mediterranean from just before dawn until just after sunset, as well as in his personal epic, *Walden* (1968).[24] And by the mid-1970s, a good many filmmakers were recognizing the possibilities of the device. For Hilary Harris, time-lapse seemed a particularly useful means for revealing the systematic structures of modern urban life; and in *Organism* (1975) he combined time-lapse photography of New York City with microphotography of the internal systems of the human body to provide a visual essay on the idea that the organization of the metropolis is a macrocosmic version of the internal systems that keep us alive.

To establish his general point of view, Harris opens *Organism* with two microphotographic images of the bloodstream and a live-action shot of people exiting a subway station. The opening titles are then presented over a live-action street scene that subsequently accelerates into the first of the film's time-lapse passages. Periodically during *Organism,* Harris reconfirms the analogy between the movements of people and vehicles in and around the city and the bloodstream, by intercutting between the two—sometimes emphasizing the connection by using out-of-focus time-lapse imagery of city traffic at night that causes headlights to look like blood corpuscles. Harris's visual argument is contextualized and confirmed through his use of a sound track that interweaves various electronic sounds and musics and two voices—one male, one female—presumably of biologists who describe various bodily processes. Harris organized the sound track so that the topics discussed by the biologists are particularly relevant to the time-lapse imagery their comments accompany: when the woman's voice explains how "food taken into the body is transformed into energy for activity," we are seeing time-lapse material of trucks delivering food to the city.

Like Menken, Harris attempts in at least one sequence to provide a more specific, moralistic message about urban life, by juxtaposing the man's statement that "not all diseases are caused by external agents" with imagery of traffic jams—suggesting the health dangers of too great a concentration of pollution-creating vehicles in the city. But as in *Go! Go! Go!*—and as in a number of other films of city life that use extensive time-lapse shooting[25]—this message is overwhelmed by the frequently magical effects of time-lapsing itself. While we may understand that, from a health standpoint, traffic jams are a problem, time-lapsing generally charms the eye into an appreciation for the degree to which the systematic processes of the city *do* function, and Harris's success in developing the analogy between city and human body suggests that the urban systems are as natural and as inevitable as the bodily systems documented in the microphotography.

While time-lapsing has become a common means for imaging city life, the very nature of the device requires a transformation of the city symphony form. The fundamental structure of the daily cycle (dawn to dusk, or dawn to night) is co-opted, since time-lapsing can reduce a daily cycle to a few seconds. Of course, the daily cycle structure of the city symphony has always been a fiction, a convenient way of organizing extensive documentation of the city over months or years. Time-lapsing exposes this fiction—in *Organism,* transforming the cycles of dawn to dusk to dawn into visual cells within a larger cinematic organism. Harris's film is regularly punctuated by extended passages of time-lapse that record metropolitan vistas as seen from the Empire State Building and the World Trade Center over considerable portions of day and/or night. Indeed, at times, Harris ingeniously explores within time-lapsed vistas. For example, one thirty-seven-second time-lapse passage begins at night with the lights of planes landing at LaGuardia Airport, then zooms back so that the plane lights are merely one part of an extended vista of Manhattan, the East River, and Long Island; then, after dawn has transformed the scene, Harris zooms in on a factory on the far side of the river. Time-lapsing also transforms the city symphony by dramatically increasing the amount of activity that can be included in even a brief film. Though *Organism* is only twenty minutes long, like *Go! Go! Go!* it includes enough vistas of enough activities to seem much longer.

As late as 1975, Harris apparently felt that time-lapsing imagery was unusual and high-tech enough to justify his frequent use of science-fictionish electronic sounds as an accompaniment. But by the mid-1970s, Harris was only one of many filmmakers interested in exploring time-lapse imagery, especially of city life. For example, the Super-8mm filmmaker John Porter had begun to record activities in and around Toronto in dozens of films, which, taken together, are a particularly extensive and inventive chronicle of city life. And by the 1980s, the device was having a considerable impact on the popular imagination: the extensive use of time-lapse material, especially of New York and Los Angeles, had much to do with *Koyaanisqatsi's* becoming one of the most frequently programmed films on American college campuses, and one of the most widely popular non-narrative films in the history of American film (this 35mm feature was directed by Godfrey Reggio and photographed by Ron Fricke, with contributions from Harris).[26]

New York has continued to inspire independent filmmakers. Notable among recent New York City films are Peter Hutton's New York portraits—*New York Portrait, Part I* (1976), *New York Portrait, Part II* (1980), *New York Portrait, Part III* (1990)—which I discuss in chapter 8: meditatively paced, silent, often Lumière-esque evocations of New York City life; Ken Jacobs's *New York Ghetto Fishmarket 1903* (1992) and other "Nervous System" performances that explore turn-of-the-century film imagery of New York City, simultaneously reviving and transforming the original 35mm imagery;[27] and Stephen Low's IMAX 3-D film, *Across the Sea of Time* (1995).

Low's film develops a flimsy, cold war plot about a Russian boy who jumps ship in New York harbor to search for the brownstone where his grandfather (who had come to America in the late nineteenth century, hoping his family would follow) had lived. To stay alive, the boy sells stereopticon images of New York City, taken by his grandfather, which he has inherited, along with his grandfather's letters. The particular tour of New York provided by the boy's wanderings is reminiscent of Browning's *City of Contrasts*. While the plot is predictable, *Across the Sea of Time* is fascinating because of Low's use of two forms of 3-D: the film intercuts between imagery of Manhattan a century ago in stereopticon 3-D and in 1995 in IMAX 3-D. Both forms of 3-D are compelling and contextualize each other: each seems fitting for the spectacular city of its time.

Do the Right Thing as City Symphony

The power of Hollywood has so informed American thinking about cinema that the long, distinguished history of independent filmmaking has remained, at best, marginal to the awareness even of many of those who consider themselves sophisticated filmgoers; moreover, the more distant from mainstream moviemaking a film or type of film is, the more thoroughly marginalized it tends to be. The converse of this pattern is that even those commercial films that do reveal considerable deviations from the Hollywood mainstream are seen almost exclusively in the context of conventional entertainment, and any connections to the more fully marginalized arenas of cinema are routinely overlooked. Spike Lee's *Do the Right Thing* is a case in point. Lee's feature is recognized as a provocative narrative entertainment with an unusual plot and a set of colorful characters, but the city-symphonic dimensions of the film have been ignored; and yet, *Do the Right Thing* can be read as a city symphony, one that incorporates crucial elements of the form as it was developed in Europe by Ruttmann, Vertov, and Cavalcanti; expands the democratic vision implicit in Burckhardt's films; and incorporates the personal expressiveness of the New York City symphonies just discussed.

The overall structure of *Do the Right Thing* is reminiscent of the traditional city symphony. Like *Berlin: Symphony of a Big City,* which begins with a prelude to the symphony of Berlin life—a dynamic visual orchestration of a train traveling the rails from the country into the city (in *The Man with a Movie Camera,* Vertov literalizes the symphony metaphor by using a movie theater orchestra that assembles near the beginning of the film and prepares to play an accompaniment to the "visual music" of its director-composer)—*Do the Right Thing* begins with a credit sequence accompanied and informed by Public Enemy's "Fight the Power." Lee's prelude simultaneously evokes the conventional introductory movement *and* invests it with a new—if (for many viewers) aggressive and abrasive—energy that suggests both the achievements and the anger of African America, as represented by Public Enemy and the dance movements of Rosie Perez. Following the prelude, the action of *Do the Right Thing* , like the action in Ruttmann's *Berlin* and other more traditional city symphonies, begins early in the morning and moves chronologically through the day and evening, revealing the typical activities and moods pertinent to the various times of day (in the case of Lee's film, a Saturday). While Ruttmann's *Berlin* ends with literal fireworks (which are echoed in various ways by other city symphonies—often in the "fireworks" of the sunset or of the lights of the city in evening), *Do the Right Thing* ends with social "fireworks" and the conflagration of Sal's Famous—a form of social rebellion Lee sees as equally inevitable and cyclical, given how modern American society functions, as the rhythms of the industrial workday in any modern metropolis (this is confirmed by Lee's closing dedication of the film to several families of young men murdered in racist outbursts).

What distinguishes *Do the Right Thing* most from *Berlin: Symphony of a Big City,* of course, is Lee's development of a sizable set of colorful characters whose activities, interaction, and commentary create an entirely different cinematic world from the one Ruttmann creates. But this deviation from Ruttmann's sense of a city symphony does align Lee's film with Cavalcanti's *Nothing but the Hours,* which, at least compared to *Berlin,* reflects a simultaneous commitment to city-symphonic structure and narrative and character. (See figs. 36, 37.) In *Nothing but the Hours* the typical day in Paris includes the activities not only of masses of people going to work, laboring for their livelihood,

Figure 36. Woman on Paris street in Alberto Cavalcanti's *Rien que les heures* (Nothing but the Hours, 1926). Courtesy Museum of Modern Art.

and returning home, but also of individuals: we get to know a young woman who delivers newspapers, a young man who seems to be unemployed, and his "girlfriend"(later, we realize she's a prostitute and he's her pimp). At the conclusion of *Nothing but the Hours,* they mug the papergirl and leave her for dead. There is also a metaphoric narrative, embodied in an old woman who staggers through the streets (is she Paris? Liberty?). These literal/symbolic narrative developments are woven through *Nothing but the Hours* and provide forms of information about city life that the more detached *Berlin: Symphony of a Big City* ignores.

Of course, *Do the Right Thing* goes much further than *Nothing but the Hours:* it is full of characters, many of whom are developed as distinct individuals in relatively limited amounts of screen time and appear as motifs throughout Lee's feature.[28] Indeed, insofar as the characters are concerned, *Do the Right Thing* is virtually an inversion of *Berlin: Symphony of a Big City.* In Ruttmann's film, individuality is subsumed within the machine of the city; in Lee's film, individuality is virtually irrepressible: people find ways of distinguishing

Figure 37. Vito (Richard Edson) and Mookie (Spike Lee) discuss race relations in *Do the Right Thing* (1989). Courtesy Museum of Modern Art.

themselves, often by directly confronting those around them. The life of Lee's city is not accomplished by a suppression of individual personality; in *Do the Right Thing* the life of the city *is* the friendly or hostile interactions of particular citizens.

That Lee's day in the life of the modern city takes place entirely on a single block, and a single block in the heart of the Bedford-Stuyvesant section of Brooklyn, is simultaneously a democratic polemic—since all New Yorkers are citizens, equally, any block in any section of the city can be used to represent the whole—*and* a (privately financed) form of affirmative action.[29] When they are depicted at all, the myriad citizens who live in predominantly African-American ghettos have usually been presented as types, and especially types of people whose lives are not to be celebrated in the commercial (or independent) cinema. Lee demonstrates the variety of these media-marginalized citizens and suggests—as does Rudy Burckhardt—that in this very variety *is* the energy of democracy: even the uprising at the end of the day that destroys Sal's Famous in retaliation for the murder of Radio Raheem (Bill Nunn) evokes the early moments of the American Revolution, when British property was attacked in the name of preserving individual liberty. While Cavalcanti suggests that crime is not only an inevitable dimension of city life, but one of the things that renders city life exciting and romantic, Lee suggests that while violence is inevitable in the racist version of capitalist democracy, it is anything but romantic. Even if the destruction of Sal's Famous provides momentary self-respect for some citizens, it impoverishes the Bed-Stuy block, both literally and democratically: Sal's pizza and his Italian presence—and all the energy they catalyze on a typical day—are gone. And yet, while the fireworks that end the "typical day" in *Do the Right Thing* are destructive, it is clear from the scenes of denouement, and especially from the scene of Da Mayor (Ossie Davis) waking up in the apartment of Mother Sister (Ruby Dee), that what has happened is merely one more momentary setback for the neighborhood in a long history of setbacks. Despite the destruction, Lee is quite clear in *Do the Right Thing* that this one block of Bed-Stuy remains not only an exciting, colorful place to live but a quintessentially American place as well.

A good many of those (especially those whites, I would guess) who have seen *Do the Right Thing* have chosen to see it as a fundamentally dangerous film in which Spike Lee urges African Americans to retaliate against European Americans: after all, the argument goes, Lee declares his loyalty to racist division and his approval of violence by having Mookie, the character *he* plays, begin the violent response to the police murder of Radio Raheem by throwing a garbage can through Sal's window. The problem with this reading is that it ignores a fundamental dimension of *Do the Right Thing:* Lee's self-reflexivity as director—a dimension of the film that echoes Vertov's *The Man with a Movie Camera.*

In Vertov's film we are not simply exploring Moscow, we are exploring the process of cinematically documenting the city (see fig. 38).[30] The man we see setting up his camera and shooting is not Vertov but his brother, Mikhail Kaufman—though Kaufman does function as an alter ego for the director, who simultaneously demystifies the process of making motion pictures and creates a new form of cine-magic by intercutting between Kaufman shooting the imagery and the imagery we saw him shooting (the editing was done by Elizaveta Svilova, Vertov's wife, who also appears as the editor *in* the film). Of course, *The Man with a Movie Camera* is full of remarkable tricks. Some draw particular attention to the camera itself, which can film from positions not

Figure 38. Moscow in Dziga Vertov's *The Man with a Movie Camera* (1929). Courtesy Museum of Modern Art.

possible for the human body; others reveal the possibilities of superimposition during the editing process. Vertov's city symphony sings the magic and excitement of mechanical technologies and their potential for allowing the individual worker and the society of which he or she is a part to move into a new era.

Do the Right Thing is self-reflexive in different but related ways. Certainly, the audience for Spike Lee's films knows who Lee is (I would guess that Lee is the most broadly recognizable American film director since Alfred Hitchcock, in large measure because of his appearances, first, in a series of Nike ads with Michael Jordan that appeared in the late 1980s and, in more recent years, on the sidelines at New York Knicks games). Indeed, even during the early stages of *Do the Right Thing,* when Lee's ideas for the film were taking shape, he was particularly conscious of his apparent impact as a recognizable personality within the fictions of his films:

Something is happening. It's not of my will, but something is happening. I'm being singled out for my acting as much as for my writing and directing. It started with *She's Gotta Have It* [1986]. I never expected such a response to Mars Blackmon.

I had a chance to forecast on my appeal as an actor at the five recruited screenings we've had to date for *School Daze* [1988]. The minute I appear on screen, the audience got excited. . . . I'm not saying I did the strongest acting in the film, but folks identified with me. I have something with people, and I think at this stage it would be a mistake not to take this into consideration as I write *Do the Right Thing.*[31]

In *Do the Right Thing,* the connection between Lee himself and Mookie is enforced in a variety of ways (see fig. 39). Mookie wears a Brooklyn Dodgers shirt with Jackie Robinson's number 42; many viewers—especially those interested in sports—know of Lee's loyalty to Brooklyn and his admiration of the Dodgers and Robinson. And anyone familiar with Lee's career knows that Mookie's sister, Jade, is played by Joie Lee, Lee's sister; that Lee's father, Bill Lee, composed music for the film; and that Mookie's affection for Da Mayor and Mother Sister is a reflection of Lee's affection for Ossie Davis and Ruby Dee. However, that Lee knows viewers will recognize that his *character* throws the garbage can through Sal's window to begin the destruction does not mean that Lee *as director* advocates destruction. Quite the contrary. To draw such a conclusion—as, apparently, many have—one must ignore the implications of the film's expressionist style.

Throughout *Do the Right Thing,* Lee uses an energetically expressionist style that owes a good bit to earlier commercial expressionists (Lee, in his *Journal:* "I want to use Chinese angles like the ones in *The Third Man* [1949, directed by Carol Reed]. They'll add an aura of uneasiness to the film")[32] and that has much in common with the personally expressionist spirit of the New American Cinema. Indeed, from its opening moments, *Do the Right Thing* is punctuated by shots that draw attention to the camera and to Lee as director. As Rosie Perez dances to "Fight the Power," the mise-en-scène within which she performs changes continually, drawing attention to Lee's fabrication of a continuous sequence from several different performances (implicitly the background provides an opening "montage" of locations around Brooklyn, seen here as stage backdrops, roughly similar to the typical American city symphony mon-

Figure 39. Spike Lee as Mookie during the shooting of *Do the Right Thing* (1989).

tage of buildings or vistas, though in this case more focused on neighborhood dwellings). The body of the film begins with such an extreme close-up of Mister Señor Love Daddy (Samuel L. Jackson) and his microphone that at first we're not sure what we're looking at. As the temperature rises through the morning, Lee demonstrates how hot it is by providing a sink-drain's-eye view of Tina with her face immersed in cold water (see fig. 40). Later, when Mookie goes into the kitchen in Tina's apartment to get some ice, we see him reach into the freezer from *inside* the freezer. When the kids open the hydrant to fight the heat of the day, and direct the stream of water, the water first flies directly at the camera, and when Radio Raheem presents his love/hate monologue to the camera, his fists and arms are distorted by their proximity to the lens. Of course, the most confrontational of such moments occurs when a series of characters hurl typical racist epithets at the camera/audience.

That Lee's expressionist flourishes make us particularly conscious of his direction of the film contextualizes his presentation of Mookie (while such

Figure 40. Sink's-eye view of Tina (Rosie Perez) cooling off in *Do the Right Thing* (1989).

self-reflexive moments appear in other Spike Lee films, *Do the Right Thing* uses them with particular frequency). Just as Mikhail Kaufman functions as an alter ego for Vertov, Mookie is an alter ego for Lee. But while Kaufman and Vertov are two representatives of the *same* process, basically ideological mirror images of each other, Lee and Mookie represent two, very different possibilities. Though his pizza delivery job is enough to keep him alive (Mookie apparently lives rent-free with Jade), this job, as Jade tells him, can take him nowhere, especially since he works halfheartedly. However, while Mookie is going nowhere, his alter ego, Spike Lee, *is* in business, as a filmmaker. Indeed, he's in business in the same neighborhood, and *his* efforts are anything but halfhearted.

The distinction between Spike Lee/Mookie and Spike Lee/director reaches a crescendo when Mookie throws the garbage can through the window. The only response Mookie can think of to the murder of Radio Raheem and to Sal's siding with the police is violence: the destruction of Sal's Famous. Lee also is responding to a series of violent incidents (including incidents of police violence) that took place during the months when *Do the Right Thing* was germinating; but his response is not to drive a business out of the neighborhood but to bring one in—a business that offers some of the kinds of opportunities Mookie doesn't have: "Sometimes on the set, while we're setting up for a shot, I look around and watch everyone working. I see all these young, talented Black artists and technicians and I feel just fine. It's a good feeling to be in a position to hire people who need jobs, people who deserve jobs. Of course, we can't hire everyone, but we're doing what we can."[33]

Perhaps the dimension of Lee's self-reflexivity in *Do the Right Thing* that most clearly distinguishes the film from the European city symphonies, including Vertov's, is its particular thematic focus on ethnicity. Like Burckhardt (and to a lesser extent Weegee), Lee locates the vitality of the modern city in the nexus of ethnicity it creates, especially on the street; and like Burckhardt's camera, Lee's meets his characters eye to eye. But Lee goes beyond Burckhardt: just as Lee himself demonstrates two different lives a particular kind of man might live, his film presents two different (and, perhaps, mutually exclusive) options for interethnic activity in New York City and in the nation New York epitomizes. One option is that African Americans, Caribbean Americans, Asian Americans, and European Americans can continue to live alongside each other as they have, as communities that often define their own individual and group worth by negating the contributions and potential of other groups: Sal maintains his Italian-American identity by including only Italian Americans on the Sal's Famous "wall of fame"; Radio Raheem and Mister Señor Love Daddy maintain their African-American identity by playing only African-American music—Radio Raheem on his giant box, Mister Señor Love Daddy on his radio show. This option can lead to violence to the spirit, to fear, and to moments of large-scale physical violence to property, people, and community.

The alternative was and is demonstrated *by the production process of the film,* which required individuals with backgrounds even more varied than those of the characters in the film to find ways to collaborate, not just for one day, but for several of the hottest weeks of a New York summer, in a neighborhood in Bed-Stuy, on a film about America's most crucial and volatile issue.[34] To put this simply: Lee *dramatizes* the periodic destruction of modern city life in a film produced by means of a process that *demonstrates* an ethnically progressive alternative.[35]

In reading *Do the Right Thing* as a city symphony, I may have seemed to ignore too fully the fact that Lee's film is a fiction feature, not a documentary or an avant-garde film, and so, any attempt to locate it in the city symphony genre remains compromised. But *Do the Right Thing* is more than a fiction film, in at least two senses. First, and most important, *Do the Right Thing* is *both* a fiction feature *and* a document that proves that the progressive production process used to create the film was successful. Lee was not content simply to provide still another delineation of the problem of racism; for him, the filmmaker's obligation was to lead the way in the direction of a solution that requires both that African Americans develop their own businesses and that European Americans overcome their alienation and fear of African-American neighborhoods—and the racism that this alienation and fear are indexes of.[36]

Second, from the beginning of the *Do the Right Thing* project, Lee made sure that the film would also have a more explicit connection with the history of documentary:

> During preproduction, Universal asked me to recommend a filmmaker to do the electronic press kit that the studio would use to promote the film. I recommended the veteran documentary filmmaker St. Clair Bourne. When I met with St. Clair to discuss the press kit, I asked him to consider directing a film about the making of *Do the Right Thing*. We were shooting in Bed-Stuy. We were taking over an entire city block for eight weeks. And we had hired the Fruit of Islam—Farrakhan's private security force—to patrol the set and to close two crack houses. Certainly, this needed to be documented. St. Clair got to work on the project immediately.[37]

The result was St. Clair Bourne's capably made, fifty-eight-minute documentation of the process of making Lee's film: *Making "Do the Right Thing"* (1989). Bourne's film extends the city-symphonic dimensions of *Do the Right Thing* by echoing dimensions of the form (Bourne interweaves several different kinds of time into *Making "Do the Right Thing,"* one of which is his review of the shooting of Lee's film as the action develops in *Do the Right Thing*: that is, from morning to evening). And he reveals dimensions of city life we could only conjecture from Lee's film: for example, while Lee dramatizes a typical day on a block in Bed-Stuy, Bourne documents the unusual event of a sustained film shoot on a block in Bed-Stuy. Bourne's film develops nonfiction "characters" who do not appear in *Do the Right Thing*—the Fruit of Islam men who assist Lee in keeping order, for example, and a wide range of people who live on this block, including a woman crack addict who works for the production and struggles with her addiction, and various men and women who reveal their support for Lee's production and their reservations about its immediate and long-term benefits. The range of personalities in Bourne's film is, simultaneously, clear evidence of the essential truth of Lee's depiction of the neighborhood and an alternative interpretation against which Lee's foci and exaggerations can be measured.

Bourne's film also confirms and extends the progressive implications of Lee's production process by recording conversations among cast and crew that relate to the issue of ethnicity. For example, during an informal conversation among several actors, Danny Aiello indicates that while he's called an "Italian American," he feels no particular connection with Italy and thinks of himself as "American Italian." Giancarlo Esposito counters by indicating that he *does* feel a connection with his Italian roots and considers himself "Italian American." In other words, Bourne's film reveals that Lee's casting models the idea that people of diverse and complex ethnic heritages can work productively with each other in empathizing across ethnic lines. In the end, Bourne's film defines *Do the Right Thing* as an event not only in Lee's career and in the history of African-American cinema (in *Making "Do the Right Thing"* Lee mentions Oscar Micheaux as an inspiration, and an appearance by Melvin Van Peebles is accompanied by excerpts from *Sweet Sweetback's Baadasssss Song* [1971]) but in the life of New York City as well: one of the final images of the film is a new street sign for this block, now Do the Right Thing Avenue; and the film's final shot, which echoes the first, is a pan up from the street to the skyline of Manhattan in the distance. Finally, as New York's particular form of multiethnicity is a notable instance of a fundamental American reality and challenge, Bourne's and Lee's efforts speak to American nationhood. As John Turturro says in *Making "Do the Right Thing,"* "This [*Do the Right Thing*] is not just a New York film; it's about any city in the country, or even a small town." Of course, multiethnicity is, increasingly, an essential reality of life in many major cities; and so, one might argue further that Lee's intense evocation of neighborhood life in Brooklyn is paradoxically a metaphor for, a premonition of, the transnational dimension of urban life around the world.

In the end, that *Do the Right Thing* stretches the city symphony form is quite fitting: the film's mixing of genres paradoxically renders it as quintessentially American (and African American) as the 1920s city symphonies now seem quintessentially *of* the nations where they were produced. America has restricted the social mobility of large groups of its citizens, including several of the groups represented in *Do the Right Thing*, but it has also regularly rewarded the defiance of social limitations (including cinematic conventions). *Do the Right Thing* remains Lee's most accomplished film, because of its director's courage and inventiveness in facing a difficult social challenge in a commercial film and in finding ways of representing this reality that simultaneously use and defy media conventions, historical categories, and production procedures for dealing with urban life.

Panorama: The San Francisco City Film

San Francisco is distinct among American cities, not only because its particular geography has always given it a distinctive look, but also because residents and visitors have been conscious of the city's appearance, proud of it, from its earliest years as a community—and have demonstrated their admiration in the visual arts, especially in the photographic arts. San Francisco was home to one of the first schools of American urban photography, if not *the* first:

> In part because of the sheer numbers of daguerreotypists, in part because its population was drawn from a pool of the most adventurous Americans, San Francisco quickly became a major innovative center for the medium and ushered in a short lived golden age of daguerreotypy [in the 1850s]. . . . Demand for contextual portraits of miners in their newly staked claims, property owners in front of their houses, and businessmen in front of their establishments forced the daguerreotypists out of their studios and into the streets of their city and the land surrounding it.[38]

Quickly the city itself became a photographer's subject and by 1852 had inspired perhaps the first American city panoramas: William Shaw's "San Francisco from Rincon Point" (ca. 1852) and a seven-plate panorama of the city by an unknown daguerreotypist (also 1852).[39] San Francisco also inspired the first American photographic book celebrating an American city: George R. Fardon's *San Francisco Album: Photographs of the Most Beautiful Views and Public Buildings of San Francisco* (1856), a tour of the city—"panoramic" in a looser sense.[40] San Francisco's importance as a location for innovative photography reached an apex in the 1870s, when Eadweard Muybridge made his remarkable panoramas from the roof of Mark Hopkins's mansion atop Nob Hill. In

1877 Muybridge completed an eleven-panel panorama, and then in 1878, the thirteen-panel panorama that remains "the finest example of the genre ever made."[41]

San Francisco's photographic importance was reconfirmed during the early history of cinematography. Again with the single exception of New York City, San Francisco may well be the most filmed American city, both because of its legendary beauty and because of its preeminence as a location for geologic drama. The Library of Congress currently distributes, online, two series of early films under the rubric "American Memory": one series of films of New York City, the other of San Francisco.[42] While the New York films are a good bit more impressive, the fact remains that San Francisco was clearly a city early movie viewers wanted to see, and the considerable number of films by the Edison Studio and American Mutoscope and Biograph of the aftermath of the 1906 earthquake make this the most thoroughly filmed American disaster of the era. If the early New York City films seem to attest to the immensity and solidity of New York, the imagery of the aftermath of the 1906 earthquake and early relief efforts attest to the resilience of San Francisco, the ability of this city to recover, which was evident in the published title of a panoramic photograph George R. Lawrence made of the results of the earthquake: "She Will Rise from Her Ashes."

Film history has confirmed, over and over, and at various levels of film production, the photographic and cinematographic significance of the Bay Area. Few American locations are as familiar to postwar film audiences. Such pop classics as *Vertigo* (1958), *Bullitt* (1968), and *Dirty Harry* (1971) established San Francisco as a location for cinema romance and suspense, which it has remained. And no city has been the location for more postwar avant-garde film, in part because of the presence of the San Francisco Art Institute, whose teachers and alumni have made regular contributions to avant-garde history. San Francisco and the Bay Area have long been a location for psychodrama, surreal humor, and spiritual exploration, in the work of dozens of filmmakers including Sidney Peterson, James Broughton, Bruce Baillie, Chick Strand, Gunvor Nelson, Robert Nelson, and George Kuchar. In more recent years, the Bay Area has been the backdrop for a variety of films that implicitly or explicitly polemicize progressive attitudes toward ethnicity and sexual freedom: Wayne Wang's *Chan Is Missing* (1981), for example, which

Figure 41. Jo (Wood Moy) in Wayne Wang's *Chan Is Missing* (1981). Courtesy Museum of Modern Art.

uses San Francisco's Chinatown as a locale for challenging the cine-traditional stereotyping of Asian Americans (see fig. 41); and the work of the gay activists Barbara Hammer and Marlon Riggs.

There is also a history of films *about* San Francisco and environs; and while the approaches of these films vary a good bit, the films tend to confirm visual approaches and themes that characterize the depiction of the city since the days of the daguerreotype.

Frank Stauffacher's *Sausalito* and *Notes on the Port of St. Francis*

By the time he made *Notes on the Port of St. Francis* (1952), Frank Stauffacher was well aware not only of the San Francisco surrealist films of the 1940s, but of the earlier history of European city symphonies, as a result of his Art in Cinema film series, which began at the San Francisco Museum of Art in 1946 and was to influence a generation of West Coast filmmakers (and to serve as a crucial resource for Amos Vogel's New York City film society, Cinema 16).[43] Art in Cinema's seventh program, "Fantasy into Documentary," presented *Nothing but the Hours* and *Berlin: Symphony of a Big City*. In fact, Stauffacher's first film, *Sausalito* (1948), was a loose amalgam of surrealist invention and the city film. Whimsical bits of observation of Sausalito—a small town just across the Golden Gate to the north of San Francisco that during the 1940s was an artists' colony with a raffish history as a port town with saloons, bordellos, and gambling joints—are combined with surrealist juxtapositions of image and of sound and image (see fig. 42). Divided into two parts ("Landscape" and "Song"), *Sausalito* reveals the various sectors of the town and some of its moods while developing a set of visual motifs reminiscent of Maya Deren and Sidney Peterson and of the French avant-garde of the 1920s: an eye looking at the camera through holes in a fence, a man carrying a violin, a phone off the hook, a seashell seen in various contexts . . .

Perhaps the most notable dimension of *Sausalito* is Stauffacher's care with the sound track, which is developed as fully as the visuals and in analogous ways.[44] For example, in the midst of a sequence of Sausalito houses accompanied by violin, Stauffacher includes a close-up of a woman peeking out a window from behind the curtain. For this one shot, the violin music stops abruptly, then continues again with the next image: a pan of a sailboat moving across the harbor, a vista that is interrupted by a pole halfway across the image—just as the sound was interrupted a moment earlier. As is true with Stauffacher's visual imagery, the sound track develops a series of motifs, and from time to time it is layered, just as images are superimposed.

Figure 42. A whimsical bit of observation in Frank Stauffacher's *Sausalito* (1948). Courtesy Museum of Modern Art.

In a sense, Stauffacher uses Sausalito as a metaphor for his own filmmaking. The unusual environment of Sausalito, just beyond the margins of the commercial center of San Francisco, is analogous to his whimsical surrealist film, which is part of a tradition that has developed outside the margins of commercial filmmaking. For Stauffacher, in fact, *Sausalito* was experimental by virtue of its very informality. In a response to a letter from Amos Vogel that included criticisms of the film by the Cinema 16 audience (*Sausalito* was presented at Cinema 16 in November 1950), Stauffacher explained, "I felt it legitimate to let it go as a truly experimental piece, with the good and the bad left as they were [rather than, as he explains earlier, to change the film in response to the "quite valid" criticisms]; in the nature of a 'sketch.' For I feel an experimental film carried to a point of perfection can really no longer be called experimental. . . . What I was trying to do was to convey a mood, an atmosphere—but punctuated with enough satire to prevent it's [sic] becoming pretentiously arty."[45]

Notes on the Port of St. Francis was Stauffacher's second foray into the city film. It, too, is distinct from the city symphonies of the 1920s, not only because—like *Sausalito*—it is not precisely a city symphony in the classic sense of the term (it does not present a composite day in the life of San Francisco), but also because it places emphasis on the city's remarkable history.

Notes on the Port of St. Francis is shaped in two ways: by Stauffacher's organization of his visuals and by the juxtaposition of these visuals and the sound track. Visually, *Notes* is divided into eight sections, each separated from the next by a fade-out, a moment of darkness, and a fade-in. After the opening credits (and a quote from Walter de la Mare, the first stanza of "An Epitaph": "Here lies a most beautiful lady;/Light of step and heart was she;/I think she was the most beautiful lady/That ever was in the west country"),[46] the opening section provides a rough overview of the history of San Francisco. The remaining sections focus on, respectively, people negotiating the city's hills via cable car, automobile, and go-cart; the speed of the city's development; the general mixture of ethnic groups and types of people; the Italian Americans and Fisherman's Wharf; the Chinese Americans and Chinatown; the fog; and, finally, the city's diverse neighborhoods—a section that leads to the concluding idea of San Francisco as a "City of Contrasts."[47] Each of the sections has its own overall structure; and some sections are structured more rigorously than others: the second section, for example, is precisely organized by means of

Figures 43–45. San Francisco harbor; street scene; and the Golden Gate Bridge; all from Frank Stauffacher's *Notes on the Port of St. Francis* (1952). Courtesy Museum of Modern Art.

intercutting, so that we see cable cars, an automobile, and several young boys with go-carts climbing hills, reaching the top (actually, the automobile gets stuck partway up a hill), and descending the other side (the automobile backs down the hill the driver apparently had hoped to climb). Throughout the film Stauffacher enforces the "City of Contrasts" idea by shooting the city from both San Francisco Bay and the hills. (See figs. 43, 44, 45.)

Stauffacher's use of sound provides a second kind of organization. During sections 1, 3, 4, 6, and 8, the visual imagery is contextualized by a spoken narration, delivered by Vincent Price, made up of excerpts from an 1882 essay about San Francisco by Robert Louis Stevenson,[48] along with assorted passages of music and environmental sound. The excerpts from Stevenson emphasize the speed with which San Francisco had developed by 1882: one generation before Stevenson wrote, the area had barely been settled, and during the span of a single lifetime, San Francisco had become a major city. The juxtaposition of Stevenson's commentary and Stauffacher's contemporary images of the city causes what we are seeing to seem further proof of Stevenson's observations: when he explains that "[a]ccording to Indian tales, perhaps older than the name of California, it [San Francisco] once rose out of the sea in a moment, and sometime or other shall, in a moment, sink again," Stauffacher provides a downward tilt shot of the city filmed from the bay that replicates the idea of the city rising suddenly out of the water. Given the introductory quotation from Walter de la Mare, it is difficult not to think of San Francisco as a goddess, like Botticelli's Venus, rising from the sea.

Overall, *Notes on the Port of St. Francis* is a relatively conventional city film that sings the city's distinctiveness and beauty without betraying much consciousness of the downsides of city life that might be a function of the city's development or of the effects of this development on the geography of California. While this film is less openly inventive than *Sausalito*, Stauffacher's imagery is capably shot and edited and his sound track is reasonably dynamic: in fact, his mixture of music, sound, and narration is thoughtful enough that he may have meant the "Notes" in his title to refer to both the informality of his visuals and his care with sound. Indeed, "Notes" may have been a subtle way of connecting his film with the European city symphonies of the 1920s.

The spirit of Stauffacher's *Sausalito* and *Notes on the Port of St. Francis* has remained alive, in Larry Jordan's *Visions of a City* (shot in 1957, edited in 1978), in Abigail Child's *Pacific Far East Lines* (1979), and in a series of recent films by Dominic Angerame: *Continuum* (1987), *Deconstruction Sight* (1990), *Premonition* (1995), *In the Course of Human Events* (1997), and *Line of Fire* (1997). All of these films combine the observation of downtown San Francisco characteristic of *Notes* with a surrealist sense of composition reminiscent of *Sausalito*. Unlike Stauffacher's San Francisco film, however (and the Stevenson essay it seems to have evolved from), the Jordan and Angerame films do not sing the excitement either of the evolution of the modern city or of the city as the culminating product of the industrial revolution.

The focus in *Visions of a City* is the way in which the reflective surfaces so common to modern urban construction shatter our sense of continuous space. People on the street and vehicles are seen as various forms of reflection (some of them reminiscent of Thompson's *N.Y., N.Y.,* made the same year). The surreal quality of many of Jordan's compositions is enhanced by the music track.

Pacific Far East Lines was shot through the windows of Child's San Francisco apartment, which offered several views of the city. Opening with a surreal combination of time-lapse imagery of buildings and passing traffic and the full moon rising in the background, and the green clock face on the Ferry Building (almost exactly the size of the moon) running in reverse, the twelve-minute, silent, color film combines imagery of a distant skyscraper being constructed (early in the film the construction has just begun, but by the end the building seems finished) with a variety of images of city lights at night, clock faces, nearby apartment buildings, clouds—each of which becomes a motif. *Pacific Far East Lines* familiarizes us with the various motifs, then gradually accelerates so that the various kinds of imagery seem to fly past, often overlapping, and San Francisco becomes a visual phantasmagoria.

The focus of the Angerame films is increasingly the precariousness of the modern city.[49] *Continuum* uses single, sometimes multiple, exposures to depict maintenance workers sandblasting, tarring, and welding in compositionally mysterious urban spaces. In *Deconstruction Sight,* the focus is on the demolishing of a large modern building by men and machines, both during the day and at night. Indeed, as the film moves into evening, the pace of the "destruction" accelerates via time-lapse photography, and the steam shovels roam around the rubble like mechanized raptors (an effect that echoes Child's imagery of a giant crane in *Pacific Far East Lines*). While the disassembling of the building in *Deconstruction Sight* seems Angerame's implicit critique of the emphasis on progress in conventional city symphonies, *Premonition,* as its title suggests, uses a notable result of the 1989 earthquake—its undermining of the Harbor Freeway (itself a symbol for many San Franciscans of the destructiveness of "progress")[50]—as a "premonition" of the second half of the Indian tale

Stevenson refers to: the possibility that San Francisco could "in a moment sink again" into the sea. Angerame's film focuses on the virtually empty freeway (used only by an occasional jogger or bicyclist, and by graffiti artists) in a series of juxtapositions to the busy downtown through which it curves—juxtapositions sometimes reminiscent of those in Stauffacher's *Sausalito*. Near the end of *Premonition*, Angerame focuses on an anonymous graffiti work, painted on the surface of the roadway, in which huge sperm seem to march forward into emptiness. As *Premonition* develops, Angerame traces the sperm to their source: a masturbating stick figure. The graffiti seems an apt metaphor for modern city building as a self-serving extravagance, in the long run an "ejaculation" into nothingness.

The implications of *Deconstruction* and *Premonition* are combined and elaborated in *In the Course of Human Events,* where the focus is on the demolition of the Harbor Freeway (see fig. 46). While Angerame is aware of the history of avant-garde depictions of San Francisco (and environs), his mood is sometimes creepy, sometimes eerily sensual. If his compositions sometimes (and perhaps consciously) evoke Stauffer's imagery, the difference in the two filmmakers' moods charts a change in attitudes toward this urban center that seems typical of at least some portion of two generations. It is, however, a

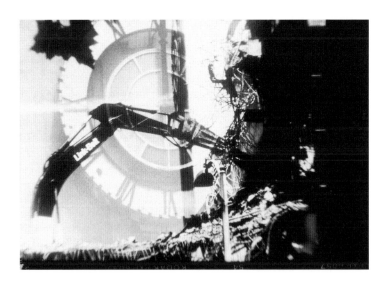

Figure 46. Clock on San Francisco's Ferry Building, seen through demolition work, in Dominic Angerame's *In the Course of Human Events* (1997). Courtesy Dominic Angerame.

complex change that is reflected in Angerame's use of black-and-white for all four films, a choice that reflects his somber vision of San Francisco while simultaneously allowing him to create frequently arresting explorations of chiaroscuro and texture that reflect his passion for the remarkable city where he has spent his adult life.

Castro Street

During the mid-1960s, Bruce Baillie became the closest thing to the Bay Area's cinematic spirit of place. He was a crucial figure in the development of Canyon Cinema, at first an exhibition cooperative and subsequently a distribution cooperative (see note 50); and his films were widely seen and admired. Baillie was instrumental in instigating a filmmaking movement in the Bay Area by demonstrating that beautiful films could be produced on minuscule budgets. Indeed, by 1963, when he completed *To Parsifal*, he had come to see himself as a cinematic knight errant, a "holy fool," his 16mm camera his sword and the resulting films, quests for the Holy Grail of cinema art. In *To Parsifal* Baillie recalls two early (and ongoing) stages of American development: "part 1" of the film—entitled "off S. Brenner's Viking" (referring to his friend Steve Brenner's fishing boat, *Viking*)—evokes the earliest stages of the transformation of North America by emigrations from Asia and from Europe: Baillie records the sea as seen first from the California coast and then from the small boat, low to the water, and the activities of fishermen (the imagery is accompanied by VHF radio transmissions between fishermen and later by excerpts from Richard Wagner's *Parsifal*). Then, after imagery of California mountains lofting up from the sea and a shot made under the Golden Gate Bridge—it "bridges" the two sections of the film—Baillie explores the transformation of California landscape by the railroad and lumbering.[51]

As a cinematic Parsifal, Baillie does not see his role either as polemicist against commercial exploitation of the landscape or as booster. His imagery of the California landscape is lovely, but his depiction of the railroad evokes the romance so many moderns have felt for things industrial. A mini-montage well into the second section of *To Parsifal* between the railroad and the spirit of the forest (as embodied in a naked woman) does suggest that the industrial development represented by the train is endangering the spirit of American place; but in other instances Baillie's imagery of the trains evokes Lionel model trains and in general has its own elegance. In the film's final shot, a train passes from right to left through the frame, against a forest background, and because the train fills the frame, we are forced to see the distant trees through the interstices between the quickly passing railroad cars. For Baillie, the modern development of California, and of America, is an evolving balance between nature and the technological exploitation of it—including the cinematic exploitation of it—that increasingly privileges technology, brings it to the foreground. And for the cinematic knight errant, the goal must be to do honor both to the pure, naked spirit of original place and to that spirit of imagination and exploration that has culminated in modern industry and in the availability of the cine-Excalibur with which Baillie can, in his own personal way, face the challenge of the ongoing transformation of his world.

Insofar as his engagement with the issue of place is concerned, Baillie faced the ultimate challenge when he came to make *Castro Street*—and as he was to say later, the effort of making the film "blew my fuses for life."[52] *Castro Street* is in no way a conventional city film, and it has nothing to do with Castro Street in San Francisco, now in the heart of the city's gay district. The Castro Street Baillie filmed is located across the bay in Richmond, California, in an industrial area dominated, in the 1960s, by railroad switchyards and a Standard Oil refinery (see fig. 47). While Castro Street, Richmond, is certainly not a cityscape in the sense that dominates this chapter, this type of industrial space is as much a part of any modern city as a cluster of skyscrapers or a ghetto neighborhood. Indeed, without such industrial zones, modern cities are inconceivable. For Baillie, this Castro Street provided a crucial challenge, precisely because such spaces are not only essential to Bay Area urbanity, but in 1966 represented the most difficult dimension of Bay Area city life to come to terms with aesthetically.

As I suggest in my introduction to this chapter, many post–Great Depression, post–World War II Americans saw active industrial landscapes in a thoroughly positive light: they were visible evidence that America had recovered from the economic disaster of the 1930s, had won a cataclysmic war, and could now lead the world in productivity. Of course, by the 1960s the environmental dangers of unbridled industry were becoming too obvious to ignore: everyone was hearing stories about how this or that river had caught fire; we were becoming aware of the dangers of air pollution . . . By the time Baillie

Figure 47. Castro Street sign, across the bay from San Francisco, in Richmond, California, from Bruce Baillie's *Castro Street* (1966).

made *Castro Street*, industrial landscapes had become "blemishes" on the landscape and, for some, visual emblems of this nation's addiction to overconsumption and wastefulness. Baillie's challenge in *Castro Street* was to make a film that would simultaneously retrieve the earlier, romantic pleasure in industrial landscape (a pleasure visualized, earlier in the twentieth century, in the painting of Fernand Leger and in Ruttmann's and Vertov's city symphonies), at least as a kind of nostalgia, and model the retrieval of nature, as an idea and as a reality, from the ravages of modern industrialization. This is the environmental version of a conflict inevitable in any evolving community: How do we honor the accomplishments of the past, accomplishments that have literally made us what we are today, while recognizing what a more contemporary consciousness understands about the injustices created by these accomplishments and the attitudes they reflect?

Baillie has described some of the specific procedures used to make *Castro Street:*

> Technically, when I made *Castro Street*, I went into the field again with my "weapon," my tools. I collected a couple of prisms and a lot of glasses from my

mom's kitchen, various things, and tried them all in the Berkeley backyard one day. I knew I wouldn't have access to a laboratory that would allow me to combine black-and-white and color, and I was determined to do it by myself. I went after the soft color on one side of Castro Street where the Standard Oil towers were; the other side was the black and white, the railroad switching yards. I was making mattes by using high contrast black-and-white film that was used normally for making titles. I kept my mind available so that as much as one can know, I knew about the scene I had just shot when I made the next color shot. What was white would be black in my negative, and that would allow me to matte the reversal color so that the two layers would not be superimposed but combined.[53]

Baillie's handcrafted techniques transform *Castro Street* into a consistently stunning phantasmagoria that looks as "high tech" as anything from the 1960s film industry. Indeed, *Castro Street*'s inventive combination of color and black-and-white predates any comparable effect I am aware of (Andrei Tarkovsky sometimes combined color and black-and-white; and in the 1990s, TV commercials—and the feature *Pleasantville* [1998]—have made such combinations familiar to a mass audience).[54] By combining multiple layers of imagery of both sides of Castro Street, much of it foregrounding movement—of the many trains in the switching yards and of the camera—Baillie creates a panoramic experience of this industrial zone that takes us up one side of the street and down the other side simultaneously: the film has a kaleidoscopic quality that effectively communicates the complex activities of these industrial spaces by making the film frame a nexus of energy and motion.

Castro Street is more than a demonstration of Baillie's capabilities as image maker, however. The particular nature of his transformation of the *Castro Street* area meets the challenge he set himself. Well into *Castro Street* Baillie presents a twenty-six-second, black-masked shot of a field on a sunny, breezy day. For a moment, a yellow industrial apparatus is visible in the distance in the center of the image; and between this apparatus and the camera, a field of weeds, full of lovely blue flowers, waves in the breeze, as clouds passing in front of the sun transform the look of the field. After a few seconds a Union Pacific train enters the frame from the right, beyond the flowering field but in front of the yellow apparatus, and comes to a stop. As complex as this shot is, it nevertheless provides a moment of comparative simplicity within Baillie's montage and superimposition: after the opening seconds, we see this image and only this image (there is no superimposition) nearly full-frame, for about fifteen seconds—with a single exception (described later), longer than any other image in the film. While *Castro Street* is generally focused on industrialization and machinery, this quiet moment reminds us, on the one hand, that in modern life technology has become the context for nature—this "garden" grows inside an industrial area, between various forms of machinery: the yellow apparatus, the train, Baillie's camera—and, on the other, that while nature may seem dominated by industry, natural growth and the natural cycles that produce growth are always present and ultimately, conceptually and in reality, provide the conditions within which industry develops.

In her analysis of *Castro Street,* Lucy Fischer demonstrates how Baillie's design for the film reflects the yin/yang duality/unity so fundamental to the Eastern thinking that was having such a powerful impact in the Bay Area (and on Baillie, in particular) during the 1960s: "It is precisely this sense of unity revealed in disunity, of resolution in opposition that reigns supreme on all levels of *Castro Street*—on the level of shot-to-shot superimposition, directionality of movement, tonal composition, sound-image relation, and spiritual sensibility."[55] And one of the two most fundamental dualities implicit in *Castro Street* is nature/culture, or more precisely, the idea of original, "pure" nature (the flowers Baillie records are, after all, weeds—flowers that have "planted themselves") and modern industry. While the area Baillie has chosen to represent is dominated by industrial process, he and we are aware that the very intensity of his focus on this space is contextualized by our sense of how such processes relate to the physical world that surrounds them and—as suggested by those flowers and that changing light—to ongoing natural processes in general. The unusualness of Baillie's focus on a dimension of California life rarely embraced by filmmakers, except in the contexts of mindless boosterism or negative polemic, confronts the repression involved in conventional attitudes toward the "more palatable" landscapes and cityscapes of the Bay Area and of other modern metropolitan areas.

In the end, the beauty of Baillie's industrial landscapes—the colors, textures, rhythms he cultivates, even his imagery of machinery—is this filmmaker's manifesto, his definition of his position as independent film poet in a commercial society. Lesser "film poets" might be satisfied to confine their attention to an easy beauty, or to ignore challenges to traditional ideas of beauty altogether. In *Castro Street* Baillie refuses such options. His film not only alchemically transforms an "ugly" space into a stunning one; but within this general retrieval of the beautiful, Baillie embeds industrial images that echo those flowers in the breeze-swept field: a poppylike smokestack in a gorgeous scarlet iris; colorful pipes, at first seen out of focus (they could be flowers), that subsequently come into focus; and a pan up a cluster of green pipes that look like stems, which lasts seventeen seconds (the only shot longer than our clear view of the field of flowers earlier in the film). As a-natural as the industrial sector of Richmond, California, might seem, Baillie suggests that it is a product of nature, not only in the obvious sense—industry is built in nature, exploits natural resources—but in a spiritual sense as well: the same force that grows those flowers (the "spiritual" force so many of us go to nature to access) has inspired human animals to "grow" the material "flowers" of their imagination. If nature is the physical manifestation of the divine spirit, modern culture—and the industrial technology that sustains it—is the manifestation of the human spirit in the process of emulating divinity. And recognizing this parallel, suggests Baillie, provides a hope that within the relentless accumulation polemicized by so many, we can recognize the original sources of our power and find new, healthier ways to honor them.

As filmmaker, Baillie stands in relation to the film industry as those flowers in *Castro Street*—the literal flowers and the "flowers" Baillie creates from the industrial machinery he films and transforms—stand to the Castro Street industrial zone. He is fully aware that his 16mm camera and the film it processes are industrial products, created in other industrial zones like this one and delivered to him through modern transportation systems: without industrial exploitation of the environment (both celluloid and film emulsion are the results of organic materials, chemically processed), and even damage to the environment (these chemical processes create pollutants), Baillie would not have the opportunity to make films; and without concentrations of population in cities, there would never have been audiences for motion pictures of any kind. But while *Castro Street* pays homage to modern industry, it also reflects Baillie's desire to transcend the technological origins of film, and to use his camera as a means for reminding us of the environmental and spiritual origins of technology and for reconnecting us with these origins. The Garden, *Castro Street* suggests, is still there: the literal ground on which the industrial zones of our cities are built, and the spiritual source of our desires to transform the world for the better.

Panorama

The most literal attempt to honor San Francisco's history as source of the American photographic panorama is Michael Rudnick's *Panorama* (1982), which was shot over the period of a year (from spring 1981 to spring 1982) from inside and around Rudnick's fourth-floor apartment in the Russian Hill area of San Francisco. Rudnick filmed in time-lapse, alternating between leftward pans (he built a device that ensured smooth panning) and a nonmoving camera: while the alternation is regular, it is not rigorously systematic (the first five shots are pans; the next eight, still; the fourteenth, a pan; the fifteenth and sixteenth, still . . .)—though the overall arrangement of what Rudnick shot is chronological. Of course, because the seasonal rhythm of San Francisco is so distinct, even from nearby areas of California, this chronological organization does not reiterate any conventional sense of temperate-zone seasonality. Within the overall rhythms of *Panorama,* Rudnick presents a range of visual experiences, some of them panoramic in the most conventional sense—time-lapse pans across broad urban vistas—others quite intimate, at least visually.

Rudnick's apartment offers a variety of vantage points that include both distant events and events taking place inside the apartment. The pans of broad Bay Area vistas, especially because of Rudnick's use of time-lapse, are reminiscent of Muybridge's panoramas, in their providing "a wealth of miniscule detail."[56] What the viewers of Muybridge's multiplate, 360-degree photographic panoramas would discover as they explored his huge photographs over time is condensed by Rudnick's time-lapsing into a few seconds: *Panorama* envisions San Francisco and environs as a phantasmagoria of human and meteorological activity. (See figs. 48a, 48b.) While Muybridge's photographic panorama is limited to the expansive vista, however, Rudnick is able to reveal not just the general but the particular as well. In many instances, he time-lapses the variations in light within his apartment and the ways in which the view of the porch and roof just outside his window varies according to weather and time of day. And in other instances, his camera is

Figures 48a–b. U.S. Steel Building, San Francisco; rainbow over San Francisco; both from Michael Rudnick's *Panorama* (1982). Courtesy Michael Rudnick.

positioned so that events inside and events outside seem coordinated: for example, in one composition, we watch, in time-lapse, as two candles on a table inside flicker and burn down, while outside the time-lapse-accelerated moon confirms the candles' flickering as it moves across the sky behind buildings and clouds.

During the year when Rudnick was filming the imagery he included in *Panorama,* he discovered tiny visual miracles made possible only by his time-lapsing and he created mini-jokes within his mise-en-scène. One of the visual miracles occurs as he is panning past the Transamerica Pyramid, when light hitting the side of the skyscraper creates a sudden arc of light. At another moment, as he pans inside the apartment, a vase spins, revealing that Rudnick is changing the position of the vase between exposures of individual frames: the spinning vase is a self-reflexive joke on Rudnick's endless panning. In other instances, Rudnick choreographs series of compositions so that movements within one composition are continued within the next. But for all the evidence of his presence as filmmaker during *Panorama,* the film is as depopulated as George R. Fardon's *San Francisco Album* and other nineteenth-century viewbooks of cities, in the sense that we come to know no particular individuals either outside or inside the apartment. We *know* Rudnick is *there,* but we see neither him nor other members of his family.

The reason for the strange emptiness, both in the imagery and in the sound (*Panorama* has a minimal sound track, credited to Rock Ross, made up of bits of environmental sound, especially wind, and of music), seems related to the depopulation of cities in nineteenth-century viewbooks. Rudnick's impetus to make *Panorama* was his wife's, Helen Almazán's, comment, on returning from a vacation, that San Francisco was dreary: "This had never occurred to me, and it caused me to begin to look more carefully at the city and especially to be more aware of light. The film developed out of my looking."[57] *Panorama* reflects Rudnick's urge to rescue his native city from the charge of dreariness. What the resulting film reveals is both the variety of San Francisco as a visual phenomenon and the frequently spectacular nature of its constantly changing vistas—and something more.

This something more—call it high spirits—is evident in many subtle ways in *Panorama;* but it is encapsulated most obviously in two passages during which we see a blimp flying over the city, accompanied, in the first instance, by sounds that emphasize the whackiness of the motion of the blimp in Rudnick's time-lapsing; and in the second, by both this sound and a bit of music suggestive of a merry-go-round. The second passage occurs at the very end of *Panorama* (immediately after the credits and a composite 360-degree pan of the city from Rudnick's apartment roof) and leads into the two final shots of the film: a downward pan—the first image in the film that is not filmed from either a camera panning left or from an unmoving camera—to boats in San Francisco Bay, apparently during a celebration (a fireboat has all its hoses spraying) and a sunset shot with pink clouds. The implication seems clear: Rudnick means to celebrate his city and its remarkable spirit, as well as the tradition that has made San Francisco one of the world's centers of photographic and cinematic experiment, and, at least for Rudnick, an endlessly enjoyable place to live. *Panorama* is a "booster" film—its pleasure in San Francisco is qualified by none of the problems of urban experience—but it is nevertheless a lovely movie that communicates the same unpretentious love of modern city life as is evident in *Weegee's New York* and in Marie Menken's *Go! Go! Go!*[58]

Eureka and *Side/Walk/Shuttle*

For anyone who has followed the filmmaking career of Ernie Gehr, the fact that he has made two of the most inventive films about San Francisco could come as no surprise. Throughout his career, Gehr has revealed himself a cinematic magician: he has continually used film technology to surprise audiences with new forms of film experience, often transforming the mundane into the extraordinary. His two San Francisco films are excellent examples. For *Eureka* (1979), Gehr took an unusual approach to the avant-garde tendency to "recycle" earlier films.[59] Using *A Trip down Market Street before the Fire* (producer unknown, ca. 1905), Gehr provided viewers with a tour not only of San Francisco just before the 1906 earthquake and fire but also of the history that had intervened between the making of the original film and Gehr's reworking the material three-quarters of a century later, as that history encoded itself in the physical decay of the original film. (See figs. 49a, 49b.) Gehr reprinted particular frames (*A Trip down Market Street before the Fire* is 9½ minutes long; *Eureka*, 30 minutes),[60] often reframing the original imagery, simultaneously reviving and exploring the original and the fading and particular tears and scratches that have damaged it. This combination of original cinematography of Market Street and material damage to the filmstrip suggests a poignant parallel: just as the *imagery* of San Francisco is damaged by the destruction of the surface of the emulsion, by friction and by fading, so the vibrant city we see *in* the imagery was about to sustain catastrophic damage as a result of changes in the Earth's surface and the resulting fires that swept through the city, burning the surface already damaged by the friction of the earth's crust.

While *Eureka* does remind us of what was about to be lost—indeed, Gehr's ever-so-slow trip down Market Street may remind those filmgoers who know

Figures 49a – b. Moments in Ernie Gehr's adaptation/ interpretation of *A Trip down Market Street before the Fire* (1905) in *Eureka* (1979). The Ferry Building at the end of Market Street is coming into view in the image below. Courtesy Ernie Gehr.

the title of the original film of the first half of James Cameron's *Titanic* (1998)—it also provides a vivid depiction of San Francisco as it was in 1905. No doubt, *A Trip down Market Street before the Fire* was made to demonstrate the vibrancy and excitement of San Francisco streets, and was, in its time, a form of cine-boosterism.[61] Gehr's reworking of the original imagery, however, allows us to see this vibrant, exciting city space so that its particulars are all the more dramatic, so that both the commonalities and the distinctions between city life then and now are foregrounded.

Perhaps the most obvious dimension of *A Trip down Market Street before the Fire* that is emphasized by Gehr's reworking of the imagery is what seems to a modern viewer the utter chaos of the activity on Market Street. Motorized and horse-pulled vehicles of all kinds vie for space with bicyclists and pedestrians who dart through the traffic seemingly with no concern for the danger. While the actual functioning of Market Street is a testimony to the energy of modern commerce at the turn of the century, the mood of *Eureka* is reminiscent of the earlier history of San Francisco as the quintessential Wild West "instant city"; the pedestrians braving the traffic, seemingly oblivious to the approach of our trolley until the very last second, seem modern versions of the jaunty San Franciscans captured in the first wave of San Francisco daguerreotypy.[62] Gehr's film also allows us to "see through" the original imagery and to recognize many of the individuals, who in the faster-moving original imagery seem merely people on the street, as individuals with their own particular energy and even a citified sense of humor: they become less human fixtures within a busy scene and more individuals with whom we can relate.

All in all, the slow trip down market Street in *Eureka* is reminiscent of two early forms of photography: the early city stereoscope popularized by Edward Anthony, beginning in 1859; and the panorama. While much of the early photography of American cities tended to depopulate urban areas, in some cases as a means of emphasizing the monumental dimensions of newer cities, their stability rather than their busyness (e.g., George R. Fardon's *San Francisco Album,* mentioned above), from the beginning Anthony's stereopticon images offered "a vision of the American city not only as a place of grandeur, but of human activity as well. With those stereo views [his "Anthony's Instantaneous Views of New York" (1859)], Anthony became the first American photographer to declare the validity of showing the city not only as *product,* but more crucially, as *process.*"[63] Anthony's use of deep focus, emphasized by the people and vehicles on New York streets, created much the same impact as does Gehr's slow movement into the deep space implied in the imaging of Market Street. The San Francisco we see in *Eureka* is a process; nothing seems still, especially because even the monumentality of the buildings along the street is compromised by the damage to the emulsion within which the imagery is encoded: the entire scene shimmers with life.

The pace of the voyage down Market Street in *Eureka* is also reminiscent of the panorama, in several senses. For one thing, it seems a literalization of

Wolfgang Schivelbusch's idea that the panorama as an entertainment form evolved out of the experience of the railroad journey.[64] As we travel along the trolley track, the panorama of Market Street seems to slide by us both to the left and to the right. That the nature of the city imagery we see is continually changing, as we move down Market Street toward the Ferry Building, also evokes the early daguerreotype panoramas of San Francisco and the Muybridge masterworks of 1877–78: as Hales explains, multiplate panoramas differed from single-plate photographs, not only because of the difficulty in making them, but also because "[t]heir long slender ribbon of view . . . demanded that viewers abandon their passive habits in favor of action. . . . The unity and identity which nineteenth-century viewers culled from their panoramas was entirely a mental image, a synthesized whole. In that sense, these multiple-plate panoramas bear closer resemblance to a day-long walking tour than to a normal photograph."[65] By slowing down the original imagery, Gehr demands a greater effort on the part of viewers, for whom the slow, painstaking trip can be as frustrating as it is revealing: we must synthesize a sense of this immense, immensely busy city space from the myriad details Gehr gradually reveals.

The trajectory of *Eureka* moves relentlessly toward the terminus of the trolley ride, and as Gehr closes in on the Ferry Building, refocusing within the original imagery so that our attention is directed to the date of completion of the building (1896), he brings together two separate historical trajectories. The terminus of *Eureka*, which is announced by a passing wagon with "Eureka, California" painted on the side, is both spatial and temporal. In the original film, the trip down Market Street doesn't really conclude; we see the trolley turning around for its return trip—suggesting that the high-energy life of San Francisco is an ongoing reality. In *Eureka*, however, the trip does conclude, with Gehr's meditation on the stone with 1896 carved into it, suggesting that the "end of the line" is, in this instance, a pivotal moment in time. The year 1896 is important, after all, not only because it marks the completion of one version of the Ferry Building, but also because it was the first full year of the public history of cinema. Eighteen ninety-six is thus the "end of the line" of those developments that culminated in cinema (whose early years are dominated by "actualities" such as *A Trip down Market Street before the Fire*)[66] and the beginning of a new form of media history that would evolve into a huge, global enterprise—and, in time, would produce forms of cinema that provide in-theater explorations and critiques of this history: *Eureka*, for instance.

Side/Walk/Shuttle (1991) takes a radically different approach to providing a panoramic experience of a major city, not only from *Eureka*, but also from any other film I'm aware of—though, like *Eureka*, *Side/Walk/Shuttle* resonates with influence from the nineteenth century. Gehr got permission to film from a glass elevator located on the outside of the Fairmont Hotel, at the top of Nob Hill, as close as possible to the spot where Muybridge photographed his San Francisco panoramas. Using this elevator, Gehr made a series of continuous shots of the city, each of which begins at the elevator's ground level and finishes on the twenty-fourth floor, or vice versa. *Side/Walk/Shuttle* is composed of twenty-five of these continuous shots, regularly alternating between upward and downward motion.[67] Each shot is extended, though the length depends on whether Gehr was filming in regular or slow motion; the entire film lasts forty-one minutes, and the average shot, well over a minute. *Side/Walk/Shuttle* evokes not only the Muybridge of the panoramic photograph, but the Muybridge who in the 1880s pioneered the study of motion, designing (in 1887) the Zoopraxiscope as a means of demonstrating that his individual representations of phases of continuous motion, when resynthesized, were in fact the components of real animal locomotion. Muybridge became famous for his highly systematized photographic method—he photographed sequences of twelve and twenty-four still images of moving subjects, against a gridwork—and his equally systematized presentation of the results, in photo-grids of several forms. Just as Muybridge created a consistent matrix along which his subjects moved, Gehr uses the continuous elevator ride as a matrix, within which he presents us with a wide range of moving panoramas of San Francisco (many reminiscent, in their expansiveness, of the Muybridge panoramas).

Gehr's choice of the moving elevator as his position from which to film also recalls early moving panoramic forms and Schivelbusch's *Railway Journey:* an elevator is, after all, a modern offshoot of railroad technology, and its comparatively gradual motion has much the effect of *Eureka*'s slowed-down journey toward the Ferry Building. This connection of elevator and railroad is emphasized by the frequent trolleys we see moving along California Street during *Side/Walk/Shuttle*—and especially by the fact that Gehr often frames his imagery of San Francisco so that the trolleys seem to be moving vertically, at virtually the same pace as we are moving in the elevator: the trolley motion echoes the elevator's motion, and vice versa.

Still another sort of "panorama" is provided by the sound track, which is sometimes silent, sometimes not. After the first shot, which is accompanied by the sounds of Austrian tourists in the elevator, *Side/Walk/Shuttle* is silent for four shots; then during the following eighteen shots sound seems continuous, though it moves through a wide range of particular moods, from groups of people having fun together to footsteps crossing an apparently big, empty space to the sounds of birds, cable cars, wind, even bits of music (the final two shots are silent).[68] In his program notes for *Side/Walk/Shuttle*, Gehr explains that "the shape and character of the work was tempered by reflections upon a lifetime of displacement, moving from place to place and haunted by recurring memories of other places I once passed through."[69] The sound track evokes a range of such memories; indeed, while the sound track appears to be seamless, it was constructed from cassette tape recordings Gehr had made over the previous years in a variety of locations: specifically (in the order we hear the excerpts in *Side/Walk/Shuttle*), in Grand Central Station, New York City; in Geneva, Switzerland; in Venice, Italy; in Geneva, again; then in London, England; and finally in Berlin, Germany.[70]

The experience of *Side/Walk/Shuttle*, however, is more remarkable than any description of the film can suggest. As the film proceeds, Gehr continually discovers new ways of framing the space outside the moving elevator, so that nearly every shot requires us to discover new aspects of this space, and often to be surprised that, in fact, we are seeing the same space we've seen before (see figs. 50a–c). Some of the vertical pans reveal relatively conventional views: for example, shot 4 climbs above nearby buildings to reveal Coit Tower atop Telegraph Hill, framed in the center of the image. But as the vertical pans accumulate, *Side/Walk/Shuttle* becomes increasingly spatially disorienting. Indeed, near the end of the film, Gehr's compositions create surreal urban vistas, more astonishing than those Francis Thompson created in *N.Y., N.Y.* with special lenses and reflective surfaces. Buildings seem to descend out of the sky; and not only are we hard-pressed to know "which end is up," but we are unclear as to the direction of our movement during the shot. I may be an unusually suggestive viewer, but at the conclusion of my first experience of *Side/Walk/Shuttle*, I was momentarily afraid to stand up, for fear I'd lose my balance. Gehr's film confronts one of the dimensions of cinema we take most for granted: that the film frame replicates our conventional sense of up and down, the upper edge of the frame being the top, the lower edge the bottom,

Figures 50a–c. Images from three of Gehr's trips up and down the elevator of the St. Francis Hotel in *Side/Walk/Shuttle* (1991). Courtesy Ernie Gehr.

not only of the film image, but of any world it represents. For Gehr, the film frame is a space within which he can see the world anew: it is a space through which we fall into a fundamentally new sense of film imagery in general and urban imagery in particular. Indeed, not since Kubrick's *2001: A Space Odyssey* (1968) has a filmmaker so thoroughly critiqued the conventional filmic depiction of space.[71]

The disorientation Gehr creates is both visceral—and has resulted in *Side/Walk/Shuttle* being among the most popular of his films (there is an amusement park ride dimension to *Side/Walk/Shuttle*)—and an expression of the mixed feelings many of us share about modern urbanity, and about San Francisco in particular. There is, for many people (and Gehr's program notes suggest he is one of them), a psychic cost to living in a major urban center. The complexity and dynamic change characteristic of the modern city can be disorienting; we sometimes don't know up from down, can't tell whether we're coming or going. The very velocity of urban change during the past century has forced all of us to continually rethink our relation to history and to the larger society of which we are part: since the life around us—as that life is embodied in our surround—is always evolving, we are never still either; we are always in motion, though the direction of this motion is often ambiguous.

That *Side/Walk/Shuttle* documents San Francisco in particular adds a further dimension to the psychic disorientation evoked by the film. No one living in the Bay Area can ignore the possibility of earthquakes. Regardless of the apparent stability, the monumentality, of modern San Francisco, the city's history—and the history of the representation of San Francisco confirms this— is punctuated by tremors, any one of which could bring buildings tumbling down. Whatever the conventional stresses of modern urban life, this dimension of living in San Francisco distinguishes the city; indeed, the very beauty of the Bay Area is, as many residents acknowledge with defiant pride, a dangerous beauty. The buildings that seem to be falling from the sky during the second half of *Side/Walk/Shuttle* suggest the particular insecurity of living in a city precarious not only geologically but morally as well: during the final decades of the twentieth century, it was not unusual to see San Francisco represented as a modern Sodom poised apocalyptically at the edge of the new millennium.

Despite all the implicit insecurity reflected in Gehr's continually disconcerting compositions, however, there is one constant that allows Gehr not only to endure the stresses of urban life, but, like the traditional jaunty San Franciscan, to have a sense of humor about them: the fact of filmmaking itself. Whatever the implicit ambiguities of *Side/Walk/Shuttle*, it is more than simply a remarkable film: it is a highly formal, serenely paced experience that provides considerable enjoyment. Like the city it images, *Side/Walk/Shuttle* is full of invention and surprise; and it suggests that not only will the energy of Bay Area residents cause San Francisco and environs to "rise from the ashes" of whatever future catastrophes occur—as the city has always recovered from previous disasters to become more impressive than it was before—but that the energy of independent filmmakers will continue to revive cinema, allowing it to rise from its regularly predicted demise, the way generations of San Francisco filmmakers have revived modern independent cinema, again and again, during the past half century.

Coda: Reinventing the City Film in *Water and Power* and *Invisible Cities*

In recent decades, we have witnessed a variety of cinematic approaches to the city that simultaneously envision urban life and critique central assumptions about the urban that characterize the long history of both the New York City symphony and the various panoramic depictions of San Francisco. Two of the most impressive instances are Pat O'Neill's *Water and Power* (1989) and Eugene Martin's *Invisible Cities* (1990). Fittingly, perhaps, both films mount their critiques from outside the traditions explored in the first two parts of this chapter: *Water and Power,* from L.A.; *Invisible Cities,* from Philadelphia.

Water and Power can be seen as a reflection on the nature of metropolitan development from a position beyond the original excitements and doubts about the accomplishment and viability of the modern metropolis. Even more fully than the San Francisco films I've discussed, *Water and Power* does not conform to the city symphony structure developed in Europe: indeed, O'Neill's depiction of Los Angeles can be read as a revision of the form that reflects the more complex relationship of city and country we have been forced to recognize as a result of the West's dwindling water resources. In *The Sky on Location* (see chap. 4), Babette Mangolte's imagery of Mono Lake is contextualized with a narration that makes clear that the startlingly beautiful tufa columns that rise out of the lake, and that presumably draw tourists (including filmmakers and photographers), are only visible because the water that would otherwise rise above even the highest of these formations has been siphoned off by one of the aqueducts that supplies L.A., hundreds of miles to the southwest. The paradox of Mono Lake's beauty—that these bizarre formations, which in another era might have caused Mono Lake to be set aside as a national park like Bryce Canyon or Arches, are a result of L.A.'s urban sprawl—lies at the heart of *Water and Power*.

For nearly thirty years, Pat O'Neill has explored the potential of the optical printer for synthesizing diverse imagery into surreal films that are simultaneously high-spirited, formally stunning, and mysterious. *Water and Power* was, at least as of 1989, the most elaborate and impressive of these films.[72] While it is only fifty-four minutes long, its impact is that of a feature film, and a complex one at that, not only because it was shot in 35mm, but also because, throughout the film, we are seeing multiple layers of image, almost all of which were originally recorded in time-lapse, accompanied by a complex and evocative sound track made up of jazz, sound effects, and bits of narration.

In recent decades the virtually inevitable use of time-lapse to reveal the representative patterns of daily life in the city—in such films as *Weegee's New York, Go! Go! Go!, Organism, Panorama, Concern for the City* (1986, by Peter von Ziegesar), as well as in Godfrey Reggio's *Koyaanisqatsi* (1984) and Ron Fricke's *Chronos* (1987), which depict urban spaces as parts of a broader survey of human experience—has rendered the representative day in the life of a city merely a cell within larger cinematic organisms. *Water and Power* represents a further step in this evolution: O'Neill reveals the modern city as layer over layer of time-lapsed cells of experience and makes no pretense of reducing Los Angeles into anything like a single, coherent understanding. In *Water and Power*, L.A. is not merely an elaborate *reality;* it is a nearly overwhelming *surreality.*

O'Neill's use of the optical printer for synthesizing each sequence of *Water and Power* is, in a sense, the film's fundamental metaphor: just as O'Neill's optical printer provides a second level of representation, where the imagery he has recorded with the 35mm camera is re-presented as a series of combinations of diverse spaces and activities, the L.A. he reveals to us is a series of conflations of divergent experiences, all of which are interwoven within the larger urban tapestry (see plates 12, 13). A series of particular conflations provide the prevailing motifs of *Water and Power*. The most obvious of these involves the depiction of indoor/outdoor spaces, of urban/rural spaces, and of present/past.

In the second shot after the title, "Water and Power," O'Neill reveals, simultaneously, the inside of a bare room with a small table and chair in front of an empty water-stained wall, filmed in time-lapse so that the sheets of light made by the sunshine coming from the window to the left and behind (the same windows, presumably, that we see in the first shot after the title) move from left to right, across floor and wall; *and* a blue sky with cumulus clouds, again recorded in time-lapse, moving from right to left on the same, far wall (a further "layer" of information is provided by an excerpt from Edgar J. Ulmer's *Detour* [1946], heard on the sound track—more on this, later). After a moment, the time-lapsed sky and clouds fade out and the movement of time-lapsed light through the bare room continues through the day until dusk and the screen fades to darkness. Next, a time-lapsed image of the moon—accompanied by the sound of a locomotive—moves diagonally across the frame from lower left to upper right (as if to signal the passing of the night following the day represented by the image of room and sky); and then, after another moment of darkness, a second "representative day" dawns, and we are tracking along the Owens Valley aqueduct from left to right (in time-lapse, to the accompaniment of jazz)—a desert mountain is visible in the background—*and,* a few seconds later, from left to right along an L.A. street where (time-lapsed) people go about their business.[73]

Even this brief opening passage (what I've described takes approximately 2½ minutes) is full of implications for the city symphony form and the city film in general. While both the European city symphonies of the 1920s and the postwar American city symphonies of New York focus on public spaces and on individuals as components of the public sphere, O'Neill suggests the obvious: the modern city is not simply a public space or a set of public spaces, it is a concentration of particular private spaces as well. And while the city symphony form has assumed that the city is a space that can be dealt with as basically separate from the country, O'Neill suggests what we know to be true: every dimension of city life is made possible by alterations in the country that surrounds the city—and further, the very social and political power of modern cities, especially those of the American Southwest, is dependent on the water table of land hundreds of miles away. Indeed, as O'Neill himself has pointed out to me, the drainage of water from the Owens Valley by the Owens Valley aqueduct has rendered it a new "death valley." In the world of *Water and Power* city and country are not alternative spaces or synergic spaces: one exists precisely at the cost of the other. (See figs. 51, 52.)

O'Neill's conflations of present and past in *Water and Power* extend these implications. In the tradition of the city symphony, the city is quite precisely the primary artifact and symbol of modernity, of the present: it is where everything is happening. But in *Water and Power*, O'Neill uses several strategies for undercutting the simplicity of this notion. For one thing, the L.A. O'Neill documents in the "present" is simultaneously the L.A. of a generation ago: we never see the current center-city skyline that has recently become so familiar; when a skyline shot is included, the centerpiece is the L.A. City Hall, that art deco landmark so familiar from 1950s and 1960s film and television. Much recent imagery of L.A. attempts to display the city's "city-ness" by revealing that, like other American cities ("*real* cities" like New York and Chicago), L.A. can boast its own distinctive cluster of center-city skyscrapers. O'Neill presents an earlier sense of L.A., closer to the one Babette Mangolte refers to in her

Figure 51. Fan and desert landscape in Pat O'Neill's *Water and Power* (1989). Courtesy Pat O'Neill.

Figure 52. Time-lapsed musician, against background of the Owens Valley, in O'Neill's *Water and Power* (1989). Courtesy Pat O'Neill.

There? Where? (1979)—a city without a focus, where "there is no *there* there." (A significant exception here is the film's longest "shot," a 1-minute, 49-second time-lapse image of a street, down which, midway through the shot, come tens of thousands of runners in the 1988 Los Angeles Marathon; on the left side of the street we do see a skyscraper of more recent vintage; nevertheless, even here, the focus of the shot is the street and the evolving activities, not this building.)

This conflation of present and past is also confirmed by O'Neill's recycling image and sound from a series of Hollywood films that suggest a skeletal history of the film industry. Near the end of the multilayered sequence described in the previous paragraph, O'Neill incorporates—within a frame-within-the-frame—imagery from Cecil B. DeMille's original version of *The Ten Commandments* (1923). At other moments in *Water and Power,* image and sound from Josef von Sternberg's *The Docks of New York* (1928) and *The Last Com-*

mand (1928), from a 1950s television commercial for General Electric, and—as mentioned earlier—from Ulmer's *Detour* become part of O'Neill's imagery. These recyclings, like the imagery of the L.A. City Hall, are a regular reminder that the present L.A. in which O'Neill is living and making film is what it is in considerable measure because of what it was during earlier decades of the twentieth century. That nearly all the recycled imagery can be read as suggesting a collapse of hope or energy—and in the case of *Detour* and *The Last Command* of failed dreams of a new life in Los Angeles/Hollywood—confirms the mix of fascination and concern evident from the opening moment of *Water and Power,* when a man, in extreme long-shot, walks out onto a high trestle and jumps off, within a gorgeous, apocalyptic composition.

A final, and crucial, interweaving of past and present is evident throughout the film in O'Neill's techniques themselves. If the sophisticated use of the optical printer (and, during indoor time-lapse shots, of O'Neill's own technique of making frame-by-frame time exposures, so that gestural movements are captured on individual frames and pile up on the retina) represents an unusually high-tech approach for an independent filmmaker, these techniques are used in such a way that they recall approaches used by the earliest filmmakers and by some of those whose work paved the way for cinema itself. The time-lapsed indoor, black-and-white imagery of men and women doing various actions—walking, playing a ukelele, climbing a ladder—are modern versions of the motion photography of Eadweard Muybridge and of Etienne-Jules Marey. The reliance on relatively long takes of (usually time-lapsed) imagery suggests the one-shot-equals-one-film approach of the early Edison and Lumière actualities. And O'Neill's complex layering of imagery to produce impossible scenes is a modern version of the trickfilm, as it was developed by George Méliès, Edwin S. Porter, and others. Of course, O'Neill's refusal to develop any sustained narrative in *Water and Power* confirms the relationship of his approach to the beginnings of cinema.

One last conflation, suggested perhaps by the foregoing discussion, deserves mention: O'Neill's combination of what in this country have traditionally been seen as quite different cinematic histories. Like his fellow southern Californian Morgan Fisher, O'Neill works *between* the history of industry filmmaking and the history of avant-garde filmmaking. *Water and Power* is a 35mm film. It was made by someone who has worked in the industry, using equipment generally reserved for big-budget movies—and it frequently alludes quite directly to this history. And yet, it is clearly an avant-garde film, one that evokes several of the forms avant-garde film has taken during the past seventy-five years. Of course, the focus of this discussion has been the relevance of *Water and Power* to the history of the city symphony; but the surreality of O'Neill's imagery—and of the brief visual texts that interrupt his more complex visual imagery (e.g., "Lucy, a man/who once made thousands of dollars a day/and who ran into trouble/ran out of luck/and now does other people's jobs/answers telephone calls/cleans up after dogs/cuts down trees/drives to the dump in a rented truck/hurls branches off the truck/hurls old televisions off the truck/boxes full of glass jars, hubcaps, mirrors/hurls everything as far as he can/and listens to the screaming of the Caterpillars")—relates the film to the history of surreal film that begins in Europe in the 1920s and becomes so typical of postwar independent filmmaking in San Francisco. Other familiar avant-garde tendencies—recycling earlier film has been mentioned—are also evident. There are even moments of abstract animation, à la Oskar Fischinger.

In its mixture of geographic and historical terrains, and of cinematic approaches, *Water and Power* can be seen as, simultaneously, an emblem of despair and of hope. That the film begins with an apparent suicide, and from time to time echoes the implications of this opening (in one three-layered sequence, time-lapse imagery of a tidal flat is layered with a time-lapsed pan of a city dump and with a time-lapsed man who paints the phrase "swamp of despair"—"despair" subsequently turns into "desire"—on a wall; in another two-layered sequence, time-lapsed imagery of a city intersection with the word "danger" painted on the street, and a time-lapsed man's shadow making an ambiguous hand gesture, is accompanied by the sound of an air raid siren) suggests O'Neill's ambivalence about the future of L.A., and perhaps of American city life in general. Certainly, the city is complex and fascinating, energetic and often beautiful. But this is a beauty leading . . . where? If O'Neill tends to take cover in an earlier sense of Los Angeles, when for most people it was an image of sunshine and Hollywood, he is haunted by a newer sense of the city as the epitome of environmental exploitation. No solution is posed; indeed, as a filmmaker who chooses to work in L.A. because of the facilities available there—and because he is rooted in this desert space—O'Neill is aware that he is more problem than solution. If the difficulty of *Water and*

Power is its very obscurity, its endless surreal pileups of image and sound that must be virtually opaque to the majority of viewers (even as we recognize O'Neill's technical dexterity and his commitment to a labor-intensive film that can hardly repay his abilities and efforts in any practical way), its strength is in its rerouting of the city symphony, a form O'Neill implicitly deconstructs in order to renew.

The implicit critique of the city film developed by Eugene Martin for *Invisible Cities* is quite different from O'Neill's critique in *Water and Power*. Indeed, the dimensions of the city film Martin responds to characterize *Water and Power* as fully as they characterize any other city film I've discussed. Like the New York and San Francisco films, *Water and Power* sees the city as the nexus of modern development. While O'Neill's *vision* of L.A. is nostalgic, his *visualization* of this nostalgia is high-tech: indeed, O'Neill's concern for the Owens Valley is balanced, even outweighed, by his desire and pleasure in working in the nation's premiere cine-industrial zone, in 35mm, and with the newest equipment. In addition, O'Neill is attached to *this* city both professionally and emotionally; and even if *Water and Power* does not picture L.A. as the essence of America, the way Ruttmann's *Berlin: Symphony of a Big City* and Vertov's *The Man with a Movie Camera* depict Berlin and Moscow as the heart of modern Germany and Russia, O'Neill's L.A. cannot be mistaken for any other urban center. The two characteristics of virtually all the city films I've discussed is that they focus on the city as quintessentially modern and they reflect a commitment to the idea of their city's distinctiveness.

Invisible Cities reveals no particular fascination for the modern; and while Martin's home base is Philadelphia, his focus is not on what he may consider quintessentially Philadelphian: in fact, Philadelphia is merely one of ten urban locations depicted in the film; and in a good many instances during *Invisible Cities* we aren't sure which of these locations we're looking at. Martin's exploration of contemporary urban space is conducted in the historical context of Atget's remarkable documentation of Old France and, particularly, of Old Paris—the Paris that was disappearing during the years just before and after the turn of the nineteenth century, during Atget's adult life (Atget was born in 1857, died in 1927) as a new wave of technology, industrial development, and urban migration was sweeping across Europe and North America. Regularly throughout *Invisible Cities* a narrator (Peter Finn) reviews

Atget's life and his documentation of Paris and environs; and a close-up of hands turning the pages of *Volume II: The Art of Old Paris* from the Museum of Modern Art's four-volume retrospective, *The Work of Atget,* is a visual motif during the film.[74]

But Martin does more than refer to Atget. For one thing, he creates a protagonist filmmaker (Eric Schoefer) whose way of working and living continually echoes Atget's. During *Invisible Cities* the filmmaker is seen using a simple, hand-wound, 1920s' Bell & Howell camera (Atget, the narrator reminds us, "liked the older tools of photography and never changed his working methods"), as he rides a commuter train into center-city Philadelphia (he sits facing in the direction opposite to the way the train is moving, looking out the window into the past) to explore older neighborhoods and to film particular spaces and moments. Like Atget, this filmmaker is a detached presence in the world he records and he avoids the tourist landmarks we identify with his city. And like Atget, the filmmaker is a loner, both in his work and in his personal life: his apartment is spare, revealing bare walls, an old stove, a small table, a dresser, and a number of old-style brown leather suitcases. At the beginning of the film the suitcases are open and arranged around the apartment; and the filmmaker carefully steps through them—a metaphor, apparently, for the filmmaker's travels and his "opening" his filmic archives to us.[75]

Basically, the character of the filmmaker represents a cinematic meeting ground where Atget, as Martin understands him, and Martin himself can commingle imaginatively. The protagonist is *not* Atget—he's a *filmmaker* working in *our* era—but he is also not Eugene Martin: Martin is not simply a silent cinematographer like the protagonist; to make *Invisible Cities* he used not only the Bell & Howell camera we see his protagonist work with but also, in some instances, a synch-sound rig and, in others, a high-8 video camera; and Martin's process included writing a screenplay, directing Schoefer and Finn, and editing the results into a coherent whole.[76] On the other hand, just as the filmmaker *in* the film emulates Atget by looking backward, literally and technologically, Martin emulates his protagonist and Atget both in the way he presents his imagery and in the imagery itself. In some instances, Martin evokes specific characteristics of Atget's approach to Paris. For example, the narrator explains that at times Atget returned to a particular location to photograph it in a different light, and Martin does the same thing, most obviously when he returns to a graffiti-covered wall along a vacant lot—seen originally when the filmmaker-protagonist is filming in front of it—and presents the same sequence of shots (sans the filmmaker) in a much yellower tone.[77]

Also, by shooting in reversal 16mm film (a type of shooting on its way out in the late 1980s), and working for months with his lab on the timing of his black-and-white and color imagery, Martin gave the entirety of *Invisible Cities* a tonal quality evocative of nineteenth-century photography (and specifically the Atget images we see in *The Work of Atget*) and of the tinting used in many early films. Indeed, because of Martin's dexterity with sepia tones and with a very limited range of color (the color in *Invisible Cities* is sometimes reminiscent of Andrei Tarkovsky, a Martin favorite), the film is consistently stunning; and Martin's careful formal control endows his imagery with a seriousness reminiscent of the Atget photographs. Martin also refers directly to early cinema, most obviously perhaps in two shots—one near the beginning of the film, the other near the end—in which Martin remakes the Lumière classic *L'Arrivée d'un train en gare de la Ciotat.*

Atget's tendency to withdraw from the world, except as a photographer, and to remain as fully invisible as possible when he was making images also finds a correlative in Martin's direction. It is easy to assume—at least on first viewing, before the credits roll at the conclusion of the film—that the filmmaker in the film is Martin and that he is also the narrator: there are a good many precedents in American independent film for such an assumption (Jonas Mekas in *Walden,* for example: see chap. 7). But when we do see the credits, we realize that Martin has disappeared behind his protagonist and narrator, in something like the way Jim McBride disappears behind the character of David Holzman (L. M. Kit Carson) in *David Holzman's Diary* (1968). This level of invisibility was something Martin sought: "if you're a good enough director, you can become invisible."[78]

Not only does Martin's presentation of his imagery evoke an earlier era, but *what* he films in *this* era reflects his interest in the passing of time, in the decay and destruction that are part of any urban environment. In general, Martin's (and his protagonist's) exploration of center-city Philadelphia focuses on spaces that, physically at least, have seen better days or imply the costs of urban development: old-style doorways, fading walls often revealing flashy new billboard signage, the rubble from demolished buildings, a graffiti-covered rusty gate, an older neighborhood in the vicinity of what was once a working factory. Even Martin's few shots of Philadelphia's center-city cluster of skyscrapers are filmed from an industrial wasteland, so that the modernity of the buildings is qualified by evidence of urban decay. Ultimately, the implication is not simply that modern cities are as full of ugliness as of beauty, or even that the modern city is a decaying organism. Martin's imagery of the "other side" of Philadelphia is consistently arresting visually and often beautiful.

Martin seems to see the city—modern or ancient—as characterized by collisions of old and new. The new is always replacing the old, for better or worse, whether we're in the Philadelphia of the late 1980s or the Paris of 1900.[79] Indeed, these collisions of old and new are more fully concentrated in urban areas than anywhere else. The popular notion that historically the rural comes first and is succeeded by the urban is misleading. The city has always been with us (the population explosion has proliferated urban areas, but the urban has been central to human society throughout recorded history); and, therefore, it has always been and will always be evolving, decaying, rebuilding, forgetting, remembering—a mix of the newest technological achievements and the remnants of ways of life in the process of being left behind. And since what is disappearing is more precarious than what is arriving, the photographer-filmmaker's job is, as the narrator explains late in the film, to pass on our memories of our moment in the ongoing evolution of city life to the next generation—and to remind viewers not only that the constancy of change *is* our connection to earlier generations but also that the evidence of this constant change within the urban environment can be celebrated as well as mourned. (See figs. 53a, 53b.)

In more than one instance in *Invisible Cities,* Martin cuts from sites of urban decay/transformation in Philadelphia to similar sites in other places, in such a way that we're not sure how we got from the one location to the other. The most obvious such invisible transition takes us from Philadelphia to Berlin, and to the vicinity of the Berlin Wall during 1989 as the wall was being dismantled. Specifically, Martin cuts from graffiti in Philadelphia to graffiti on and around the wall, and by doing so, he reminds us that in the twentieth century urban evolution has become increasingly transnational: the new developments in an urban area in one nation can be counted on to reverberate in cities around the globe, whether we're talking about mainstream culture (e.g., the recent proliferation of once-American-style clusters of skyscrapers in urban centers in cities on six continents) or countercultural responses to the mainstream (e.g., writing graffiti on the walls of established institutions). In

Figures 53a–b. Wall with graffiti in Philadelphia; arcade and scaffolding along street in Torino, Italy; both from Eugene Martin's *Invisible Cities* (1990). Courtesy Eugene Martin.

other words, the traditional assumption in city films that major urban areas are visually distinctive, the essence of *this* nation and no others, is increasingly open to question.

Martin's movement from one urban center to another is a pervasive gesture throughout *Invisible Cities*. The ten cities listed in Martin's closing credits as locations are—this is Martin's order—Philadelphia, Las Vegas, Turin, Berlin,

Venice, Verona, Paris, Rome, Caracas, and New York. Of course, some of these cities remain quite distinctive in *Invisible Cities*—Las Vegas and Venice, most obviously—but even when a location is immediately recognizable, Martin places it in a larger context that tends to emphasize the location's typicality as well as its distinctiveness. For example, early in the film Martin intercuts between Las Vegas and Turin; but as different as these two urban spaces are, the focus is on light signs at night—a dimension of city life in urban areas around the world. Similarly, later in the film Martin cuts from a sequence filmed on the narrow streets of Venice to a galleria-type retail space in Verona: again, as different as these two cities are, we have no way of being sure that the galleria is not in Venice, as so many cities now have retail spaces based on the model of the original Galleria in Milan.

The transnational complexity of *Invisible Cities* is confirmed by the sound track: for example, in Martin's decision to use Peter Finn as narrator. Finn is a native Dubliner (currently he is a foreign correspondent for the *Washington Post*), and his Irish accent adds another "location" to those present visually. Further, Martin often uses ambient sound from one location (Rome, and sometimes Venice) in combination with imagery recorded in Philadelphia. The results are virtually seamless, and the fact that the people on the sound track speak Italian doesn't necessarily interrupt the illusion of continuity, because almost every urban area is now home to people speaking many languages; and the Italian-American community is one of Philadelphia's largest.

The transnational emphasis of *Invisible Cities* has become a characteristic of a good many films that depict modern urbanity. The second half of Godfrey Reggio's *Powaqqatsi* (1988), for instance, cuts from one urban area to another without identifying locations, as a way of seeing modern urban development as a transnational issue. *Baraka* (1993), Ron Fricke's exploration of spiritual sites around the world, often involves jumping from an urban center in one part of the world to an urban center in a very different part of the world. And, of course, television advertising in the 1990s frequently highlights a transnational sense of the world that has much in common with Reggio's and Fricke's work. The tendency is also evident in Rudy Burckhardt's *Around the World in Thirty Years* and in the sound track of Gehr's *Side/Walk/Shuttle*.

Late in *Invisible Cities* Martin includes 8mm home-movie footage that seems to belie his tendency to minimize the distinctiveness of his locations. The source of these home movies is not specified in the film; Martin himself came upon the imagery when a colleague gave him a box of film, assuming he might want to use the reels and cans, and he decided to incorporate portions of the footage in *Invisible Cities*, "as a naive eye," an unprofessional eye, in contrast to the more art-professional eye evident in the 16mm and video imagery of Martin's travels. In the home movies the travelers record standard tourist landmarks (the Bridge of Sighs, the Eiffel Tower, the Statue of Liberty), and the consistency of their focus on themselves amid this particular imagery provides a contrast with both the filmmaker *in* Martin's film, who records neither the conventional landmarks nor himself, and Eugene Martin, who films a fictionalized protagonist and combines the identifiable locations he records with other locations that suggest not just the past/present composite nature of all urban areas but the combination of the distinctive and conventional that increasingly characterizes urban centers around the world.[80] These home movies add a further layer of transnationality to *Invisible Cities* and remind us that even this seemingly new dimension of urban life and of cinema has precedents, including the traditional home-movie travel film. Indeed, early Lumière programs are probably the original models of cinematic transnationality.

In the end, Martin's reframing of the city film allows *Invisible Cities* to speak to the inevitably composite nature of urban identity and of the identity of individuals living in an urbanized culture, which is certainly all of us who see his film. Cities are, intrinsically, past *and* present, local *and* transnational; and the energy of city life is a function of the inevitable collisions between the old and the new, the native and the foreign. Since all of us live in or near cities, either literally or by virtue of being connected to networks that emanate from urban centers, our experience is equally composite, and energetic to the degree that we engage the inevitable conflicts between where we come from and where we are, both historically and geographically. The particular power of *Invisible Cities* is a result of Martin's willingness to work against the grain of the traditional city film in the interest of creating a more complete, more evocative sense of how the experience of the urban figures in his and our lives.

chapter 7

The Country in the City

On a map or from the air, nothing defines New York City more clearly than the rectilinearity of Central Park at the heart of the curvilinear island of Manhattan. And nothing encodes the paradox of the thinking that created Frederick Law Olmsted's first great park—and simultaneously distinguishes it from many of the parks inspired by Central Park—than the virtually perfect geometry of its outline. The park simultaneously confirms the grid structure of the streets of Manhattan and dramatically interrupts this structure: streets that run vertically uptown and downtown or horizontally across town must, when they reach the horizontal and vertical boundaries of the park, leave their verticality and horizontality behind to traverse the park before rejoining the grid of streets and avenues at the far boundaries of the park's expanse. If the Cartesian clarity of

midtown Manhattan has come to represent the efficiency of American capitalism that was making the United States a major industrial power during the
years when the Greensward Plan (fig. 54) was designed and Central Park constructed, the park represented (and continues to represent) a countersensibility: as Olmsted and Calbert Vaux predicted,

> The time will come when New York will be built up, when all the grading and
> filling will be done, and when the picturesquely-varied, rocky formations of the
> Island will have been converted into foundations for rows of monotonous straight
> streets, and piles of erect, angular buildings. There will be no suggestion left of its
> present varied surface, with the single exception of the few acres contained in the
> Park. Then the priceless value of the present picturesque outlines of the ground
> will be more distinctly perceived, and its adaptability for its purpose more fully
> recognized.[1]

Of course, this countersensibility has as its ultimate benefit the refresh-
ment of those who use the park and, at least implicitly, their return to their
workaday worlds in better frames of mind for productive labor and effective
citizenship in a capitalist republic. Indeed, the very complexity of the Olmsted-
Vaux design for Central Park was itself a product of the interest in efficiency
that is encoded in the graphlike design of the surrounding city: the articulation of the park's considerable acreage in a wide variety of mini-terrains, each
with particular kinds of experiences to offer, was a way of ensuring not only
the maximum options for individuals interested in using the park, but the
longevity of its ability to function as a relief from the commercial energies of
the city. Over time, any individual could use the park in many different
ways—and, in effect, have many different reenergizing experiences.

For those of us who grew up during the second half of the twentieth century
(or, at least, for me), the overall shape of the park is also suggestive of the

Figure 54. Map of the Greensward Plan submitted
by Frederick Law Olmsted and Calbert Vaux.

cinematic image, especially of the various wide-screen images that became so popular as television began to threaten the economic viability of the motion picture industry (fig. 55). Obviously, the length-to-width ratio of the park (approximately 5 to 1) is of a different order from even the widest of wide-screen cinema aspect ratios (Cinerama's ratio is 2.77 to 1; Cinema Scope, 2.55 to 1), but this discrepancy seems less an issue if we remember that the panoramic views offered by wide-screen cinema are contemporary versions of the full-fledged panoramas that were so popular in this country and in Europe during the years preceding the development of Central Park and during the period when the park was under construction (Paul Philippoteaux's 1884 panorama of Pickett's Charge in Gettysburg, for example, is 356 feet in circumference and 26 feet high). And it is also less an issue once we remember that Central Park and modern cinema have a good bit more in common than the graphic rectangularity of their visible shape, most obviously a commitment to a fundamentally narrative form of visual experience that is meant to provide at least the momentary illusion of "escape" from the demands of the workplace. In Olmsted's view, according to Bruce Kelly, the park was consciously designed so as to provide a sequential experience in which the viewer's eye would be gently led by the continual discovery of new vistas.[2] If the Ramble—the series of woodsy paths laid out between Belvedere Castle to the north and Bethesda Fountain and the Lake to the south—was the first sequentially designed section of Central Park to be constructed and, as a result, of particular importance in Olmsted's thinking, the entirety of the park, in one sense or another, reflects this commitment to sequential visual experience.

Central Park is more than a remarkable intervention in the geography of Manhattan, however. Both in theory and in practice the development of the park has reflected the complex realities of social class and ethnicity. Certainly, class and race played a crucial role in Olmsted's life and his design for the park. Olmsted's brilliance was, first, to recognize that the benefits of gorgeously designed landscape should *not* be confined to the wealthy, as it tended to be in England (and in his father's generation); *and then,* to have the ability and perseverance to convince people in power—many of them with little interest in parks or democracy—that such spaces should become a reality. After all, the richest class didn't need public parks; they could enjoy their financial superiority on their own estates. Olmsted *was* from a wealthy background; nevertheless, his passion was not simply landscape design but democratic access to it. Olmsted made this quite clear during the early planning of Central Park:

> The primary purpose of the Park is to provide the best practical means of healthful recreation for the inhabitants of the city, of all classes. . . .
>
> No kind of sport can be permitted which would be inconsistent with the general method of amusement, and no species of exercise which must be enjoyed only by a single class in the community to the diminution of the enjoyment of others. Sports, games and parades, in which comparatively few can take part, will only be admissible in cases where they may be supposed to contribute indirectly to the pleasure of the majority of those visiting the Park. The Park is intended to furnish healthful recreation for the poor and the rich, the young and the old, the vicious and the virtuous, so far as each can partake therein without infringing on the rights of others, and not further.[3]

Ethnicity was equally important in Olmsted's thinking. Like Central Park, which is divided into two distinct sections—a smaller, more sylvan northern section and a larger, more heterodox section below the reservoir—Olmsted's career in the 1850s and 1860s had two different phases. During the 1850s, Olmsted was a travel writer whose books about the pre–Civil War South—*A Journey through the Seaboard Slave States* (1856), *A Journey through Texas* (1857), *A Journey through the Back Country* (1860), and *The Cotton Kingdom* (a conden-

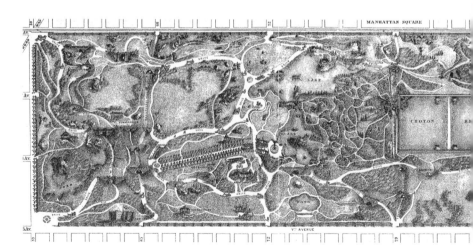

sation of the previous three books, published in 1861)—remain important descriptions and indictments of slavery. During the same years that his final contributions as travel writer were written and published, Olmsted's interest in public parks was coming to fruition in his collaboration with Vaux on the Greensward Plan for Central Park (submitted in 1858). Though these two interests—slavery and public parks—may seem distinct, they are related.

Olmsted concluded that one of the major disadvantages of slavery, above and beyond its indefensible inhumanity, was its impact on land: in those areas of the South where human beings were enslaved, there was also less respect for natural resources than he had observed in free states; those crops that "required" slave labor also did the most damage to the soil. If one considers the obverse of this conclusion, Olmsted's commitment to well-designed, public lands is no surprise: a society that values human beings, regardless of their origin or class, might be expected to devote not just land but beautiful, enjoyable, accessible land to the public good. Of course, Olmsted and Vaux designed Central Park, not only in light of the problematic urban realities of their own era, but because they could see that urbanization was the trend, and effort was needed immediately to avoid future problems.

On the other hand, whatever the theory behind the Greensward Plan, the actual building of the park was problematic with regard to both class and ethnicity. In *The Park and the People*, Elizabeth Blackmar and Roy Rosenzweig are

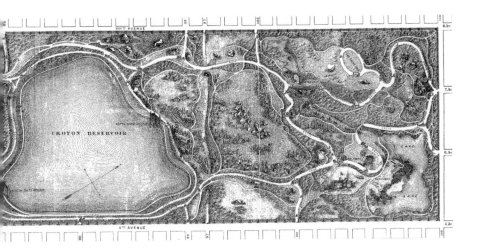

Figure 55. Map of Central Park as it was actually built by Olmsted and Vaux.

at pains to balance several generations of Olmsted worship with a detailed history of Central Park as a social space. As the authors make clear, in making the Greensward Plan a reality, the park builders trampled the interests of many of those who made their homes on the land bounded by what is now 59th Street and 110th Street, Fifth Avenue and Central Park West. Ninety percent of these sixteen hundred people were immigrants (primarily Irish and German) and African Americans, many of whom resided in what was called Seneca Village, one of the most economically successful largely African-American communities in New York state (in 1855 African Americans living in Seneca Village had a rate of home ownership five times greater than New Yorkers in general and thirty-nine times greater than other African-American New Yorkers). Whatever interests in beauty and healthy living for the less privileged classes underlay the Olmsted-Vaux design and whatever the aesthetic distinctions of this design and of the finished park, the sociopolitical history that made the building of Central Park possible was *also* one more instance of the racism and religious intolerance (churches displaced by the park included two African-American Methodist churches—AME Zion and African Union—one racially integrated Episcopal church, and Mount St. Vincent Convent, established by the Sisters of Charity in 1847) so evident in American society then and now.[4]

Almost exactly a century after the construction of Central Park, anti–Vietnam War demonstrators gathered in Central Park Mall for a rally that was followed by a march down Fifth Avenue. This March 26, 1966, event was only the second oppositional political event ever held in the park (the first was a 1914 women's suffrage meeting); and it was to be the first of many such gatherings that characterized the 1960s and 1970s. Of course, the same period saw a flowering of oppositional cinematic activity, including the completion of the two most distinctive films to have used Central Park as a primary location: Jonas Mekas's *Walden* (shot from 1964 to 1968 and completed in 1969) and William Greaves's *Symbiopsychotaxiplasm: Take One* (shot in 1968, completed in the earliest version in 1972, and revised in 1995). That Mekas is a Lithuanian immigrant (he escaped his native land as Nazi Germany invaded and spent several years in a prison camp in Germany before emigrating to the United States in 1949) and Greaves is an African-American native of Manhattan makes the fact of these two films a poignant historical note, especially as both film artists use the making of these films as demonstrations of political viewpoints critical of an "upper-class" Hollywood film industry that has been, for most of its history, as oblivious to the interests of immigrant groups and African America as were those who wiped out Seneca Village to make way for what Vaux called the "big art work of the Republic."[5]

Walden

Jonas Mekas began his career as a filmmaker almost immediately on his arrival in the United States—Mekas's *Lost Lost Lost* (1976) begins with the intertitle "A WEEK AFTER WE LANDED IN AMERICA (BROOKLYN) WE BORROWED MONEY & BOUGHT OUR FIRST BOLEX"—almost as if his arrival in America necessitated a transformation, if not of his artistic consciousness, at least of the means with which he would express it. By the time he left Lithuania, Mekas had established himself as a significant poet with a defiantly personal sensibility, deeply hostile to the interests of major conglomerate nation-states like Nazi Germany and Communist Russia.[6] Once he and his brother Adolfas had purchased their Bolex, Mekas transformed the diaristic tendency of his written verse into a diaristic cinema with few predecessors either in this country or abroad. From late 1949 on, Mekas chronicled first the New York City community of Lithuanians-in-exile and his own personal explorations of the city, and subsequently the development of what was to become the New York art scene of the 1960s and, for Mekas himself, a new, artistic "homeland." By the early 1960s he was completing films, though it was not until 1969 that his first major diary film—known at first as *Diaries, Notes and Sketches (also known as Walden)* and more recently simply as *Walden*—was finished.

Mekas's *Walden* is a 177-minute film divided into four sections (six in the video version) of approximately equal length. Each section includes two types of visuals—Mekas's generally hand-held chronicling of the events he sees and the frequent intertitles (visual texts intercut with a film's other imagery) that introduce imagery we're about to see or identify imagery we've just seen—and three types of sound—environmental sounds taped by Mekas (most frequently, the sound of subways), narration by Mekas, and music. The particular quality of these various sources of information and to a certain extent their organization are implied by the film's opening intertitle, which precedes even the title of the film: "DEDICATED TO LUMIERE." For Mekas, and for some other filmmakers emerging from the New York underground during the 1960s, the Lumière Brothers' earliest films were an inspiration. The inspiration they provided was less a function of their original, commercial concerns (the Lumières were camera manufacturers and their one-shot films were a function of their interest in marketing the Cinématographe and their Cinématographe presentations) than of what was for a time a widespread idealization of the comparative simplicity and directness of the earliest films. For 1960s filmmakers interested in providing a critique of commercial culture and commercial media—and especially of the visual and auditory overload increasingly characteristic of television and of a film industry desperately trying to compete with the new mass medium—the Lumières' single-shot, extended views of what seemed to be the everyday realities of 1895–96 offered a useful alternative, just as Thoreau's decision to live at Walden Pond half a century earlier was an alternative to what he saw as the fast-paced life of Concord and Boston.[7]

Another part of Mekas's defiance of contemporary film standards is his consistent use of intertitles to introduce and interpret the events and experiences he chronicles. Intertitles had been an essential dimension of Hollywood films until the advent of sound-on-film, at which point they quickly became at most a visual vestige of a bygone era. In other words, like the informality of Mekas's hand-held imagery, his frequent intertitles (themselves presented in a typewriter typeface that provides a handcrafted feel) declare his alliance with the cinematic past, with his own past as a poet, and with the literary past represented by Thoreau's *Walden; or, Life in the Woods,* which Mekas read in German translation in the mid-1940s while living in a German prisoner-of-war camp and, again, in English in 1961.[8]

While Thoreau's *Walden* provides the title for Mekas's film and the film's central metaphor (the intertitle "Walden" is juxtaposed with images of Central Park lakes three times; see plate 14 and fig. 56), Mekas's relationship to Thoreau, as evidenced in the film, is complex and even paradoxical. One obvious similarity between the two *Walden*s is evident in the particular ways in which the authors draw attention to their authorship. Thoreau's narrative of his personal experiences at Walden Pond is from the outset defiantly personal. Of course, Thoreau not only writes in the first person, his narrative is about his largely solitary life in the woods, a life so solitary—at least as it is depicted in *Walden*—that while he is "naturally no hermit," most of those with whom he communes on a regular basis during his two years at Walden Pond are

"brute neighbors." Indeed in the second paragraph of "Economy" Thoreau
confronts the issue of his use of the first person:

> In most books, the *I*, or first person, is omitted; in this it will be retained; that, in
> respect to egotism, is the main difference. We commonly do not remember that it
> is, after all, always the first person that is speaking. I should not talk so much
> about myself if there were anybody else whom I knew as well. Unfortunately, I am
> confined to this theme by the narrowness of my experience. Moreover, I, on my
> side, require of every writer, first or last, a simple and sincere account of his own
> life, and not merely what he has heard of other men's lives; some such account as
> he would send to his kindred from a distant land; for if he has lived sincerely, it
> must have been a distant land to me.[9]

Mekas's film is as fully first person as Thoreau's written narrative, a choice
that for Mekas was at least as defiant of contemporary standards and expectations as was Thoreau's use of *I*. The first visual image in Mekas's *Walden* is the
filmmaker waking up, and from the beginning Mekas's visual imagery is
framed as a first-person activity. In the opening minute of the film we see
Mekas playing the accordion and read the intertitle, "I CUT MY HAIR, TO RAISE

MONEY. HAVING TEAS WITH RICH LADIES [fig. 57]" (followed by images of Mekas having his hair cut). Mekas's first-person approach was so unusual for a film in 1969 that he printed a broadside guide to *Walden,* with this introduction:

> This film being what it is, i.e. a series of personal notes on events, people (friends) and Nature (Seasons)—the Author won't mind (he is almost encouraging it) if the Viewer will choose to watch only certain parts of the *work (film),* according to the time available to him, according to his preferences, or any other good reason. To assist the Viewer in this matter, particularly in cases of repeated viewings (forgive the Author this presumption), the following Contents, a list of scenes and their time tables, reel by reel, have been prepared.
>
> A note in the beginning says, that this is the First Draft of the Diaries. Why should the Author permit then, one may ask, the unpolished or half-polished edition to come out? His answer is, he thought that despite the roughness of sound and some parts of the images, there is still enough in them—he felt—to make them of some interest to some of his friends and a few strangers. In order to go to the next stage of polishing, he felt, he had to look at the footage as it is, many many more times, and gain more perspective to it—that's why this edition. There is another reason. A few months ago, suddenly he saw his room filling up with smoke—he couldn't even see the film cans—and only a very lucky coincidence stopped the fire next door which would have consumed five years of his work. So he gave himself word to bring out as soon as he can this First Draft version, and there he stands, and hopes that some of you will find some enjoyment in what you'll see.[10]

This "First Draft version" was never substantially revised.

Mekas's determination to make and release what would come to be known as a "diary film" not only defied the Hollywood tradition of suppressing directorial identity and the process of producing the film we're seeing (Mekas was not alone in this particular defiance; even as he was shooting the footage that would later become *Walden,* Fellini's *8½* [1963] was a hit on the art house circuit), but his decision to make a longer-than-feature-length film as a solo enterprise defied the even more fundamental corporate tradition of American cinema (and of popular European cinema as well). Further, his assumption that individual viewers should decide how much of the film they should experience during any one time period ignores the tradition that films are consumed in their entirety in a public forum controlled by distributors and exhibitors, in favor of the kind of access readers have to literary texts.[11]

If *Walden* is characterized by Mekas's consistent defiance of film industry

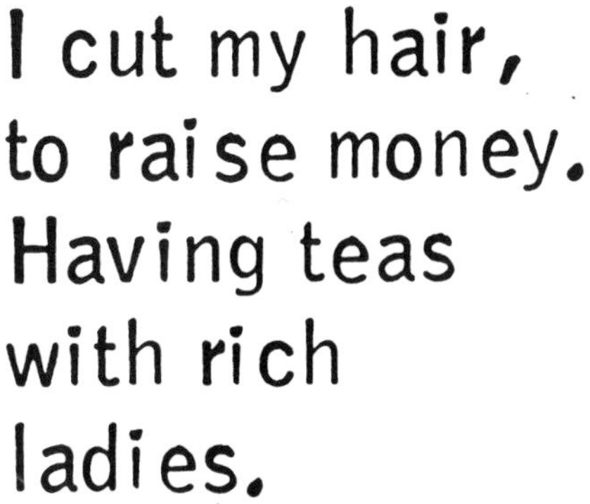

I cut my hair,
to raise money.
Having teas
with rich
ladies.

Figure 57. An early text from Jonas Mekas's *Walden* (1968). Courtesy Anthology Film Archives.

traditions and the audience expectations these traditions have created, he is quite explicit in seeing an alliance between his "film diary" and another popular film tradition: home movies. Early in *Walden,* Mekas sings (while accompanying himself on what looks to be a child's accordion),

> I live—therefore I make films.
> I make films—therefore I live.
>
> Light. Movement.
>
> I make home movies—therefore I live.
> I live — therefore I make home movies.

While Mekas does focus on weddings, on children, on vacation trips—the stuff of most home-movie and video making—the alliance he proposes is at best rather disingenuous.[12] Most home movies have a very limited audience—the family itself and a few friends—but *Walden*'s focus on those who were important in the New York art scene of the 1960s, and, to a degree, *their* family life gives this project a much larger potential audience. Further, while home-movie makers in the 1950s and 1960s tended to emulate Hollywood standards for making "good shots" and "good movies,"[13] Mekas's style in *Walden* is aggressively "personal": he refuses to hold the camera still, preferring an openly gestural style, and he often single-frames in a wildly erratic manner as he films—an approach that for audiences accustomed to more stable imagery is difficult to watch. Mekas defies the production standards for commercial cinema *and* the home-movie tradition of suppressing personal style in order to honor the nuclear family. In this, Mekas again goes further than Thoreau in his defiance of convention: if the writing in Thoreau's *Walden* is more openly self-involved than was usual at the time, it is not grammatically rebellious: readers need not learn to read in a new way.

Of course, it is the centrality of the idea of nature in the literary and the cinematic versions of *Walden*—not each work's emphasis of its author's defiantly personal stance—that accounts for Mekas's decision to use Thoreau's work as the central, guiding metaphor of his film. And it is the idea of nature that suggests the most fundamental distinction between the visions of the two works. That Thoreau's *Walden* was part of a particular American cultural moment when writers and painters were realizing the degree to which industrialization was threatening America's distinctive access to "wilderness" and to the connection with God available through the Book of Nature made it of particular relevance for Mekas whose personal history had threatened a comparable loss.

Mekas had spent most of his life in rural Lithuania, but after the arrival of the Nazis had forced him to flee his homeland and once the partition of Europe at the end of the war had put Lithuania into Communist hands, Mekas found himself exiled both from Lithuania and from the immersion in nature he had experienced there as a child and an adolescent. Not surprisingly, this loss of access to homeland created a considerable nostalgia that is often a central issue in Mekas's diary films: *Lost Lost Lost,* for example, chronicles Mekas's gradual personal evolution from Lithuanian-in-exile to American artist; and *Reminiscences of a Journey to Lithuania* documents the filmmaker's return to his mother and his motherland for the first time in twenty-seven years. *Walden* is the earliest of Mekas's completed diaries to express this nostalgia. About three minutes into the film, we see Mekas in bed, apparently unable to sleep, followed by the intertitle "I THOUGHT OF HOME." The suggestion is that the pain of his exile has kept him awake, or is a bad dream he has just awakened from. The intertitle is immediately followed by an image of the Lake in Central Park, which is in turn followed first by the intertitle "WALDEN" and then by a series of sequences filmed in Central Park.

Thoreau's decision to leave Concord and live at Walden Pond for two-plus years in the hope that the privacy and serenity offered there would allow him to plumb the depths of his soul was an attempt to defend his psychic health from what he saw as the increasingly pervasive tendency in modern man to have "no time [in his life] to be anything but a machine,"[14] a human machine at the mercy of the larger machine of industrialization. As is suggested in Mekas's introduction of Central Park-as-Walden (and as is consistently confirmed during the remainder of the film), for Mekas, the "natural" environment of the park is a way of making contact with his rural origins and the source of his identity, both of which he has been separated from by the industrial machines of modern Germany, the Soviet Union, and the other major nation-states whose decisions have determined Lithuania's modern history.

While both men see nature as a refuge from the machine of industrialized society, the century that separates them causes their depictions of nature to seem at first like inversions of each other. In 1845 Thoreau needed to go no farther than a couple of miles outside of Concord to achieve the feeling of solitude, and had he wished to be even more fully isolated, he need only have traveled a few miles farther. The location of Central Park on what was then the outskirts of New York City was a result of a combination of economic practicality (the less densely inhabited land was less expensive for the city to acquire) and of the same urge that took Thoreau to Walden Pond: the desire to leave the city behind, in order to access what the city could not offer. But judging from the imaging of the park in photography and cinema, the modern eye is less astonished by nature itself than by the spectacle of nature walled in by skyscrapers in virtually all directions, and by the "seam" between park and city. For Mekas, the beauty of Central Park was no longer a function of its being outside the city. Indeed, the park's location so dramatically inside the city provided Mekas with his *Walden*'s most essential insight into nature:

> In general I would say that I feel there will always be Walden for those who really want it. Each of us lives on a small island, in a very small circle of reality, which is our own reality. I made up a joke about a Zen monk standing in Times Square

with people asking, "So what do you think about New York—the noise, the traffic?" The monk says, "What noise? What traffic?" You *can* cut it all out. No, it's not that we can have all this today, but tomorrow it will be gone. It *is* threatened, but in the end it's up to us to keep those little bits of paradise alive and defend them and see that they survive and grow.[15]

The motif of Mekas's use of the various Central Park lakes in conjunction with his intertitle "WALDEN" is essentially a paradox: on the one hand, Mekas recognizes that his filming of the lakes and the crowds of walkers, ice skaters, and rowers who frequent them is virtually the opposite of the Thoreau of *Walden*, alone, gazing deep into the unruffled waters of Walden Pond at the dazzling pickerel and his soul. Indeed, on this level, Mekas's references to Walden might seem a form of humorous irony. On the other hand, however, this seeming irony unites the author and the filmmaker as fully as it distinguishes them.

While in the popular imagination, Walden Pond's isolation and Thoreau's solitude there seem at the heart of *Walden,* in fact, Thoreau was not a chronicler of "wilderness": even the pond's isolation was compromised, though not in a way he resents, by the train tracks that run past it across from his cabin. In fact, one of the most elaborate descriptions in *Walden*—a description located strategically in "Spring," the penultimate chapter of Thoreau's chronicle—focuses on the thawing of sand and clay on the sides of a deep cut "on the railroad through which [he] passed on [his] way to the village, a phenomenon not very common on so large a scale, though the number of freshly exposed banks of the right material must have been greatly multiplied since railroads were invented." For Thoreau, what happens on this hillside "illustrated the principle of all the operations of Nature. The Maker of this earth but patented a leaf."[16] That is, the essence of creativity and the hand of the Divine are as fully evident in those spaces where we feel nature and technology intersecting as in an "untouched wilderness." Mekas's *Walden* expands on Thoreau's insight by recording the myriad such spaces offered by Central Park and the New York City environment in general and by chronicling the many creators he meets who, like himself, do honor to the divine creativity in all of us. Mekas's camera is a twentieth-century version of Thoreau's house by the pond, and the legendary frugality of Thoreau's budget in "Economy" finds its modern echo in Mekas's low-budget, high-art "home movies."

Symbiopsychotaxiplasm: Take One

Central Park allows Mekas to pursue his solitary way within a "natural" environment. He is the quintessential "American" individualist. Indeed, even when he is with someone—as when he films Stan Brakhage crossing the park—Mekas remains a detached observer.[17] On the other hand, for William Greaves, who was an actor (dancer, songwriter) on Broadway and in commercial movies before he became a director, filmmaking is a fundamentally social activity, and he chose Central Park as the location for what became *Symbiopsychotaxiplasm: Take One* not only because it is a social space but also because of the kind of social space it is. While Mekas wanders through the park, recording what interests or touches him, Greaves uses the park as a background and a resource for a cinematic engagement of the ways in which creative individuals relate to one another when they find themselves outside the institutional structures within which their creativity is usually exploited. Indeed, for Greaves himself, the opportunity to participate in the project that generated *Symbiopsychotaxiplasm: Take One* came as an interruption of a busy career of producing sponsored documentary projects for such institutions as the United Nations and the U.S. Intelligence Agency.

Greaves made a name for himself in the 1940s on Broadway, where he was among the most sought after African-American actors of the period. His stage roles led to his appearing in several of the last Black Underground films of the 1940s—Herald Pictures' *Miracle in Harlem* (1948), Powell Lindsay's *Souls of Sin* (1949)—and to a small but crucial role in one of the major Hollywood "problem pictures" of the time: *Lost Boundaries* (1949), produced by Louis de Rochemont and directed by Alfred L. Werker. By the 1950s he had become interested in filmmaking, and in particular, in documentary. Seeing no way to develop a career as a documentarian in the United States, Greaves found his way to the National Film Board of Canada where he worked on dozens of Canadian productions, returning to the United States in 1963 a capable filmmaker. Since the 1960s Greaves has produced and directed dozens of films for others and for his own production company. A good many of these films chronicle aspects of African-American history, an ongoing interest that also found an outlet in the television series *Black Journal*, which Greaves produced, directed, and cohosted. By the time a well-heeled former acting student agreed to provide "angel" financing for a fully experimental film project of

Greaves's own devising, Greaves had a range of accomplishments and skills to call on, and he combined them in one of the most bizarre film productions of the 1960s—and a remarkable document of the attitudes of that era.

Greaves wrote a brief script for an argument between a man and a woman reminiscent of Edward Albee's *Who's Afraid of Virginia Woolf?*: the woman complains bitterly about the abortions her partner has pressured her into having and charges him with being a homosexual; the man denies he is gay, claiming the time just isn't right for them to have children (see fig. 58). The script for this argument was used as a screen test for five pairs of actors who were asked to perform the scene in a variety of ways. Don Fellows and Patricia Ree Gilbert, the leads in *Symbiopsychotaxiplasm: Take One*, played the scene as conventional melodrama; another pair performed it as a musical; still another, as a psychodrama. In addition to filming the various versions of the argument, the crew was directed to film themselves filming the actors: that is, Greaves conceived the various performances of the scene as a catalyst for the interaction of crew, performers, and director that was the real focus of the project. And, finally, Greaves also directed the crew to film their Central Park surround, whenever the activities of those observing the shoot seemed particularly interesting or energetic.[18]

Figure 58. The arguing couple in William Greaves's *Symbiopsychotaxiplasm: Take One* (shot in 1968, finished in 1972). Courtesy William Greaves.

Originally, Greaves's plan was to use the considerable footage recorded of the performances, the production process, and its Central Park environment for a series of five films: *Symbiopsychotaxiplasm: Take One, Take Two, Take Three, Take Four, Take Five,* each of which would center on one of the five pairs of performers. But the decision to run several cameras at once—necessary since the process of a cameraperson filming the performance could only be filmed by another camera—quickly used up Greaves's financial resources. The result was that sufficient material for all the projected "takes" was recorded, but only *Take One* was finished—and not for several years.

The intellectual sources for the *Symbiopsychotaxiplasm* project were several. Perhaps the most crucial of these is the source of the film's title, which is a take-off on "symbiotaxiplasm," the philosopher–social scientist Arthur Bentley's term (in his *An Inquiry into Inquiries*) for any particular social organism within which human beings interact with each other.[19] Greaves added "psycho" to Bentley's term, "to focus more acutely on the role that psychology and creativity play when a group of people come together and function as a creative entity charged with the responsibility of making a film."[20] Bentley's exploration of the various approaches to investigation in the social sciences is analogous to Greaves's project both on the level of the actors performing the screen test (which is always an inquiry into the abilities of the actors who perform it) and on the level of the crew recording the action of screen test and surround. Indeed, Greaves planned from the beginning to reveal his own personal vulnerability in the hope of energizing a multilayered inquiry into the cinematic process. For a crew accustomed to professional directorial decisiveness, this "vulnerability" appeared to be confusion, even incompetence—and it provoked rebellion. At one point, Gilbert becomes furious that she can't perform the scene the way she thinks Greaves wants her to and storms off, with Greaves following. Instead of recording their subsequent discussion, the crew, alienated from Greaves's process, remains behind. They also demonstrate their alienation by meeting together without Greaves's knowledge to discuss what seems to many of them the fiasco of the production. They filmed their discussion and gave the material to Greaves at the end of the production.[21]

In the end, Greaves was able to edit *Take One* so that viewers can sense the developing frustration of this particular social organism—but also to reveal his fascination with two scientific principles, the Heisenberg principle of uncertainty,

I began to think of the movie camera as an analog to the microscope. The reality to be observed is the human soul, the mind, the psyche. Of course, as the camera investigates that part of the cosmos, the individual soul or psyche being observed recoils from the intrusion. On-camera behavior becomes structured in a way other than it would have been had it been unperceived.

and the second law of thermodynamics,

In *Symbiopsychotaxiplasm,* the cameras trace the flow of energy in the social system I had devised. If the cameras focused on one person and the energy level of spontaneous reality began to decline as a result of their being under observation, that energy would shift and show up somewhere else—behind the cameras or among the bystanders, for example.[22]

Greaves's decision to use Central Park as the (only) location for his project has both general and particular relevance to the issues raised by the film. Most obviously, Greaves, like Mekas, sees the park as a space that allows people to leave—for a limited time—the rigidity of their workaday schedules and enter a more "creative" environment. This understanding of the park is relevant on all three levels of *Symbiopsychotaxiplasm: Take One.* For Alice and Freddy, the arguing couple, the expanses of Central Park provide both the psychic space and the comparative privacy to express their frustrations. The level of Alice's frustration and Freddy's surprise at her confronting him suggest that they have lived together, while repressing their problems, for some time; and this walk in the park is a result of Alice's desire to leave the puzzling "wonderland" of repression and let some fresh air into her life.

The park is equally relevant for the production process Greaves instigated. While the filming was done by men and women who had had considerable experience working on more conventional films, the very point of Greaves's method was to force both actors and crew into unfamiliar ways of working, in the hope of freeing them to be more openly creative than conventional film production allowed. The comparatively open spaces of Central Park are analogous to the creative space Greaves offered cast and crew, though ironically—like Freddy, who claims over and over not to know what Alice is talking about—they have come to be so at ease with their more usual (controlled, repressed) ways of working that they cannot make sense of what Greaves is doing. And even on the level of the park surround, those visiting the park who come across the production are rewarded with the spectacle of creative activity within a space originally created, at least in part, for their aesthetic pleasure.

The analogy of Greaves's film and Central Park goes deeper than the general idea that, as a created, artistic space, the park is an appropriate environment for creative activity. For one thing, the economic background of the *Symbiopsychotaxiplasm* project recalls the economic history of the park. The economic realties of commercial film production would never have allowed Greaves to conceive a feature-length experimental film—much less a set of five features.[23] Greaves's experiment was only possible because of the trickle-down effect of Greaves's "angel's" business success, combined with a respect for the creative process in general and Greaves as a creative person.[24] Further, just as Central Park, during its earliest years, was used primarily, or at least most visibly, by the rich,[25] *Symbiopsychotaxiplasm* was not only funded by independent wealth and shaped by the support of Greaves's patron (whose generosity made possible the extensive shooting and the shooting of the shooting), it was and has been available only to those with considerable cultural resources: *Symbiopsychotaxiplasm: Take One* has been seen primarily at film festivals, in colleges and universities, and in art museums, by people with sufficient leisure to pursue an interest in experimental cinema—that is, by people who are a modern version of "the carriage trade."[26] To put this another way, just as Central Park provides only the illusion of escape from the realities of New York City—"illusion" because it is surrounded by and, in the long run, serves the capitalist energies of businesses and businesspeople—*Symbiopsychotaxiplasm: Take One* is a brief cinematic "fling" made possible by a business success, which was followed by Greaves's quick return to a more conventionally productive filmic life in the city surrounding the park.[27]

Having said all this, however, I must make a substantial qualification. Even if one were to decide that Central Park was a result of nothing more noble than a combination of the financial interests of those who stood to gain from its construction and the self-serving, class-inspired, paternalistic romantic egos of Olmsted and Vaux,[28] in the long term the democratic idealism that Olmsted and Vaux claimed as the basis of the Greensward Plan has, in fact, become a reality: Central Park *is* used by a huge, diverse population in a very wide variety of ways, only a few of which can be said to be the property of the rich. This contemporary democracy of the park is clearly demonstrated by *Take*

One. The only "character" in the film who might be said to represent the rich is a woman who rides past the production on horseback early in the film.[29] And if the characters in the film's melodramatic story and those men and women doing the filming are middle-class professionals, the people who are watching the production appear more broadly representative economically.

In general, Greaves is at pains to assure a broad representation of park-goers. In the opening credits, for example, the names of those who worked on *Symbiopsychotaxiplasm: Take One* are superimposed over a montage of people using the park. This montage, which is so fully reminiscent of Edward Steichen's *The Family of Man* (1955) as to be virtually an homage, presents hundreds of people, seemingly of many heritages and a wide variety of economic circumstances, as representatives of the cycle of life: there are parents and babies, parents with older children, adolescent and young adults playing soccer, lovers . . .

Further, in the body of the film, Greaves and his crew interface with a number of bystanders, most notably a middle-aged, alcoholic, homeless man who "sleeps in the bushes." Though this homeless man represents the most economically disenfranchised class of New York City residents, the film gives him a substantial voice—indeed, he has the film's last words—and reveals him as an (at least accidentally) astute commentator on the production. His entrance into the film is announced on the sound track as we hear him say, "What is this thing? What is this thing? . . . Oh, it's a *movie*—so who's moving whom?" If this man (and others like him: he explains that there are "many sleeping in the bushes") has been excluded from or has dropped out of the economically productive sector of society, and is, as he explains, unrepresented politically, he has found at least a temporary refuge in the park, just as Greaves's film has provided the man with a momentary escape from his social invisibility by offering him at least one brief moment of democratic "representation."

A final dimension of the analogy between Central Park and *Take One* involves the issue of race. As mentioned earlier, at the outset the Central Park project displaced the particularly successful African-American community at Seneca Village. Whether or not this was part of a conscious plan, the comparative sacrifice of African Americans in the interest of goals devised by European Americans seems of a piece with the history of American racial politics (a history also evoked by the fact that this community was named *Seneca* Village). Regardless of the racial attitudes of those who planned and developed

Central Park, however, the forces of history have encouraged the racial integration some nineteenth-century New Yorkers might have avoided. By the 1920s African-American migration from the South had transformed Harlem, which lies directly north of the park, into one of the largest and most visible African-American communities in the nation. And by the 1960s the northern migration of Hispanics had further transformed sectors of this community into "Spanish Harlem." These transformations of Central Park's surround have transformed the nature of the community using the park for recreation, and this transformation is visible in *Symbiopsychotaxiplasm: Take One*. For example, a group of adolescents observing the filming with whom Greaves and the crew interact early in the film are primarily African American and Hispanic.

The integration evident within the park is also visible on the production level of the film, not only in the fact that Greaves himself is African American, but also in his mixed-race crew and cast. Two crew members (Clive Davidson and Phil Parker) are black, and one of the five pairs of actors who dramatize the argument is a mixed-race couple: the 1972 version of *Take One* ends with final credits superimposed over shots of an African-American woman (Audrey Heningham) and her European-American partner (Shannon Baker); the 1995 revision ends the same way, but shots of this mixed-race pair also introduce the film. There seems little ethnic friction between cast and crew. Indeed, Greaves claims, "The people who worked on *Symbiopsycho-taxiplasm* were Age-of-Aquarius-type people who were in many respects shorn of the racist encumbrances that many White Americans are burdened with"[30]—though when Don Fellows jokingly says to Greaves, "You wanted to say a few words for George Wallace," Patricia Ree Gilbert's laughter seems forced and embarrassed, revealing perhaps that for the cast and crew race was not entirely invisible.

More suggestive than the fact of Greaves's decision to use a mixed-race cast and crew is the way in which Greaves conceptualized his role as director vis-à-vis race:

> [C]learly we were working in a context of the urban disorders of the Sixties and the rage of the African-American community against the tyranny and racism of the American body politic. Plus the more specific struggles: the Civil Rights marches[,] . . . the whole Vietnam War problem and the growing dissent over it. There was the emerging Feminist movement. . . .
>
> This film was an attempt to look at the impulses and inspirations of a group of

creative people who, during the making of the film, were being "pushed to the wall" by the process I as director had instigated. The scene that I had written was fixed, and I was in charge. I was insisting that this scene would be done by the cast and crew, even though it was making them very unhappy. The questions were, When will they revolt? When would they question the validity, the wisdom, of doing the scene in the first place? In this sense, it really was a metaphor of the politics of the time.[31]

If in the mid-nineteenth century even the most successful of African-American communities could not slow the development of the park, by 1968 an African-American director could not only take charge of a mixed-race production, but he could also see himself as a representative of "the Establishment." No one could argue that racism had disappeared by the mid-1960s, even in Central Park; but by 1968 Greaves himself had lived through substantial changes insofar as his own access to the means of film production was concerned.

That Greaves functions as the Establishment in *Take One*, however, will not blind anyone familiar with American film history to the fact that Greaves's access to directorial control in this instance is anything but representative of the era. (See fig. 59.) Indeed, one could argue that in the 1950s and 1960s opportunities for African Americans to direct commercial film were at a nadir: the increasing inclusion of black performers in some Hollywood films had cost the Black Underground cinema its audience, and it was not until the 1980s that some African Americans began to have anything like a regular opportunity to direct. At most, Greaves enacts a metaphor for the Establishment: he *is* in charge of this particular production, but the project itself is as distant from the established, white-dominated business of cinema as Central Park is from Hollywood.

Symbiopsychotaxiplasm: Take One is rich with paradox. For one thing, it was precisely Greaves's distance from the commercial mainstream that allowed him the opportunity to experiment with the film process and form and provided him with a mind-set that saw improvisation—on location and later in the editing room—as a logical creative option (an option located within the larger history of African-American creativity by Greaves's use of Miles Davis's "In a Silent Way" to accompany the credits and as a motif during the rest of the film). Further, even if Greaves's sense of himself as the Establishment is, in a larger sense, ironic, considering the general lack of opportunity for

Figure 59. William Greaves shooting what became *Symbiopsychotaxiplasm: Take One* in 1968. Courtesy William Greaves.

African Americans to direct, nevertheless, the visual motif of Greaves and his cast and crew moving through Central Park provides us with at least an image of film history moving in the direction of equal opportunity. In this context we can see a poignancy in the fact that one of the few identifiable locations in the park, other than the bridge at the northwest corner of the Lake, is a monument located just to the west of the Sheep Meadow and to the north of Tavern on the Green, erected in honor of fifty-eight men of the New York National Guard's Seventh Regiment who were lost during the Civil War. The monument, which is one of several locations where Alice and Freddy argue, is a reminder (a conscious one, according to Greaves) of the centuries-long road toward societal freedom and equal access African Americans had had to travel before even the *metaphor* of cinematic power provided by *Symbiopsychotaxiplasm: Take One* would be possible.

From our perspective at the beginning of the twenty-first century, it is difficult to imagine New York City without Central Park. Even if we see the park as merely a space in the service of capitalist goals, that it continues to exist in a section of the city where land values are as high as anywhere in the world is a testament to the fact that the idea of nature has remained a crucial component of the American psyche, so crucial that anyone interested in transforming the park must confront considerable resistance on the part of New Yorkers from a variety of classes. Central Park remains not only another instance of capitalist development, but a space that a good many of us continue to find startlingly beautiful and an aid to both physical and spiritual health. Similarly, even if we see all forms of "experimental" or "personal" cinema as trickle-down results of the moneyed commercial film industry, the cinematic alternatives demonstrated by Mekas's *Walden* and Greaves's *Symbiopsychotaxiplasm: Take One* reveal that as long as the industry remains powerful, those willing to offer creative alternatives to it will not only continue to work, they will evolve in stature. While Mekas may have assumed that *Walden* would be of interest only "to some of his friends and a few strangers" and even if *Symbiopsychotaxiplasm: Take One* represents a momentary interruption of a more conventional documentary career, these two films have become increasingly interesting as time has passed—at least for that substantial group of us who remain fascinated by the full spectrum of film history. Indeed, it is difficult to think of two commercial films of the 1960s that look more impressive today than these alternative films do. Whatever the nature of their limitations, Central Park and the films by Mekas and Greaves for which the park has served as explicit location and implicit inspiration offer a set of visionary experiences that continue to enrich our sense of the past and the present.[32]

chapter 8

Rural (and Urban) Hours

[T]he contrast of the country with the city and the court: here nature, there worldliness. This contrast depends, often, on just the suppression of work in the countryside, and of the property relations through which this work is organised, which we have already observed. But there are other elements in the contrast. The means of argricultural production—the fields, the woods, the growing crops, the animals—are attractive to the observer and, in many ways and in the good seasons, to the men working in and among them. They can then be effectively contrasted with the exchanges and counting-houses of mercantilism, or with the mines, quarries, mills and manufactories of industrial production. That contrast, in many ways, still holds in experience.

But there is also, throughout, an ideological separation between the processes of rural exploitation, which have been, in effect, dissolved into a landscape, and the register of that exploitation, in the law courts, the money markets, the political power and the conspicuous expenditure of the city.

The rhetorical contrast between town and country life is indeed traditional.

RAYMOND WILLIAMS, *THE COUNTRY AND THE CITY*

From our perspective at the beginning of the twenty-first century, the fascination of so many nineteenth-century American painters with rural and wilderness landscape can seem—depending on one's predilections—a poignant, quaint, or silly refusal to come to terms with the arrival of the industrial revolution in North America. Some painters saw that further development was inevitable but used painting to warn those indifferent to the beauties of nature about what, in a spiritual sense, the transformation of nature into modern culture might cost. Others saw development itself as the divine plan for the Western Hemisphere and traveled to the farthest reaches of New World territory to celebrate Manifest Destiny while avoiding its results, at least for the moment. And still others looked for ways to maintain forms of spiritual contact through nature regardless of the extent of development, and even within development itself.

On another level, however, virtually all the painters who committed their art to the representation of landscape were men of the city. They may or may not have been born in cities, but they came to live in major urban centers because that's where paintings were bought and sold. Indeed, while they may have made frequent trips into rural areas, and to wilder regions as well, to make pencil and oil sketches, generally they returned to the city to produce their paintings.[1] In some cases—Thomas Cole and Frederic Church are examples—long-term economic success enabled painters to finally leave the city and take up permanent or seasonal residence in a rural surround. But by the time Church was settled in Olana, high above the Hudson, the river had become one of the major industrial thoroughfares of the republic and New York City businessmen were increasingly concerned that the continued denuding of the

Adirondack forests might lower the water levels of New York rivers and the Erie Canal and slow the exploitation of the continent.

A century or so later, a generation of American independent filmmakers were confronting the urban/rural distinction, but in a new way. While nineteenth-century landscape painters had focused their painting on what was disappearing or, really, had already disappeared—a rural or wilderness experience unaffected by urban realities and stresses—this generation of filmmakers lived lives that made impossible any pretense of being able to avoid the urban: indeed, as they were well aware, their chosen art form—their "paintbrush"— was one of the quintessential products of the industrial revolution (Hollis Frampton called cinema "the last machine," a gesture that on the one hand suggested his pride in being part of modernity and on the other, perhaps, betrayed a Thomas Cole–like hope that that the domination of the continent by the machine would have a limit). For this generation of artists, the issue was not how to reverse or slow or even ameliorate the impact of the urban on the rural and the wild, but how to create a livable integration of the inevitable (and often wonderful) urban and the historically modified (but still salutary) rural.

Life Considered/Life Experienced: Hollis Frampton's *Zorns Lemma* and Robert Huot's *One Year (1970)* and *Rolls: 1971*

> Sometimes I try to imagine what it must be like to be illiterate. Of course, it's impossible to imagine. Once we can read, and a word is put before us, we cannot not read it. —HOLLIS FRAMPTON[2]

> There was no bullshit about Bob Huot; he didn't have the time or language for it. He was always about his business. —TWYLA THARP[3]

During the late 1960s and early 1970s, a variety of factors was contributing to a more complex balance between urban and rural life on the part of a good many independent filmmakers. Improved and cheaper transportation was making it easier for filmmakers to live in two regions at once. Perhaps the most famous and elaborate double existence was for a time Stan Brakhage's. Brakhage's domestic life with his wife, Jane, and their six children (a domesticity Brakhage chronicled in dozens of films) was spent at nine thousand feet in the Rockies, twenty miles outside of Boulder, Colorado; his work life—that is, the job that earned him sufficient money to support his family and his filmmaking—was at the School of the Art Institute of Chicago. For well over a decade, beginning in the late 1960s, Brakhage commuted from the Rockies to Chicago on a biweekly basis. If few commutes from home to job, from rural to urban, were as elaborate as Brakhage's, many filmmakers of the time— filmmakers who realized that the kinds of films they were committed to making were *not* going to provide them with a livable income—were accepting jobs in educational institutions in urban areas but developing domestic and filmmaking lives at a considerable distance from their jobs. Two such filmmakers were Hollis Frampton and Robert Huot, who had become close friends in New York City and then moved upstate—Huot to live on a farm outside of New Berlin, in central New York State, about four hours from his teaching job in the Art Department of Hunter College in Manhattan; Frampton to teach in the Department of Media Studies at the State University of New York at Buffalo and to live in rural central New York (near Eaton, a three- to four-hour drive from Buffalo). Huot arrived in central New York in 1970 and helped Frampton find a house, about twenty miles to the west of Huot's farm, in 1971. Both commuted between work and home weekly; and both made films that reflect their attempt to adjust to this new life. Indeed, their filmmaking of the early 1970s can be understood as a cinematic dialogue, or perhaps more precisely, a point-counterpoint in which Huot's first two "diary" films suggest an answer to Frampton's *Zorns Lemma* (1970).

In the cinematically marginal world of "avant-garde" film, Frampton's *Zorns Lemma* is relatively well known as one of the classic "structural films" of the late 1960s and early 1970s.[4] *Zorns Lemma* is about epistemology—specifically, the process of learning to understand in a modern, literate society—a process Frampton divides into three parts. During the brief (2 minutes, 14 seconds) opening passage, viewers watch a dark screen and listen to a schoolmarmy voice read alphabetic verses from *The New England Primer* (1683), one of the most widely read books in seventeenth-century New England. This experience is a metaphor for the "darkness" of childhood, before the ability to read has freed the young child's intellect; and perhaps (if one also reads *Zorns Lemma* as a metaphor for American history) for the "dark ages" of the early settlement of New England when, at least from a modern perspective, religious intolerance constricted intellectual freedom. *The New England Primer* verses have the twofold goal of teaching the alphabet (each verse includes an alphabetized word—"In *Adam's* fall we sinned all"; "Thy life to mend God's *Book* attend"; "The *Cat* doth play, and after slay"[italics mine])—and of promulgating a Puritan brand of Protestantism.[5]

The second part of *Zorns Lemma* is by far the longest (47 minutes) and most complex. While there is virtually nothing to see in the opening section,[6] there is almost too much to see in the second section (this part of the film is silent). Frampton uses the twenty-four-letter Roman alphabet (*I* and *J*, *U* and *V* are treated as single letters) taught in *The New England Primer*—an implicit allusion to the normal running speed of sound film of twenty-four frames per second—as a structuring device for arranging 2,640 one-second shots into a giant montage. At the beginning of this montage, viewers are seeing set after set of alphabetized environmental words,[7] nearly all of them filmed in Lower Manhattan, where Frampton lived at the time (each set of 24 one-second shots is divided from the next by one second of dark leader). Letter by letter, each position in the alphabetic sequence is replaced by one-second segments of ongoing activities (A: hands turning the pages of a book; B: a close-up of an egg frying . . . Z: waves breaking on a beach) (see figs. 60, 61). The changeover from alphabetized environmental words to ongoing imagery is gradual and unpredictable: first-time viewers have no way of knowing when a letter will be replaced, or which letter will be replaced next; the final replacement—of a red ibis flapping its wings, for C—occurs in the final set of images in the section.

The second part of *Zorns Lemma,* like the first, creates an essentially metaphoric experience. In Frampton's view, the phantasmagoria of language that begins once a child has isolated the concept of the alphabet from the moralistic yeses and nos of early childhood is simultaneously thrilling and a bit overwhelming, but in any case, a wonderful change from the intellectual "darkness" of the child's first years.[8] The environmental words are quite various and unpredictable, and their environmental contexts are generally colorful and dynamic: Frampton's camera is hand-held and words, for example, in store windows, are often filmed so that one can see, reflected in the window glass, pedestrians and moving traffic behind and around the camera. Once the initial excitement wears off and replacement of the words begins, the "work" of seeing the experience through to a conclusion takes over. In fact, this process suggests the rigors of workaday life (Frampton: "Image B is the frying of an egg; it is, after all, breakfast time; we have turned a new leaf in the book,

Figures 60-61. Turning the pages of Antonio Pigafetta's diary of the voyage of Magellan, the replacement image for the letter *A;* and frying an egg, the replacement for the letter *B;* both in Hollis Frampton's *Zorns Lemma* (1970). Film stills by Biff Henrich. Courtesy Marion Faller.

and we're at the start of a new day. . . . Image W is at the end of the day; it's a journey through an urban environment, through the night streets where only the lights are visible, and that is the last part of the [daily] cycle proper. I did try to take a little care . . . to present things at the appropriate times of day in relation to the frying of the egg and the journey through the night").[9] The relentless, repetitive process of the second section leaves most first-time viewers exhausted and relieved when the section concludes. Epistemologically, the experience represents the process of language-centered education, which, in American life, begins in early childhood and ends, at least in the popular mind, when adult students are released from the time-organized rigors of academic life and must learn to function in the "real world." The stamina asked of the viewer suggests the stamina required for any serious learning experience.

The twelve-minute, final section includes both sound (six women read a passage from Robert Grosseteste's *On Light, or the Ingression of Forms*—an eleventh-century treatise on the structure of the universe—alternating one word at a time, in conjunction with a metronome that continues the one-second rhythm of the previous section) and imagery (four 100-foot-roll-long shots reveal a man, a woman, and a dog traversing a rural winterscape: they begin in the foreground and move away from the camera until they enter a woods on the far side of a small dell) (see fig. 62). Frampton focuses the section on two forms of motion: the movement of man/woman/dog into the distance and the subtle changing of natural light that regularly punctuates their journey across the field, as the winter wind periodically blows clouds across the sun. The section as a whole is punctuated by Frampton's need to remove one roll of film from the camera and put another in—changeovers evident in the combination of the walkers standing still, of slightly more dramatic alteration in the light from the end of one roll to the beginning of the next, and of tiny bits of flare evident at ends and beginnings of the rolls of film.[10] The final roll—the final shot in the section and in *Zorns Lemma*—ends with an extended flare that turns the winterscape to pure light.

Just as the experience of the first two sections of *Zorns Lemma* can be read metaphorically, the final section can be understood as Frampton's recognition that the forms of intellectual development suggested by the earlier parts of the film can, and perhaps in his personal case did, lead to a fuller, "more philosophical" sense of the world and of the human journey through it. That the final section of *Zorns Lemma* represents a spiritual quest is suggested by Frampton's visual emphasis on light and is confirmed by the reading of Grosseteste's text, in which the universe is seen as an emanation of divinity (Grosseteste was bishop of Lincoln when he composed *On Light*).

The three sections of *Zorns Lemma* can also be read historically. The brief, early section can be seen as representing the opening moments of European settlement in New England (and elsewhere): only a faith in the Word and the divinity of their mission allowed the Pilgrims to deal with what they saw as the

Figure 62. Robert Huot, Marcia Steinbrecher, and Colonel, the
dog, begin the walk across Huot's farm in the final section of
Zorns Lemma (1970).

great darkness of the Wilderness. The exhaustive, and exhausting, excursion
around Lower Manhattan during the second section of *Zorns Lemma* recalls
the urbanization and industrialization that made New York the prototype for
the American city. And the rural winterscape of the final section suggests the
American pastoral mode, which came of age in the work of Thomas Cole,
Frederic Church, and Asher B. Durand and later took a more ethereal form in
the work of the Luminists.

That Frampton's spiritual appreciation of the countryside was motivated by
the exhausting rigors of city life seems implicit in his decision to have the
Grosseteste text read, one word at a time, by six women, during the majority of
the final section. Indeed, the distracting quality of the reading is a means of
suggesting that, once the individual intellect has escaped early fears and has
developed within an urbanized cultural system, the rhythms of this system are
virtually impossible to escape: we can only long for a return to innocence, to
the Garden. Or, to return to the final section of *Zorns Lemma*, we can only see
a pastoral vision within the rhythm of language our culture has taught us.

This longing for a comparatively pristine nature (and all that it represents) from within a technologically mediated, urbanized world is encoded visually within the imagery of the final section of *Zorns Lemma*. Frampton framed the four roll-long shots so that the field is roughly bisected by a fence that the man and woman step over about halfway through their walk to the woods. Nine fence posts, each more or less equidistant from the next (and at the right and left sides of the frame, from the vertical frame-line) are visible. In a context of Grosseteste's numerology ("When the Number One of Form and the Number Two of Matter and the Number Three of Composition and the Number Four of Entirety are added together, they make up the Number Ten")[11] the fence posts suggest points along the horizontal axis of the fence, and the walkers' trajectory is suggestive of a vertical axis. In other words, the more closely one looks at the rural field that at first seems so distinct from the city environment of the central section of *Zorns Lemma*, the more evident is the fact that even this space encodes a Cartesian grid, on at least two levels: not only does Frampton's framing suggest a two-dimensional graph, but on the most literal level, the rectangular organization of these fields, emphasized by the fence, is as much a part of the overall Cartesian organization of space as is the film frame itself.

And yet, it is precisely our containment within physical limitations that makes a spiritual quest interesting and necessary. We may be separated from the innocence represented in so much of Western culture by the forest—and in America by the "wilderness"—by our cultural history and the geography that encodes it (as Frampton's camera is separated from the distant woods by the intervening fields), but in the end it is our awareness of this separation that inspires in us a desire to "see the light"—and in Frampton's case, to reframe cinema and cinema spectatorship. By the time he made *Zorns Lemma*, Frampton was—like anyone growing up in American society—well aware that cinema had become not only the quintessential industrial art form but also one of the most pervasive emblems of commercial culture. To make a film as thoroughly *intellectual* as *Zorns Lemma* was his way of critiquing and countering this powerful history, and of creating a (cinematic, intellectual) "Garden" where at least some filmgoers in the old age, "the winter," of film history could go to meditate on higher things.

To understand *Zorns Lemma* as part of a cinematic conversation between Frampton and Robert Huot, it is helpful to consider the biographical background of the imagery of the final section of *Zorns Lemma*. The specific field crossed by the man, woman, and dog was (and is) owned by Huot. In fact, it is Huot we see traversing the field with Martha Steinbrecher, Frampton's lover at the time.[12] Identifying Huot, and Frampton's relationship with Huot, has several implications. Just as Frampton's camera "follows" Huot's walk across his field, Frampton was literally to follow Huot to central New York. Indeed, to go one step further, Huot's dynamic way of experiencing life and relating to art— well known at the time—seems to have made a powerful impression on the younger Frampton. Huot's power and defiance of convention (see fig. 63) have been remembered by both Don McDonagh and Twyla Tharp.

In *The Rise and Fall and Rise of Modern Dance*, McDonagh describes one of Huot's early performances, *Wall*, at the Angry Arts Festival:

> Painter Robert Huot has some of the clean intellectuality of Alex Hay, but he possesses a belligerent forcefulness that removes his work from the fastidious. "Wall," . . . shows a clean sensitive feeling for motion overcoming obstruction. Having placed a white wall on stage, he demonstrated its strength by having a performer fling a hard rubber ball against it. After it had rebounded a number of times, the solidity of the wall was established. Suddenly a burly figure (Huot) burst through the wall in a physical demonstration of the power of determination. The wall was soundly constructed but the "dancer," moving with the requisite force, was able to break through the barrier it constituted.[13]

Tharp's memory is more romantic: in 1964, on a morning after attending a party at Huot's loft (he was then her downstairs neighbor), attended by, among others, Larry Poons, LaMonte Young, Yvonne Rainer, Robert Morris, Carl Andre, Rose Marie Costaro, Al Held, and Frampton, Tharp went down to help Huot clean up:

> As I picked up the last of the paper cups, I stopped to look at the [Huot] painting that had been the evening's center of attention. I saw now that the masking tape the hard-edge painters used to assure a razor-sharp line between color areas was still in place. Bob explained it hadn't been quite dry enough to strip off last night. He asked if I would like to pull the tape. I was a little nervous about ruining the painting, but Bob showed me that a steady, even pull would keep the paint from "chipping"—adhering as the masking tape came up. As I gently lifted the tape, Bob took my hand, guiding my motion. My body heated instantly, I loved his strength and size. I loved feeling his authority, feeling I could trust him with my body, feeling he knew what he was doing. We kissed gently. Then he lifted me off the ground and swung me round and round, ending the moment but increasing the desire.[14]

Figure 63. Robert Huot in costume for *War* (1961), a performance at Judson Church on Washington Square, by Huot and Robert Morris, with sound by LaMonte Young. Courtesy Robert Huot.

Figure 64. *Hero,* the word photograph Hollis Frampton gave to Robert Huot. Courtesy Robert Huot.

In the kitchen of Huot's farmhouse hangs a Frampton photograph from the series of photographs of environmental words that was the predecessor of the central section of *Zorns Lemma*—a gift from Frampton (see fig. 64). The photographed word is *Hero.* I read the final section of *Zorns Lemma* as a late-twentieth-century version of Asher B. Durand's *Kindred Spirits* (1849; see fig. 65), Durand's homage to Thomas Cole (who is seen near Kaaterskill Falls, teaching William Cullen Bryant about nature): as an homage to a teacher whose dynamic life, and work, had played a considerable role in his life, and in *Zorns Lemma.*

Both Frampton and Huot began to make films in 1966. Frampton, who had the necessary equipment first, helped Huot learn to use a motion picture camera and to splice 16mm film. Huot's earliest films confirmed tendencies already evident in his minimalist painting of the time. At first he used the strip of celluloid as a new surface on which to explore painterly interests: for *Spray* (1967), he spray painted eleven-plus minutes of clear leader; for *Scratch* (1967), he scratched into the emulsion for eleven minutes. But for his first long film—*One Year (1970)* (1971), which got under way just as Frampton was finishing *Zorns Lemma*—Huot changed his approach and began applying minimalist procedures to an ongoing documentation of his experiences adjusting to his new farm.[15]

Figure 65. In a Catskill Mountain landscape, Thomas Cole instructs William Cullen Bryant on using the natural world as the source for art, in Asher B. Durand's *Kindred Spirits* (1849), oil on canvas, 46" × 36". Collection of the New York Public Library, Astor, Lenox and Tilden Foundations.

One Year (1970) documents Huot's life from January 1970 until New Year's Eve, when he and Twyla Tharp, Huot's wife at the time, share a champagne toast. The film is organized chronologically and structured in the most straightforward way: Huot apparently shot a complete one-hundred-foot roll of 16mm film each time he worked on *One Year (1970)* (roughly once a week) and at the end of the year simply strung the rolls together. While *Zorns Lemma* is a heavily, even compulsively, edited film, Huot's *One Year* is a series of (silent) sketches of Huot's new farm (and an exploration of the filmic means at Huot's disposal), some of them subtle and lovely: the film's ninth roll, for example, is a mounted-camera meditation on a tiny crystal rivulet flowing through a snow-covered field. In this instance, Huot's technique matches his subject so closely that they become metaphors for each other. Just as the flow of the rivulet is interrupted and energized by a tiny "waterfall" in the center of the image, the flow of Huot's film through the camera is interrupted every thirty seconds and reenergized, when he must stop to rewind his Bolex.

Unlike Frampton, however, Huot refuses to make a clear distinction between country life and city life: *One Year (1970)* tends to alternate between the rural and the urban and sometimes records the trips from one to the other. Several rolls were shot in the neighborhood of Huot's Lower Manhattan apartment (the film's first four rolls are city scenes), three during automobile trips to and from New York City, and various rolls document Tharp and her dance troupe at work in a makeshift studio in the attic of the farmhouse and Frampton and Steinbrecher working with Huot to fix up Huot's new home. Further, instead of confirming, as Frampton—and most nineteenth-century painters—did, the traditional distinction between city life as conducive to busyness and rural life as conducive to serenity, Huot makes no filmic distinction between these disparate environments. Some rolls record farm and city in a manner that expresses a meditative sensibility; other rolls of both city and country do not. Of course, the length of *One Year (1970)*—160 minutes—and its generally serene pace reflect Huot's thoughtful seriousness in reorienting his life, now that he had the farm; but even this "meditative" dimension of the film is complex: at various times, Huot has presented *One Year (1970)* as a forty-minute, four-image piece (two images mounted directly above the other two), in which all four reels of the film—and in a sense all four seasons—are projected simultaneously.

After exploring his new environment and the new organization of his life necessitated by the farm in *One Year (1970)*, Huot made a second diary that confirmed the aesthetic approach developed in *One Year (1970): Rolls: 1971* (1972). And he began to make diary paintings as well as diary films (see fig. 66).[16]

At least implicitly, *Rolls: 1971* provided a more coherent answer to both *Zorns Lemma* and the traditional attitude toward city and country life Frampton's film shares with so many nineteenth-century paintings. In *Rolls: 1971*, Huot found a way to integrate a meditative sensibility with a more coherent vision of how this sensibility fits into day-to-day life. In *One Year (1970)*, Huot accepts the calendar year as an overall structure within which his activities are modularized into one-hundred-foot rolls of film, but for *Rolls: 1971*, he developed a more complex structure—a structure particularly reminiscent of *Zorns Lemma*—based, how-

Figure 66. During the years when Huot made his early diary films, he was also beginning what would become an extensive series of "diary paintings": he would buy ends of rolls of canvas from canvas wholesalers, and, rolling out one section at a time onto the floor of his studio, he would paint the canvas roll from one end to another, day by day. One of the roll-long shots in *Rolls: 1971* shows Huot and Twyla Tharp rolling out *Diary #16*. Pictured here is Huot's diary painting *Diary #28* (1973), oil on canvas (96" × 900" [approx. 25 yards]), photographed at Paula Cooper Gallery in New York City by Robert E. Mates and Paul Katz. Courtesy Robert Huot.

ever, not on a theoretical breakdown of the process of learning and the intellectual construct of the alphabet, but on his practical experiences working as a pigment chemist in New York City during the mid-1960s. *Rolls: 1971* alternates regularly between roll-long shots (thirteen altogether) and heavily edited passages made up of these same shots, divided—like the shots in the long middle section of *Zorns Lemma*—into one-second segments and arranged into visual versions of what pigment chemists call a drawdown (samples of pigment are placed on a sheet of glass and "drawn down" so that each sample can be seen next to all the others). Since thirteen different rolls make for a sizable and varied set of "samples," Huot's drawdown organization is complex.

Rolls: 1971 opens with the first drawdown, followed by the opening roll-long shot, and intercuts between drawdowns and roll-long shots throughout the film's ninety-six and a half minutes.

The fourth roll-long shot is of the same field filmed in the final section of *Zorns Lemma,* in the changing light of a cloudy summer day. However, Huot's shot of his dell doesn't betray the sense of a prearranged event so obvious in Frampton's imagery; it is varied only by subtle changes of chiaroscuro as a result of clouds passing over the summer sun (the entirety of *Rolls: 1971* is silent). That is, Huot's image of the dell is less an epistemological metaphor for the wisdom achieved in the "winter" of life and more a meditation on the moment itself.

After the first two or three drawdowns, the excitement generated by the quickly changing imagery tends to dissipate—just as does the visual excitement of the changing environmental words in the second section of *Zorns Lemma*. Of course, Frampton's choice of color for *Zorns Lemma* (except for two rolls, *Rolls: 1971* was shot in black-and-white) and the variety of both the environmental word images and the replacement images does mitigate against monotony, but *Rolls: 1971* has a more direct sensuality. Huot's compositions are generally arresting, either for their formal beauty (the film's opening roll of snowfall is stunning; a later roll of Twyla Tharp breast-feeding their son, Jesse, is simultaneously simple and mysterious; see fig. 67) or for their shock value: in the fifth complete roll, for example, Huot stands nude *on* a mirror, masturbating and filming simultaneously (the camera is mounted so that it points downward into the mirror)—a defiant response, perhaps, to the frequently expressed attitude at the time that "underground" or "experimental" film was a masturbatory exercise. Viewers tend to be repelled by the imagery

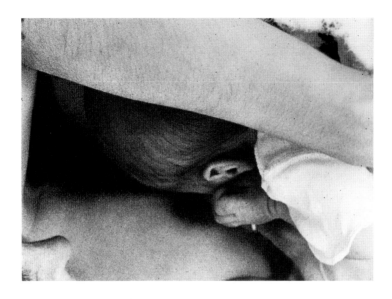

Figure 67. Twyla Tharp nursing Jesse Huot in Robert Huot's *Rolls: 1971* (1972). Courtesy Robert Huot.

(the roll flares out as Huot ejaculates onto the mirror) and dumbfounded by the strange, almost Escher-like composition.

In general, *Rolls: 1971* provides both of the experiences created by the second and third parts of *Zorns Lemma* but in an alternating, rather than a single, "progressive" overall design. Indeed, whereas *Zorns Lemma* must be seen in its entirety to be understood, Huot's serial organization allows *Rolls: 1971* to be sampled (the first reel would be plenty for most viewers). Huot's variation on the *Zorns Lemma* organization can be read as his answer to the vision provided by the earlier film—and unwittingly dramatized in Frampton's positioning of his camera, and himself, in the final section of *Zorns Lemma*. If one tends to stand ouside life, to contemplate the entirety of life as a theoretical enterprise, one might deduce that life is a period of intellectual darkness, followed by an exciting and exhausting period of education, followed by a period of serenity and wisdom. But for someone like Huot, who has never been comfortable in an intellectually detached stance toward experience, there is simply no point in pretending that life can be categorized the way *Zorns Lemma* presents it. For Huot, moments of serenity alternate with periods of frenzied activity, regardless of what age we are or where we happen to be living. Indeed, to go a step further, each type of experience continually makes the other necessary and possible. Both Frampton and Huot commuted from their teaching jobs to their country homes for sustained periods (Frampton from 1971 until his death in 1984), Huot from 1968 until his retirement from Hunter College in 1991). Both lived lives that literally took them back and forth from country to city. But while Frampton, as artist, tended to ignore the practical realities of his everyday life—a pattern equally traditional among nineteenth-century landscape painters—in favor of an intellectual interpretation of life's "essential" pattern, Huot's actual experience provided the model for the extended self-portrait accomplished in *Rolls: 1971*, a self-portrait that models the existential reality of most lives.

From our position more than a quarter century removed from the years when Frampton and Huot began to live their double lives, *Zorns Lemma* and the first Huot diary films have taken on a certain poignancy (see fig. 68). Frampton's early death from lung cancer (he was 49) in 1984 brought him to those snowy woods sooner than he might have considered likely in 1970. On

Figure 68. Robert Huot *(left)* and Hollis Frampton during the shooting of Huot's *Third One-Year Movie—1972* (1973). Courtesy Robert Huot.

the other hand, after Huot retired from Hunter College in 1991 (a decision that may have had something to do with Frampton's early demise), he became increasingly engaged with his farm and *in* that very field imaged in *Zorns Lemma* and *Rolls: 1971*. Indeed, he has come to see himself as a farmer, as well as a painter (Huot remains an active painter), and to recognize that raising quality Holstein heifers is a creative activity, that indeed it is just the sort of hands-on, working-class activity Huot always attempted to incorporate into his painting and filmmaking (and that Frampton recognized in having Huot paint a wall as the replacement image for the letter *K* in *Zorns Lemma*).[17] Huot has also become involved in local politics (he has served on the town council of Columbus, New York) and in trying to support what has, in recent years, become the increasingly marginal small dairy farm in central New York State.

Sacred Speed: Nathaniel Dorsky's *Hours for Jerome*

> What have the best of us done to merit one such day in a lifetime of follies, and failings, and sins? The air we breathe so pure and balmy, the mottled heavens above so mild and kindly, the young herb beneath our feet so delicately fresh, every plant of the field decked in beauty, every tree of the forest clothed in dignity, all unite to remind us, that, despite our own unworthiness, "God's mercies are new every day." . . .
>
> Christian men of ancient times were wont to illustrate the pages of the Holy Scriptures with choice religious paintings and delicate workmanship; they sent far and wide for the most beautiful colors; they labored to attain the purest lines, the most worthy expression, the most noble design. . . . And thus, to-day, when the precious Book of Life has been withdrawn from the cloisters and given to us all, as we bear its sacred pages about in our hands, as we carry its holy words in our hearts, we raise our eyes to the skies above, we send then abroad over the earth, alike full of the glory of Almighty Majesty,—great and worthy illuminations of the written Word of God. ——
> SUSAN FENIMORE COOPER, *RURAL HOURS*, "TUESDAY, [MAY] 16TH"[18]

Virtually from the beginning of what in recent years has come to be called "American Nature Writing," the cycle of the seasons has been seen as a useful structuring device: it informs James Fenimore Cooper's *The Pioneers* (1823), Susan Fenimore Cooper's *Rural Hours* (1850), and, of course, Thoreau's *Walden* (1854), as well as such modern landmarks of the genre as Aldo

Leopold's *A Sand County Almanac,* part 1 (1948), and Josephine Johnson's *The Inland Island* (1968). In all these works, the seasonal organization—whether it's constructed from more than a single year, as in *Walden,* or it is a record of a particular calendar year—provides a rough grid within which the author can present the sorts of precise observation that are the hallmark of nature writing. While some writers focus on more remote biota and others on biota already bounded or surrounded by development, the tendency has been to isolate oneself from the forces of transformation as fully as possible and to see how the seasonal cycle develops in these isolated places. Of course, even in the nineteenth century, real isolation was tenuous at best: Thoreau sees the train go by Walden Pond; Josephine Johnson's "island" is invaded by the sounds of nearby farmers, by the poisoned runoff of pesticides, and even the Vietnam War makes itself felt.

Like much nineteenth-century landscape painting, nature writing is generally elegiac, a plea—to put it in Leopold's words—"for the preservation of some tag-ends of wilderness" within the unpreventable, combined forces of the "exhaustion of wilderness in the more habitable portions of the globe" and the "world-wide hybridization of cultures though modern transport and industrialization."[19] By the 1960s, in fact, the hunger for solitude in nature could be (momentarily) assuaged in only three ways: by going to the remotest areas left on the globe (as Barry Lopez does in *Arctic Dreams* [1986]—indeed, his remoteness allows him a new sense of temperate zone seasonality itself);[20] by learning to focus with great intensity on extremely limited spaces, as is done in many Japanese gardens and in the painter Charles Burchfield's explorations of his backyard; and, finally, by learning to see the interplay of development and natural biota with new eyes. This last approach informs the two most remarkable seasonally structured American independent films I'm aware of: Larry Gottheim's *Horizons* (1973), the subject of chapter 2, and Nathaniel Dorsky's *Hours for Jerome* (1982).[21]

By the time he completed *Hours for Jerome,* Dorsky had completed a trilogy of short films on growing up in small-town America: *Ingreen* (1964), *A Fall Trip Home* (1964), and *Summmerwind* (1965). Shot in Millburn, New Jersey, a small suburb west of New York City, the triology dramatizes a young, gay man's coming-to-awareness, focusing on three aspects of personal development: the sensual (*Ingreen*), the social (*A Fall Trip Home*), and the aesthetic (*Summerwind*). Throughout the trilogy, the young Dorsky's talent as a visual artist is obvious; but in the middle of shooting *Summerwind,* his taking a cube of LSD transformed his way of seeing, allowing him to focus more intensely on the forest scenes that frame the film—"I had thought I was in rural New Jersey; but under the influence, I saw it was the Forest Primeval!"[22]—and on his images of small-town life. The new clarity and intensity of vision that developed in *Summerwind* also informed the imagery Dorsky shot in the late 1960s for what would, a decade later, become *Hours for Jerome,* and it has continued to be a hallmark of his films.[23]

The title of *Hours for Jerome* is a reference to the medieval *Book of Hours,* the prayer book that was produced in many versions in various European countries from the mid-thirteenth to the mid-sixteenth century (see fig. 69). Generally, each version of *The Book of Hours* included a variety of information crucial for Catholics, in this order: a calendar of fast days, a set of Gospel lessons, and the following prayers: the Hours of the Virgin (the Infancy Cycle and the Passion Cycle), the Hours of the Cross and the Hours of the Holy Spirit, the "Obsecro Te" and "O Intemerata" (two special prayers to the Virgin), the penitential Psalms and Litany, a set of Accessory Texts, "a nearly inexhaustible array of ancillary prayers," and finally the Office of the Dead.[24] Of course, a central interest of *The Book of Hours,* then and now, was its extensive and widely varied "illumination." The elaborate illustration of the texts of *The Book of Hours* seems to have served something of the purpose of modern motion pictures. The illustrations visualized and energized the daily and yearly motion of life; and, like particular movie genres, were able to entertain a mass audience (the Catholic laity, not the church-ordained, were the primary users of *The Book of Hours*) by providing nearly endless visualizations and interpretations of familiar texts and well-known stories.[25] While *The Book of Hours* represented a democratic development in medieval society, and thus, in a sense, a movement in the direction of modern life, Dorsky's decision to evoke *The Book of Hours* in *Hours for Jerome* was an attempt by a modern, working in one of the quintessential modern media, to use cinema as a means connecting the viewer with a sense of experience more medieval than modern: specifically, to reaccess something of the sacred.

Like Susan Fenimore Cooper's journal entries in *Rural Hours,* Dorsky's images in *Hours for Jerome* are conceived as prayers—in this case dedicated to his lifelong partner, Jerome Hiler, as a way of honoring their connection.[26] But while Cooper's "Hours" are rural, Dorsky's are both rural and urban; and

Quadã die leo claudicãs monasteriũ igrellus
est ieronimi aurc aim ceti fugent q̃ hospin obui
at leo pede ohdit q̃; adhibita aira diligent̃
librat̃ur er oĩ feritate ꝓposita inter eos habitat

Figure 69. *Story of Saint Jerome: Jerome Heals a Lion,* from *The Book of Hours, The Belles Heures de Jean de France* (ca. 1412), as reproduced in *The Belles Heures of Jean, Duke of Berry, Prince of France* (New York: At the Cloisters/Metropolitan Museum of Art, 1958). This particular catalog's depiction of Saint Jerome was an important influence on Dorsky's *Hours for Jerome* (1982). The pages of the original manuscript measure 6⅝" × 5⅜". Courtesy Metropolitan Museum of Art.

these visual prayers make no spiritual distinction at all between country and small-town living and life in New York City, America's quintessential metropolis: for Dorsky, *all* locations offer the possibility of spiritual life. While the overwhelming majority of films are in the service of the forces of development and financial accumulation, Dorsky sees his own films as ways of being in touch with a higher self, a cinematic space wherein the viewer can reassess, for brief moments, a visual innocence—Edenic instants outside conventional time and day-to-day stress.

Hours for Jerome includes sixty-six visual "prayers," organized into two sections: Part One (spring and summer: twenty-eight prayers); and Part Two (fall and winter: thirty-eight prayers). Seen at eighteen frames per second, the film lasts fifty-five minutes (more on the "correct" projection speed for Dorsky's films later). *Hours for Jerome* creates a composite year: Dorsky shot imagery from 1966 to 1970 and didn't begin editing until 1980. Within this meta-year each individual section is separated from the one that follows by two seconds of deep blue; and each section, each prayer, is composed as a mini-film in its own right *and* as a piece that has a variety of relationships with the mini-films that precede and follow it. Further, each "prayer" is an instance of one or another of the motifs that Dorsky develops during the film, the most general of which is the alternation between imagery of the country—in and around Lake Owassa in northern New Jersey (to the east of Kittatinny Mountain in the Delaware Water Gap National Recreation Area), where Dorsky and Hiler had a summer home—and of New York City, where Dorsky and Hiler had an apartment.

An individual section of *Hours for Jerome* can be a single shot (the film concludes with a single, six-second shot of Lower Manhattan), or a few shots, or a complex montage. The beginning four sections of Part One can serve as a representative passage. *Hours for Jerome* opens with a thirty-three-second shot of light breaking through an early spring woods; it is dawn, the coming of "new light" in the daily cycle, the yearly cycle, and cinematically: this was, at least in Dorsky's mind, the beginning of a new approach to filmmaking. This long first shot introduces the first "prayer," which altogether is made up of eleven subsections, ten of which are single shots (the eleventh is a mini-montage of a single space in which each pair of frames involves enough of an adjustment of the camera to create almost a strobe impact). All eleven subsections are images of a woods in early spring, though Dorsky constructs the ninety-six-second passage so that it has a particular contour, visually and rhythmically.[27] The passage provides counterpoints between longer and shorter takes, between long shots and close-ups, between gold and green, between changes in nature and visual variations created by the camera.

A different form of organization is evident in the second section of Part One, which is made up of twenty-nine shots in thirty-five seconds. In this case, Dorsky uses an intercutting strategy, at first cutting between color shots of clouds moving quickly across a blue sky and black-and-white close-ups of a TV screen on which no imagery can be identified: there is only a distorted signal. Near the end of the passage, a third element is added: three panoramic long shots of Appalachian mountains and clouds (altogether, there are eighteen shots of clouds moving across blue sky and eight close-ups of the TV screen). The generally high-speed intercutting of the passage is emphasized by the fact that the eighteen shots of clouds were composed and arranged so that the direction of the cloud movement is obviously different each time we see the clouds. This disparity in direction is counterpointed by the relative consistency of the imagery on the TV screen and by the fact that the three panoramic landscape shots are virtually identical. In addition to the formal rhythms of section two, Dorsky implies a conceptual connection between the clouds moving through the atmosphere and the television signal, which also (this is the late 1960s) comes by air, and perhaps is distorted by the weather.

Sections three and four form a counterpoint to the visual complexities of sections one and two (which, of course, are also in a contrapuntal relationship with each other). Both the third and fourth sections are brief (eight seconds and nineteen seconds, respectively), and each is composed of two shots. Section three is two shots of a man at a service station wiping the windshield of a station wagon, the first filmed at a slightly greater distance than the second. The first shot of section four is of a woods (similar to the woods in the first and third shots of section one, though there is more green now) shaking in a breeze; the second shot is of Jerome Hiler sitting by a window (outside of which we can see a bit of woods) on a sunny day, reading the paper. About halfway through the shot, he turns a page—a movement contrapuntal to the consistent shaking of the trees in the first shot. The clear difference in the two shots of section four is a "response" to the similarity of the shots in section three—just as the pair of brief passages "respond" to the two longer passages that precede them. Of course, as different as the four opening sections are in a more general sense, they are all dimensions of country living: section six brings us into New York City, adding still another variable to the opening and establishing the rural/urban rhythm that dominates the film.

While the overall structure of *Hours for Jerome* is sequential both in its presentation of the yearly round and in Dorsky's organization of successive sections so that they, to use Sergei Eisenstein's phrasing, create a series of formal and conceptual "collisions" that drive the film forward from day to day and season to season,[28] Dorsky has also shaped Parts One and Two so that every new subsection provides a variation on one or several motifs established and confirmed by earlier sections, *and* so that the two major subdivisions of the film can function as a diptych. Two memorable instances of Dorsky's using a passage in Part Two to echo a passage in Part One (there are many such echoes in *Hours for Jerome*) involve, in the first instance, the use of slow motion and, in the second, a vivid sense of three-dimensionality.

Late in Part One (in the twenty-third subsection, 1 minute, 49 seconds long), Dorsky presents two views of people walking along New York streets, in slow motion. Because of Dorsky's framing and his use of slow motion, the sequence is evocative of Eadweard Muybridge's motion photographs and his use of the Zoopraxiscope to present everyday human activities. These slow-motion walkers are echoed in section twenty-eight of Part Two: six shots of people walking, again in slow motion, in this instance in a park (I assume Central Park). There are obvious differences in the two sequences (city street/park; summer/winter; camera filming across the flow of pedestrian traffic/camera positioned so walkers walk toward and away from the camera), but the similarity of the passages—walkers in slow motion—is obvious.

The 3-D "echo" involves a passage early in Part One (section six) and another early in Part Two (section five). For the spring sequence Dorsky filmed branches of trees just after the green-gold leaves have appeared; and by carefully controlling his distance from the branches, the number of frames he exposed, and the particular sequencing of his brief shots, and by using the varying qualities of light this particular day gave him, he creates an astonishing sense of three-dimensionality. The sequence is magical. In the fall, a similar three-dimensional effect is created in an apple orchard; this time the magical impact of the sequence is a function of time-lapsed natural light illuminating different spaces within the overall compositions of the shots. The more fully viewers attend to *Hours for Jerome,* the more complex Dorsky's development of similarities within the differences and differences within the similarities becomes.

That Jerome is seen in the orchard sequence, picking and eating an apple, can serve as a metaphor for the visual experience Dorsky means to create. During the shooting of this sequence, Dorsky and Hiler joked about Hiler's being "Adam," and for Dorsky this connection is essential.[29] He means to return us to an innocence of vision, a way of seeing film imagery, not only outside the usual demands of commerce and narrative thrust, but even outside those forms of polemic so popular in the world of independent cinema in recent years. While Dorsky certainly admires the best of the commercial cinema and is in sympathy with many independent critiques of industry ideology, his commitment is to use filmmaking as a spiritual practice that can help us refine our vision in an era he sees as addicted to distraction.

For Dorsky, as for many artists of the era, the discovery of LSD and marijuana led to a new sense of the visual that was simultaneously—paradoxically—more meditative and more intense than the more "practical" ways of seeing implicitly polemicized by social institutions, including the conventional cinema. For those using LSD and marijuana, time often seemed to slow down as space opened up, revealing the spectacularity of the everyday visual world. *Hours for Jerome* is the quintessential "psychedelic" film, not in what has become the pejorative sense of the word (Dorsky does not provide us with hallucinations verging on the psychotic), but in the liberating sense of the term so widespread in the late sixties: it sings the possibility of an experiential ecstasy not dependent on material acquisition, the possibility of Vision accessible directly through vision.[30]

Dorsky's commitment to using cinema not as part of our culture-wide technological acceleration but to slow things down is also evident in his preference that, with few exceptions, his films be shown not at normal projection speed—24 frames per second (fps)—but at what for many years was called "silent speed," that is, 18 fps.[31] During the past quarter century, Dorsky's preference has become a challenge, since the most recent generations of 16mm projectors no longer offer the double option of sound speed and silent speed.[32] In 1998 Dorsky reedited *Hours for Jerome* and in the newest *Canyon Cinema Catalog,* No. 8 (1999), asks that Part One be shown at 18 fps and Part Two at

24 fps, though *ideally* he prefers that *both* parts be run at 21 fps (an option on only a tiny handful of available 16mm projectors)! Of course, Dorsky recognizes that most people who rent his films will decide to screen them at 24 fps—and certainly *Hours for Jerome* (and other Dorsky films, too) look wonderful at sound speed: even at a faster pace they interrupt most viewers' conventional rhythms. But he continues to ask that those committed to exhibiting his films make the extra effort to show them "correctly," because of his determination to resist the velocity of commercial life: "When I hear a projector running at twenty-four frames per second, I think of planes taking off; but when I hear a projector running at eighteen frames per second, it sounds like a cat purring. I want a more domestic, intimate, serene film experience. I'm not in a hurry to take off."[33]

If Dorsky cannot stop the acceleration of modern life, if he cannot do away with machines, he can at least do his best to slow the machines down, and to use them in ways that remind us that our spiritual options have nothing at all to do with whether we live an urban or a rural existence or a combination of the two.

Peter Hutton as Luminist

> The new landscape mode expressed—and in turn shaped—a growing mid-century appreciation for nature as a complex organic realm surrounding the human world. . . . The aesthetic of atmospheric luminism was grounded . . . in an identification with nature rather than an insistence on one's physical separation from it. . . . Instead of temporalizing space through planar divisions, atmospheric luminism spatialized time. In doing so it freed landscape art from its loyalties to a narrative or literary meaning.
> —ANGELA MILLER, *THE EMPIRE OF THE EYE*[34]

Barbara Novak's famous distinction between two approaches to American landscape in nineteenth-century painting—"grand opera" and "the still small voice"—remains useful for twentieth-century film, and not merely as a theoretical construct that assists in distinguishing different kinds of work developing from different aesthetic sensibilities.[35] The two areas of contemporary cinema that conform to Novak's categories are responses to the same set of historical developments that produced the paintings her *Nature and Culture*

Figures 70–71. Two "Luminist" paintings that achieve a quiet stillness analogous to the mood Peter Hutton creates in his films. *Above:* Fitz Hugh Lane's *Ipswich Bay* (1862), oil on canvas, 20" × 33⅛". Gift of Mrs. Barclay Tilton in memory of Dr. Herman E. Davidson. Courtesy Museum of Fine Arts, Boston. Reproduced with permission. © 2000 Museum of Fine Arts, Boston. All Rights Reserved. *Opposite:* Martin Johnson Heade's *Newburyport Meadows* (ca. 1875), oil on canvas, 10½" × 22". Metropolitan Museum of Art, Purchase, the Charles Engelhard Foundation Gift, in memory of Charles Engelhard; Morris K. Jesup, Marie DeWitt Jesup and Pfeiffer Funds; John Osgood and Elizabeth Amis Cameron Blanchard Memorial Fund; Thomas J. Watson Gift, by exchange; and Gifts of Robert E. Tod and William Gedney Bunce, by exchange, 1985 (1985.117).

surveys; and their positions vis-à-vis contemporary commercial culture are analogous to the positions occupied by the "grand operatic" painters and the "Luminists" with regard to mid-nineteenth-century commercial development. To a significant degree, the grand landscape epitomized by Frederic Edwin Church and the "Rocky Mountain school" (Albert Bierstadt, Thomas Moran, Thomas Hill) became, and has remained, the literal, as well as historical, background of epic commercial films, from the earliest attempts to interest filmgoers in natural scenes[36] to John Ford's *Stagecoach* (1939), *Fort Apache* (1948), and *The Searchers* (1956) to such recent popular hits as *Dances with Wolves* (1990) and *Legends of the Fall* (1995); and it has played a major role in the his-

tory of independent feature filmmaking, from Robert Flaherty's *Nanook of the North* (1921) to Godfrey Reggio's *Koyaanisqatsi* (1984) and Robert Fricke's *Baraka* (1993).[37] But the "still small voice" also seems alive, not as a major influence on commercial cinema, but as a sensibility of considerable use in coming to terms with a number of landmark American independent films of recent decades.

Art historians have defined "Luminism" in a variety of ways since John Baur coined the term in the 1940s,[38] to refer to the work of John Frederick Kensett, Sanford Gifford, Martin Johnson Heade, and Fitz Hugh Lane and to selected paintings by some Hudson River school painters, especially Cole and Church (see figs. 70, 71). Generally, Novak and others have described the Luminists as reflecting and offering a more meditative route to the spiritual than that provided by the awesome paintings of Church, Bierstadt, and Moran: "In contrast to the operatic landscape, Luminism is classic rather than baroque, contained rather than expansive, aristocratic rather than democratic, private not public, introverted not gregarious, exploring a state of being rather than becoming."[39] Stylistically, Luminism is identified with a particular rendering of atmospheric effects—specifically, as Angela Miller puts it, "a resonant, light-suffused atmosphere [that] melded topographic divisions into a visually seamless whole,"[40] often presented in comparatively small compositions extended along the horizontal. Generally, the paintings betray little or no evidence of the artists' "labor trail" so obvious in contemporaneous impressionist painting and in modernist work in general.

For an American cinematic progenitor of the Luminist sensibility evident in more recent independent films, there seems little point in exploring the origins of cinema. Faced with the challenge of turning the new medium of cinema into a popular, economically successful enterprise, filmmakers did the obvious: they attempted to impress viewers; and the last thing they could be expected to produce is a film that appealed to a meditative sensibility. By the late 1920s, however, as filmmakers began to reflect on cinema's high-speed commercial development, premonitions of a more meditative sensibility are evident in the films of Ralph Steiner and especially his H_2O (1929).

By the time he made H_2O, Steiner was already an accomplished still photographer. His interest in motion pictures seems to have developed from an ongoing commitment to more alert and precise visual perception, and from a feeling that the film industry had not begun to tap the aesthetic resources of the motion picture camera:

> During the twenties we grew disgusted with the philistinism of the commercial film product, its superficial approach, trivial themes, and its standardization of film treatment: the straight-line story progressing from event to event on a pure suspense basis, unmarred by any imaginative use of the camera. . . . The important thing, we felt, was to do those things which the film was capable of, but which the commercial film didn't and couldn't possibly do. There seemed unbounded possibilities for the use of film as a visual poetry of formal beauty.[41]

The resulting film, Steiner's first, was a demonstration of the possibilities of the motion picture camera in the hands of an artist perceptually alert to the visual world around him and willing to focus on aspects of it consistently ignored by commercial filmmakers.[42]

Specifically, Steiner's short (9 minutes) film focuses on water, especially on reflections of light on water, a subject common in Luminist painting, though in one obvious sense H_2O could hardly be less meditative: the film includes ninety-one separate shots. However, as many of the shorter shots occur near the beginning of H_2O, by the conclusion of the film viewers are asked to focus on limited expanses of water for durations that, in any conventional film, would seem rather extended: the final twenty-two shots of the film are on-screen for an average of eleven seconds each.[43] Much has been made of the tendency of Luminist painters to efface evidence of their actually producing their paintings.[44] In H_2O, Steiner was clearly interested in revealing what could be done with the camera without camera trickery; he used nothing but composition—framing—to create his effects. His commitment was to reveal what could be seen by the naked eye, if only our sight were not distracted from everyday visual miracles.[45] Steiner's choice of water, in some of its most common and unspectacular forms—small streams, a pond—seems a conscious refusal of the grandiose, a refusal Steiner confirmed later in life in *Beyond Niagara* (1973), in which he makes a point of focusing on the rapids above Niagara Falls rather than on the falls themselves.[46]

H_2O begins with a "prologue" of brief shots that suggest elements of the visual terrain the remainder of the film explores: a waterfall, raindrops hitting the surface of a lake; and continues first with a sequence revealing water under one or another form of technological control (water gushing out of pipes, being regulated by pumps) and then, with longer sequences, made up of longer shots. Increasingly, the film focuses on the reflections of light on the surface of water (see figs. 72a, 72b). H_2O includes passages of visually exquisite imagery that often approach the abstract, though the imagery is always contextualized by our awareness of the real surface of the water, an awareness continually reenergized by raindrops and by the tiny particles of debris that float through the phantasmagoria of light and shadow Steiner reveals. Ultimately, for the Steiner of H_2O, the world *is* a motion picture, and the central responsibility of the visual artist is to help people enjoy this "movie" as fully as possible. The film's title is ironic. We may think of water as simply two parts hydrogen, one part oxygen, but for Steiner, water includes such a wealth of visual possibilities that any schematic description of it is rendered laughable. Unlike the Luminists, however—and this *is* a crucial distinction— Steiner seems to have been uninterested in revealing anything like a spiritual dimension in what he observes. His interest was in helping all citizens to see more of what surrounds them—a noble and democratic quest, but not necessarily a spiritual one, at least not in the sense that informs so much nineteenth-century painting. In his later years, when he turned to landscape as a subject, Steiner's sensibility was sometimes close to that of some nineteenth-century landscape painters—as it is in the lovely *Hooray for Light!* (1975), where Steiner's depiction of a campfire; a mountainous, tropical landscape; a

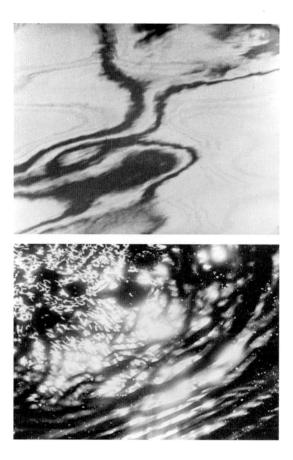

Figures 72a–b. Two images of water from Ralph Steiner's H_2O (1929). Courtesy Museum of Modern Art.

waterfall; grass and trees blowing in the breeze; ferns deep within a forest; a winter landscape; and mountains covered in mist evokes a variety of nine-teenth-century paintings.[47]

For a filmmaker more thoroughly and consciously in touch with Hudson River and Luminist painting, however, we need to go to Peter Hutton. During his thirty years as an independent filmmaker, Hutton has made a meditative gaze, especially a gaze on qualities of light and atmosphere, his fundamental rhetorical gesture, and in many instances he has, quite consciously, provided viewers with film experiences that stand in relation to popular moviegoing and to the dynamics of most independent cinema, precisely as "the still small voice" of Luminist painting stands in relation to the more aggressive dynamics of the more widely popular "operatic" school of nineteenth-century landscape painting. Hutton:

> Most people go to films to get some kind of hit, some kind of overwhelming experience, whether it's like an amusement park ride or an ideological, informational hit that gives you a critical insight into an issue or an idea. But for those few people who feel they need a reprieve occasionally, who want to cleanse the palate a bit, whether for spiritual or physiological reasons, these films seem to be somewhat effective.
>
> I've never felt that my films are very important in terms of the History of Cinema. They offer a little detour from such grand concepts. They appeal primarily to people who enjoy looking at nature, or who enjoy having a moment to study something that's not fraught with information. The experience of my films is a little like daydreaming. It's about taking the time to just sit down and look at things, which I don't think is a very Western preoccupation. A lot of influences on me when I was younger were more Eastern. They suggested a contemplative way of looking—whether at painting, sculpture, architecture, or just a landscape— where the more time you spend actually looking at things, the more they reveal themselves in ways that you don't expect.
>
> For the most part, people don't allow themselves the time or the circumstances to get into a relationship with the world that provides freedom to actually look at things. There's always an overriding design or mission behind their negotiation with life. I think when you have the occasion to step away from agendas— whether it's through circumstance or out of some kind of emotional necessity— then you're often struck by the incredible epiphanies of nature. These are often very subtle things, right at the edge of most people's sensibilities. My films try to record and to offer some of these experiences.[48]

In Hutton's films, meditative moments are not incidents in a larger, more varied filmic structure that includes other types of experience. Each of his mature films—and especially the films discussed in detail here: *Landscape (for Manon)* (1987) and *New York Portrait, Part I* (1976)—offers an extended meditative experience made up of a series of individual meditations. I mean "extended" not literally—*Landscape* is only eighteen minutes long, *New York Portrait, Part I*, sixteen minutes—but because for most viewers the experience Hutton provides *feels* extended, as a result of his timing and the unusual serenity of his images and especially their remarkable silence. Earl A. Powell has discussed the "contemplative sublime" of Fitz Hugh Lane and Martin

Johnson Heade as characterized by the "stillness and serenity of frozen time" and, in the case of Lane's paintings of Brace's Rock (*Brace's Rock*, 1864; *Brace's Rock, Brace's Cove*, 1864; *Brace's Rock, Eastern Point*, 1864), by "the extreme sublime of silence" (see fig. 73).[49] Hutton's films create an analogous silence, and just as the silence of the Brace's Rock paintings seems especially powerful because of the historical context of the Civil War, the silence of Hutton's films is particularly dramatic because of the nature of our era and the "noisy" way in which film generally functions in our lives. For a contemporary audience weaned and socialized by television and film, Hutton's combination of a meditative gaze on serene, black-and-white imagery presented in total silence can be almost shocking: some first-time viewers are dumbfounded.[50]

Hutton makes films in conscious homage to nineteenth-century painting. Indeed, he believes he was hired at Bard College in some measure because Bard, located in Annandale-on-Hudson, has often marketed its Hudson Valley locale. Since moving to Bard, Hutton has completed four films in an ongoing series conceived as a tribute to Hudson River painting. Much of the imagery in *Landscape (for Manon)* is suggestive of Cole's Catskill paintings—some of Hutton's imagery was made in and around Kaaterskill Clove—and the title of

Figure 73. Fitz Hugh Lane's *Brace's Rock, Brace's Cove* (1864), oil on canvas, 10¼" × 15¼". Terra Foundation for the Arts, Daniel J. Terra Collection, 1999.83. Photograph courtesy Terra Museum of American Art, Chicago.

the second film, *In Titan's Goblet*, refers to Cole's 1833 painting, *The Titan's Goblet*.[51] The third and fourth of his Hudson Valley films, *Study of a River* (1996) and *Time and Tide* (2000), explore the Hudson River itself, often from a position *on* the river (see figs. 76a, 76b). In general, *Landscape (for Manon)* recalls those Cole paintings usually seen as forerunners of Luminism—*The Clove, Catskills* (1827), for example, and *Catskill Creek* (1845)—though the sensibility it reflects and the experience it provides is quite close to Lane, Heade, and Kensett.[52]

Landscape (for Manon) is made up of twenty-two shots. The first and last shots frame the film as a tribute to Hutton's young daughter, Manon (the inscription "for Manon" concludes the film): in the film's delicate and arresting final shot, we see her face in close-up, double exposed with mottled light. The film's opening image, of a toy train moving along an isolated track seen from above (that it *is* a toy train is not clear until late in the twenty-five-second shot), not only confirms his use of the film as a tribute to Manon, it also suggests that Hutton saw the move to the Hudson Valley as rendering him a "visual child" and providing him with a new world to explore—though, of course, the specific reference to the train is a reminder that his exploration follows a long tradition of exploration and development in this particular region.

The organization of the other twenty shots of *Landscape (for Manon)* is rigorous, though less formally determined than the organization of either *Zorns Lemma* or *Rolls: 1971*. With two exceptions, each individual shot is separated from the next by two to five seconds of darkness (the exceptions are two "couplets"—one made up of shots 3 and 4, the other of shots 15 and 16, where Hutton cuts directly from one image of a subject to a somewhat closer shot of the same subject).[53] The timing of the particular images is quite sedate, and indeed seems calculated to confront the tendencies of commercial film editing: in general, the more "exciting" a commercial film becomes, the more heavily edited the film is; in fact, the best-known contribution of the Soviet montage school of editing was the "montage" itself, a device for intensifying the density of editing, in particular, climactic sequences, so as to thoroughly engage viewers in their secondhand participation in the action depicted and to force them to feel its symbolic import. The average length of a shot in a contemporary commercial film is under ten seconds, and, of course, in advertisements and in music videos, individual shots are often much shorter. In contrast, the lengths of the twenty-two shots in *Landscape (for Manon)*, in seconds, are 25, 27, 11/27, 18, 27, 27, 15, 21, 38, 49, 49, 53, 45, 39/34, 26, 28,

15, 25, 19, 31. The particular length of any one shot is a function of the subtle events revealed in the shots, but even a cursory look at Hutton's overall timing reveals that *Landscape* begins quietly and then dramatically *slows down* and that the moments where the editing is least frequent occur almost at the center of the film.

The development of the overall timing of *Landscape (for Manon)* is confirmed by the specifics of the imagery. After the toy train shot and a remarkable shot in which a bare tree seems to develop a glow, shots 3 through 8 focus on trees blowing in the breeze or, sometimes, a wind, in early autumn. These relatively active images lead to a series of much quieter images of landscape, most of which include views of the Catskills (see figs. 74a, 74b) . These landscape images generally develop in a manner that creates—at least for those viewers who don't tune out—an unusual perceptual process. In nearly every instance, the landscape images seem, at first, like still photographs (this is particularly the case once the film's first eight images, as slow-paced as they are, have provided immediately apparent motion). It is only if and when one accepts this apparent stillness that a subtler form of motion begins to tease the eye and mind, and we realize that what looked to be still is actually a part of a much larger order of motion: the cloud masses are gradually, relentlessly shifting through the space defined by the frame; the subtleties of chiaroscuro and composition are continually evolving; and what originally seemed (at least to a commercial filmgoing sensibility) "dead" is, in fact, not only very much "alive," but part of an order of motion that dwarfs the rectangular world delimited by the camera.

What the Luminists accomplished by making their presence as working artists invisible—except in the general sense that the implicit dexterity of their "frozen" views allows particular spaces to speak directly to the spectator's senses, mind, and spirit—Hutton accomplishes by making his presence as filmmaker invisible: except for the play of the toy train image, the double exposure at the film's conclusion, and a subtle moment of zooming at the beginning of shot 20, Hutton's only filmic "device" is spatial and temporal composition. Hutton allows a revelation of the motion of the world to speak directly to the viewer's senses, mind, and spirit. Indeed, this perceptual subtlety and implicit spiritual connection is Hutton's gift to the sleeping child in the film's closing shot, and to the filmgoer-as-sleeping-child. We are often more oblivious than real children to the visual subtleties of the world.

Figures 74a–b. Two Catskill Mountain landscapes, from Peter Hutton's *Landscape (for Manon)* (1987). Courtesy Peter Hutton.

While *Landscape (for Manon)* and *In Titan's Goblet* are Hutton's most obvious tributes to nineteenth-century painting, Hutton's Luminist sensibility is not confined to his landscape work. Indeed, Hutton's portraits of cities—New York: *New York, Near Sleep, for Saskia* (1972), *New York Portrait, Part I, Part II* (1980), *Part III* (1990); Budapest: *Budapest Portrait* (1986); and Lodz: *Lodz Symphony* (1993)—resonate with the same meditative approach evident in the landscape films (see figs. 75a, 75b). In several instances, in fact, his New York City images provide obvious parallels to the Luminists, especially to Heade

Figures 75a–b. Images of New York City, from Peter Hutton's *New York Portrait, Part I* (1976). Courtesy Peter Hutton.

and Lane. That a cityscape of Manhattan can remind us of a Fitz Hugh Lane harbor is less surprising if we remember that what may seem a quiet location to early-twenty-first-century eyes—a harbor with sailing ships—was, a century ago, a dynamic industrial arena. Of course, Lane's handling of a harbor had the impact of freezing this activity into a protosurreal frozen moment— an effect very similar to what Hutton achieves by choosing quiet moments in a metropolis and cinematically meditating on them in extended shots. In *New*

York Portrait, Part I, this meditative sensibility is confirmed not only by Hutton's tendency to divide individual shots (or in a few cases, pairs or triads of shots) from one another by moments of darkness, as he does in *Landscape (for Manon),* but also by his frequent use of fades in and out to introduce and conclude particular shots. The fades eliminate virtually all abruptness from the beginnings and ends of images.

Several particular shots of *New York Portrait, Part I* (the 15-minute film includes 32 shots) deserve comment. In shot 6, for example, we observe a downtown Manhattan skyline in silhouette, stretching across the bottom of the image; above the buildings is a sky full of clouds. As happens so often in *Landscape,* the image is so still that, at first, we are not sure it isn't a still photograph. But the length of the shot allows us to adjust and realize that the image *is* changing, that the clouds are gradually shifting through the space of the frame: instead of taking the conventional route of locating a moment of "action" within the "world" of the frame, Hutton implicitly locates the space delimited by his frame within the shifting forces of the larger world that surrounds his filmmaking. By far the longest shot in the film (2 minutes, 18 seconds) confirms the implications of shot 6. The image is a "skyscape"; all we see are sky and clouds—and at first one, then several distant flocks of pigeons looping through the sky, moving in and out of the framed space and, within the framed space, in and out of the light so that at one moment the birds seem white, the next moment black. One minute into the shot, an even more distant airplane enters the frame and for a full minute is seen moving into the distance, from the upper left toward the lower center of the image. At some point during this accidental choreography ("accidental" because Hutton obviously couldn't control the particular motions of birds and plane; "choreography" because he chose the space knowing birds and plane would move through it), we become aware of a third "layer" of motion—visible in the distance beyond the birds and plane but implicitly conditioning every motion they make: the gradually shifting clouds that are altering the look of the frame and breathing new graphic life into the space even as we focus on the activities in the comparative foreground. The shot is an emblem of Hutton's commitment to an intensification of our sense of the particular as a means of putting us in touch with the general, of helping us to see what is within our world as a means of providing us with a spiritual awareness of the world he and we are within.[54]

My arguing for an analogy between Luminist painting and Peter Hutton's filmmaking has ignored one central dimension of Hutton's work, a dimension evident in virtually every shot in both *Landscape (for Manon)* and *New York Portrait, Part I.*[55] And it's a dimension of Hutton's imagery that, at least on one level, conflicts with my analogy. While it is true that Hutton, as film artist, "gets out of the way" of the scenes he depicts, as fully as Lane, Heade, and Kensett efface themselves from the scenes they depict, Hutton is trapped, in a way the painters were not, by the limitations of the mechanical-chemical technology he uses. To put it more precisely, Hutton is attracted to visual scenes that foreground the fact that all imagery depicted by the movie camera tends, to one degree or another, to depict the cinematic apparatus: Hutton's attraction to low-light outdoor conditions in both *Landscape (for Manon)* and *New York Portrait, Part I* (and in other films) causes much of his imagery to be somewhat grainy. This graininess is the mechanical-chemical version of the particulars of moment-to-moment perception that fascinated Monet, Seurat, and other impressionists and produced paintings of rural and urban scenes that critics have seen as fundamentally different from Luminist work: paintings that reveal the fundamental transience of perception and experience, rather than—as in Luminist work—the fundamental, divine harmony and stability behind, or within, momentary appearance. However, while the subtle "dance" of the film grain in Hutton's films does undercut my identification of Hutton as a Luminist, there is one dimension of some Luminist paintings that can be seen as a parallel to the texture of Hutton's imagery. In certain Martin Johnson Heade paintings—*Approaching Storm: Beach Near Newport* (ca. 1860) and *Twilight, Singing Beach* (1863), for example—the application of paint to canvas is so delicate that the weave of the canvas itself is visible, adding a layer of texture to the composition. While Hutton's grainy texture is a function of his choice of low-light conditions and Heade's is a result of the painter's decision, there seems an analogy in both artists' willingness to allow the medium to show through (in a sense, as the ground on and within which their own creativity must manifest itself).

In any case, while the graininess of Hutton's shots may contradict the desire to "get out of the way" so obvious in Hutton's timing and composition, it is most usefully positioned as a synthesis of what at one time seemed conflicting concerns. Because Hutton, child of the twentieth century that he is, has chosen to be a *film* artist, he cannot help but confront the implications of this choice, even when he is using his mechanical-chemical apparatus to

Figures 76a–b. Two Hudson River scenes from Hutton's homage to the Hudson River school, *Study of a River* (1997): above, a tug pulls a tanker down the Hudson; below, a train moves along the river near Bear Mountain Bridge. Courtesy Peter Hutton.

achieve a meditative sensibility akin to that of nineteenth-century American painters. But he has also realized that the very set of orderly natural processes that transforms the particular, "static" images I've discussed into instances of a more fundamental motion is *also,* and simultaneously, transforming the surface of the filmstrip as we watch. The wind that moves across the mountainscapes and fields in *Landscape (for Manon)* and above the city in *New York Portrait, Part I,* continually altering the light and the composition, is "blowing" across the "field" of the film image as well. Indeed, the individual frame of Hutton's film is a microcosm that, by means of film grain, encodes the macrocosmic developments the shots depict: the particular *is* the general. Just as his meditative gaze makes no fundamental distinction between rural and urban locales—both are places in which people live, and both are in a continual process of transformation by both societal and natural forces—Hutton makes no fundamental distinction between material realities outside and inside the camera. The function of filmmaking, for Hutton, is to use the camera as a means of revealing outer and inner realities, the material and the spiritual, as the fundamental unity that in fact they are.[56]

chapter 9

Expulsion from the Garden

I am nobody:
A red sinking autumn sun
Took my name away.

RICHARD WRIGHT

Thomas Cole's Garden of Eden

> It [American scenery] is a subject that to every American ought to be of sur-
> passing interest: for whether he beholds the Hudson mingling waters with
> the Atlantic—explores the central wilds of this vast continent, or stands on
> the margin of the distant Oregon, he is still in the midst of American
> scenery—it is his own land; its beauty, its magnificence, its sublimity—all
> are his; and how undeserving of such a birth right, if he can turn toward it
> an unobserving eye, an unaffected heart! ——THOMAS COLE, "ESSAY ON AMERICAN
> SCENERY, 1835"[1]

Since the idea of America as a new Eden—Thomas Cole: "We are still in
Eden; the wall that shuts us out of the garden is our own ignorance and
folly"[2]—was widespread during the nineteenth century, one might assume
that, as the continent was changing rapidly, the theme of the expulsion from
Eden might also have been popular among artists and writers. And yet,
because of the widespread assumption that the natural resources of North
America were virtually inexhaustible and that it was not only our right but also
our manifest destiny to exploit these resources, few artists or writers felt called
upon to depict the trauma of Adam and Eve's exit from Paradise. In fact,
Thomas Cole's pair of pictures, *The Garden of Eden* (1827–28; see fig. 77) and
Expulsion from the Garden of Eden (1828; see plate 15), are America's most
accomplished rendering of the theme.[3] While there is some doubt that the two
paintings were originally conceived as a pair, it is clear that as Cole began his
Expulsion, he saw it as "a companion picture to the Garden of Eden."[4] Indeed,
as a pair, the two paintings represent a turning point in Cole's career, both in
terms of the landscapes presented (they are allegorical landscapes, not painted

versions of real places) and because they are Cole's first sequential paintings and, therefore, premonitions of the distinguished series that would follow: *The Course of Empire* (1834–36), *Departure* and *Return* (1837), and *The Voyage of Life* (two versions: 1839–40 and 1842; see chap. 2).

As sequential paintings, *The Garden of Eden* and *Expulsion from the Garden* have generally been understood as depicting Adam and Eve, first, before Evil has entered the Garden (there is no indication of a serpent in *The Garden of Eden;* and even the dark cave on the right was, in Cole's mind, not foreshadowing: "The poets often speak of caves and grottos as pleasing objects, and I do not know why the painter may not think as a poet—it is a cool retreat during the Noon-day heats"),[5] and then, just after they have been driven out of Paradise (just as no serpent is visible in *The Garden of Eden,* no figure of God or angel is visible in *Expulsion,* except in the form of divine light shining out through the gate). Cole dramatizes the pre- and postlapsarian worlds through the physical forms of nature. In *The Garden of Eden,* Cole's image of Paradise before the fall is organized in a form that roughly suggests a mandala, with the waterfall in virtually the dead center of the image, measured either from left to right or from top to bottom, or implicitly from the distant mountain to the pool in the foreground. Around this central point are arranged idealized versions of the four components that, seven years later, in "Essay on American Scenery, 1835," Cole would use to analyze American nature: mountains, water (lakes, waterfalls, rivers), forest, and sky.[6] Adam and Eve, standing and sitting, respectively, in the middle distance seem engaged in a prayer of thanksgiving focused on the divinity of the world, while the painting guides the viewer's gaze to the essential unity within the diversity of the world God has created.

Just as in Milton's *Paradise Lost* (presumably, one of Cole's sources for the pair of pictures) Satan has been considered more interesting than the angels who remained loyal to God, Cole's *Expulsion from the Garden of Eden* has generally been considered more compelling than its companion, in part because the later painting images the Garden *and* the postlapsarian world.[7] The Garden in the upper right quadrant of the painting, in its overall impact and in its particulars, seems an echo of the earlier painting, though here seen from outside Eden's walls, across a dark chasm. To the left of the gate through which Adam and Eve have exited Paradise is a very different world, with an erupting volcano in the upper distance and the dark chasm that Adam and Eve

Figure 77. Thomas Cole's *The Garden of Eden* (1827–28), oil on canvas, 38½" × 52¾", 1990.10. Amon Carter Museum, Fort Worth, Texas.

cross on a precarious rock bridge as they walk toward a forest of blasted trees where animals are battling over a carcass. While commentators have tended to see *Expulsion from the Garden of Eden* as dramatizing a two-sided, prelapsarian/ postlapsarian dynamic, there are problems with this dualistic sense of the painting, as obvious as it may seem.

To interpret *Expulsion from the Garden* simply as embodying the contrast of prelapsarian Good and postlapsarian Evil in the peaceful and violent forms of natural process seems out of character for Cole. If one jumps forward eight years to Cole's *The Oxbow* (see chap. 1), we see another painting divided into two halves, but here Cole has clearly aligned himself with the left side of the painting, dark sky, blasted trees, and all. In his paintings of the Catskills and the Adirondacks, Cole sometimes imaged mountain scenes as emblems of serenity—*Mount Chocorua* (1827, a source for the mountain in *The Garden of*

Eden) and *Lake Winnipiseoogie* (1828) can serve as examples—but just as often, perhaps more often, embraced the high energy of nature in the mountains: for instance, in *Landscape with Tree Trunks* (1828), *A Tornado in the Wilderness* (1831), *View of Schroon Mountain, Essex County, New York, after a Storm* (1838), and *A View of the Mountain Pass Called the Notch of the White Mountains (Crawford Notch)* (1839). To resolve this issue, as Bryan Jay Wolf does, by suggesting that Cole rejects the view of nature expressed in *The Garden of Eden* in favor of the more romantic commitment to the sublime and to the divinity of individual expression evident in *Expulsion* seems contradicted by Cole's considerable commitment to *The Garden of Eden* and to his subsequent commitment to comparable Edenic scenes in later years.[8] Cole seems to have continued to see the peaceful *and* the violent aspects of nature as equally interesting, equally divine.

As a film historian, I am led, albeit indirectly, to a somewhat different reading of the space of *Expulsion from the Garden of Eden,* one that seems more consistent with Cole's other depictions of nature. I want to argue for a tripartite division of the space depicted in *Expulsion,* one that recognizes that Adam and Eve are as fully separated from the distant volcano as they are from the Garden—by the steep, dark wall of rock that extends to the left of the gate. For someone familiar with the early history of cinema and with precinematic forms of entertainment and visual illustration, the volcano in *Expulsion* and the semicircular space that defines it (along with the waterfall just below the volcano) looks like the circular inserts used by early filmmakers. Well-known examples occur in Georges Méliès's *The Magic Lantern* (1903) and Edwin S. Porter's *The Life of an American Fireman* (1903), though this way of combining two spaces using superimposition was common. Méliès's film in particular makes explicit early cinema's incorporation of nineteenth-century magic lantern shows, during which imagery on circular glass slides was projected for audiences (see figs. 78–80).

It is not simply the idea of a circular insert that seems relevant here, but the subject matter evident in Cole's "insert." Volcanoes were a popular subject of precinematic entertainments, from the eruption of Mount Etna at the Ranelagh Gardens (1741–1803) well into the nineteenth century, when the Paris Diorama "finally got around to portraying that old faithful subject of London pictorial exhibitions, the eruption of a volcano, in this case Mount Etna."[9] In the years just before Cole painted *Expulsion from the Garden of Eden,* volcanoes were

Figures 78–80. *From top to bottom:* Nineteenth-century magic lantern show; magic lantern projection in Georges Méliès's *The Magic Lantern* (1903); fireman thinks about his family at home (in circular insert), in Edwin S. Porter's *The Life of an American Fireman* (1903).

discussed in geologic texts and represented in illustrations, scale models, and transparencies. Indeed, Elwood Parry argues that *Expulsion* and *The Subsiding of the Waters of the Deluge*, painted the same year, suggest that "in 1828–29 Cole's geological views tended to lean toward catastrophism," the idea that the terrain of Earth was achieved through a series of geologic cataclysms.[10]

In early cinema, visual inserts often suggest that the imagery enclosed within the insert exists in a time and/or space different from the larger surrounding image. My conjecture is that Cole means for us to read the cataclysmic events depicted in his insert as taking place as the Earth was being formed, at a moment farther in the past than the Garden itself; and that the painting represents a tripartite history, beginning with the process of the geologic formation of the Earth by God, followed by the final product of God's creation, the Garden, followed by the temporal and environmental challenges of a postlapsarian world. The historical trajectory of the painting would thus move from the volcano in the upper left to the right into the bright Garden space of the upper right, then down across the image, through the gate to the lower left of the painting where Adam and Eve make their way, now in human historical time, toward the blasted forest. While this implicit historical trajectory is certainly more complex than the trajectory usually assumed, from the Garden on the right into the fallen world on the left, it is a form of movement familiar from other Cole paintings. In both *The Voyage of Life: Youth* and *The Voyage of Life: Manhood*, the River of Life flows in one direction and then bends dramatically into nearly the opposite direction.

If one accepts my reading of the space in *Expulsion from the Garden of Eden*, the sequence of the two paintings can be understood as representing, first, the timeless, ahistorical peace and perfection of the original Garden; and then, the delivery by means of the Fall, into the full spectrum of geologic, biological, and human history. And it allows the two paintings to fit more comfortably into the mythic sense of American history that seems embodied in Cole's other work. For Cole, both the more sublime manifestations of nature and nature's more peaceful interludes are divine; indeed, they define each other. At the same time, the desecration of America's Edenic heritage by overdevelopment remains a possible historical future for the New World Adam and Eve, as represented by the fact that in *Expulsion* the blasted forest is the *only* living nature other than the predators. Cole may have wanted viewers to understand that unless we look back at our Edenic natural heritage and recognize its value, we cannot help but move forward to an entirely "blasted" America (where all relationships are predatory). Such an America may seem inevitable, given the forces of development, but it remains—even in our time—only one of the possibilities. It may be true that in America "the most noble scenes [of American nature] are made desolate, and oftentimes with a wantonness and barbarism scarcely credible in a civilized nation"; nevertheless, that God could create the peaceful harmony of Eden out of the chaos that existed before the Garden suggests that if those made in His image are creative, they may be able to reverse the contemporary motion of history and re-create what must not be lost.[11]

Racism as the Fall

> A black winged butterfly hovered at the water's edge. A bee droned. From somewhere came the sweet scent of honeysuckles. Dimly they could hear sparrows twittering in the woods. They rolled from side to side, letting sunshine dry their skins and warm their blood. They plucked blades of grass and chewed them.
>
> "Oh!"
>
> They looked up, their lips parting.
>
> "Oh!"
>
> A white woman, poised on the edge of the opposite embankment, stood directly in front of them, her hat in her hand and her hair lit by the sun.
>
> "It's a woman!" whispered Big Boy in an underbreath. "A *white* woman!"
>
> They stared, their hands instinctively covering their groins. ——RICHARD WRIGHT, "BIG BOY LEAVES HOME"[12]

In fall 1992 I designed a special course in American studies in an attempt to take advantage of Utica College's unusual (for a small private college) mixture of upstate, small-town white students and New York City blacks and Hispanics. The course was divided into two units, each of which culminated in a field trip: the first unit focused on developments in nineteenth-century America, especially on American nature; the field trip was a two-day Hudson Valley experience: a hike to Kaaterskill Falls, a visit to Frederic Church's Olana, a screening of Peter Hutton's landscape films at Bard College, a tour of Clermont Mansion on the Hudson, and an overnight stay in some rustic cabins in Bear Mountain State Park. The second unit focused on the twentieth century and the American city; the field trip was a weekend in New York, during which the upstate students stayed in the homes of the city students.

For me, one of the more memorable moments of that fall occurred as we were checking into the virtually empty Bear Mountain cabin village. As I filled out the necessary forms in the office and saw the students to the cabins on a late September evening that was becoming dark and rainy, I noticed that a young Hispanic man would not leave my side. Finally, I asked him what was the matter, and he made it clear that he was terrified. "Of what?" I asked. "We're the only ones in the cabins." "How do you know," he countered, "that some redneck won't attack us with a chainsaw?" As I was developing this special course, I knew that the upstate students would be nervous about staying in New York City neighborhoods and that the city students might be nervous about hosting them; but it had not occurred to me that anyone would fear Bear Mountain State Park. Of course, once Raphael had expressed his fear, I was reminded that in America, feeling at home in what is understood by some as an Edenic natural surround has a good bit to do with one's ethnic heritage— and always has.

It is painfully obvious to us now that, in order for American nature to become a metaphor for God's original Eden, it first had to be cleared of those indigenous people and ways of life that offered implicit alternatives to European Christianity. Cooper's Leatherstocking tales often reveal the author's apparent regret at the devastation of the indigenous; and his nostalgia for the Lenni Lenape, particularly the Mohicans, is confirmed not only in Thomas Cole's *Falls of Kaaterskill* (1826), an homage to chapter 26 of Cooper's *The Pioneers* (1823) but also in other paintings—*Autumn in the Catskills* (1827), *Distant View of Niagara Falls* (1830), *Indian Pass—Tahawus* (1848), for example— where isolated Indians add a melancholy note to Cole's evocation of American nature before development.

American racial politics intruded a note of grim reality into nineteenth-century American landscape painting at other moments as well. The widespread fascination with swampy terrain, particularly the Great Dismal Swamp (in Virginia and North Carolina), beginning midcentury, functioned not only as a complex metaphor for dimensions of the human psyche not represented in earlier, and other, landscape paintings; but at times it allowed for representation of the plight of American slaves (see figs. 81–82).[13] Novelists—Harriet Beecher Stowe, for example, in *Dread, a Tale of the Dismal Swamp* (1956);

Figure 81. Thomas Moran's *Slave Hunt, Dismal Swamp, Virginia* (1862), oil on canvas, 43" × 44". Gift of Laura A. Clubb. Courtesy The Philbrook Museum of Art, Tulsa, Oklahoma.

poets—Henry Wadsworth Longfellow, for example, in "The Slave in the Dismal Swamp" (1865); autobiographers—Henry Bibb, in *Narrative of the Life and Adventures of Henry Bibb, an American Slave, Written by Himself* (1850); and visual artists—Thomas Moran, in *Slaves Escaping through a Swamp* (1865), often depicted the swamp as a hideout for runaways.

Moran's remarkable painting—especially in the context of his other paintings of the early 1860s, which (to quote one of Moran's titles) suggest that "The Woods Were God's First Temple"—dramatically suggests how slavery defiles God's nature. Here the solitude and quiet so obvious in Moran's other landscapes is destroyed by the vicious dogs close on the heels of terrified slaves—one of whom, judging from his or her dress is a Carib or an Indian— and by the slave hunters approaching through the shadows in the woods. Indeed, for those familiar with Cole's *Expulsion from the Garden of Eden*, the

Figure 82. Detail from Moran's *Slave Hunt, Dismal Swamp, Virginia.*

fugitives' positions with regard to their pursuers are roughly reminiscent of the positions of Adam and Eve leaving the Garden.

While the defilement of nature by slavery did not continue to interest Moran as a painter, and while American landscape painting and culture in general soon moved on to other concerns, there have continued to be instances in which the issue of race and the American fascination with the idea of a pristine nature have intersected. Some of the most notable instances have occurred in cinema; and perhaps the most obvious of these is the original version of *King Kong* (1933), directed by Ernest P. Schoedsack and Merian C. Cooper (Kong was animated by Willis O'Brien) (fig. 83). Though the discovery of Kong and his prehistoric jungle takes place on the remote Scull Island in the South Pacific—and is easily read as the Cooper-Schoedsack team's mythification of their earlier adventures in Asia, which resulted first in *Grass*

(1925) and subsequently in *Chang* (1927)—this South Sea island seems inhabited entirely by African Americans! Presumably, the directors assume that, because the actors are dark-skinned, the audience will not recognize that *these* dark-skinned people don't look like South Sea islanders; but from our vantage point, this casting "glitch" seems to offer Cooper and Schoedsack an opportunity to exploit conventional American attitudes about race.[14] *King Kong* creates a tripartite world: a prehistoric jungle behind the giant wall (the jungle seems to owe a good bit to nineteenth-century American representations of jungles and swamps); the primitive native village outside the wall; and Manhattan, the epitome of modernity, with its elevated trains, huge theaters, and brand-new Empire State Building, which had opened during the production of the film. The film's geography simultaneously confirms a number of widely held racist notions (most obviously, that blacks are farther down the evolutionary ladder, closer to the prehistoric, more apelike than whites) *and* creates sympathy for the captured Kong, who becomes a metaphor for the enslavement and destruction of nature (and implicitly African America) by urban development.[15] Of course, Kong escapes only to be killed by a combination of his adoration of a white woman and modern military technology.

Figure 83. King Kong does battle for Anne Darrow (Faye Wray) in a prehistoric swamp, production still for *King Kong* (1933). Courtesy Museum of Modern Art.

Figure 84. Family members arrive for reunion on Sea Island off the coast of South Carolina in Julie Dash's *Daughters of the Dust* (1992). Courtesy Kino Films.

In more recent years, African-American directors have begun to have the still-rare opportunity to use feature filmmaking as a forum for dealing with America's racial history. A number of their films have explored the intersection of race and American nature: most notably, Julie Dash's *Daughters of the Dust* (1992) and Carl Franklin's *One False Move* (1991). *Daughters of the Dust* is the story of the Peazant family, who meet for a reunion on St. Helena, one of the Sea Islands off the coast of South Carolina, where Nana Peazant, the great-grandmother of the family, and some other family members continue to live (see fig. 84). It is a special reunion, as most of the family has decided to leave the South and begin the new century (the film takes place in 1902) in the North. While the island is physically Edenic—Dash and cinematographer Arthur Jaffa emphasize its beauty—this beauty is compromised by the island's racial history and by the continuation of this history in the film's present.

Near the beginning of *Daughters of the Dust*, just after we see a flashback of a younger Nana Peazant's indigo-stained hands in the island's dusty soil (later she explains, "Our hands [were] scarred blue with the poisonous indigo dye that built up all those plantations from swampland"),[16] Dash shows an island inlet with a sign identifying it as Ibo Landing, a now-mythic location where a group of captives of the Ibo tribe rebelled against slavery and, depending on the version of the myth, walked on water back to Africa, flew back to Africa, or walked into the water and drowned themselves.[17] While slavery is in the past by the time the action of the film begins, its vestiges are in evidence, most obviously in the apparent rape that has resulted in Eula's pregnancy: one of the central dramatic issues in the film involves the struggle of Eli, Eula's husband, to accept the unborn child (who appears in the film as a spirit, functioning as one of two narrators—Nana Peazant is the other) as his own.

As the Peazant family celebrates their coming migration North with what Dash calls their "Last Supper," the family divides into two groups. The bulk of the family leaves the island the next day. But Eula and Eli and the coming child; Iona, another of Nana's granddaughters, who is in love with the Cherokee St. Julien Last Child; and Yellow Mary, still another granddaughter and a lesbian prostitute, all remain behind with Nana on the island. The island is reclaimed as an Eden, not because it is not fallen or will not remain fallen (the unborn child explains that in the years that followed Eli would become involved in the anti-lynching movement), but because, as Dash has explained, the Sea Islands were "the region with the strongest retention of African culture," and a maintenance of connection with ancestors is essential for moving out of a troubled history into a better future.[18] For Dash, and for the characters in *Daughters of the Dust,* the idea of a natural Eden remains a crucial element in any recovery from the racial horrors that brought Africans to America and kept them in chains to develop the land.

Whereas *Daughters of the Dust* is a challenging experimental feature (Dash aimed the film at an audience of African-American women and hoped others would also be drawn to it),[19] Carl Franklin's *One False Move* is in many ways a conventional suspense thriller, though it provides an implicit analysis of America's racial history that is unusually astute for a commercial feature. *One False Move* begins in L.A., where one of the film's two triads of main characters—Fantasia/Lila (Cynda Williams), Pluto (Michael Beach), and Ray (Billy Bob Thornton, who cowrote the screenplay with Tom Epperson)—breaks into a party where cocaine is being used and threaten the party guests until the host agrees to take them to their drug source. Pluto stays behind to guard the guests while Ray and Fantasia accompany the host to the supplier's house, where they steal his cocaine and $15,000. Ray calls Pluto to tell him they've been successful; Pluto kills the party guests, and Ray murders the supplier and the other adults present.

These opening sequences are unusually powerful, even for a 1990s American film, especially because of Pluto's and Ray's calculated violence toward both men and women: we see Pluto cover the head of a woman with a pillowcase and passionately and repeatedly stab her in the stomach; Ray is consistently violent—he punches and pistol-whips men and women—and kills his bound victims by suffocating them in plastic bags. The grisly opening sequence ends when Ray sends Fantasia to check the house and be sure they leave no witnesses behind. Fantasia searches the house, finally finding a young black boy who is shivering with terror in his room. We do not immediately find out what happens to the boy; as we look at him, we hear a scream— "Mommy! Mommy!"—and then see a young white girl in rural Arkansas awaking from a nightmare. She turns out to be Bonnie, the eight-year-old daughter of Dale "Hurricane" Dixon (Bill Paxton), a small-town sheriff who soon becomes a member of the film's second triad of protagonists: Dixon and two L.A. detectives, McFeely (Earl Billings) and Dud Cole (Jim Metzler). McFeely and Cole investigate the scenes of the crime in L.A. and soon head to Star City, Arkansas, where, they have discovered, the fugitives mean to hide out (both Ray and Fantasia are Star City natives).

The opening of *One False Move* develops an urban/rural opposition that seems to reflect the widespread American notion that violence and drugs are an urban black phenomenon; or, to put it in the terms the opening sequence sets up, that urban drug violence is the nightmare of rural America. At first, the issue of race seems nearly peripheral to the action (except for the fact that all the men and women at the party and the supplier's house are black): both triads of protagonists are mixed race—Pluto and Fantasia are black, Ray is white; McFeely is black, Cole and Dixon are white—and both triads seem to work across racial distinctions. However, as *One False Move* develops, and the film's two plot lines converge—the fugitives travel from L.A. to Star City; the police gather in Star City and make ready for the fugitives' arrival—not only is the urban/rural opposition undermined, but the subtle racial politics within each triad is exposed.

The characters themselves confirm the rural/urban opposition I've described. When Dixon first talks with the L.A. police by phone, he tells them, "Now you got six people dead out there at the same time. Well, we don't get much of that down here in Star City"; and in the hope of being as fully involved in their investigation as possible, he makes clear that "you boys bein' from the city and all, you'd be lost [in this area] in ten minutes." Later, when the L.A. detectives are driving from the airport in Little Rock to Star City, a drive that is taking them through dense, forested swampland, Cole comments, "It's really beautiful, man," and McFeely responds, "It sure is green as hell."[20] This urban/rural distinction culminates when Dixon is called to the scene of a domestic dispute—a husband is furiously trying to break into his house with an ax, supposedly to kill his wife—which Dixon resolves by wrestling the man to the ground and talking sense into him. The wife seems less frightened of her husband than of the L.A. cops, who have drawn their guns—to the amusement of Charlie, Dixon's deputy. Dixon brags later, "I been police chief here for goin' on six years. I never even had to draw my gun," and subsequently approaches Cole about moving to L.A., where the real criminal action is, and joining the LAPD. The L.A. cops respond in kind later when they agree that the likable but naive Dixon wouldn't last ten minutes in L.A.

While the violence of the film's opening defines Ray and Pluto as quintessential violent urban criminals, the film gradually makes clear that the urban/rural opposition is more complex than it may first seem. During the opening sequence, it is obvious that Fantasia is uncomfortable with the extent of Ray's brutality; and during the remainder of the film, she seems to stay high on cocaine in large measure to overcome her guilt at being a part of the violence (her refusal to participate fully is demonstrated by her allowing the child she finds in the supplier's house to live). And later when she must kill a Texas Ranger who is holding Pluto and Ray at gunpoint, she is clearly upset about it. Near the end of the film, when she travels to Star City ahead of Ray and Pluto, she has her younger brother put the $15,000 (which she's taken with her, unbeknown to Ray and Pluto) in the bank for her five-year-old child, Byron, who lives with her mother and brother.

While Fantasia reveals herself to be less an abject criminal than Pluto or Ray, Hurricane reveals himself to be a less thoroughly upstanding law officer than his urban colleagues. Early in *One False Move*, when McFeely, Cole, and Dixon have their first meal in the town diner, Dixon asks the waitress about herself, and when she begins to tell about her husband's recent surgery, Dixon, who is star-struck by the L.A. cops, rudely ignores her and leaves the restaurant not only without leaving a tip but also without entirely paying the bill (he leaves a $10 bill for a $12 check), apparently not unusual behavior for him. Gradually, it becomes clear not only that Dixon knows Fantasia and her family, but that Byron is his child—though Dixon denies it until the final moments of the film. When he and Fantasia talk just before the film's final showdown, we realize that, six years earlier, he had taken advantage of Fantasia after arresting her for shoplifting when she was a seventeen-year-old virgin and had maintained a sexual relationship with her—despite his marriage with Cheryl Ann and the birth of Bonnie—only to break it off around the time Fantasia became pregnant with Byron.[21]

Other dimensions of the implicit racial politics in *One False Move* become increasingly evident as the film develops. Pluto, the L.A. police decide, is a racially atypical mystery: his 150 IQ and college degree don't jibe with his criminal record and remarkable callousness. While Pluto seems personally unaffected by the mixed-race relationship of Fantasia and Ray, he becomes angry only when Fantasia makes fun of him for his obliviousness to pleasure—he doesn't use coke, drink, or seem interested in sex—and Ray calls him a "brown turd." And he reveals his awareness of the social implications of their relationship: when the Texas Ranger is following them, his explanation is "white boy and nigger girl in Texas—that's all it is." The three law officers also seem to get along comfortably, despite Hurricane's tendency to stereotype blacks in conventional ways and, at times, to use "nigger." At the same time, it's clear that McFeely and Cole respond differently, in ways that have to do with their ethnic difference. Early in the film, when Cole, responding to the beauty of Arkansas, tells his partner, "You know, I'm a country boy, John," McFeely responds, "That's a bunch of crap; you were born in L.A.," confirming the slight cynical tone evident earlier in his comment "It [Arkansas] sure is green as hell." McFeely is also the first character to deduce the nature of the relationship between Hurricane and Fantasia/Lila. He understands racial power in the South (and knows the truth of what Fantasia says later, to her brother: "Lookin' guilty is bein' guilty for black people") and recognizes the unlikelihood of Hurricane's helping Lila and being positive about her innocence unless more has gone on between them than Dixon is willing to admit (see fig. 85).

The relentless convergence of the film's two plots, and its undermining of the clear distinctions between the triads of protagonists, is the film's fundamental statement about American racial relations. The idea that blacks and whites live in two different worlds is an illusion. While American history has certainly affected whites and blacks differently, these histories are hardly

Figure 85. Sheriff "Hurricane" Dixon (Bill Paxton) and Lila/ Fantasia (Cynda Williams) reunited just before the conclusion of *One False Move* (1991).

separate even when they may seem to be, even when they have legally been defined as separate. Dixon's taking advantage of Lila is "one false move" that evokes the whole history of white men using their power to achieve illicit sex with black women. And Dixon's actions ultimately determine Lila's subsequent life: she moves to California in the hope of making enough money to support her fatherless son, an action that echoes the history of American black migration first to the North and subsequently to the West from a South unwilling to provide generations of African Americans with a reasonable opportunity at a decent life. Of course, no group has done more to obscure the realities of America's racial history than the movie studios in Hollywood, the "star city" that for better than a century has been content to provide feel-good cartoons so that a population that continues to benefit from the American history of racial exploitation can continue to escape that reality (that the two black criminals have renamed themselves Fantasia and Pluto is an obvious allusion to Disney). Indeed, Sheriff Dixon's name could be a reference to *The Birth of a Nation* (1915)—that landmark in the development of cinematic language (the intercutting structure of *One False Move* echoes D. W. Griffith) and in the stereotyping of African Americans—the second half of which was adapted by Griffith from the racist novel and play *The Clansman* by Thomas Dixon.

Though *One False Move* doesn't say so, we might conjecture that Pluto's cold brutality toward everyone could be a result of his being ignored and denied, as Byron is, by his father and his society solely on the basis of his skin color. Pluto's real name in the film is Lane Franklin; is it too much to suggest that he bears a similar relationship to director Carl Franklin as Bigger Thomas in *Native Son* (1940) bears to Richard Wright? Like Bigger, Lane Franklin is what, given another scenario made very possible by a cold, white society, Carl Franklin might have become.[22] On the other hand, that Franklin was able to get *One False Move* made does suggest a hopeful dimension to the film, one confirmed by Dixon's apparent acceptance of Byron at the end of *One False Move*. As Dixon lies on the ground, Byron asks his father, "Are you dead, Mister?" and the sheriff replies, "Not quite." Dixon's earlier refusal to accept the results of his irresponsibility toward Lila can function as a metaphor of white America's refusal, so far, to do what needs to be done to assure that black America, and America as a whole, will recover from the traumas visited on African Americans during the nation's early development. Too often we have hidden—and continue to hide—within mythic fantasies, including the fantasy that in "the good old days," in small-town rural America, where men and women were close to nature, "we" lived in an Edenic paradise. There is still time for change—we're "not quite" dead yet—but the longer we wait to deal with our "urban" nightmare . . .

J. J. Murphy: Choosing to Fall

> [T]his much is crystal clear: our bigger-and-better society is now like a hypochondriac, so obsessed with its own economic health as to have lost the capacity to remain healthy. . . . Nothing could be more salutary at this stage than a little healthy contempt for a plethora of material blessings.
>
> Perhaps such a shift of values can be achieved by reappraising things unnatural, tame, and confined in terms of things natural, wild, and free.
> —ALDO LEOPOLD, MADISON, WISCONSIN, MARCH 4, 1948[23]

Near the end of *Lost Lost Lost* (1976), Jonas Mekas describes a cultural "guerrilla action," during which he, Ken and Flo Jacobs, and some others attempt to invade the 1963 Robert Flaherty Seminar, in the name of Jack Smith's *Flaming Creatures* (1963) and Ken Jacobs's *Blonde Cobra* (1963).[24] Rejected by the seminar, they sleep outside; and in the morning, to quote Mekas's voice-over narration, "Slowly we woke up. No, we didn't sleep well. But it was beautiful. . . . We felt a part of the morning, of earth. It was very, very quiet, like in a church, and we were the monks of the order of cinema." Mekas's voice-over is immediately followed by the sound of church bells and of a mass; and in the visuals, Mekas, Jacobs, and the others pretend to be monks, using their blankets as vestments; Mekas holds a camera as if it were an incense holder. The idea that those who have committed themselves to forms of cinema outside the mainstream are spiritually committed and that, like monks, they have turned their backs on American commercial culture to nurture the purity of this spiritual commitment was widespread during the 1960s and early 1970s. Indeed, for some of us, the willingness of filmmakers to make defiantly noncommercial films, and the willingness of audiences to receive this work in a mood of deep respect, was akin to the establishment of a new cinematic religious order that ministered to the worship of the human spirit in a network of Edenic screening spaces, cinematic Gardens within the fallen world of commercial capitalism.[25]

While there were many filmmakers and film enthusiasts who were *not* interested in such a "pretentious" attitude toward cinema, and some who were revolted by it, this sense of filmmaking/filmgoing as a spiritual engagement was productive of an impressive body of work and a considerable number of alternative filmmaking careers, generally characterized by an assumption that patience, even serenity, and often silence were the marks of enlightened viewership. One noteworthy instance of this historical moment was the early career of J. J. Murphy—I say *early* career because the trajectory of Murphy's development as a filmmaker would by the 1980s take him out of this cinematic "order" in a way that, while providing us with a sense of an "expulsion" from Eden different from those I've been discussing, ultimately returns us to the theme of race and nature.

Murphy began his filmmaking career (having earlier on, as an undergraduate at the University of Scranton, become a devotee programmer)[26] as a graduate student at the University of Iowa, with a series of distinctive films that explored the interface of landscape and cinema: *Highway Landscape* (1972); *In Progress* (made with one of his professors, Ed Small, in 1971–72); *Sky Blue Water Light Sign* (1972), discussed in chapter 1; and *Print Generation* (1974).

Highway Landscape is a six-and-a-half-minute, single-shot film in which the camera is positioned to look across a rural Iowa roadway at ground level: some bare trees are visible on the far side of the road; a dead rabbit lies on the highway in the right foreground of the composition. The energy of *Highway Landscape* is a function of the sound track, which was recorded in synch with the image: while viewers gaze at the narrow space delimited by the composition, we hear the approach of vehicles that flash through the image, going one way or another (the monaural sound does not indicate direction). *Highway Landscape* suggests that filmmaking can function from a position on the margins of commercial development, that it need not be confined to the commercial "highway"; if we cannot escape the industrialization of the Garden, we can learn to slow down and contemplate the trajectory and velocity of our culture.

In Progress is a longer (18 minutes), silent meditation on an Iowa farmscape, for approximately six seconds a day, from late summer 1971 to early summer 1972. The changing world outside the window through which the mounted camera gazes causes myriad variations in the scene, many of them a function of the changing seasons, others caused by the impact of the variable levels and directions of natural light on the filmstock. Few films demonstrate as effectively the complexity of temperate-zone seasonality and cinema's capacity for witnessing/participating in this complexity.[27] Indeed, *In Progress* performs a kind of magic by revealing such dramatic variations in the scene that most viewers have difficulty believing that the camera has not been moved, the composition adjusted. The irony is that Murphy and Small devised the project so that their imagery would be, as fully as possible, the result of the interface of the environment and cinema technology, rather than of human pre- or post-conception: once they had decided on the specific composition and had bolted the camera to the floor, they paid little attention to what was outside the window when imagery was exposed (indeed, at times they asked others to expose imagery in their absence). When the film was developed at the conclusion of all the shooting and the collaborators discovered the imagery their process had produced, Small suggested they choose the "best" imagery for their final product, an idea that Murphy strongly and successfully opposed on the grounds that the totality of the imagery was the most legitimate record of this novel interface of nature and machine.[28] The resulting film is precisely what came out of the camera: sequential rolls of film were simply spliced together. The film reveals a literal garden continually "in progress"—whether a camera is there to record it or not—and reflects on the filmmaking process producing the imagery we're seeing, at times, literally: the circular reflection of the lens of the camera is seen on the window pane, creating a mechanical metaphor for the cyclical process being recorded. Nature and machine are in a synergic relationship in *In Progress:* the land outside the window is maintained by the (often visible) farm machinery; the camera inside the window records what the natural processes outside the window determine.

Murphy's most elaborate early film and most ingenious investigation of landscape is *Print Generation,* a fifty-minute exploration of the process of contact printing (that method of making photographic imagery that involves laying already developed imagery against unexposed film, exposing the interface to light, and creating a second print through this "contact"). Those of us who teach film history must inevitably—*inevitably,* because film itself is a material object, subject to decay over time—deal with the fact that some prints are better than others, either because more or less damage has been visited on a particular print or because the process of making prints from prints (necessary when an original negative is no longer available) automatically results in diminished clarity and detail. In recent years, the advent of cheaper color film has exacerbated this inevitable problem, since nearly all color filmstocks are less stable than black-and-white stocks: it is not at all unusual to rent a film made in the 1960s in which the color has decayed to the extent that we cannot be sure what the original colors were. Having come to grips with this issue as both filmmaker and teacher, Murphy decided to see if he could use filmmaking itself to come to a fuller understanding of the implications of this process of decay.

Murphy made a one-minute diary of imagery recorded in summer 1973—sixty one-second shots, most recorded in rural Vermont where he stayed with his friend and fellow filmmaker Norman Bloom;[29] the remainder, at his mother's home in Bayonne, New Jersey—and gave the little film to a lab in Houston, Texas, with directions to generate a series of contact prints (a contact print of the original, a contact print of the contact print, a contact print of *that* contact print, and so on) until the original imagery had disappeared. The lab made sixty prints, though Murphy ended up using only fifty—no significant change was occurring in the final ten generations. The fifty contact prints were divided into an "A Wind" and a "B Wind" (necessary because successive prints are mirror images of each other) and arranged in the finished film so that all the prints are seen in the same right-to-left configuration—that is, the B Wind prints were flipped to match the A Wind prints—beginning with the most decayed A Wind print and moving successively to the least decayed A Wind print (see plates 16–18); then beginning with the least decayed B Wind print and moving print by print to the most decayed B Wind print. For a sound track, Murphy made an analogous experiment with magnetic tape: he recorded one minute of ocean waves breaking, then made a tape of that tape, a tape of *that* tape, and so on, for fifty generations. The results are arranged in *Print Generation* so that we hear the least decayed sound with the most decayed imagery and proceed to the most decayed sound (and least decayed imagery), and back again.

The finished film creates an experience that is dense with implication. As the viewer moves through the "strata" of emulsion during A Wind (each contact print removed a thin layer of emulsion), from the layers closest to the celluloid toward the layers farthest from the celluloid, the imagery becomes, slowly but surely, roughly, then precisely identifiable—though we are never able to read any of the images with complete confidence, because of the brevity and sometimes the visual complexity of the individual one-second shots.[30] In other words, as we move toward the surface of the emulsion and the least decayed print, we are increasingly able to recognize the imagery, much of it landscape, that Murphy originally recorded. And since the film colors closest to the surface, and thus most subject to decay, are greens and browns, the stratification of the emulsion evokes the stratification of the Earth itself; and the precariousness of these greens and browns, the precariousness of the Earth's surface ecology.[31] That the mechanical apparatus of cinema inevitably destroys the imagery it has created can easily be read as an index of the destruction of "original" American nature by the processes of industrial development—processes that first made original American nature accessible, then exploited it to such a degree that it subsequently became valuable in new ways to those who came to see a tragedy in its disappearance.

During *Print Generation,* we gradually reaccess, for a moment or two, the Edenic summer Murphy spent in Vermont (and his relationship with his mother, whose walk through her yard/garden is for nearly all viewers the first recognizable image in the film; see fig. 86), only—during B Wind—to lose it again, as the clarity of the original images and our memories of what we finally saw in the prints closest to the original begin to fade. Of course, we,

Figure 86. J. J. Murphy's mother walking in her backyard, midway through the contact print generations in *Print Generation* (1974). This image is usually the first a viewer can identify with any accuracy. Courtesy J. J. Murphy.

and the cinema that represents us, are inevitably creatures of decay, subject to the swift, inevitable passing of time: what Eden we *can* find, in our fallen state, is at best an elusive memory of an illusory perfect moment—though this image of perfection (imaged so often in American culture as the kind of rural, northeastern moment Murphy records) remains crucial, at least conceptually, as the measure of the extent of our "expulsion" from the Edenic state.

Print Generation remains a landmark independent film and in my view Murphy's "best" film;[32] but for Murphy it was merely one moment in an ongoing career that has involved a second kind of "expulsion from the Garden." In the years immediately following the completion of *Print Generation*, Murphy explored a variety of other filmmaking approaches, with varying degrees of success.[33] By the end of the 1970s, however, he had become increasingly interested in making "movies"—not Hollywood spectaculars, certainly, but narrative films with plots and speaking characters. While this may seem to many— to *most*—of us a perfectly obvious, even a "natural," inclination, for Murphy it represented a major revision of his sense of himself as a filmmaker and a considerable change in his reputation in the field. For a good many of those who had committed themselves to avant-garde film during the 1960s and early 1970s, anything approaching conventional commercial film storytelling was anathema, a surrender to the corruption of the mass media. With *Print Generation* Murphy had established himself as a major force in the avant-garde; and many of his colleagues and admirers probably assumed that, during the coming years, he would continue to confirm his significance in this field and perhaps find some sort of academic niche that would allow him to continue this work. When it became clear that Murphy was moving toward more conventional filmmaking, there were those who said that he was betraying the cause of film art, that he was succumbing to the lure of the movies, taking the easy way out.[34] At the time, many avant-garde film artists seemed to feel that, especially in America, narrative filmmaking was so conventional that, given the budgets Hollywood directors had access to, virtually any artist could direct a movie; and given the size of Hollywood advertising budgets, be financially successful with it. The considerable success of so many thoroughly mediocre films certainly seemed evidence for such a conclusion—and for a related one: the rarity with which anything like true film art came out of Hollywood proved that commercial filmmaking was and is not an appropriate arena for an artist. For those criticizing Murphy, film art was, essentially, sophisticated *individual* expression, more suited to the forms of artisanal production that characterize the avant-garde.

For Murphy, however, the interest in making narrative, synch-sound movies was anything but an escape from difficulty or an abandonment of film art. It is one thing to condemn the industry for the compromises of so much of what it produces; it is quite another to prove that you can do something better, without compromises. And it is obvious that, in fact, the industry's collaborative system has produced a considerable history of film art, a history that has made the ongoing availability of film equipment and filmstock possible: without the industry, all forms of filmmaking, including the most individual, would probably be doomed to extinction. And Murphy was *not* aiming at a commercial career; he was trying to work in the gap between avant-garde cinema and commercial movies, to see if he could make narratives that would interest audiences larger than the small groups that were finding their way to avant-garde screenings. Or to put this another way, he was willing to risk *expelling himself* from the Edenic security of his avant-garde reputation, in order to prove he was a "filmmaker," not simply an "avant-garde filmmaker."

During the 1980s, Murphy produced a trilogy of narrative films, evocative of *cinema noir*—*The Night Belongs to the Police* (1982; 29 minutes), *Terminal Disorder* (1983; 43 minutes); and *Frame of Mind* (1985; 80 minutes)—that allowed him to explore central Wisconsin (where he had moved in 1980 to teach at the University of Wisconsin–Madison), both as a specific geographic region and as a space involved with characteristic American sociopolitical issues—race relations, the drug trade—just the sorts of issues that so many of his avant-garde colleagues were able and willing to ignore, at least during their "spiritual quests" as filmmakers. While none of these films is perfect—the way one might argue that *Print Generation* or *Sky Blue Water Light Sign* are perfect films—they do reveal a progression in Murphy's ability to handle the collaborative filmmaking process and cinema storytelling. They are also evidence of Murphy's willingness to take on the inevitable stresses of even semicommercial production. To express this in financial terms, *Print Generation* cost approximately $4,000 (and Murphy remembers that it "felt shocking" to owe the laboratory $2,000);[35] *The Night Belongs to the Police* cost between $5,000 and $8,000; *Terminal Disorder*, between $10,000 and $15,000—actors and crew were not paid in either production; and *Frame of Mind*, a feature in which actors and crew were paid, albeit at a virtually minimal rate, $100,000.[36] And for *Horicon* (1993; 90 minutes), his next and so far most interesting narrative film, Murphy needed to find $165,000, which he did by forming a general partnership with film-interested Madison locals, by investing $30,000 of his own money, and by applying for a variety of university, state, and regional grants. The irony is that, while *Horicon* has a good bit to recommend it— including a fine performance by Eva Loseth[37]—and did a reasonable business regionally, it was not picked up for national distribution—and so lost much of the investment Murphy had labored to find.

Horicon has much in common thematically with *One False Move*. Set in the area of Wisconsin's Horicon Marsh—famous as the home of Aldo Leopold and the location described during Part 1 of his landmark *A Sand County Almanac*—*Horicon* centers on sixteen-year-old Rachel (Loseth), a high school dropout who helps her mother, Dolores (Margie Weaver), eke out a living from a small motel and diner in Wampun, frequented mostly by visitors to the Wampun State Prison. Her boyfriend, Quiz (David Gregory), works as a tour guide, taking people on boat tours of the marsh, which is famous as a stop for

Figure 87. Rachel (Eva Loseth), with Barnum (Peter Holland), visiting the Horicon Marsh in J. J. Murphy's *Horicon* (1993). Courtesy J. J. Murphy.

migratory birds. *Horicon* focuses on the days leading up to the release of Nichols (Ed Holmes), an African American who—we learn from Wright (Edmund Wyson) and Barnum (Peter Holland), a hustler and an ex-con from Chicago who are staying at the motel—has hidden stolen money in the marsh. Barnum's plan is to kidnap Nichols on his release (see fig. 87). Dolores is also involved—though it is not clear until near the end of the film (which was adapted by Murphy and James Vculek from one of Vculek's short stories) that Dolores knows about the money, which she too hopes to steal from Nichols when he retrieves it from the marsh. In the end, Rachel discovers that she is the mixed-race child of Dolores and Nichols; and Rachel and her father are left to deal with their relationship (Dolores never told Nichols about the child or Rachel about Nichols). Having killed Wright (who has murdered Barnum earlier), Dolores drives off with the money, leaving Rachel and

Nichols in the marsh. That Rachel and Nichols are the most humane characters in the film gives the ending a hopeful edge, though it is also obvious that they are left with nothing but each other.

The juxtaposition of the Horicon Marsh and the Wampun State Prison, in which, as in so many American prisons, an unrepresentative percentage of prisoners are African Americans (most of the visitors to the prison in *Horicon* are African American), suggests that the events that play out in *Horicon* encapsulate American development during the past two-plus centuries: the native population was eliminated (as Rachel explains, "Wampun" is an Indian name) to make way for the agricultural exploitation of the Horicon wetlands (what remains of the original marsh is fenced off and controlled by a dam) and for the commercial development of the Midwest, which by the early part of the twentieth century was luring African Americans from the South to settle in urban areas, where for many virtually the only option was crime. The irony is that the combined pressures of economic development and social control have regularly conspired, as they've conspired in Wampun, to locate minority prisoners in economically "underdeveloped," that is, more natural, areas—conflating the economic downside of American racial politics and the apparent contempt of so many in power for natural landscape.

While on one level the marsh and the prison may seem like opposites, both are maintained in the interests of a safer and healthier society, and the larger institutions they represent—the system of protected lands, the penal system—are evidence of major systematic failures of American development: American slavery was eliminated but without any workable provision for the former slaves; American nature was so consistently decimated that we can only (partially) protect some tag ends of what once seemed a continental Eden.

As fully as any of his narrative films, *Horicon* suggests Murphy's awareness of his position as an independent film artist within these larger sociohistorical realities. During the boat tour of the marsh that opens the film, Quiz points out a wood duck nesting box, fastened to a small tree, and explains that the box is necessary because there are no longer enough trees in the marsh to provide nesting habitats for the migrating ducks. When we discover at the end of *Horicon* that Nichols has hidden the stolen money in one of these boxes, it is difficult not to read this gesture as a metaphor for the tendency to look for psychic security and renewal in what remains of original nature. But it also suggests Murphy's attempt to evolve into an effective moviemaker in a cinematic "region" where even when one is able to find money for the production of a politically intelligent and aesthetically satisfying film—a low-budget production that seems to imprison one's creative mobility at every turn—the hope of completing such a project and finding it at least marginally profitable can seem an elusive fantasy.

Like so many independent filmmakers committed to regions outside the media-industrial centers of New York and Los Angeles, Murphy remains a prisoner of his own desire to have at least a modest progressive impact on a reasonably sized audience of moviegoers, without giving in to the forces of wholesale greed and exploitation. What makes Murphy's career particularly poignant is the very success of his original films. As he wrestles with his ongoing financial struggles as an independent narrative filmmaker—struggles that, again and again, leave him in the position of starting over with nothing—he must at times look back wistfully at the Edenic cinematic moment he was able to achieve in the early 1970s.

chapter 10

Satan's National Park

In the beginning there were days set aside for various tasks.
On the day He was to create justice
God got involved in making a dragonfly

and lost track of time.
It was about two inches long
with turquoise dots all down its back like Lauren Bacall.

God watched it bend its tiny wire elbows
as it set about cleaning the transparent case of its head.
The eye globes mounted on the case

rotated this way and that
as it polished every angle.
Inside the case

which was glassy black like the windows of a downtown bank
God could see the machinery humming
and He watched the hum

travel all the way down turquoise dots to the end of the tail
and breathe off as light.
Its black wings vibrated in and out.

ANNE CARSON, "GOD'S JUSTICE"

The concept and the accomplishment of the American national park system and comparable, more localized accomplishments—the systems of state parks in New York and other states;[1] of Olmsted-inspired city parks in many cities and restored or protected historical landmarks—remain one of the more convincing arguments for federal governmental action in the public interest during an era of privatization and transnational capital. And the success of this concept and accomplishment is confirmed by the degree to which it has been emulated around the world by nations hoping to preserve some crucial physical remnants of their natural (and national) history from the destructive results of the population explosion, industrialization, and urbanization. However, there is no point in ignoring those aspects of the national park idea/reality that are a function of the sociohistorical problems that necessitated the idea itself. While few of us (I hope) would like to see such forms of public protection curtailed, we can also recognize the historical and ideological compromises implicit in the public protection of the naturally beautiful and the historically important, compromises explored or suggested in a number of independent films.

Beginnings of the End? Bruce Conner's *Crossroads* and Werner Herzog's *Lessons of Darkness*

Ernest Hemingway's *Green Hills of Africa* (1935), one of the least recognized major contributions to American nature writing, includes the longest sentence Hemingway ever published. It comes almost exactly halfway through the nonfiction novel (in part 2, "Pursuit Remembered") during a moment when

Hemingway is distinguishing between the necessity of being involved in politics—where "you serve time for society, democracy, and other things"—and an equally compelling necessity to decline "any further enlistment" in politics and "make yourself responsible only to yourself." Hemingway departs from his paean to the Kenyan countryside to explain this second commitment:

> That something I cannot yet define completely but the feeling comes when you write well and truly of something and know impersonally you have written in that way and those who are paid to read it and report on it do not like the subject so they say it is all a fake, yet you know its value absolutely; or when you do something which people do not consider a serious occupation and yet you know, truly, that it is as important and has always been as important as all the things that are in fashion, and when, on the sea, you are alone with it and know that this Gulf Stream you are living with, knowing, learning about, and loving, has moved, as it moves, since before man, and that it has gone by the shoreline of that long, beautiful, unhappy island [Cuba] since before Columbus sighted it and that things you find out about it, and those that have always lived in it are permanent and of value because that stream will flow, as it has flowed, after the Indians, after the Spaniards, after the British, after the Americans and after all the Cubans and all the systems of governments, the richness, the poverty, the martyrdom, the sacrifice and the venality and the cruelty are all gone as the high-piled scow of garbage, bright-colored, white-flecked, ill-smelling, now tilted on its side, spills off its load into the blue water, turning it a pale green to a depth of four or five fathoms as the load spreads across the surface, the sinkable part going down and the flotsam of palm fronds, corks, bottles, and used electric light globes, seasoned with an occasional condom or a deep floating corset, the torn leaves of a student's exercise book, a well-inflated dog, the occasional rat, the no-longer-distinguished cat; all this well shepherded by the boats of the garbage pickers who pluck their prizes with long poles, as interested, as intelligent, and as accurate as historians; they have the viewpoint; the stream, with no visible flow, takes five loads of this a day when things are going well in La Habana and in ten miles along the coast it is as clear and blue and unimpressed as it was ever before the the the tug hauled out the scow; and the palm fronds of our victories, the worn light bulbs of our discoveries and the empty condoms of our great loves float with no significance against one single, lasting thing—the stream.[2]

In the context of *Green Hills of Africa,* Hemingway's faith in "the stream" to outlive all human striving is something of a paradox, as his essential motivation in writing the book is to create a vision of the Kenyan landscape that will communicate the experience of being *in* that landscape to someone who has never been there, and, more important, to capture this landscape in words so that once it has been destroyed, it can be reaccessed, at least in the imagination.[3] Hemingway's gulf-stream sentence is a form of whistling in the dark—a way of holding onto some sense of the wonder of original nature, in the midst of a premonition of its imminent demise.

Until the end of World War II, American writers and painters had usually understood the long-term impact of the industrial machine on the Garden of the New World as a slow, relentless accumulation of destruction, but the dropping of the atomic bombs on Hiroshima and Nagasaki and the subsequent nuclear arms race made obvious that while human impact on the environment might still be relentless, there was no longer any point in hoping that it would continue to be gradual. Indeed, in the 1950s the increasingly frequent appearance of imagery of atomic and nuclear detonations, especially of the Crossroads nuclear test in the Pacific, in film and on TV, was a signal that the "American Technological Sublime" had evolved to a new stage in which human technology could instigate an instantaneous expression of natural energy as sublime as virtually any natural display.[4] No filmmaker was more aware of the horrific beauty of the nuclear blast than Bruce Conner; indeed, since his early films incorporating the detonations were widely shown (and rented by advertising agencies), they may be partly responsible for the frequency of nuclear detonation imagery in subsequent years, not only in independent films (e.g., Andrew Noren's *Scenes from Life,* 1972) but in commercial films (e.g., Stanley Kubrick's *Dr. Strangelove,* 1964). Detonation imagery was so pervasive during the 1960s and 1970s that by 1983 when Peter Watkins was preparing to shoot *The Journey* (1987), his fourteen-and-a-half-hour critique of the failure of media and educational systems to deal with the global arms race, one of his first decisions was that the film would include no motion picture imagery of nuclear detonations, because such imagery had become so pervasive in the culture as to be endangering the planet by naturalizing the sight of bombs going off.[5]

While imagery of nuclear detonations appears throughout Conner's ouevre—in *A Movie* (1958), *Cosmic Ray* (1962), *Report* (various versions, 1963–67), *Mongoloid* (1978)—it is also the subject of by far his longest film: *Crossroads* (1976). While Conner is generally known not merely as one of cinema's most accomplished "recyclers" but also as a master editor—his syncopated montage in *Cosmic Ray* may have been a major influence on the acceleration of the editing in television commercials during the 1960s—*Crossroads* is

Figure 88. Nuclear detonation during Crossroads testing, from Bruce Conner's *Crossroads* (1976). Courtesy Pacific Film Archive.

an excursion into minimalism. Once he had bought the Crossroads footage from the National Archives, he decided to present a portion of the material in unusually long shots: the thirty-six minutes of *Crossroads* require only twenty-six shots.[6] During the first third of the film, we see a series of detonations from a variety of viewing positions (see fig. 88)—at sea level and from the air—accompanied by what may seem (after a birdcall) to be the original sound, though in fact it is a reverberant Moog synthesizer piece by Patrick Gleeson. During the remainder of the film, music by Terry Reilly accompanies a variety of other images of the testing on Bikini, including one shot that lasts more than seven minutes.

Conner's use of a minimalist approach for dealing with this material tends to confuse our usual categories. Since the detonations are visually arresting, even gorgeous to look at, and since this aesthetic impact is enhanced by the frequent slow motion and by the Reilly score, one is tempted to fall into a meditative sensibility akin to that evoked by such films as Larry Gottheim's

Fog Line and Peter Hutton's *Landscape (for Manon)* (see chaps. 1 and 8). And yet our consciousness of the *function* of this visually sublime process—its function in history, its implicit goals—renders any such meditation conflicted at best. The very power of these new bombs clearly places us at a crossroads in terms of our ability to adjust to the pressures of technological and industrial development. The "beautiful" detonations imply the potential for *total* transformation of both the human population and the diverse biota of the world.

If moratoriums on nuclear testing and the end of the cold war have kept nuclear detonations more or less out of sight in recent years (except on the Indian subcontinent), political events continue to provide imagery of comparably conflicted sublimity. The most obvious recent instance is the Gulf War, which provided CNN with astonishing imagery of the attack on Baghdad, and Werner Herzog (and others) with equally remarkable imagery of the war's aftermath. *Lessons of Darkness* (1992), Herzog's forty-seven-minute documentation/interpretation of the postwar disaster, begins as if its imagery were science fiction: the opening narration identifies "[a] planet in our solar system/ wide mountain ranges, clouds, the land shrouded in mist." Indeed, the film sometimes evokes Chris Marker's apocalyptic *La Jetée* (The Jetty, 1963), the seed for both *Terminator* films (*The Terminator,* 1984; and *Terminator 2: Judgment Day,* 1991, both directed by James Cameron) as well as *Twelve Monkeys* (1995, directed by Terry Gilliam).

Lessons of Darkness is divided into a prologue and thirteen sections. The prologue presents several shots of a strange, smoky landscape, followed by an image of a man near a huge fire gesticulating toward the camera, perhaps demanding that the filmmakers cease filming, though the meaning is ambiguous. The following numbered sections are titled, in English translation, "A Capital City" (it is Kuwait City just before the war),[7] "The War" (a brief passage of the television imagery of the bombing of Baghdad), "After the Battle" (shards of destroyed machinery, bombed-out industrial installations and bunkers), "Finds from Torture Chambers" (hand-held imagery of tools laid out on a table and other refuse, an "interview" with a woman whose sons were tortured to death in front of her: she attempts to speak to the camera), "Satan's National Park" (a destroyed oil field, with immense fires), "Childhood" (a mother tells of soldiers' brutalization of her now-mute son and the murder of her husband), "And a Smoke Arose Like a Smoke from a Furnace" (more imagery of the destroyed oil field, the fires), "A Pilgrimage" (American oilmen fight the fires with hoses, bulldozers, steam shovels—this imagery makes the prologue clearer: though we don't find out what the man's ambiguous gesture means, we realize who he is and what his job is), "Dinosaurs on the Go" (huge machines fighting the fires), "Protuberances" (burning, bubbling oil), "The Drying Up of the Source" (men plus machines bringing the fires and the spouting oil under control), "Life without Fire" (the men *start* two fires that had been put out), and "I am so tired from sighing; Lord, let it be night" (several final shots of the burning oil fields). The majority of the film focuses on the spectacular burning oil fields; indeed, the war that produced this disaster (and the brutality described in sections 4 and 6) accounts for only forty seconds of the film, reflecting both the general media blackout and the speed with which this environmental disaster was produced.

Like the imagery of nuclear detonations in *Crossroads,* Herzog's imagery of the Kuwaiti disaster is simultaneously politically troubling and visually sublime (see fig. 89). The sublimity is a function of the immensity of this disaster, of the size of the fires and the towering billows of black smoke; and it is powerfully confirmed both by Herzog's use of helicopter shots to survey the oil

Figure 89. Abandoned tank in Kuwaiti oil fields after the Gulf War, from Werner Herzog's *Lessons of Darkness* (1992). Courtesy Museum of Modern Art.

fields and by his accompanying the imagery with a sound track composed of excerpts from classic works that suggest the epic scope and historical significance of what we're seeing: Grieg's *Peer Gynt*, Mahler's *Symphony No. 2*, Arvo Pärt's *Stabat Mater*, Prokofieff's *Sonata for 2 Violins, Opus 56*, Schubert's *Nocturne, Opus 48*, Verdi's *Requiem*, and Wagner's *Das Rheingold, Parsifal*, and *Göttendammerung*. The overwhelming sublimity of *Lessons of Darkness*—all the more powerful, of course, because it was filmed in 35mm—is regularly reenergized during the film by Herzog's depiction of the men who are work- ing to control the disaster: they provide a continual reminder of its scale (as well as a heroic subtext, since we know that, in time, their efforts were able to bring the forces unleashed by the war under control).

Herzog's tour of this "national park" includes meditations on its more spec- tacular vistas and sites, and on less extensive "wonders." The close-up imagery of the burning and bubbling lakes of oil in "Protuberances," for example, pro- vides a detail of this disaster that is fascinating in a manner reminiscent of the tufa columns of California's Mono Lake: these remarkable formations, created when calcium from fresh spring water encounters the carbon in the alkaline salt water of the lake, were revealed by the lowering of Mono Lake's water level when an L.A. aqueduct drained the lake's feeder streams. In other words, like Kuwait's strangely lovely black oil lakes, they are a "natural wonder" revealed by a lack of human concern for the landscape.

The sublimity of Herzog's imagery is also a function of its mythic implica- tions. That Herzog sees the burning oil field as an apocalyptic vision of Hell come to Earth is clear both from his quotations from *Revelations* in the narra- tion of sections 4 and 6 and from the way in which the scenes in Herzog's film recall the history of the imaging of Hell[8]—most especially perhaps, Pieter Brueghel's *The Triumph of Death* (1527). The biblical connection is also, of course, a function of the fact that geographically Iraq is what was Babylonia; and this war is (still another) battle in the centuries-old confrontation between the Judeo-Christian and non-Judeo-Christian Middle East, a confrontation now so old as to seem nearly a part of the region's natural history.

For students of American culture, Herzog's choice of the title "Satan's Na- tional Park" for his introduction of the burning oil fields, and much of his sub- sequent imaging of this disaster, is evocative in a very different, though not entirely unrelated, way. In *Sacred Places: American Tourist Attractions in the*

Plates 12 – 13. Two composite shots from Pat O'Neill's
Water and Power (1989). Courtesy Pat O'Neill.

Plate 14. The Lake in Central Park in Jonas Mekas's *Walden* (1969). Courtesy Jonas Mekas.

Plate 15. Thomas Cole's *Expulsion from the Garden of Eden* (1828). Oil on canvas, 39¾" × 54½". Gift of Martha C. Karolik for the M. and M. Karolik Collection of American Paintings, 1815–1865 (47.1188). Courtesy, Museum of Fine Arts, Boston. Reproduced with permission (1999).

Plates 16–18. Three phases of a rural Vermont scene, from J. J. Murphy's *Print Generation* (1974). Courtesy J. J. Murphy.

Plate 19. Mountainous terrain in Utah, from James Benning's *Deseret* (1995). Courtesy James Benning.

Plate 20. The concluding image from James Benning's *Deseret* (1995). Courtesy James Benning.

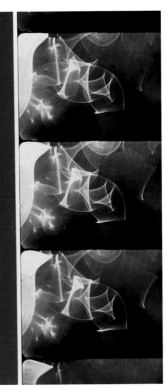
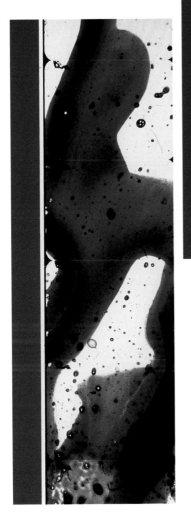

Plates 21–22. Two filmstrips from Stan Brakhage's *Commingled Containers* (1997). On the left strip, Brakhage has hand-painted imagery that evokes water; on the right, he has captured reflections within the flow of Boulder Creek, in Boulder, Colorado. Courtesy Anthology Film Archives.

Plates 23–24. Two images from Leighton Pierce's *50 Feet of String* (1995): *(above)* a man mows a lawn; *(below)* a toy tractor. Courtesy Leighton Pierce.

Nineteenth Century, John F. Sears reminds us that while the Yellowstone region, which became our first national park, has become one of the nation's foremost symbols of natural grandeur, during the nineteenth century the view of Yellowstone's magnificence epitomized by Thomas Moran's monumental painting, *The Grand Canyon of the Yellowstone* (1872), was not the only response to the region. Some well-known visitors found the Yellowstone area unpleasant, disgusting, even horrific: "Because of the strange, underworld features of its landscape, Yellowstone appeared to the nineteenth-century visitor to provide access to the infernal rather than the heavenly regions."[9] In an article in *Scribner's Monthly*, Nathaniel P. Langford extolled the beauty of some sections of the Yellowstone area but also described a "hideous glen filled with the sulphurous vapor, emitted from six or eight boiling springs," comparing it to "the entrance to the infernal regions."[10] The naming of various sectors of the park "Devil's Well," "Hell's Acre," and "the Devil's Kitchen" confirmed this connection.

Of course, the Yellowstone region is entirely a production of natural history, while the hellish landscapes recorded in *Lessons of Darkness* are, to adapt a Goya title, a natural disaster of war. And yet underneath this obvious difference lies an "infernal" connection. Herzog's use of the title "Satan's National Park" should remind us that, on one level, the national park system and the "sacred spaces" it preserves—or pretends to preserve—is a set of monuments to American imperial designs and successes; the parks are the remnants of our battles with "the wilderness" and with the indigenous peoples we decimated in our relentless expansion westward. The sublimity of the spaces enclosed by the parks, their power in the American imagination, is complex: it *is* a function of nature; but it is also, at least implicitly (and explicitly for the indigenous peoples whose loss was our gain), a function of the military power of the American nation, which, as a monument to itself, has defined these special spaces as symbols within its continental domain—symbols, ironically, of a respect for landscape that has hardly been a consistent dimension of our exploitation of the continent.

The horrific beauty of the burning oil fields in *Lessons of Darkness* is merely a twentieth-century version of a nineteenth-century pattern: we (and I mean all of us involved in such events as the Gulf War) are still demonstrating our nationhood by exploiting whatever landscapes we deem necessary for the maintenance of our way of life and the relentless expansion of our economic power—regardless of what it means for these landscapes and for the people native to them. If the national parks are symbolic gardens within the continental machine of capitalism, "Satan's National Park" in Kuwait is a transnational monument to our seemingly insatiable desire for power and to the "satanic" response of those who resist us.

Shoah as Landscape Film

> The Industrial Revolution . . . was a complex process of denaturalization.
> —WOLFGANG SCHIVELBUSCH, *THE RAILWAY JOURNEY*[11]

> The greatness of Claude Lanzmann's art is in making places speak.
> —SIMONE DE BEAUVOIR, PREFACE TO *SHOAH: THE COMPLETE TEXT*[12]

For a young American with German roots, growing up just after World War II, the Holocaust was an evolving realization and a formative warning. I do not remember when I first knew there had been a "Holocaust," though it did seem implicit in some of the war films I saw and in some of what I heard people talk about; and it was explicit in the ubiquitous high school dramatic versions of *The Diary of Anne Frank*. Of course, in college we learned more about the events and were outraged that "such things could happen." But my first powerful sense of what the Holocaust *was*—and I'm sure my experience is not unusual—came as a result of films that offered visual evidence: those piles of naked, emaciated corpses, shoved by bulldozers and, somehow even more horrifying, carried by soldiers, one by one, to be tossed into burial holes. Nothing in my experience did more than these images to undercut the 1950s American palaver about how modern progress was making everything better, and to deflate the seeming innocence of the new American suburban "paradise" in which I was living.

Of course, the preeminent Holocaust film in revealing this imagery was, and remains, Alain Resnais's remarkable *Night and Fog* (1955)—"remarkable" for both its power and its brevity: in only thirty-two minutes the film offers a history and an interpretation of the Holocaust. *Night and Fog* is about memory, and Resnais's attempt to bridge the gap between the crumbling, overgrown death camps in the 1950s and the astonishing events that had taken place there scarcely more than a decade earlier is ultimately a means to an end: the memorable reminder with which *Night and Fog* concludes:

Who among us is on the lookout from this strange tower to warn us of new executioners? Are their faces really different from our own? Somewhere among us, there are lucky Kapos, reinstated officers, and unknown informers. There are those of us who refused to believe this, or believed it only from time to time. And here we are, with all good intentions, looking at the ruins today as if the old concentration camp monster were dead and buried beneath the debris; and we pretend to take hope as the image recedes, as though one could be cured of the concentration camp plague; we pretend to believe that all this happened only once, at a certain time and in a certain place, and we refuse to look around us, we who do not hear the endless cry.[13]

I feel sure that few films, and no documentary, had a more powerful impact on the academic generation that came of age in the 1960s, the generation that made film studies (and Resnais's film) part of American academe. Indeed, in the four-plus decades since *Night and Fog,* only one of the dozens of subsequent films about the Holocaust seems to have had a comparable impact on thinking about the Nazis' Final Solution: Claude Lanzmann's *Shoah* (1985).[14]

When *Shoah* was released, its length (9 hours, 23 minutes) seemed remarkable, though few would argue that the Holocaust is not deserving of an unusually expansive film. And yet perhaps the most fundamental irony of Lanzmann's "epic" is that despite its length and despite the fact that Lanzmann needed eleven years to make the film, *Shoah* is a synecdoche: it uses interviews with twelve survivors, twenty or so Polish "bystanders," and four Nazis to represent events that involved millions.[15] Similarly, though Lanzmann takes us to the sites of the major camps and interviews survivors (and others) living in Germany, Poland, Switzerland, Greece, Israel, and the United States—watching *Shoah* is a thoroughly transnational experience—the film's primary focus is on a few, very particular locations that are seen over and over. Further, whereas *Night and Fog* gains much of its impact through the revelation of the literal evidence of the death camps, recycling the documentation of the corpses discovered by the Allies at the end of the war, *Shoah* presents no grisly documentation of the Holocaust at all. As we tour the locations where the events took place, we listen to and/or read (in subtitles) the stories told by those interviewed by Lanzmann. As we internalize these stories, we inevitably visualize the events, "shoot" the grisly imagery ourselves, internalizing not only the facts but also something of the experience of living through the horror.

Overall, *Shoah* is divided into two halves: the "First Era," which focuses on the earlier months of extermination; and the "Second Era," which focuses on the full-scale industrialization of death. While Lanzmann distinguishes the two eras in his titles (both "First Era" and "Second Era" conclude with detailed rolling credits, as if they were separate films), the film's internal structure is more complex than this division suggests, because the various histories included in *Shoah* are woven into a tapestry during which our awareness of the various locations and many of the events are all developing simultaneously.

One of the major trajectories that develops during the film—a trajectory that to some degree inverts the chronology of the Holocaust—is the movement from rural, village, and small-town locations to an increasing focus on the huge death factory at Auschwitz and, finally, to urban Warsaw and what was the world's largest Jewish ghetto. While on one level, this trajectory recalls the history of the urbanization of Europe (and North America) during recent centuries, Lanzmann recalls this history in part as a means of critiquing the myths that modern industrialization and urbanization have produced, myths that are encapsulated in three forms of public space we honor as parks and monuments: reservations of original, or at least earlier, natural landscape; significant historical ruins or restorations; and the maintenance of open spaces in highly developed urban environments as a means of maintaining the long-term efficiency of the modern, mechanized city.

Shoah begins with one of the most remarkable images in the history of film, a continuous (1-minute, 22-second) shot of the beautiful countryside along the Narew River in western Poland, in late summer: through the trees we see a rowboat in which one man rows and another sings a song. Translated, the lyrics mean, "A little white house/lingers in my memory./Of that little white house/I dream each night."[16] This long opening shot is followed by an extended (48-second) close-up of the singer, shot from inside the boat so that the lovely landscape along the river moves past him. This opening is dense with evocations of the past, of the traditional pastoral landscape and of the nostalgia for earlier, simpler ways of life "closer to nature" that has become one of the characteristics of nations in the midst of industrialization.[17] Indeed, Lanzmann's composition in the two shots suggests the history of landscape painting: specifically, the tradition of the calm, winding river from Claude Lorrain to the Hudson River school and the nineteenth-century moving panoramas of river journeys that helped to pave the way for cinema.[18]

Of course, by the time we see the conventional, traditional beauty of these opening shots, we already have a context for them that inverts their usual significance—a context created by our general awareness that these are the opening images in an epic film about the Holocaust and by the specific rolling text that immediately precedes the shots, which identifies the singer as Simon Srebnik, one of two survivors of the exterminations at Chelmno, whose father was murdered in front of him in the Lodz Ghetto and whose mother was killed in a gas van at Chelmno. Srebnik was forced to sing for the Nazis during his trips up the Narew to gather alfalfa for the rabbits grown by the SS and at the end of the war was shot through the head but lived. As a result of this context, the two opening images, which otherwise might seem the quintessential emblem of the simple and the beautiful, of "the good old days," are revealed as elements of a social system that was at least complicit in, if not a cause of, the most horrific inhumanity of modern times.

In the sequence that follows the opening two shots, Lanzmann's simultaneous recognition of the beauty of the pastoral and the dangers it hides, both philosophically and historically, is elaborated. Srebnik's rediscovery of the location of the mass graves and incinerations is also presented in a series of slow serene shots that capture the seeming paradox of natural beauty and cultural horror. What Srebnik and Lanzmann reveal here (and this realization is confirmed, again and again, in several different locations, in the company of other witnesses, during the "First Era" of Shoah) is that it was precisely the solitude made possible by the nearly pristine nature in these locations that made them perfect for death camps. Since the Nazis wanted both to exterminate the Jews and to exterminate any memory of the extermination itself, these gorgeous, unspoiled forests were perfect: not only did the forests help to hide the horrors (and allow many of the locals to feel detached from what was going on), but the very power of these biota to renew themselves allowed for the evidence of the horrors to be quickly overgrown. Srebnik's first words in the film are, "It's hard to recognize, but it was here. They burned people here." This sequence is followed by a third image of Srebnik singing in the boat—another conventionally beautiful, nearly two-minute panorama.

Much of the first half of Shoah focuses on the events that transpired in Chelmno and in other rural and small-town extermination camp locations; and a good many of Lanzmann's interviewees are small-town farmers and others "close to the land" and thus, at least in one quite conventional reading of country living, less corrupt than those living in more urbanized areas. During

Lanzmann's discussions with the residents of Chelmno, it becomes increasingly clear that most of these Poles are less than distressed by the horrors that occurred in their town: indeed, many see their lives as having been improved by the elimination of Chelmno's Jewish community. If they are still comparatively poor, some live in the better housing vacated by the extermination and in general their status is no longer contextualized by a richer, more sophisticated Other. Near the conclusion of "First Era," Lanzmann visits Chelmno on a Sunday when the locals are celebrating the birth of the Virgin Mary. This passage—which comes at the end of a long series of interviews with Polish witnesses to the extermination—is introduced by a final shot of Srebnik singing on the Narew River (this one, a more than two-minute panorama that includes the steeple of the lovely Chelmno church in the background). We then see Srebnik among the villagers as the church ceremony ends and a procession leaves the church to walk through the village. With Srebnik positioned in the center of the frame, the villagers discuss the former "procession" of the Chelmno Jews out of this same church on the way to extermination. The discussion ends with the explanation by two outspoken villagers that the murder of the Jews by the Nazis was the expiation (understood, say these villagers, by the Jews themselves) of the murder of Christ by the Jews of Bethlehem. The "First Era" of *Shoah* thus critiques not only the tradition of the classic pastoral landscape but also the Christian use of the pastoral idea. Here in front of this country church, during a celebration for the Mother of God, these Christians reveal that not only underneath their land, but within their most sacred ideology, lies an acceptance of violent revenge—their version of the Nazi mythology that resulted in the extermination itself.

The first half of *Shoah* concludes with a reading of a letter that suggests improvements to the gas vans used in the Chelmno exterminations, accompanied by a sequence of shots, filmed from a moving vehicle, of factories in the Ruhr Valley—a premonition of the full-scale industrialization of the Holocaust that culminates in the film's exploration of the ruins of Auschwitz-Birkenau. These ruins are the heart of *Shoah,* as the Birkenau extermination complex was the heart of the Holocaust; in fact, the image used on the jacket of the VHS version of *Shoah* is the gateway into Auschwitz-Birkenau, at the end of the railroad line. It is an image reiterated regularly during *Shoah*—and a metaphor for the film itself: the space beyond the gate revealed by the more or less rectangular gate opening is the world to which the film ultimately delivers us, though of course what we come to know is only the most constricted version of, a cinematic "gateway" to, the immensity of these events. The combination of the desire for gas-van efficiency and the imagery of the German "industrial sublime" so evident in the Ruhr Valley suggests what the entirety of *Shoah* confirms: the Holocaust itself is a culmination of the industrial revolution. In *The Machine in the Garden*, Leo Marx sees the arrival of the railroad in the American "Garden" as a watershed moment in the transformation of America; in *Shoah*, Lanzmann's many images of trains arriving at the rural Polish railroad stations where European Jewry was decimated becomes a metaphor for that culmination of modern industrial efficiency that must transform our sense of history, our faith in progress—including our conventional sense of the evolution of cinema.

It is a common trope of film history that with *L'Arrivée d'un train en gare de la Ciotat* (1895) the industrial history of the projected motion picture begins; and the conventional understanding of the evolution of the medium sees film history as parallel to the larger history of industrially produced machinery of which cinema is one small part. As the medium becomes increasingly sophisticated, it develops more characters and more elaborate plots that move more and more quickly. Of course, central to the improvement of narrative efficiency is the evolution of editing, first in the hands of Edwin S. Porter and D. W. Griffith and subsequently during the 1920s, when Sergei Eisenstein and others recognized that montage "should be compared to the series of explosions of an internal combustion engine, driving forward its automobile or tractor."[19] By the 1960s the acceleration of film (and TV) history in general and of individual films (and the TV hour) was instigating responses from independents who recognized the limitations of cinematic velocity and who committed themselves to filmic approaches that ran counter to this relentless acceleration.[20] Of course, *Shoah* is among the most accomplished, if not *the* most accomplished and suggestive instance of this pattern. Lanzmann tours the physical ruins of the Final Solution, using a cinematic approach that reverses the direction of modern media evolution: virtually every shot in the film is a long, continuous shot, many of them more than twice the length of the original Lumière films: that is, *Shoah* goes back to the arrival of the train at la Ciotat and demands that we slow down and consider the full range of implications of the historical "triumph" of the modern industrialized state (see figs. 90, 91).[21]

Figure 90. The Lumière Brothers' *L'Arrivée d'un train en gare de la Ciotat* (1895).

In the history of parks in America and elsewhere, the convention—at least for places considered to be of historical importance—is to use modern technology to provide detailed historical restorations of the past (as has been done in the Colonial Williamsburg National Historical Park in Virginia and, more recently, in the Lowell National Historical Park in Massachusetts), or at least, to prevent the further decimation of what remains of particular ruins (the 1906 Antiquities Act was passed to preserve what remained of such Native American landmarks as Mesa Verde and Chaco Canyon). Presumably, the reason for such preservation, and especially restoration, is to honor earlier steps in the progressive evolution of modern America: *this*, suggest the preserved monuments, is how we came to be the remarkable modern nation we are![22] Lanzmann's tour of Auschwitz inverts this paradigm. His film uses a historically "primitive" visual approach to meditate on the *un*restored ruins of one of the twentieth century's pivotal accomplishments, revealing the most catastrophic flaw in the development of modern life—a flaw that is the result of the very industrial efficiency we define *as* the essence of modernity, and for which we strive so relentlessly.

The final section of *Shoah*—the fifth and final tape in the VHS version—

Figure 91. The gate to Auschwitz-Birkenau, from Claude Lanzmann's *Shoah* (1985). Courtesy Museum of Modern Art.

focuses on the earliest events reviewed in detail in the film: the events that transpired in the Warsaw ghetto following the sealing off of the ghetto's half-million Jews in 1940, and leading to the transportation of the ghetto population to extermination camps in 1942. This section begins with Jan Karski's narrative of his visit to the ghetto in 1942 and is followed by visuals that, in another film, might seem like a city symphony of modern Warsaw, [23] including three long, rightward pans (45 seconds, 38 seconds, 51 seconds, respectively) across the city of Warsaw, apparently from the roof of a skyscraper. Taken together, these three pans are reminiscent—at least for an American—of Eadweard Muybridge's panoramic photography of San Francisco. But here again, Lanzmann's panorama of Warsaw, and the imagery of street scenes in Warsaw that comes later, inverts the conventional celebratory implications of such depictions. From Muybridge's panorama of San Francisco through the entire history of the city symphony form, the vista of the modern industrialized city has become a visual icon of the magnificent intricacy of modern, urbanized life: "Look," such vistas seem to say, "at all these people working together to keep this astonishing meta-machine running efficiently!" In *Shoah,* however, the areas of Warsaw we are seeing were the locations where the Nazis turned modern city life into hell on earth, where the intricacy and efficiency of modern life functioned both to destroy lives and to render that destruction virtually invisible to those outside the ghetto.

In a sense, the Warsaw ghetto is a nightmare version of the idea of protecting open, natural spaces within the modern city. Great public city parks, like Central Park or the Tier Garten in Berlin, allow city dwellers to free themselves from the inevitable pressures of modern urban population density. The Warsaw ghetto, like other Nazi-defined ghettos, was precisely the opposite: a space of *more* than the usual urban density within which residents were *less* free and certainly more stressed than their counterparts outside the boundaries of the ghetto.[24] While the urban park usually protects those in it from stress, the ghetto simultaneously created additional stress for those inside and protected those outside from being aware of it, so they could continue about their business.

Lanzmann's serene pacing during this final section of *Shoah* (and throughout the film) bears the same relationship to conventional film pacing, even documentary pacing, as the pace of life in a city park (at least theoretically) bears to the pace of the urban life that surrounds it.[25] The paradox is that Lanzmann's serene pacing means to give us time—more time, indeed, than we might wish—to ponder, not natural *beauty,* but the remarkable *horror* that is described by Jan Karski, Raul Hilberg, and Franz Grassler as they sit in their living rooms being interviewed by Lanzmann. Lanzmann does not strive to assist us in *forgetting* the stresses of urbanized living but means for us to remember—and to a degree, even *feel*—the stresses of those who were to become the casualties of industrial "efficiency."

Because the Nazis were obsessively careful to use so many of the most cherished assumptions of Western culture, especially those about nature, in ways that invert any sane understanding of those assumptions, Lanzmann had no choice but to invert the conventional use of the machine of cinema in order to provide a sense of the Holocaust that he and we can live with and learn from. For most of us, moviegoing has come to function in much the same way that natural and historical reserves are meant to function: that is, as time-limited "escapes" useful for general stress relief and for confirmation of national identity. Lanzmann means to transform this "escape" into a more thorough engagement with crucial historical realities, realities that have everything to do with how we moderns live our lives. *Shoah* does more than require us to remember what the Nazis wanted forgotten; the experience of *Shoah* requires that we open spaces within our obsessively scheduled, efficient lives wherein we can confront the dangers implicit in societal tendencies that we continue to consider not only normal but worthy of distinction and reward.

James Benning: Two "Westerns"

A surveyor from each state shall be appointed by Congress or a Committee of the States, who shall take an oath for the faithful discharge of his duty, before the Geographer of the United States. . . .

The Surveyors, as they are respectively qualified, shall proceed to divide the said territory into townships of six miles square, by lines running due north and south, and others crossing these at right angles, as near as may be, unless where the boundaries of the late Indian purchases may render the same impracticable. . . .

The first line, running due north and south as aforesaid, shall begin on the river Ohio, at a point that shall be found to be due north from the western termination of a line, which has been run as the southern boundary of the State of Pennsylvania; and the first line, running east and west, shall begin at the same point, and shall extend throughout the whole territory. Provided, that nothing herein shall be construed, as fixing the western boundary of the State of Pennsylvania. The Geographer shall designate the townships, or fractional parts of townships, by numbers progressively from south to north; always beginning each range with No. 1; and the ranges shall be distinguished by their progressive numbers to the westward. The first range, extending from the Ohio to the lake Erie, being marked No. 1. The Geographer shall personally attend to the running of the first east and west line; and shall take the latitude of the extremes of the first north and south line, and of the mouths of the principal rivers.

The lines shall be measured with a chain; shall be plainly marked by chaps on the trees, and exactly described on a plat; whereon shall be noted by the surveyor, at their proper distances, all mines, salt-springs, salt-licks and mill-seats, that shall come to his knowledge, and all water-courses, mountains and other remarkable and permanent things, over and near which such lines shall pass, and also the quality of the lands.

The plats of the townships respectively, shall be marked by subdivisions into lots of one mile square or 640 acres, in the same direction as the external lines, and numbered from 1 to 36; always beginning the succeeding range of the lots with the number next to that with which the preceding one concluded. . . . —LAND ORDINANCE OF 1785[26]

Benning came of age as a filmmaker during the heyday of two cine-cultural projects in American independent cinema (see chapter 4 for background on Benning). One was what P. Adams Sitney called "structural film": many filmmakers were devising new formal structures that would create types of in-the-ater experience that interrupted the smooth narrative continuities of Hollywood movies.[27] The other was a broad-ranging rebellion against both Hollywood and the "arty," formal concerns characteristic of structural film, in the interest of a more thorough cinematic engagement with political issues. Feminist filmmakers were questioning the gender politics of all cinema, including the avant-garde;[28] punk filmmakers, the mechanics of modern, consumer-culture fascism; trash films, "good taste." And African-American filmmakers were countering the absence of African Americans in both the commercial and the independent cinema in films that were "avant-garde" simply because of the presence of the issue of race. The films of Benning's maturity, including his films about the West, are a weave of these two projects. In *Deseret* (1995), a highly formal structure is used as a scaffolding that allows Benning to construct an examination of the impact of human settlement—including the collisions of different ethnicities—on the landscape of Utah. In *Four Corners* (1997), a different but equally rigorous formal structure allows Benning to explore the same issues, in this instance, foregrounding the conflict of ethnicities in the geographic region where Utah, Colorado, New Mexico, and Arizona meet.

Deseret gets its title from the Jaredite word for "honeybee" in the *Book of Mormon* ("Deseret" was the Mormons' original choice for what we know as "Utah"). The film is organized into a precise, though unconventional, structure. The sound track of *Deseret* is made up of a series of ninety-three stories about Utah taken from the *New York Times* and arranged chronologically, beginning with the *Times*'s first story about Utah, published on March 19, 1852 (a story about non-Mormon settlers being "despoiled of their goods" by Mormons—the story indicates that the rumors are exaggerated), and ending with a December 21, 1992, story about a stand of aspen trees in the Wasatch Mountains having been identified as "the world's largest organism." To find these news stories, which are narrated by Fred Gardner, Benning read every *New York Times* story about Utah, from the founding of the newspaper in 1852 until 1992, chose ninety-three, and condensed each to a maximum of eight to ten sentences (Benning was careful to retain the original language of the news stories, so that the slow evolution of journalese becomes one of the historical threads in the weave of *Deseret*). Then, having collected a considerable range of images of Utah, Benning matched the imagery to the text in a predetermined organization. (See fig. 92; plate 19.)

Each sentence in the spoken text is accompanied by a single, continuous shot; and each story and mini-sequence of shots is separated from the next by a single shot. The publication date of the news story is superimposed over the first shot of each story. While the length of shots during the stories is determined by the length of the sentences we are hearing, the length of each shot that divides one story from the next is a bit shorter than the previous "divider" shot. The continuing reduction in the length of the shots that separates the news stories has a number of effects, one of which is to suggest the shortening time between the occurrence of a news event and the reporting of it, from the middle of the nineteenth century to the present (the second story in *Deseret* describes the massacre of a Lieutenant Gunnison and eleven of his men by a band of Utes: the massacre occurred on October 26, 1853; the *Times* story is dated January 25, 1854, three months later). On another level, the

Figure 92. Desert in southern Utah in James Benning's *Deseret* (1995). Courtesy James Benning.

shortening duration echoes the speed-up created by the shortening of sentences in reportage, which itself seems an aspect of the ever-accelerating pace of modern life.

A further, general dimension of Benning's organization is his division of the film in half: the first half of *Deseret* is in black-and-white (and the superimposed dates are printed in an antique typeface); the second half—which begins with the fortieth story, just after the announcement of Utah's achieving statehood on January 5, 1896—is in color (dates are printed in a more modern typeface).

Ironically, the organizational complexity of *Deseret* creates what for most viewers is a relatively slow-paced experience: we *hear* the history (or the "history": Benning chose the *New York Times* in part because he wanted to recall the history of a sector of the *West* as it was interpreted by the quintessential *Eastern* newspaper; and because he wanted to depict the history of a religious sect that emigrated to Utah to be *outside* the United States, as it has been interpreted by a newspaper that, as fully as any, proposes to be the *inside* word on the American nation), as we *see* the geography.[29] If the formal design of *Deseret* is more felt than conceptualized by the first-time viewer, intersections of text and image continually tease the mind. One of the "rules" of the film is that within the sequence of shots that corresponds to each *Times* story, one shot bears a literal relationship to the story we are hearing: that is, one of the shots was recorded precisely where the events described in the news story took place. Sometimes this visual/auditory connection is obvious, sometimes not. As a result, we are often in the position (as no doubt Benning himself often was) of wondering, Is *this* the place where it happened? or is *that*?

The interplay between imagery and narrated story can be complex—an engaging game, for those who agree to play. For example, the "October 14, 1867" story about illness includes four sentences: "This is the sickliest season of the year in this locality though this is not considered the most sickly year we have had, by far. The mortality is chiefly among children. It is no easy matter to raise children in this place, however famous the country for the production of them. During the period of teething the percentage of mortality is great: Diarrhea, dysentery, canker and consumption being the chief causes of death." This text is accompanied by five shots (Benning interprets the final sentence as two, cutting after the colon): a minimal image of water and sky; an image of a child's grave; a shot of what looks like a homestead in a state of decay; a desert landscape; and a factory. The literal connection is obviously between the brief second shot and the second sentence; but there are other possible connections as well: the third shot may suggest a failed attempt to establish and raise a family, and the juxtaposition of the factory with the phrase "the chief causes of death" is a premonition of the theme of the dangers of industrial development that becomes increasingly important as *Deseret* develops. Even the fourth shot, of a few bushes growing in the sand, may visually evoke—it's a stretch—a baby's teeth beginning to appear.[30]

The overall experience of *Deseret,* however, is a combination of the visual pleasure of touring this remarkable region—Benning's imagery is consistently elegant and, especially during the second half, stunning—and the accumulating impact on our perception of a set of suggestive visual motifs and historical echoes. Two central themes dominate *Deseret:* the development and decay of that series of ways of life that are encoded in this particular geographic area; and the health of the land itself. Of course, as the title indicates, the most obvious way of life developing in Utah is Mormonism (the first twenty-four *Times* stories are about the establishment of Mormonism), but evidence of the various Indian societies that were established in Utah before the arrival of the Mormons—the Anasazi, the Shoshoni, the Goshute, the Ute, the South Paiute, and the Navajo—is obvious from the beginning of the film, in the form of two visual motifs: pictographs from many eras; and the ruins of Indian pueblos, many of them cliff dwellings. The ongoing collisions of the Mormons, the local Indians, and the U.S. government that began during the early years of Mormonism are referred to in various *Times* stories.

Other "ways of life" also develop, and fade, in *Deseret*. There are dinosaurs whose remains were chiseled out of Split Mountain ("March 22, 1925"). A January 8, 1944, *Times* story announces the establishment of Topaz, the Japanese internment camp that for a time was the fifth largest city in Utah (Benning includes a shot of the ruins of Topaz).[31] And there are the many anonymous individuals whose lives have ended or changed, leaving behind the decaying factories, homes, trailers, trucks, cars we see in Benning's imagery, as well as those people involved in the new stores and developing industries Benning records. This multifaceted overlapping of cultures is poignantly encapsulated in several images of rock faces where pictographs are defaced by, or at least coexist with, modern graffiti. Benning depicts Utah as a place of endless comings and goings, beginnings and endings—a distinctive region and a microcosm of America.

The second general theme, the health of the land, becomes more and more obvious during the second half of *Deseret,* as an increasing percentage of *New York Times* stories involve environmental issues—though this is visually implicit through much of the film. Benning's structure enacts a rough balance between the early years (the first third of the film covers only the period from 1852 until the Civil War—in twenty-six stories) and the years since the Kennedy administration, when Benning came of age (the final third of the film covers twenty-nine years—in thirty-seven stories). The middle third of *Deseret* covers nearly a hundred years in only thirty stories. Each third of the film places a different kind of emphasis on the environment. None of the *Times* stories during the opening third of the film refers to the natural environment, except as the location of a contest for space—though the visual imagery does reveal a variety of interventions into the landscape that have environmental implications. During the middle third of the film, *Times* stories chronicle events that were, especially in their time, seen as improvements to the land—for example, the completion of the transcontinental railroad ("May 11, 1869")—*and* events that may have seemed positive at the time but now seem ambiguous at best—for example, the slaughter of predatory animals ("May 2, 1970"), which is accompanied by an image of a dead coyote. But from the 1950s on, and increasingly during the final third of the film, the *Times* stories cover a variety of events that have done, and continue to do, serious damage: radioactive fallout and cancer from nuclear testing in Nevada; chemical and biological weapons development, testing, and stockpiling at Dugway Proving Grounds, ninety miles west of Salt Lake City; major toxic waste sites in Utah and the trucking of toxic waste from other regions *to* Utah; and air force plans to build a $3 billion electronic battlefield on 1,400 square miles of the Utah desert.[32]

While the central dramatic tension in the first half of *Deseret* is the viewers' attempt to imagine what *really* happened in Utah, judging from the *Times* stories and the imagery Benning presents (while simultaneously trying to make sense of the complex structure of the film), the central dramatic tension of the second half is the combined effect of Benning's switch to color and the information we're learning in the *Times* stories (regularly confirmed in the imagery) on our perception of the landscape. The change to color, on Utah's becoming a state in 1896, has the impact of the shock of the new—especially because of Benning's sensitivity to the remarkable range of color that characterizes a year in Utah.[33] Benning's color gives the second half of the film a new immediacy and sensuality, and a precariousness that is emphasized by the gradual acceleration of the pace of Benning's editing. Because sentences in *Times* journalese (and therefore Benning's shots) have become shorter during the past century and because the "divider" shots have grown shorter throughout the film, the gorgeousness of Benning's imagery must be apprehended more and more quickly.

At the same time, as the *Times*'s chronicling of environmental damage increases, our sense of the beauty of Benning's imagery evolves. After we learn that the sego lily, the state flower of Utah, is doomed to extinction in Utah by urban spread, Benning's image of a sego lily is both lovely and bittersweet. After we learn that an aboveground nerve-gas test conducted at Dugway killed 6,400 sheep and that the dangerous chemical agent can be "isolated in snow, water, sheep blood, sheep liver tissue, and in the grass taken from sheep's stomachs" ("March 24, 1968")—Benning presents a snowscape at the moment when the narrator says, "snow"—our perception of Benning's subsequent snowscapes renders them as problematic as they are beautiful. Indeed, by the conclusion of *Deseret* virtually every place we see is felt to be simultaneously beautiful and endangered. While ways of life in Utah may continue to come and go (and while some of these ways of life continue to be confronted with the same challenges that confronted them a century ago), the land itself seems, increasingly, a casualty of American progress, despite lip service to the idea of environmental cleanup.

Benning's increasingly frequent imaging of Robert Smithson's *The Spiral Jetty*, built in a remote part of the Great Salt Lake in 1970, is a central reference during *Deseret* and a clue to both the implications of the film's unusual structure and Benning's concern for the environment (see fig 20). *The Spiral Jetty*'s imaging of the concept of entropy (popularly understood, the idea that in a closed system, energy runs down)[34] is represented symbolically in the shape of the spiral; it is demonstrated by the fact that Smithson's original work is in an advanced state of decay and will soon cease to be visible; and it was implicit in Smithson's decision to build the jetty in the Great Salt Lake: as Benning explains in *North on Evers*, "Smithson described the surrounding salt flats in his writings. Caught in their sediments were countless bits of wreckage. He said that the site gave evidence of a succession of man made systems mired in abandoned hopes."[35]

The structure of *Deseret* echoes Smithson's spiral. Just as *The Spiral Jetty* spirals in on itself until there is no space for further looping, the "divider" shots continue to shorten until they provide virtually no division between the *Times* story sequences. And this entropic dimension of the film's structure reflects the theme of environmental damage. As the exploitation of the region has accelerated, so has the damage to the environment: the faster *we* go, the faster *it* goes. On this level, the ever-shortening "divider" shots suggest both the decrease in space between people in Utah (and everywhere else on Earth) and the ever-shortening time we have left to do something about this process before the "flower" of *our* culture is extinct.

Benning sees the danger of our current cultural trajectory *and* the importance of not giving in to it: he uses his gorgeous imagery to energize us. Indeed, his concluding with the *Times* story about the stand of aspens as "the world's largest organism" is a reminder that our stake in the viability of the environment is global; we are all part of a single "root system." *Deseret* was finished on the centennial anniversary of Utah statehood: the concluding image is of a billboard that says "Utah 1896–1996/Still the Right Place" (see plate 20). Utah *is* "still the right place," not merely in the senses that the designers of the sign may have had in mind (the "right place" for still *more* development; the morally "right" place, the politically "right" place), but in the environmental sense: Utah remains the, or at least *a,* right place for coming to grips with our environmental crisis.

Deseret is a record of Benning's *exploration* of Utah. In *Four Corners* he slows down to meditate more fully on the issues the experience of making *Deseret* defined for him. *Four Corners* uses the intersection of Utah, Colorado, New Mexico, and Arizona as horizontal and vertical axes—a synecdoche of Jefferson's grid system for America, which was formally instituted by the Continental Congress in the Land Ordinance of 1785—against which he and we can measure four kinds of history/geography that have evolved in the Four Corners area: *geologic history,* which has been readable ever since Clarence Dutton published his *Tertiary History of the Grand Cañon District* (1882), summarizing two decades of geologic observation by John Wesley Powell, Dutton, and others; *sociopolitical history,* including the long complex Indian history that began with the first peoples to cross the Bering land bridge and subsequent Native American migrations and continued with the several histories of emigration from Europe (and Africa and Asia); *art history,* as represented (in image and text) by Yukuwa, a Native American woman artist whom Benning imagines painting canyon walls in the 100s A.D., Claude Monet, Alabama folk artist Moses Tolliver, and Jasper Johns; and *Benning's personal history,* which intersects with each of these other histories in a variety of ways.

Structurally, *Four Corners* divides into four rigorously organized sections of equal length and identical design, each made up of four different kinds of information. The four sections are introduced by a continuous two-and-a-half-minute close-up of a campfire, accompanied by the sounds of a fire and of a traditional chant, "Song for a Journey," sung by the Little Wolf Band—suggesting that *Four Corners* is a modern form of campfire storytelling. Each of the four sections of the film begins with eighty seconds of visual text, white on black, that is at first still, then begins to scroll upward: the text summarizes the life of a particular artist, leading to the creation of a particular artwork.[36] Each text is composed of the same number of typographic characters (1,214). Following the visual text, we see a single, continuous shot of the artwork mentioned at the end of the text; and we hear a particular history read by a narrator: each history consists of exactly the same number of words (1,186), though the lengths of the readings vary slightly. The narrators, all of whom are filmmakers and speak differently accented English, are Hartmut Bitomski (a German American who works with Benning at the California Institute of the Arts in Valencia, California); Yeasup Song (a Korean who went to school at the California Institute of the Arts); Billy Woodbury (the African-American director of *Bless Their Little Hearts,* 1984); and Benning, who has retained his Milwaukee accent. Each of the four subsections concludes with a sequence of thirteen forty-second shots—each sequence a visual and auditory tour of locations mentioned in the previous history.[37] The four thirteen-shot sequences are arranged seasonally: summer, fall, winter, spring. *Four Corners* concludes with an epigram by Black Elk—"Sometimes dreams are wiser than waking"—and with a continuous two-and-a-half-minute shot of two homes on the Hopi reservation, accompanied by "I Sang the Blues" by the Lost Poets, a piece that reviews the history of the brutalization of African Americans in North America.

All in all, the experience of *Four Corners* is more serenely paced than the experience of *Deseret.* Not only are all the individual shots considerably longer than most viewers are accustomed to (the forty-second shots in the thirteen-shot "tours" are the *shortest* in the film), but each of the four sections of the film is identical to the others: by the conclusion of the second section, any potential for surprise has vanished. The result, at least for those willing to engage what Benning *does* provide, is space for careful observation of what is presented to the eye and ear and for extended thought about the implications of the spaces we see and the stories we hear. In many cases, Benning frames imagery so that particular details declare themselves gradually, or so that implicit connections between sound and image develop. For example, in the thirteenth shot of Benning's tour of Milwaukee, we see the outside of a church in what looks to be an empty, lifeless neighborhood, but we *hear* a congregation singing with energy: the implication is that even a neighborhood that by conventional cultural definitions is bottoming out and has, for all commercial purposes, been forgotten, hides within it not just spirit but enthusiastic hope for the future. Of course, in general, Benning's extended shots of artworks and of landscape/cityscape (all the images in the thirteen-shot tours are of spaces in which human habitation and natural environment have intersected and continue to have an impact on each other) suggest that *these* artifacts of cultural development are worthy of our sustained attention.

While the rigorous, even obsessive organization of *Four Corners* echoes the geometric rigor of the boundaries (territorial in the 1860s and subsequently state) that meet at the Four Corners, and while the serene pace of Benning's editing captures something of the expanse of the Four Corners area, the complexity of the stories told in Benning's visual and narrated texts and the intersections between them echo the historical complexity of the region. Indeed, at times the texts seem as unruly as the film's structure is precise. Perhaps the most unruly of the texts is the second narration (presented as we look at Moses Tolliver's *George Washington*), Benning's own history, narrated by Benning himself. This text, which focuses on Milwaukee, begins with a brief discussion of Benning's father rebuilding what became the family home during World War II and the neighborhood's German roots; it then switches to a review of the early geologic history of the region and in more recent eras its settlement by Paleo-Indians, the arrival of French fur traders, and the wars between the Menominee and Potawatomi Indians and the expanding American nation; the influx of Germans in the mid-nineteenth century after the 1848 German cultural revolution; and the influx of Poles in the 1880s and of two hundred thousand African Americans in the 1940s. Next, Benning reviews aspects of his childhood, including his white neighborhood's fear of blacks, and the white exodus to other neighborhoods; then briefly reviews the history of political resistance in Milwaukee during the twentieth century—the city's socialist government, the civil rights marches in the sixties organized by Father James Groppi (during one of which Benning "was beaten unconscious in Kosciuszko Park")—and concludes with a description of the current state of Benning's old neighborhood, now the center of "the worst poverty in Milwaukee." Milwaukee is a nexus of so many strands of history—and so many kinds of explicit and implicit collision: Native American/European American; German/Polish; white union members/blacks—that Benning's narration is virtually a historical, auditory montage within the serenity of the extended shot of the Tolliver painting.

That the entire text focuses on the history of *Milwaukee* may seem a glitch in Benning's focus on the Four Corners. And yet, Benning is well aware that to see the history of the Four Corners as separate from the larger history of the sociopolitical evolution of the American West would be a fiction: after all, until the nineteenth century, the Milwaukee area was part of the "Northwest Territory," and the issues that developed as *this* territory became part of the American nation were precisely the issues that developed as the territories of Colorado, Utah, New Mexico, and Arizona became part of the United States. That one of the four artists Benning profiles in the rolling texts is Claude Monet seems a similar "glitch"; but again, to see the evolution of American art as separate from the history of European art would be as arbitrary as the geometric boundaries at the Four Corners, and would ignore Benning's own use of an artistic tool that is a product of the European Renaissance and the industrial revolution.

While the four narrated texts explore widely diverse histories, they do reveal certain parallels. Each history is much involved in collisions between ethnicities and cultures, collisions that result in violence: in narration 1 (the story of James Wetherill, who made a living selling Indian artifacts to the Museum of Natural History in New York), the murder of James Wetherill by Navajo Chrischilling-begay; in narration 2, the beating of Benning by a group of whites during the civil rights march; in narration 3 (a history of Native America in the Four Corners area), Cortés's massacre of the Zuni in the name of Christianity; the Hopi massacre at Awatovi; disputes between Mexico and the United States

Figure 93. Navajo cemetery in Farmington, New Mexico, some-
times called "Moccasin Hill" (as opposed to "Boot Hill"), where
Herman Dodge Benally is buried, from James Benning's *Four
Corners* (1997). Courtesy James Benning.

and between the Hopi and the Navajo; and in narration 4 (a history of
Farmington, New Mexico, the largest city in the Four Corners), the murder of
Navajo Herman Dodge Benally by three white teenagers and the resulting riot.
And each of the four histories intersects with the others: Wetherill's visits to
Farmington are described in the fourth narration; the murder of Herman
Dodge Benally is part of the larger history described in the third narration;
Benning visits the sites "discovered" and exploited by Wetherill (now Mesa
Verde National Park and Chaco Canyon National Park) and the locations in
and around Farmington mentioned in the fourth narration (see fig. 93).

Another form of interplay between the four sections is a function of the
film's seasonal structure: Benning's beautiful imagery of Chaco Canyon in
summer and Mesa Verde in winter provides a counterpoint to his imagery of
Milwaukee in fall and Farmington in spring, especially since, comparatively
speaking, we see almost no people in Chaco Canyon or in Mesa Verde, while

people and vehicles regularly punctuate Benning's imagery of Milwaukee and Farmington. If cities are now the more obvious battlegrounds of culture, the places where American cultural diversity and change are most obvious, Benning's depiction of two national parks, two of the first to be dedicated to Native America, is a poignant reminder that while these two parks honor histories that indeed should be honored, the ruins tourists now visit within these remarkable landscapes are the empty shells of worlds that expired before we could know them (before we could contest *their* ways of life in the name of *our* cultural norms), worlds that became national parks only after they were fully exploited and on the verge of total decimation. *Four Corners* reminds us that we are surrounded by, and surround, worlds currently full of life but endangered by the same patterns of bigotry and economic exploitation: surely it is our obligation to these still-living communities that Benning means to place within the crosshairs of our thinking.

All in all, the complex personal/ethnic/national histories reviewed in Benning's texts and imagery are like vines growing on the trellis of his structure; and together, Benning's point/counterpoint of structure and event define our current situation. As a people, or a set of peoples (and in this we are little distinct, if distinct at all, from any other geographic region on Earth), we have the desire for order, clarity, and coherence and for beauty and a memory of the complex histories that have produced us, histories defined in large measure by collisions of varying *definitions* of beauty and brutal excesses perpetrated in the name of beauty. In its own small way, *Four Corners* models one artist's vision of an integration of the ideal and the real that allows for diversity *and* unity, formal beauty *and* a respect for the realities of history as they are embodied everywhere in our increasingly interconnected and inescapably diverse world. Ultimately, the unusual cinematic structures of Benning's two "Westerns"— recent evidence of this filmmaker's lifelong, ongoing resistance to Hollywood ways of depicting human experience—*are* his fundamental argument. So long as we follow the Hollywood model and continue to repress the complex realities of geography and history on the assumption that there are no real alternatives, we will not find our way out of the dilemmas that face us.[38] But if we can begin to confront these issues in all their complexity, with patience and commitment and the faith that experience can be restructured in progressive ways, we may be able to grow beyond our current sociocultural limitations, doing honor both to our ethnic diversity and to our physical environment. [39]

chapter 11

Benedictions/New Frontiers

Scenery seems to wear in one's consciousness better than any other element in life. In this year of much solemn and idle meditation, I have often been surprised to find what a predominant part in my own spiritual experience it has played, and how it stands out as almost the only thing the memory of which I should like to carry over with me beyond the veil, unamended and unaltered.

We of the highly educated classes (so called) have most of us got far, far away from Nature. . . . We are stuffed with abstract conceptions and glib verbalities and verbosities; and in the culture of these higher functions, the peculiar sources of joy connected with our simpler functions often dry up.

WILLIAM JAMES

Few words are more likely to cause consternation in recent generations of American academics than "the spirit" and "spiritual." Whether in the context of traditional religion or in the more recent New Age context, admitting to a spiritual connection seems to a good many educated people tantamount to admitting to a disease of the intellect. There are, of course, good reasons for this state of affairs. Those of us who grew up in the wake of the horrors of Nazism were quickly aware of how easy it has been to use religion as a cover for monstrous acts; the use of the swastika—an ancient cosmic and religious symbol, both in Europe and in Native America—as the symbol for National Socialism has been a reminder of the pattern, which was also evident, closer to home, in the tendency during the 1950s to use religion to enforce rigid conformity and the status quo in a society rife with racism and sexism. For many academics, the assumption has been that only a rigorous intellectual clarity, unmarred by sentimental ideas like a "higher power," can train new generations to face up to social inequity and transform society for the better.[1] That one of the most courageous and effective social transformations in American history was a project of the undeniably religious Southern Christian Leadership Conference might be expected to give pause to progressive academics, but the irony is that the work of the Reverend Martin Luther King, Jr. (and so many others) has often been patronized by an academic establishment that feels more comfortable with approaches to social change based on more intellectually complex social theories. The irony here is that, recently, when I showed a class segments of *Eyes on the Prize* (1980), they were astonished at what "unsophisticated" young people and adults could undertake and accomplish in the name of the spirit; these students, like so many of us, were *theoretically* aware but could barely imagine having the "spirit" to take the kinds of action they saw in *Eyes on the Prize*.

In the world of academic film studies, and in the more academically marginalized world of independent filmmaking, this same suspicion of "the spirit" and "spiritual" is obvious. Recently, I had a conversation with Chick Strand, who has made a number of films that I would classify as "spiritual," and when I told her I thought that her *Kristallnacht* (1979) could be categorized as a cinematic prayer, she quickly responded, "Well, a prayer for the Godless!" I said, "How about a prayer for the spiritual?" And she responded, "Whatever *that* means." Certainly, I understand her embarrassment with the term "prayer" applied to her film: it has come to sound pretentious and mindless at the same time. The paradox is that *Kristallnacht* is resonant with spirit, and only a spiritually driven filmmaker could have made it.

Throughout the previous chapters, I have regularly invoked the idea of the spiritual in connection with the films I've discussed. Indeed, the assumption of *The Garden in the Machine* is that a century of industrial development and social transformation has inverted the locale of the spirit. Nineteenth-century painters and writers made it a convention to see spirit in the landscape, to image New World Nature as God's Eden, and to understand the advent of the machine (epitomized by the railroad) as a fall from innocence; in *this* century, however, a good many artists have used the quintessential aesthetic machine—cinema—as a way of tracking the spirit, of reaccessing Edenic moments within the camera and screening room, and within the machine of postmodern, transnational society. The films discussed in this chapter continue this theme; but, more fully than many of the films and videos I've discussed so far, they can be understood as cine-prayers, prayers with a variety of personal and social functions.

Segue: Chick Strand, *Kristallnacht*

Given the particular nature of Chick Strand's short film, *Kristallnacht* (the film is a bit over seven minutes), the title might seem strange—even an insult to the events that occurred on November 9 and 10, 1938, the "Night of Broken Glass," during which the Nazis in Germany and Austria destroyed two hundred synagogues, looted seventy-five hundred shops, and arrested tens of

thousands of Jewish males and sent them to concentration camps.[2] This pivotal moment in the acceleration of systematic persecution of European Jewry
at first seems quite irrelevant to Strand's film, which begins with a haiku (in
white text on a black background):

> White chrysanthemum
> before that perfect flower
> scissors hesitate.[3]

The haiku is followed by a sequence of exquisite imagery of two young women
swimming in what appears to be a lake at night (while we do not hear the
young women speak, we do hear their splashes and a variety of nighttime
sounds: crickets, frogs . . .), exquisite because of the way in which the light
sparkles and shimmers on the water.[4] The sequence ends with the sound of a
distant train whistle, the sounds of the train arriving at a station; and then,
accompanied by the sound of a gong, a dissolve forms a segue into a nearly
three-minute shot of water rippling through the frame from upper right to
lower left (imagery as exquisite as the imagery of the young women swimming, and for the same reason: the complex reflections of light off the dark
water), accompanied by a haunting, rhythmic music.[5] *Kristallnacht* concludes
with the dedication—white on black, echoing the opening haiku, "For Anne
Frank."

It is, of course, the beauty of Strand's film in conjunction with the horrific
reality of the original Kristallnacht that may seem, at first, inappropriate; but
the power of the film rests in this very disjunction, a disjunction evident in her
pun on the term "kristallnacht." On the most literal level, the term means
"crystal night," and thus can refer to the lovely evening evoked by Strand's
crystalline water and sensual sound track: the very image of growing up in an
Edenic, rural America. Even the distant sounds of the train confirm the
romance of the moment Strand captures: for many of us who grew up in midcentury, the distant sound of (especially nighttime) train whistles resonated a
combination of nostalgia, security, and excitement about the future. On the
other hand, the historical implications of the title, the dedication to Anne
Frank, and the startling gong that accompanies the transition from swimmers
to rippling water demand that we also respond to Strand's "Edenic moment"
as a haunting allegory for the Holocaust. The absence of the young women

after the arrival of the train and the gong recall the destruction of the world's innocence by the near-extermination of European Jewry; and in this context the persistence of the motion of the ripples and the consistent rhythm of the sound track evoke the relentlessness of the Nazi horror in the wake of Kristallnacht. Even the haiku with which the film begins can be seen to confirm this dimension of the film, since Anne Frank was in the flower of innocence when her life was cut off.

For Americans growing up in the aftermath of World War II, with a slowly growing consciousness of the immensity of the Holocaust, the nagging question has been how to recognize and remember these atrocities *and,* in a world denuded of an essential innocence by these events, maintain a healthy, even hopeful attitude toward experience. Strand's *Kristallnacht* models an answer. Of course, there must be no forgetting of what happened in Europe at the hands of the Nazis and those who collaborated with them; we must not even forget that the sounds that *meant* security and romance for *us* were the sounds of the arrival of horror for so many others. And yet, we—non-Jews and Jews alike—must continue, not only to live, but to treasure life's beautiful experiences, and the continuing potential for Edenic experience, both for ourselves and for our children.

Claude Lanzmann's *Shoah* remains the most compelling response to the Nazi desire not only to implement the Final Solution but to erase all traces of its implementation as well; *Shoah* is a remembering of what the Nazis wanted forgotten. On a far humbler level, Strand's *Kristallnacht* bears a similar relation to Nazi policy. The Nazis attempted to reserve the good things of life for only certain people, and to relegate Jews and other "inferiors" to an earthly hell. Strand's film suggests that, in our anger at what the Nazis did, in our determination to see that such crimes are eliminated from the world, we must not become complicit with them in destroying either the idea of innocence or the ability to enjoy, and honor, what the earth provides for all people. *Kristallnacht* is a cinematic haiku that suggests that the innocence natural to all of us must not be cut off by any societal machinery, including the commercial machinery of cinema. Strand's cine-prayer for Anne Frank is also a prayer for our present and future. Of course, Strand hesitated, as filmmaker, before the daunting task of filmically confronting the reality of Anne Frank's experience and the larger crimes for which her experience became a metaphor, but

Strand's care in cutting the lovely imagery she uses honors both the memory of the past and the experience of the present—even as it defies the tendency of commercial media to either ignore or exploit both human suffering and healthy, innocent sensuality.

Of Time and the River: Stan Brakhage, *Commingled Containers*

> With their acute awareness of the power of language—both the potential damage of words as well as a sense that words should flow from the depths of a pure heart—the desert fathers had a genuine appreciation of the practical value of silence. Not only was silence the quickest way to cut off the cancerous growth of slander and gossip, it was seen as the atmosphere in which a spirit of prayerful awareness of God could thrive. —DOUGLAS BURTON-CHRISTIE, *THE WORD IN THE DESERT*[6]

No independent filmmaker has been more forthright or persistent in identifying filmmaking as a spiritual quest than Stan Brakhage. He has regularly claimed that during the process of filmmaking, he finds himself in a trance state and produces the films that "are given to me to make." Indeed, Brakhage's famous commitment to silence has always seemed to me more fully an attempt to emulate the importance of silence in a variety of religious and spiritual practices than a polemical assertion that film is essentially *visual* art. While Brakhage has made his living with words, as a legendary teacher and lecturer (Andrew Noren remembers Brakhage in the sixties: "Brakhage would descend on New York from the mountains once a year or so, grandiloquent and Promethean, lightning bolts in one hand and film cans in the other, talking everyone under the table—what a talker!"),[7] he has seen his filmmaking as a means to reaccess a sense of the divinity of the moment of innocence into which we are born and within which we continue to live until words, the language of the society in which we are living, incorporate us into a contemporary social order and lock us away from our Edenic origins.[8] Brakhage has attempted to create cinematic metaphors for the experience of the individual soul prior to its consciousness of being bound by societal controls over perception.

Brakhage's commitment, as filmmaker, to the image before the word has resulted in films that are notoriously difficult to write about. Not that there is any shortage of commentary about Brakhage: he has been so prolific and so influential, there is no avoiding him. And yet, even in the 1990s, most writing about Brakhage remains focused on a set of relatively early films—films that are metaphorically dense enough to support a variety of explications—and on the general implications of Brakhage's gestural camera work and complex editing in these early films.[9] While at one time the early films—specifically, *The Way to the Shadow Garden* (1955), *Anticipation of the Night* (1958), *Window Water Baby Moving* (1959), *Mothlight* (1963), *Dog Star Man* (1961–64), *The Act of Seeing with One's Own Eyes* (1971)—seemed a major challenge for the historian, they have continued to dominate writing about Brakhage, not only because of their undeniable quality and influence, but also because much of Brakhage's later work defies the kinds of explication that seem appropriate in academic contexts. Indeed, while earlier Brakhage films seem to have been generated by the *idea* of being beyond the verbal, much of his filmmaking for the past quarter century has more fully achieved this state. While the power of the best of the early Brakhage continues to move viewers, even in some cases (*Window Water Baby Moving*, *The Act of Seeing with One's Own Eyes*) to shock viewers, and to function as a means to the end of extended intellectualization and discussion, in most of his recent work, Brakhage seems content to provide *experiences* of light, color, and rhythm that confirm his sense of the divinity that lies at the edge of the everyday, of the Light encoded within the light his camera records. In these films he seems less interested in instigating intellectual discussion than in creating a sense of awe.

During summer 1997, Brakhage discovered that there was a possibility that he had developed cancer of the bladder, a possibility that became a reality during the following fall and led to surgery to remove the bladder in December. During the years just previous to the discovery of the cancer, Brakhage had stopped photographing imagery, for financial reasons: the breakup of his thirty-plus-year relationship with Jane Collum Brakhage, his second marriage to Marilyn Jull, and the arrival of children had put enough of a strain on Brakhage's always-limited finances that he decided to return to the less-expensive process of working directly on the celluloid—not, on one level, a sacrifice for Brakhage, as he continues to see himself as fundamentally a painter, but certainly a limitation on his creative abilities in general, and more particularly, on his ability to use the movie camera to work directly with light.[10] Just previous to the exploratory surgery that would determine that the growth in his bladder was in fact malignant, Brakhage bought a Bolex camera that had been offered for an unusually good price (he had worn out his previous Bolex), with a thirty-day warranty. Soon after the purchase, he was passing Boulder Creek, near his home, and, thinking he needed to run a test for the camera before the warranty ran out, he went down to the stream and, for some reason, pulled out of his camera case several extension tubes he had been carrying around for more than thirty years (since his father had bought him his first camera), attached them to the lens of the Bolex, and proceeded to film the stream:

> all of which is quite silly: if you're trying to test a camera to see if it's okay, you don't stick some tubes on it and take a guess on the aperture! I guess I just went into a fit. All of this of course was an expression of what was tearing me up inside: what's the point of checking this camera out anyway? One, you don't intend to photograph anymore; two, you're probably going to die, which is really what I thought. But I also thought, if you're going to die, what does it matter if you have the right light reading![11]

Brakhage spent hours filming, not the surface of the water—"which is like all the fussiness of daily life"—but "this very organic-feeling 'bubbleworld,' that was slowly evolving under the surface—there was something spiritual about it." The resulting film, *Commingled Containers,* was completed during the period between Brakhage's learning that the growth *was* cancerous and the removal of the bladder and subsequent chemotherapy.

Commingled Containers is a short film (about 2½ minutes) that includes both the imagery Brakhage shot at Boulder Creek and bits of hand-painted film—hand-painted in a mottled blue, as if the celluloid strip were the bed of a creek (see plates 21, 22). The film begins with a passage of relatively heavy editing (two longer shots—8 and 14 seconds—of the water, then a moment of intercutting between clusters of frames of photographed water and painted "water") and then gradually focuses in on the bubbles under the surface as they evolve in the light, filming them for increasing, unedited durations (near the conclusion of the film, in shots of 21 and 53 seconds). This imagery of the bubbles is both ineffably beautiful and suggestive of the spiritual dimension of human life that lies just under the surface of everyday experience. As an emblem of Brakhage's state of mind at this pivotal moment in his life, the imagery reflects both his determination to make the most of whatever time remained to him and a willingness to discover in the very limitation of time and in the friction of decay (bubbles are "the result of the friction of air on water")[12] something beyond conventional limits, something that transcends the machinery we have devised to replicate the surface of experience—and to share the results with those willing to watch. It is, in short, a prayer of thanksgiving for the Light that was making it possible for Brakhage to go forward, at least for a bit longer.

The title of the film is a reference to one of the categories of recyclable refuse in Boulder, and, clearly, a multileveled metaphor, for the creek represented in the film, which commingles water, air, rocks . . . ; for the film, which commingles and contains two different kinds of representation of the creek; and for Brakhage, whose body contained/commingled both healthy and unhealthy tissue and something more—something that drew him to "commingle" with Boulder Creek by half-submerging his lenses in the water, as a way of accessing something beyond physical limits through an act of perception—as extended/limited by, of all things, a machine.

The most visceral of Brakhage's filmic confrontations of death takes place in *The Act of Seeing with One's Own Eyes,* the film that resulted from his witnessing autopsies conducted at the Pittsburgh morgue. During *The Act,* Brakhage's imagery reveals a gradual change in his relationship to the horrific imagery he records, from terror to an increasing visual freedom. It's a change some members of the audience may share—though for a good many viewers (especially first-time viewers), the imagery remains horrific throughout. Near the conclusion of *The Act,* as Brakhage's camera seems to fly through the eviscerated corpses like a helicopter over a grisly landscape, he hovers for a moment to meditate on a tiny blue, shimmering membrane that looks like a lake among the surrounding "mountains" of flesh. It is a moment that can be read as a premonition of *Commingled Containers:* in 1971, Brakhage could only find his way *to* this lake through his horror at the fact of death; in 1997, facing the opening of his own body and the possibility of imminent death itself, he was able to look into the shimmering water of Boulder Creek and revel, for a moment, in the light/Light beyond—and then share the revelation with us.

Beyond Words: Andrew Noren, *Imaginary Light*

For nearly thirty years, I taught American literature at Utica College, in Utica, New York—specifically, the period of American fiction bracketed by Gertrude Stein and Richard Wright: Stein, Sherwood Anderson, Theodore Dreiser, Willa Cather, F. Scott Fitzgerald, Hemingway, Faulkner . . . Wright. It is, of course, a remarkable era for American prose, and every year I would grapple with the demands of reducing this prolific period into a syllabus for a fourteen-week course. Inevitably, the institutional shape of the college semester would determine not only which authors would, to put it crudely, make the final cut; but which of the chosen authors' books would "fit" within the requisite time span and within the capabilities of students taking not just my course, but several others, and in many cases working full-time jobs to support their education. No matter that, each year, I would consider defying what seemed the inevitable choices, in the end the institutional *shape* of academic life always seemed to force me in the direction of brevity, and I would choose Stein's *Three Lives* over *The Making of Americans,* Fitzgerald's *The Great Gatsby* over *Tender Is the Night,* Hemingway's *In Our Time* and/or *The Sun Also Rises* over *For Whom the Bell Tolls,* Cather's *O Pioneers!* over *My Ántonia,* even Wright's *Native Son* over John Dos Passos's *U.S.A.* and James T. Farrell's *Studs Lonigan.*

In that other teaching arena, scholarship (teaching oneself and one's field), the inverse tends to be true: the more words the scholar produces, the more distinguished the career and the more consistent the rewards—assuming, of course, that the scholar is reasonably thoughtful as well as prolific. Especially in the area of film studies, a relative newcomer to academe, the pressure to demonstrate one's intellectual mastery by means of the production of written theory and analysis has been particularly strong, and this pressure has had a considerable impact on which films have become inevitable in film courses. The need to produce increasing amounts of writing on film has tended to privilege the narrative fiction feature, even the popular fiction feature: the pop cinema's position not only as a producer of works of cinema art, but as an industrial polemicizer of widely held cultural attitudes has made it a fertile field for the production of a substantial literature.

The academic pressure to produce verbal discourse has also had an impact on avant-garde cinema, which has always been underrepresented in the discourse of academe, and in the college classroom. But even in this lesser-known cinematic arena, films have generally become distinguished to the degree to which they are able to sustain extended verbal discourse. And the converse is true: those films that tend to leave viewers speechless, that exist primarily as evanescent film *experiences*—rather than as texts that can be verbally represented, even photographically represented, outside the screening room—have tended to become invisible to film history, no matter how powerful the in-theater experience of seeing these films, no matter how distinctive and dynamic the Vision of these filmmakers *is*. No one better represents this tendency than Andrew Noren; his *Imaginary Light* (1995) is one of recent cinema's most remarkable "secret gardens."

Noren has always been fascinated with light. One of his earliest memories has to do with his consciousness of light in his native Santa Fe: "An early memory is of sitting under a cottonwood tree behind my parents' house, September afternoon light of great clarity with a wind blowing—you know how cottonwood leaves shiver and tremble in the wind. I sat there watching the light and the leaf shadows dancing on the dust, listening to the wind in the leaves. It was my first movie and a great one. I was bewitched by it."[13] Noren's films have always been distinctive in their depiction of light, from the lovely meditation on light coming through an open window in the early *Wind Variations* (1969), throughout *The Adventures of Exquisite Corpse: Part I: Huge Pupils* (1968); Part II: *False Pretenses* (1974); Part III: *The Phantom Enthusiast* (1975); Part IV: *Charmed Particles* (1979); Part V: *The Lighted Field* (1987); and Part VI: *Imaginary Light*.[14] Indeed, for Noren, the 16mm movie camera has been an instrument for "playing" light and shadow, and few filmmakers in the history of cinema have played this instrument with more dexterity.

Imaginary Light is just under thirty-five minutes, but it seems far more substantial because of the density of Noren's imagery. The film is divided into three sections, bracketed by a visual frame. The beginning half of the film includes, first, imagery of light and shadows recorded, one frame at a time, in the yard of Noren's then-home in Monmouth County, New Jersey (just south of the New York metropolitan area); and then, imagery of light and shadow recorded—again, one frame at a time—inside the house. During the second half of *Imaginary Light*, Noren filmed light and shadow as it was reflected in and on the water of a small creek near the house, using the one-frame-at-a-time procedure, but also adjusting the aperture for each frame. These three sections are visually framed by a passage of imagery taken (one frame at a time) on a walk along a road through a woods, presented at the beginning right side up and forward and at the end upside down and in reverse; and the entire film is accompanied by a sound track made from the sound of an old

clock in Noren's home: the repeated sound of the striking of the hours is gradually slowed down (at the beginning the gong strikes at five-second intervals,
but by the middle of the film, the intervals are as much as fifteen seconds),
until, at the center of the film, just as the imagery of the inside of the house
ends and the imagery of the water begins, the sound is reversed and proceeds
in reverse until the conclusion of *Imaginary Light*, slowly accelerating until at
the conclusion the intervals are, once again, approximately five seconds.[15]

While *Imaginary Light* was shot one frame at a time, it is not time-lapsed:
that is, the frames were not exposed automatically by the camera, or even at
predetermined, equal intervals. The result is that the experience Noren provides is not the familiar one in which the film frame becomes a window that
allows us to see the patterns of motion during a particular period; rather,
Imaginary Light is a record of Noren's *interaction* with light and shadow, his
use of the camera to engage and be engaged by the phenomenon of light—a
fact made evident during the opening section of the film by the frequent presence of Noren's own shadow among the shadows flowing through the yard
(see fig. 94). This shadow, which becomes a motif in this section (and only in
this section), is complexly evocative: it suggests a monk or priest, a wizard,
even a demon (at times, the shape is reminiscent of Murnau's Nosferatu).
However we interpret Noren's shadow, his presence within the world he
reveals is obvious: the phantasmagoria of light and shadow we see is consistently alive, not only within the inevitable, regular motion of the daily cycle,
but also within Noren's perceptual/psychic "dance" with what he sees—apparently a kind of ecstasy resulting from a relentless, even obsessive need.

Having said this much, I must return to the issue with which I began my
discussion of Noren. While it is tempting to "read" *Imaginary Light*, to articu-
late a discourse "about the film" either by verbalizing what seems to happen as
I experience it or by formulating specific metaphoric comparisons between
this experience and others; in fact, I see *Imaginary Light* as fascinating precisely in its resistance to conventional academic procedures for "dealing with"
film. Anything *Imaginary Light means,* or seems to mean, is less interesting to
me—and less relevant to the film—than the experience of being in a screening room *as the film is happening.* I am less concerned with understanding the
film than with participating, with Noren, in an experience that not only honors—even worships—a natural phenomenon we take for granted and the
capacity of a human technology to transform the everyday into the miraculous

Figure 94. Two successive frames of Andrew Noren filming in his backyard, from *Imaginary Light* (1995). Courtesy Andrew Noren.

(a suburban yard into a visual Garden) but also confronts and revises—from within the flickering theater space itself—our sense of what a film and a filmmaker can do and be.

Even Noren himself has no interpretation of *Imaginary Light,* and accepts the film as a mystery: "It is a sort of visitation or inhabitation . . . which is the literal meaning of 'inspiration,' I guess. Unconscious urgings? Dictation from a higher authority, as Rilke might say? I can't say. My take on this these days is

. . . 'I just work here. You'll have to talk to the owner.' . . . [W]hen I was making *The Lighted Field*, I dreamed one night that I was presented (I don't know by whom) with a huge book, *The Instructions of the Sun.*" To the extent that his motives *are* conscious, Noren is a kind of documentarian "of the flow of light and shadow in that particular 'home' place[,] . . . part of the eternal cosmic dance that goes on and on, whether or not we humans are here to see it and be in it. We are irrelevant to it, though we are privileged to participate if we have the mind for it. It was in progress long before our recent, ill-omened appearance on the stage, and will continue long after we've made our exit."[16]

Since Noren has made his living working as a news archivist in New York, often dealing with raw news footage coming in from around the world ("The stock in trade is war, murder, death, destruction, grief and weeping, disaster and degradation, greed, starvation. . . ."),[17] it is tempting to think of his filmmaking as the means by which he is able to maintain a psychic balance—though Noren himself sees such a reading (and I'm sure, correctly) as simplistic and reductive. Nevertheless, the intensity of his focus, and especially in the first half of the film—judging from the shadows—during the early morning and the evening hours, along with the repeated sound of the clock, causes *Imaginary Light* to evoke the prayer ritual of matins and vespers, the first and sixth of the canonical hours in *The Book of Hours* (see chap. 8). The intensity of his focus on water during the second half of the film—his variation of the exposure of successive frames and the ways in which his single-framing transforms the movements of the water—is also evocative of Eastern mandalas and the process of focusing attention during meditation.

However we understand the relationship between Noren's filmmaking and his practical life, *Imaginary Light* offers viewers an escape, not only from practical day-to-day realities, but also, in an academic context, from the requirement to use every film experience as raw material for the production of verbal discourse—a discourse that, all too often, obfuscates the sense of mystery that has always brought us into the darkened space of the movie theater.

Transcendental Domesticity: Leighton Pierce, *50 Feet of String*

During the 1970s, feminists called for a reorganization of domestic politics, questioning the assumption that child care was biologically determined "women's work" and demanding that men learn to function as true domestic *partners* in the quest for economic stability and personal fulfillment, rather than exclusively as "breadwinners." That the domestic round was the new frontier in cultural development was clear in the landmark film by Laura Mulvey and Peter Wollen, *Riddles of the Sphinx* (1977), which argued that who takes care of young children is *the* issue on which the organization of modern society turns. *Riddles* is one of the remarkable independent features of the last quarter century—though it can be a challenge in an undergraduate class-room—because of the precision and intricacy of its structure and mise-en-scène.[18] For me, and I assume many, seeing the film in the late 1970s (and this may still be true), the most powerful moment in *Riddles* was the opening shot of the body of the film, "Louise's story told in thirteen shots," a stunning 360-degree pan, more than six minutes long, during which we see Louise's kitchen as she prepares a scrambled egg for her two-year-old daughter, Anna (the sound track combines Mike Ratledge's haunting music and a voice-off poem that evokes the daily round of child care: "Time to get ready. Time to come in./Things to forget. Things to lose./Meal time. Story time . . ."). Mulvey and Wollen reveal the kitchen, a location peripheral at best in the history of film, as a space where a great drama is occurring, something crucial and mythic, something worth our sustained cinematic attention.

While domestic partnership has evolved, at least in some sectors of society, during the decades since *Riddles of the Sphinx* was so widely discussed, cine-matic attention—or, really, inattention—to the domestic has changed little. The realities of domestic work, especially child care, have remained virtually invisible. Perhaps it is this continued invisibility that causes Leighton Pierce's films and videos of the 1990s to seem so remarkable. In Pierce's work, the domestic arena becomes the site of visual-auditory dramas that have the potential to undermine conventional ideas about the domestic. Indeed, Pierce's understanding of how media making fits into daily life is nearly the inversion of the conventional assumption shared, it would seem, by both com-mercial media makers and most of those who provide independent, even "avant-garde" critiques of the commercial. The general assumption, of course, is that the domestic world and the art-making world must remain separate.[19] One may create a life that includes both, but such a life requires us to "inter-cut" between the two spheres, moving back and forth between them.

While Pierce earns his living outside the home (since 1985 he has taught media production at the University of Iowa), he has built his reputation as a major contributor to independent film and video history within his home, as *part* of his day-to-day domestic experience. *Thursday* (1991), for instance, is a visual-auditory evocation of his kitchen, shot during the quiet moments of his son's naptime on Thursdays: images and sounds—Pierce pouring coffee, washing dishes; a tree blowing in the breeze outside the window, the sound of a distant train, a rainstorm—are combined into what Peter Hutton might call "a reprieve" from the tendency of modern life and most cinema to project us speedily forward.[20] *Thursday* is an exquisite rest for the audience, as naptime is for the child. Similarly, the video *If with Those Eyes and Ears,* the first section of *Principles of Harmonic Motion* (1991), was made soon after the child was born. Pierce spent time in the baby's room, exploring visual and auditory details of the space and combining them into a lovely, haunting experience that simultaneously evokes the baby's fascination with his new world and the father's excitement at sharing life with this mysterious new being: "It's not an attempt to see the way the baby sees, but just to be *with* this tiny newborn—trying to do parallel play in a way."[21]

Pierce's output, in both film and video, has been considerable in the 1990s, but certainly his most impressive work to date is his domestic "epic," *50 Feet of String,* now in two versions: the original (1995, 53 minutes), which I'll discuss here; and a condensed version (1998, 35 minutes).[22] The film *50 Feet of String* depicts domestic life in and around Pierce's home (see plates 23, 24), by combining imagery and sounds collected from midsummer to fall and organizing them into an intricate montage, broken into a series of segments, each with its own title: "E"; "corner of the eye"; "12:30"; "lawn care"; "white chair"; "50 feet of string"; "two maples"; ".29 inches"; "lawn care 2"; "pickup truck"; "implement"; "red-handled scissors."

One of Pierce's "rules" for the film was that he would not film beyond one hundred yards from his kitchen.[23] Each section of *50 Feet of String* explores a particular visual and auditory dimension of Pierce's domestic surround that is suggested more or less directly by the title (".29 inches," for example, focuses on a rainstorm; "lawn care" focuses on cutting grass; "lawn care 2," on raking leaves), though the sections are unified not only by Pierce's repeated use of particular aspects of a single, limited indoor-outdoor space in section after section but also by a particular motif that provides the film with its title and most pervasive metaphor: a string drawn taut, often seen near the sink, where water drips into a glass and, seemingly, causes the string to vibrate. Visually, the string seems to suggest the measure of domestic space (and time) explored by the film, evoking plumb lines, measuring tapes, time lines; auditorily, it suggests a string that can be plucked to make music. Indeed, the double, visual-auditory nature of the string makes it a particularly appropriate metaphor for *this* film (and for Pierce's 1990s work in general), as few filmmakers or videomakers have been as successful as Pierce in integrating sound and image into works so that they are absolutely equal contributors to the resulting experience.[24]

What makes *50 Feet of String* and Pierce's other films of the 1990s distinctive, however, are the particulars of his exploration of the domestic. Pierce's consistent use of a variety of subtle dimensions of lens technology and camera placement transforms the spaces he records, so that only one narrow plane of the space is in clear focus at any moment; the remaining aspects of the framed space are in varying degrees of blur.[25] In addition to causing his imagery to combine spaces of great clarity with impressionistic renderings of color and shape, Pierce's technique determines the nature of the developments that can occur within any given image, in two ways. For one thing, the narrow breadth of the space revealed by any given image allows for the sudden transformation of an image by the movement of a human or a vehicle into or out of the frame. In "two maples," for example, movement into and out of the frame is the central visual motif. This short section (a bit more than a minute altogether) includes eight shots, each separated from the next by a moment of darkness. The first shot is taken from a moving hammock; in the second, a young boy runs into the distance, apparently having left the hammock; and in the following five shots, we see the boy on a distant swing, as he swings into or out of, or into and out of, the frame, within three different compositions, so that each repetition of the movement provides a visual surprise (in two instances, the same composition is used, but in each case, the direction of the swing in the second shot is the opposite of its direction in the first shot—Pierce has apparently divided a single up-and-down motion into two halves and has separated them). The final shot of "two maples" reveals a "yard-scape" across which a blurred car moves left to right, confirming and concluding the movements of the swing in the previous seven shots.

The second result of Pierce's combination of techniques has to do with the drama he achieves by manipulating the available layers of focus. In "pickup truck," for example, Pierce creates an astonishing moment by extending a single shot for more than two minutes.[26] The shot begins with extended images of several distant trees with yellowing leaves, blowing in the wind, as seen through a blurry "curtain" of plants in the foreground. Because this particular focus plane is maintained for a minute and a half, the subsequent refocusing onto the curtain of weeds comes as something of a surprise (made more dramatic by the fact that it is timed so as to coincide with the auditory passing of a truck we never actually see that has moved closer and closer during the previous minute). This refocusing continues, as weeds nearer and nearer to us come into focus, and culminates with the sudden coming into pristine focus of first one stalk, then two even closer, and finally at the conclusion of the shot a single, thin stem. Each of these final changes in the image has the impact of magic: because our training as filmgoers is to notice what is in focus and to ignore what is not, each new visual revelation seems to come out of nowhere.

Pierce was a musician before he was a filmmaker (as a student at the Museum School of the Museum of Fine Arts in Boston). He made *musique concrète* and became attracted to film in part because "there was this problem with *musique concrète;* once you've constructed this music electronically on tape, what do you do at a concert? It's very awkward sitting in an auditorium listening to a tape."[27] Once he began to work with imagery as well as with sound, he was quickly aware of the wide range of visual possibilities film offers. Nevertheless, his consciousness of sound and his dexterity with it in conjunction with visual imagery are unusual for a filmmaker; indeed, he continues to return to sound as the primary pleasure in film- and videomaking: "I shoot now, and have for years, with the goal to get to the part where I can do sound."[28] Pierce edits his imagery silent, but with a sound track in mind; and subsequently coordinates what is heard and what is seen.

In "two maples," for example, Pierce uses two different sounds that suggest the movement of a hammock and a swing (Pierce collects sound as a separate process from filming imagery and is more likely to create the illusion of continuity by combining a sound from one source with an image from a different source than by recording the sound actually made by what he films); these sounds punctuate the imagery, providing a second rhythm in subtle syncopation with the rhythm of the visual editing and at times coming together with imagery in surprising ways: for example, the sound of what we assume is the squeak of the swing is, in two instances, present in synchronization with the fade-out of an image to darkness. The "two maples" section concludes with the shot of the car, which is presented "in synch" with the sound of a vehicle passing; the two separate rhythms of image and of sound come together to bring the passage to a formal resolution, followed by the silence leading to the next title and next section.

For the long, continuous shot from "pickup truck," Pierce constructed a series of sound events that "fit" the experience and give it a powerful impact, but which were in some cases recorded in an entirely different locations. Indeed, while the visuals are recorded in a rigorously limited space, Pierce explains, "*50 Feet* has sounds from all over in it (east, west, midwest, France); and thinking about those sounds evokes my memories of those places. . . . Sound seems to bring me deeper into memory than photos."[29] At intervals throughout this passage we hear the distant "toots" of a foghorn recorded during a vacation to Lubec, Maine. At the beginning these toots are heard in conjunction with the sound of a breeze blowing through leaves, and are joined, for a while, by the distant sounds of a chainsaw (recorded in Iowa) and by the nearer sounds of what I assume is a frog. After thirty seconds or so, the sound of a distant truck becomes increasingly evident (both truck and frog were recorded along County Road 33 in the Finger Lakes region of New York State, where Pierce spent his formative years), and as the truck comes closer, it becomes the foreground not only of the sound track but of the film as well, as Pierce's continuous, unchanging focus on the distant trees tends to draw the audience's attention to the changes in the sound. Just as the truck "passes us," the focus of the image shifts from the distant trees to the nearby weeds, drawing attention back to the imagery.[30] During the remainder of the shot, the distant toots of the foghorn are evident again, as is, for a moment, the distant chainsaw, and, very subtly, the sound of nearby water (recorded at Seneca Lake, one of the New York Finger Lakes), and at the very end the sound of a car door closing, which forms an auditory segue into the sound of a car leaving and accelerating through the moment of darkness that follows the end of "pickup truck" and leads into "implement."

Each of the two general figures of style evident in the passages discussed above can be read as an aesthetic manifesto that reflects Pierce's commitment to domestic space. The first of these figures of style has to do with the interplay between the space defined by the film frame and Pierce's evocation of what lies beyond the frame. We are always seeing a very particular image *and* seeing and hearing a variety of events that are occurring at the edge of the frame (like the child swinging into the image or the car moving through the image in "two maples") or entirely outside the frame, either nearby (like the wind in the weeds or the frog in the passage from "pickup truck") or at a considerable distance (the chainsaw, the foghorn). This particular dynamic is a visualization of the idea that the limited frame of the domestic is, in fact, a more energetic space than it may seem: it is a nexus of those human/environmental comings and goings that provide the fundamental rhythms of experience. The other figure of style, Pierce's layering of visuals and sounds, suggests that the excitement of life is not simply a function of accessing new places, but can lie in recognizing the astonishing complexity of the spaces nearby. The long continuous shot from "pickup truck" is a powerful visualization of the idea that the most crucial drama of experience can be our discovery of what was in front of us all along.

What close attention to the particulars of Pierce's imagery and sound reveals is that, while 50 *Feet of String* does locate viewers within his domestic space in Iowa City, the film we watch is an experience that lies somewhere between perception and memory, between fact and fiction. It is fundamentally a *cinematic* reality, rather than a simple diary of Pierce's personal life—a transformation of the particular into the mythic, of domestic space into Domestic Space (see fig. 95). Further, it is a confrontation of the traditional assumption that Eden is a distant place that we must journey to. For Pierce, the screening room is a space of perceptual concentration that can train us to recognize and appreciate the "Gardens" that surround us and those we have internalized:

> I embrace Zen. . . . I'm not sure it's correct to say that shooting the films is like a Zen practice, but it is almost meditation. . . . The editing is like meditation, too. . . .
>
> Making the films *is* kind of like making a garden, though I hate to be so presumptuous as to say I'm making a beautiful Zen garden. And I'm trying to invite people into that "garden."[31]

There is also a political dimension to Pierce's work. Pierce draws an analogy between his work and a story about nature writer Terry Tempest Williams:

> I've heard that when Terry Tempest Williams takes people on nature walks, she'll walk out the back door and stop right there. Then she'll ask that those with her look down to see what's right in front of them. It's a form of deep looking.
>
> I see my work as closely related. If I can help the audience to see and hear more

Figure 95. Umbrella and raindrop in Leighton Pierce's *50 Feet of String* (1995). Courtesy Leighton Pierce.

carefully, maybe I can change people's perception—if only briefly—so that when they walk out of my film, suddenly they *notice* the sidewalk, that tree. There is value in noticing *exactly* where you are, *exactly* what is happening. Once you *know,* you can consider if things need to change, and how.[32]

For Pierce, personal, domestic space is also political space, and the reverencing of domestic space in film is a form of environmental politics, related to that expressed by Emerson in "Self-Reliance":

Traveling is a fool's paradise. . . . Beauty, convenience, grandeur of thought and quaint expression are as near to us as to any, and if the American artist will study with hope and love the precise thing to be done by him, considering the climate, the soil, the length of the day, the wants of the people, the habit and form of the government, he will create a house in which all these will find themselves fitted, and taste and sentiment will be satisfied also.[33]

and by Thoreau in his famous line from *Walden,* "I have travelled a good deal in Concord." Pierce *has* stayed at home, both as a domestic partner and as an artist, but he has learned how to travel a good bit—both physically and spiritually—without leaving the premises.

Envoi: David Gatten, *What the Water Said, nos. 1–3*

> Though for some time I have not spoken of the roaring of the breakers, and the ceaseless flux and reflux of the waves, yet they do not for a moment cease to dash and roar, with such a tumult that if you had been there, you could scarcely have heard my voice the while; and they are dashing and roaring this very moment, though it may be with less din and violence, for there the sea never rests.
>
> The sea, vast and wild as it is, bears thus the waste and wrecks of human art to its remotest shore. There is no telling what it may not vomit up. It lets nothing lie; not even the giant clams which cling to its bottom. —
> THOREAU, CAPE COD[34]

In the 1960s, television seemed to be in the process of destroying the commercial film industry; and now, though the film industry has recovered from that scare, the new wave of digital technologies, especially coming on the heels of the increasing accessibility of video equipment, seems to have put independent film in general, and many of the kinds of work I've been discussing in this and previous chapters, in a similarly precarious position. And yet, I am hopeful about the future, not only because the recovery of the commercial film industry has shown that the "inevitable" is not always inevitable, but also because there has never been a moment when the spirit has moved more independent filmmakers to risk their resources on more interesting films than during the past few decades. I am also hopeful that the new wave of interdisciplinary thinking that is inundating a good many institutions of higher learning will provide new opportunities for using the full range of independent cinema, and create new classroom and extracurricular audiences for this work. Indeed, it is the mission of this book to suggest the pedagogical (and, of course, the personal and social) value of one noteworthy set of independent films and videos. I would ask the reader to consider David Gatten's *What the Water Said, nos. 1–3*, as a metaphor for the body of work represented in this book, a body of work that itself is meant to represent a far more extensive field.

That the commercial cinema has recovered from its crisis of the 1960s is a function of the ability of inventive producers and directors to reinvigorate the forms of popular film experience that have always drawn moviegoers to theaters. James Cameron's remarkable success with *Titanic* (1997) can serve as an emblem for the industry's capacity to transcend its own seemingly inevitable demise. Who could have imagined that Cameron could raise two hundred million dollars for another retelling of *this* story? And that the film would be a success? At the margins of cinema, a similar resilience remains evident. Who could have imagined that avant-garde cinema could continue throughout the 1980s and 1990s to produce new forms of film experience (and to reinvigorate earlier innovations) when, only a few years ago, even some of its more distinguished chroniclers were claiming that we'd seen the last of important work and that the entire field would soon disappear from view?[35] A perfect example has been the recent work of David Gatten, one of a number of contemporary filmmakers who are finding new ways of working collaboratively with the natural environment and natural processes.

In 1997 Gatten decided to bring a dimension of his personal history together with his current interests as a filmmaker in a new set of filmmaking (and, he hoped, film *viewing*) experiments. The personal element of what was to become *What the Water Said* involved what had for years been an important location for Gatten: the southern tip of Seabrook Island, South Carolina (about twenty miles down the coast from Charleston), where the Edisto River joins the Atlantic: "That whole area—the Kiawah-Seabrook-Edisto-St. Johns Islands area—has been really important in my life. Starting when I was 14, we began taking our annual family vacation down there [Gatten grew up in Greensboro, North Carolina]. . . . [The ocean] was something I loved and trusted for more than half my life, watched it change with the seasons, listened to it in darkness, walked along it, swam in it." As a filmmaker, Gatten had become interested in the possibility of a nonlinear film: "This seems to be a sort of buzz word in avant-garde film, but in the end nearly everything is both made and presented in a linear fashion. . . . I was intrigued that I could at least *make* the sound and image in a film in a truly non-linear fashion, even if it would be presented in standard linear format with a projector."[36] Specifically, Gatten decided to put unspooled rolls of film stock into a crab trap (since the filmstrips were unrolled, "spaghetti style," inside the trap, "any given frame on the strip could have been created in any possible relationship to the other frames on the strip: before, after, at the exact time"), and to throw the trap into the surf at various times for various durations so that the ocean itself would inscribe both image and sound onto the filmstrip.

Gatten threw the crab cage into the ocean on three separate occasions. On January 1, 2, and 3, 1997, he marked the turn of the year by immersing a high-contrast black-and-white print stock (7378 Optical Sound Film) during a "cold, blustery January week. The varying results in the three sections [were] likely due to changes in tide and length of time soaked." Later that same year, he returned to immerse a color film stock usually used to make positive prints from camera negatives (7386 Color Positive Print Stock) on October 13, 14, and 15, a period characterized by "interesting variances in the weather": "The first day the water was beginning to get rough, with signs that a storm was approaching. The second section was made at the height of a huge storm— and I think it shows! Standing knee deep in the ocean I felt sure I was going to be electrocuted any minute! The final section was made in the nearly still ocean following the storm. Dolphins . . . came over to check out what I was up to." Finally, on August 22, 1998, Gatten unrolled an older color reversal stock occasionally used for making prints from color reversal originals (7399 Color Reversal Print Stock: "7399 . . . does not have the Kodak pre-hardening agent built into more recent stocks") into the crab trap, and on a "beautiful, clear, and sunny day" swam out into deep water and let the cage go, first at high tide, then during ebb tide, and finally at low tide.

The results of Gatten's "trapping expedition" vary with the film stocks and the weather conditions. What the water said in response to Gatten's first experiment varies with each day.[37] During "1/10/97," we see white flecks and scratches of light on a black background and hear what sounds like radio static (the various film stocks Gatten immersed all had sound tracks, so immersion affected image and sound simultaneously); the shorter "1/11/97" section (the lengths of the various sections for *nos. 1, 2, and 3* are a result of how much film stock remained in the crab trap after immersion and was usable: the three sections of *no. 1* are 1 minute, 20 seconds; 40 seconds; and 3 minutes, 10 seconds, respectively)[38] reveals similar but more "energetic" flecks and scratches, on a background that varies from black through various grays, even to white. The final section of *no. 1* reveals much scratching on a tan background; at times the scratching becomes so dense as to create a curtain across the filmstrip. The effect on the sound track is a sound reminiscent of ocean waves. A secondary layer of black dots is also evident within the continually changing patterns of white flecks and scratches.

While the first section of *no. 2* is reminiscent of the first two sections of *no. 1*, "10/14/97," the section made during the storm, is radically different: against a tan background, curvy, organic-looking shapes are etched into a lighter tan-yellow, and this overall pattern is supplemented by less dense overall patterns of white flecks and subtle bits of battleship gray. The density of the scratching varies, at times nearly whiting out the frame. The sound too reveals various "layers," one of which is the "surf sound" mentioned earlier. The final section of *no. 2*, "10/15/97," is similar to "10/13/97," with the exception of some popcorn-shaped flecks.

No. 3 provides an entirely different experience from *nos. 1–2*: here, the sections are vividly colored—the first passage revealing translucent violet-purple shapes against a white background; the second, alternating between full-frame pink-violet and yellow-gold, and concluding with various overall organic designs suggestive of plant leaves, amoebas. "Low tide" concludes *no. 3* with a gorgeous passage of pink-highlighted, scratched-out areas against a black background punctuated by a moment or two of full-frame pink.

Ultimately, of course, the particular nature of the results is less significant than the imagination behind Gatten's experiment. Whatever the effects Gatten's flinging the crab trap into the sea would have created, his gesture in making *What the Water Said, nos. 1–3*, reveals not only a faith in the possibility of collaborating with the environment in a more direct way, but a confidence in the ongoing capacity of a remnant of the mechanical age to continue to bring body and spirit together. Obviously, throwing the crab cage into the sea is a kind of prayer, a spiritually driven gesture that means to effect a material result, a petition to nature in the hope of a response. And the result is a set of inscriptions on the filmstrip that the projector transforms into light. As viewers sit in the darkened space of the theater, they are face-to-face with the inevitable cinematic paradox: once again, a machine (indeed, for all practical purposes, a vestige of nineteenth-century technology) confronts us with the ineffable.

Like so many independent filmmakers of the past quarter century or so, Gatten continues to find new creative possibilities in the continuing premonitions of film's demise. Whether he and the other filmmakers discussed in these chapters will continue to reinvigorate cinema during its second century or are merely creating an elegy to its ultimate disappearance remains to be seen. Either way, those of us who have the capacity to program independent film and video, in educational contexts or elsewhere, still have time to expose ourselves and those we care about to one of the remarkable cultural achievements of modern history—and, as I cannot help but repeat, to make use of our most underutilized pedagogical resource.

Distribution Sources
for Films and Videos

Two lists follow: first, a listing of distributors and their abbreviations; second, a listing of films and videos mentioned in the text—both arranged alphabetically. Film and video titles are followed by abbreviations indicating the distribution sources for prints of films and copies of videos. When film prints for films are not available, I've also provided at least one source for video copies of the films. NA indicates that a film or video is not currently in distribution.

Distribution Sources and Abbreviations

Allen	Austin Allen, 1523 East Blvd., #203, Cleveland, OH 44106 (216–721–4241; a.allen@csuohio.edu).
Benning	James Benning, California Institute of the Arts, Film/Video School, 24700 McBean Parkway, Valencia, CA 90038 (805–255–1050 X2017; jbenning@muse.calarts.edu).
Bloom	Norman Bloom, 53 Weybridge St., Middlebury, VT 05753 (802–388–9703).
CC	Canyon Cinema, 2325 Third St., Suite 338, San Francisco, CA 94107 (415–626–2255; films@canyoncinema.com; www.canyoncinema.com).

CFDC	Canadian Filmmakers Distribution Centre, 37 Hanna Ave., Suite 220, Toronto, Ontario M6K 1W8, Canada (416–588–0725; barbara@cfmdc.org; www.cfmdc.org).
Cinenova	113 Roman Road, London E2 OQN, UK (44–181–981–6828; admin@cinenova.demon.co.uk).
Direct Cinema	P.O. Box 10003, Santa Monica, CA 90410 (800–525–0000; directcinema@attmail.com).
EmGee	6924 Canby Ave., Suite 103, Reseda, CA 91335 (818–881–8110).
FACETS	1517 W. Fullerton Ave., Chicago, IL 60614 (800–331–6197; rentals@facets.org; www.facets.org).
FDK	Freunde der Deutchen Kinamathek, Welserstrasse 25, Berlin D10777, Germany.
FMC	Film-makers' Cooperative, 108 Leonard St., 13th floor, New York, NY 10013 (212–267–5665; film6000@aol.com; www.film-makerscoop.com).
FR	First Run Features, 153 Waverly Pl., New York, NY 10014 (212–243–0600; mail@frif.com; www.frif.com).
Friedrich	Su Friedrich, 118 N. 11th St., Brooklyn, NY 11211 (718–599–7601; Sufriedrich@cs.com).
Gatten	David Gatten, Park School of Communications, Ithaca College, Ithaca, NY (607–274–1548; dgatten@ithaca.edu).
Greaves	William Greaves, 230 W. 55th St., New York, NY 10019 (212–265–6150; 800–874–8314).
Jacobs	Ken Jacobs, 94 Chambers St., New York, NY 10007 (212–227–3144).
Kino	333 West 39th St., Suite 503, New York, NY 10018 (212–629–6880; kinoint@infohouse.com).
KP	Kit Parker, P.O. Box 16022, Monterey, CA 93942–6022 (800–538–5838).
LC	Light Cone, 12 rue des Vignoles, 75020 Paris, France (33–1–46–590–153; lightcone@club-internet.fr; www.lightcone.org).
Library of Congress	http://lcweb2.loc.gov/ammem/papr/mpixhome.html.

LUX	Lux Centre for Film, Video and Digital Arts, 2-4 Hoxton Square, London N1 6NU, UK (44–020–76–842–844; dist@lux.org.uk; www.lux.org.uk/distribution/)
Mangolte	Babette Mangolte, University of California at San Diego, Visual Arts Dept., 9500 Gilman Dr., La Jolla, CA 92093–0327 (858–755–0567); 319 Greenwich St., New York, NY 10013 (212–925–6319; bmangolte@cs.com).
Martin	Eugene Martin, City Story Pictures, 32 Strawberry St., 2d floor, Philadelphia, PA 19106 (215–413–0960; Eugenem@bellatlantic.net).
Milestone	275 West 96th St., Suite 28C, New York, NY 10025 (800–603–1104; MileFilms@aol.com; www.milestonefilms.com).
Miller	Franklin Miller, Dept. of Communication Studies, University of Iowa, Iowa City, IA 52242 (319–353–2261; fmiller@blue.weeg.uiowa.edu).
MoMA	Museum of Modern Art Circulating Film Program, 11 W. 53d St., New York, NY 10019 (212–708–9530; 212–708–9531 [fax]).
Murphy	J. J. Murphy, 6110 Vilas Hall, 821 University Ave., Madison, WI 53706 (608–263–3965; jjmurphy@facstaff.wisc.edu).
New Day	Community Media Production Group, 22D Hollywood Ave., Hohokus, NJ 07423 (tmcndy@aol.com; www.newday.com).
NL	New Line, 575 Eighth Ave., 16th Floor, New York, NY 10018 (212–649–4900; www.newline.com).
Noren	Andrew Noren, 10 Ladwood Dr., Holmdel, NJ 07733 (732–946–8390;anoren@msn.com; www.archive-search.com).
NY	New Yorker Films, 16 West 61st St., New York, NY 10023 (212–247–6110; info@newyorkerfilms.com; www.newyorkerfilms.com).
O'Neill	Pat O'Neill, 8331 Lookout Mountain Ave., Los Angeles, CA 90046 (323–650–1933).
Robertson	Anne Robertson, 69 Dennison Ave., Framingham, MA 01701 (508–872–4611).
Rudnick	Michael Rudnick, 312 Texas St., San Francisco, CA 94107 (415–824–8079).

Samuel Goldwyn	1023 Santa Monica Blvd., Los Angeles, CA 90067–6403 (310–284–9278).
Swank	P.O. Box 7008M, St. Louis, MO 63195 (800–876–5445; www.swank.com).
Thomas	Michael Thomas, c/o September Films, 535 East 6th St., New York, NY 10009 (212–460–8888).
UConn	University of Connecticut Center for Instructional Media and Technology, 249 Glenbrook Rd., University of Connecticut, Storrs, CT 06269–2001; c/o Patricia Miller (860–486–2530; mfladml@uconnvm.uconn.edu).
VDB	Video Data Bank, School of the Art Institute of Chicago, 112 S. Michigan Ave., Chicago, IL 60603 (312–345–3550; info@vdb.org; www.vdb.org).
WMM	Women Make Movies, 462 Broadway, Suite 500E, New York, NY 10013 (212–925–0606; orders@wmm.com; www.wmm.com).

Films and Videos Mentioned in the Text

Across the Sea of Time: IMAX
The Act of Seeing with One's Own Eyes: CC, CFDC, FMC, LUX
The Adventures of the Exquisite Corpse (in several sections): FMC, Noren
Akran: CC, FMC
All Major Credit Cards: CC, FMC
American Dreams: CC, CFDC
The Animals of Eden and After: CC, CFDC
The Answering Furrow: CC, FMC
Anticipation of the Night: CC, CFDC, FMC, LUX
Around the World in Thirty Years: CC
L'Arrivée d'un train en gare de la Ciotat: MoMA
Autumn Fire: MoMA

Back and Forth: CC, CFDC, FMC, LFC, MoMA
Backyard: FR
Baraka: Samuel Goldwyn
Barn Rushes: CC, FMC, LFC, LUX
Berlin: Die Sinfonie einer Grosstadt (Berlin: Symphony of a Big City): MoMA
Beyond Niagara: Thomas
Black and White Movie: FMC

Blazes: ACGB, CC, FMC, LC, LFC, MoMA, LUX
Bleu Shut: NA, CC
Blonde Cobra: FMC, MoMA
Bouquets 1–10: CC, CFDC, LC, LUX
Budapest Portrait: CC, FDK

Castro Street: CC, CFDC, FMC, LC, LUX, MoMA
Central Park in the Dark: FMC
Cerveza Bud: CC, FMC
Champ Provençal: CC, FMC, LC, LUX
Chang: Milestone
Chan Is Missing: NY
Un chant d'amour: FMC, LUX
Chelsea Girls: MoMA
Chicago Loop: FMC
A Child's Garden and the Serious Sea: CC, CFDC, LUX
Chronos: FACETS, IMAX
The City: MoMA
City of Contrasts: MoMA
City Pasture: CC, FMC
Claiming Open Spaces: Allen
The Climate of New York: FMC
Commingled Containers: CC
Concern for the City: FMC
Continuum: CC, LUX
Cosmic Ray: CC
Critical Mass: FMC, MoMA
Crossroads: CC, LUX

Daughters of the Dust: Kino
David Holzman's Diary: Direct Cinema
David: Off and On: UConn
Deconstruction Site: CC, LUX
Deseret: CC
Detour: FACETS, KP
Dog Star Man: CC, CFDC, FMC, MoMA
Doldrums: FMC
Do the Right Thing: Swank

Eastside Summer: FMC
Eaux d'artifice: CC
8 ½ × 11: FMC

11 × 14: CC, CFDC
Encyclopedia of the Blessed: CC, FMC
Eureka: CC, FMC
Evolution of the Skyscraper: MoMA

The Fall of the Romanov Dynasty: MoMA
A Fall Trip Home: CC
Female Trouble: NL
Film about a Woman Who . . . : BFI, CFDC, Zeitgeist
Fireworks: CC
Fist Fight: CC, CFDC, FMC, LUX, MoMA
Flaming Creatures: CC, FMC
Fog Line: CC, FMC, LUX
Four Corners: CC
Frame of Mind: Murphy
Fuses: CC, FMC, LUX

Garden at Target Rock: NA
The Garden of Earthly Delights: CC, CFDC, LUX
Gladly Given: NA
Glass: Memories of Water #25: CC
Go! Go! Go!: FMC
The Gold Diggers: BFI, WMM
Grand Opera: Benning , FDC, LUX
Grass: Milestone, MoMA
Greetings from Out Here: VDB

Highway Landscape: CC, FMC
Him and Me: Benning, CFDC, MoMA
Hold Me While I'm Naked: CC, FMC
Hooray for Light: Thomas
Horicon: Murphy
Horizons: CC, FMC
Hotel Terminus: Swank
Hours for Jerome: CC
House of the White People: CC, FMC
House Painting: Bloom
H_2O: MoMA

Ice: CC, FMC, MoMA
If with These Eyes and Ears: CC
Images of Asian Music: CC, FDK
Imaginary Light: Noren

Impromptu: CC, CFDC, FMC, LC, LUX
Inauguration of the Pleasure Dome: CC
Ingreen: CC
In Progress: CC, FMC
In the Course of Human Events: CC, LUX
In the Street: MoMA
In Titan's Goblet: CC, FDK
Invisible Cities: Martin

Jamestown Baloos: BFI, CC, FMC, LUX, MoMA
Jeanne Dielman, 23 quai du commerce, 1080 Bruxelles: NY
La Jetée: EmGee, UConn
The Journey: CC, FACETS
July 1971 in San Francisco Living at Beach St. Working at Canyon Cinema, Swimming in the Valley of the Moon: CC, FDK

Koyaanisqatsi: NY
Kristallnacht: CC
Kristina Talking Pictures: BFI, CFDC, Zeitgeist

Landscape (for Manon): CC, FDK
Landscape Suicide: CC, CFDC
The Lead Shoes: CC, MoMA
Lessons of Darkness: NA
Line Describing a Cone: CC, FMC
Line of Fire: CC
Lives of Performers: BFI, CFDC, Zeitgeist
Lodz Symphony: CC, FDK
A Look at Laundry: Thomas
Look Park: Thomas
Lost Boundaries: Greaves
Lost Lost Lost: CFDC, FMC, LC

The Machine of Eden: CC, CFDC, LUX, MoMA
Making "Do the Right Thing": FR
Manhatta: LC, MoMA
Manual of Arms: FMC, MoMA
The Man with a Movie Camera: MoMA
Melon Patches: Robertson
Meshes of the Afternoon: FMC, MoMA
Metamorphosis: FMC
Miracle in Harlem: NA
Moana: MoMA

Mondo Trasho: NL
Mongoloid: CC, LUX
Moon's Pool: CC
Moscow: NA
Mothlight: CC, CFDC, LUX
A Movie: CC, LUX, MoMA
Movie Stills: CC, FMC
Multiple Maniacs: NL
Munchen-Berlin Wandering: LC, MoMA

Nana, Mom and Me: New Day
Nanook of the North: MoMA
Natural Born Killers: Swank
New York Ghetto Fish Market 1903: Jacobs
New York Near Sleep, for Saskia: CC, FDK
New York Portrait, Parts I, II, III: CC, FDK
Night and Fog: KP
The Night Belongs to the Police: FMC
9−1−75: FMC
Nobody's Business: Milestone
Non Legato: Rudnick
North on Evers: CC
Notes on the Port of St. Francis: MoMA
N:O:T:H:I:N:G: CC, FMC
Nothing but the Hours (Rien que les heures): MoMA
Nude Descending the Stairs: CC
N.Y., N.Y.: MoMA

One False Move: Kino
One Man's Island: Thomas
One Way Boogie Woogie: Benning, CFDC
One Year (1970): CC
Organism: NA

Pacific Far East Lines: CC
Panorama: Rudnick
Peace Mandala/End War: CC, CFDC, FMC
Pink Flamingos: NL
Premonition: CC
Principles of Harmonic Motion: CC
Print Generation: CC, FMC, MoMA

Puce Moment: CC
The Pursuit of Happiness: FMC

Quixote: CC, FMC, LC, MoMA

Recreation: ACGB, CC, FMC, LC, LUX, MoMA
Red Shovel: CC
Reflections on Black: CC, CFDC, FMC, LC, LUX
Reminiscences of a Journey to Lithuania: CC, FMC, LC, MoMA
Report: CC
Retour d'un repère: FMC, LC, LUX
Riddles of the Sphinx: BFI, MoMA
Rien que les heures (Nothing but the Hours): MoMA
Roam Sweet Home: VDB
Rolls: 1971: CC
Rue des Teinturiers: CC, CFDC, FMC, LC, LUX

Sausalito: MoMA
Scenes from Life: FMC
Science Fiction: CC, FMC, MoMA
Scorpio Rising: CC
Scratch: CC
She's Gotta Have It: Swank
Shift: CC, FMC, MoMA
Shoah: FACETS, NY
Side/Walk/Shuttle: CC
Sigmund Freud's Dora: BFI, CFDC, McCall
Signal—Germany on the Air: CC
Sink or Swim: CC, CFDC, Friedrich, LFC, MoMA, WMM
Sky Blue Water Light Sign: CC, FMC, MoMA
The Sky on Location: Cinenova, FMC, Mangolte
The Sorrow and the Pity: FACETS
Souls of Sin: Archived at Donnell Public Library, New York City
Spray: CC
Square Times: FMC
Star Garden: CC, CFDC, LUX, MoMA
Summerwind: CC
Surface Tension: CC, CFDC, FMC, MoMA
Symbiopsychotaxiplasm: Take One: Greaves

Terminal Disorder: Murphy

There? Where?: FMC, LC, Mangolte
Thursday: CC
Time Indefinite: FR
To Parsifal: CC, FMC
T,O,U,C,H,I,N,G: CC, CFDC, FMC, LC
Les tournesols: CC, CFDC, FMC, LC, LUX
A Town Called Tempest: NA
Trash: FACETS
A Trip down Market Street before the Fire: Library of Congress

Under the Brooklyn Bridge: FMC
The United States of America: FMC
Up and Down the Waterfront: CC, FMC
Utopia: CC

Vietflakes: FMC
Visions of a City: CC, FMC

Walden: FMC
The War Game: EmGee, FACETS
Water and Power: CC, O'Neill (for 35mm)
Wavelength: BFI, CC, CFDC, FMC, MoMA
The Way to the Shadow Garden: CC, CFDC, FMC, LFC
Weather Diary 1, 2, 3 . . . Present: VDB
Weegee's New York: NA
What Maisie Knew: Cinenova, FMC, LC, Mangolte
What Mozart Saw on Mulberry Street: FMC
What the Water Said, nos. 1–3: CC, Gatten
Whose Circumference Is Nowhere: Miller
Wild Night in El Reno: CC, FMC
Window Water Baby Moving: CC, CFDC, FMC, LUX, MoMA
The Wind Variations: Noren

Zipper: CC, FMC
Zorns Lemma: FMC, LC, LUX, MoMA

Notes

Introduction

Epigraph: John Elder, *Reading the Mountains of Home* (Cambridge, Mass.: Harvard University Press, 1998), 163–64.

Chapter 1. The Garden in the Machine

Epigraph: Leo Marx, *The Machine in the Garden* (London: Oxford University Press, 1964), 251.

1. While I am not entirely comfortable with the term "avant-garde film," I use it here because it has somewhat broader currency than other terms used to refer to this general cinematic terrain: "experimental film" is a term many filmmakers dislike (they do not see their films as "experiments," but as finished works); "independent film" has been used to refer to many kinds of film that share only an independence from big Hollywood budgets; "underground film" and "the New American Cinema" seem closely connected with the particular social-historical context of the 1960s. In my own writing and teaching, I prefer the pragmatic "critical cinema," as a way of emphasizing the pedagogical value of the films discussed here for critiquing mainstream commercial cinema and television (and as a way of polemicizing the importance of these films as accomplished works of art).

2. As is discussed later, Richard B. Altick's *The Shows of London* (Cambridge, Mass.: Harvard University Press, 1978) is a most valuable introductory overview of many forms of precinematic motion picture entertainment, including still and moving panoramas, Daguerre's Diorama, and Loutherbourg's Eidophusikon.

Gerald C. Carr discusses the phenomenon of the "Great Picture" in connection with Frederic Church's work, in *Frederic Edwin Church: The Icebergs* (Dallas: Dallas Museum of Fine Arts, 1980), chap. 1. Stephen Oettermann's *The Panorama: History of a Mass Medium*, translated by Deborah Lucas Schneider (New York: Zone, 1997), is a remarkable overview of the international phenomenon of the panorama.

3. For a review of some of the many "single-shot films" that were made during this period, see Scott MacDonald, "Putting All Your Eggs in One Basket: A Survey of Single-Shot Film," *Afterimage* (U.S.A.) 16, no. 8 (March 1989): 10–16. During the early years of cinema, some filmmakers marketed "nature films"—single-shot films of waterfalls, single and multiple shots of trains traveling through famous landscapes. For a listing of such films—none of which were seen by the filmmakers I'm discussing in chapter 1—see Iris Cahn, "The Changing Landscape of Modernity: Early Film and America's 'Great Picture' Tradition," *Wide Angle* 18, no. 3 (July 1996): 85–100.

4. This is Gottheim's own metaphor. I have heard him compare the clearing of the fog in the landscape to achieving intellectual clarity, during in-person presentations of his films. (It has become a convention in avant-garde filmmaking for filmmakers to appear with their films, to introduce screenings and answer questions afterward.)

5. Of course, Muybridge was not the only important motion-study photographer whose work often focused on animals. The Frenchman Etienne-Jules Marey provided major contributions to photographic motion study. See Marta Braun's definitive history of Marey's work (which includes a detailed comparison of the contributions of Muybridge and Marey): Marta Braun, *Picturing Time: The Work of Etienne-Jules Marey (1980–1904)* (Chicago: University of Chicago Press, 1992).

6. If one can accept the horses as an implicit reference to Muybridge's study of horses, the flight of the bird may provide an even subtler, if accidental, reference to Marey's (and to a lesser degree, Muybridge's) motion photography of flying birds.

7. For a time in the late 1960s and early 1970s, it seemed de rigueur for some film artists to forswear credits, as if their identities were implicit in their imagery; some of these filmmakers have continued to abjure credits, presumably in defiance of the tradition of the commercial cinema.

8. The particular look of *Fog Line*—and Gottheim's other early films—has changed over the years, not simply because all film, and especially color film, decays, but because certain printing stocks that were available in 1970 are no longer manufactured. The early *Fog Line* prints were a gorgeous pea green; the green in recent prints is a bit grayish—and less memorable as a film color, though the film remains lovely.

9. See Angela Miller, *The Empire of the Eye: Landscape Representation and American Cultural Politics, 1825–1875* (Ithaca: Cornell University Press, 1993), 42.

10. Lynne Kirby explores the cinema-railroad connection in *Parallel Tracks: The Railroad and Silent Cinema* (Durham: Duke University Press, 1997).

An early experiment in what would now be called "virtual reality," Hale's Tours was introduced by George C. Hale and Fred and Ward Gifford at the 1904 St. Louis Exposition. "Passengers" interested in embarking on a Hale's Tour would enter a railroad car and take seats. Movies taken from moving trains would be projected onto the windows from outside the car so as to cover the entire field of vision, and the car itself would be moved slightly from underneath so that the passengers would feel and hear the typical sensations of rail travel. Hale's Tours became popular in American amusement parks from 1905 to 1907 and may have lasted as late as 1912. See Raymond Fielding, "Hale's Tours: Ultrarealism in the Pre-1910 Motion Picture," in John L. Fell, ed., *Film before Griffith* (Berkeley: University of California Press, 1983), 116–30.

11. While few viewers who see the film now are familiar with the actual light sign, much of Murphy's original audience in Iowa City would have recognized the sign, though he did not make the film solely for that local audience.

12. See Altick, *The Shows of London*, chapter 12, p. 167. Even taking into account the somewhat more spectacular effects provided by the transformations in the Diorama images and the tendency of Diorama performances to condense time, that audiences were enthralled by Daguerre's invention is a further indication of the changes in taste between the early nineteenth century and the twentieth century, and it suggests that there is nothing about *Fog Line* that renders it intrinsically "boring": the most we can say is that *Fog Line* provides a type of experience most audiences are no longer prepared to enjoy.

13. See Altick, *The Shows of London*, 129. Altick's history of still panoramas is useful: see chapters 10, 11, 13, and 14, though the most extensive history of the panorama, both the still and the moving variety, is Oettermann, *The Panorama*.

14. The Gettysburg Cyclorama is currently presented in a manner analogous to a movie. Viewers gather on a central platform in the semidarkness. The painting is contextualized by narration and is revealed, first, in a series of "close-ups"—a rectangular light source reveals details of the painting—and "medium shots," as Pickett's Charge is contextualized historically and geographically. The presentation culminates in Pickett's Charge itself, with the entire panorama illuminated and the visual action accompanied by sound effects.

15. Elaborate discussions of the St. Louis panoramas are available in John Francis McDermott, *The Lost Panorama of the Mississippi* (Chicago: University of Chicago Press, 1958), and Angela Miller's " 'The Imperial Republic': Narratives of National Expansion in American Art, 1820–1860," a Ph.D. dissertation completed at Yale University in 1985, section 2: "The Moving Panoramas of the Cultural Colonization of the West." See also Miller's "The Panorama, the Cinema, and the Emergence of the Spectacular," *Wide Angle* 18, no. 2 (April 1996): 34–69.

16. The original moving panoramas were hand-cranked from one side of the viewing rectangle to the other. The Hamm's light sign imagery is printed on a plastic loop that is lit electrically from the inside and revolves continuously.

17. Many scholars have noted the relationship (or at least the analogy) between the moving panorama and the modern motion picture, including McDermott, *The Lost Panorama of the Mississippi*, and Charlotte Willard, "Panoramas, the First Movies," *Art in America* 47, no. 4 (1959): 64–69. See also Barbara Novak's and Ellwood C. Parry III's discussions of Thomas Cole in Novak, *Nature and Culture: American Landscape Painting, 1825–1875* (New York: Oxford University Press, 1980), 20; and Parry, *The Art of Thomas Cole: Ambition and Imagination* (Newark: Associated University Presses, 1988), 124–25.

18. See Miller, " 'The Imperial Republic' ": "Implicit in the panoramic narrative was the image of the river linking together both the regions of the republic and the stages of national progress. A great artery running the entire length of the valley, the Mississippi encapsulated in its two thousand mile length the phases of western community, from its wilderness beginnings to its fully realized urban form in New Orleans" (409); "As a popular art form, the panoramas identified geography with cultural identity, and brought both into the service of America's collective mission, the colonization of the continent" (419).

19. All in all, the effect of Murphy's film for most viewers is a bit surreal, and reminiscent of the scene in Marcel Duchamp's peep-hole erotic landscape composition, *Étant donnes: 1° la chute d'eau 2° le gaz d'éclairage* (1946–66), an installation at the Philadelphia Museum of Art.

20. See Joni Louise Kinsey, *Thomas Moran and the Surveying of the American West* (Washington, D.C.: Smithsonian Institution Press, 1992), for the details of Moran's involvement with the Northern Pacific Railroad.

21. Miller, " 'The Imperial Republic,' " 276–77.

22. This "accuracy" could be of more than one kind. Cole's *The Oxbow* paints a real turning in the Connecticut River as seen from the Mount Holyoke hills but avoids revealing the degree to which that vista had already become a popular tourist attraction. That is, Cole paints "reality" but distorts our sense of the space in the interest of demonstrating his attitudes toward development. Further, Cole, and other artists, often designed composite, "fictional" images of wild scenes, on the basis of precise accurate plein air studies of the geologic, biological, and atmospheric particulars of a region.

23. Murphy interviewed in Scott MacDonald, *A Critical Cinema: Interviews with Independent Filmmakers* (Berkeley: University of California Press, 1988), 182.

24. Murphy might have used a recording of a stream, of course—though, in fact, he recorded the stream "live."

25. Gottheim has maintained a practical interest in the nineteenth-century visual arts since 1982, when he established Be-hold, Inc., through which he sells vintage

photography: daguerreotypes, tintypes, cartes de visite, stereopticon images, etc. Be-hold can be reached at behold@be-hold.com; http://www.be-hold.com; and at 914–423–5806.

Chapter 2. Voyages of Life

1. Cole painted two versions of *The Voyage of Life*. The version in Utica was painted first, as a commission for the New York banker and philanthropist Samuel Ward, who stipulated that the four-part series was to be executed in the style of Cole's previous series of paintings, the five-part *The Course of the Empire*, painted for Lumen Reed, a wealthy New York merchant, from 1833 to 1836. Ward died soon after Cole began *The Voyage of Life*, and though Cole was finally paid $5,000 for the series (after litigation and following a free exhibition of the paintings at the National Academy of Design in New York), his frustration with the fact that *The Voyage* would be hidden away in a rarely visited private gallery led him to paint the series a second time during a visit to Rome. This second version, completed in 1842, was widely exhibited and is now part of the National Gallery of Art in Washington, D.C.

For information on *The Voyage of Life*, see William H. Truettner and Alan Wallach, eds., *Thomas Cole: Landscape into History* (New Haven and Washington, D.C.: Yale University Press/National Museum of American Art, 1994), a catalog for a major Cole retrospective exhibited at the National Museum of American Art in Washington, at the Wadsworth Atheneum in Hartford, and at the New York His-torical Society from March 18, 1994, until March 25, 1995; and Paul Schweizer, ed., *The Voyage of Life by Thomas Cole* (Utica: Munson-Williams-Proctor Institute, 1985), a catalog for an exhibition of paintings, drawings, and prints relating to *The Voyage of Life*, at the Munson-Williams-Proctor Institute in Utica, N.Y., from October 5 through December 5, 1985.

2. Each of Cole's paintings is approximately 52" × 78", a ratio of 2:3—not pre-cisely the aspect ratio of the conventional film image (the standard aspect ratio for 35mm, 16mm, and Super-8mm, at least until the advent of wide-screen film, was 3:4) but certainly comparable to it.

3. Griffith discovered and perfected those means of articulating a sequence that are now considered standard: inheriting the shot from the Lumières, the simple narrative from Georges Méliès, and the beginnings of more complex storytelling from Edwin S. Porter, Griffith was able to use editing to deepen viewers' engage-ment with character and action. Griffith is also given credit for adapting the nine-teenth-century novel's complex plotting to cinema, through his development of intercutting.

4. Sergei Eisenstein, "The Cinematographic Principle and the Ideogram," in

Film Form, ed. and trans. Jay Leyda (New York: Harcourt, Brace and World, 1949), 37; emphasis in the original.

5. In Eisenstein's theory, the more dynamic the film, the more thoroughly dialectical it is, in both composition and editing. During many of the most energized sequences in *Potemkin* (1925), for example, individual shots are often designed to reveal different oppositional forms of movement simultaneously (e.g., movement from right to left in the upper half of an image, left to right in the lower half), as well as movement in opposition to the motion in the previous and subsequent shots. In this context, one might argue that "Youth" is the most energetic of the four *Voyage of Life* paintings, since viewers can see that the Youth's movement leftward "collides," at least conceptually, with the river's rightward movement in the background of the image.

6. In a letter of March 21, 1840, Cole explains to the Reverend J. F. Phillips (who seems to have criticized Cole's decision not to design the four paintings so that the River of Life flowed consistently in the same direction),

> There are many windings in the stream of life, and on this idea I have proceeded. Its course toward the Ocean of Eternity we all know to be certain, but not direct. Each picture [in *The Voyage of Life*] I have wished to make a sort of antithesis to the other, thereby the more fully to illustrate the changeable tenor of our mortal existence. . . .
>
> In order to give the same direction to the stream in each picture, I should be constrained to have the same view of the boat and figure or figures—nearly the same all through the several parts of the work: this would be monotonous, and would strike the beholder as having arisen either from incompetency to execute, or from poverty of invention, and that pleasure which arises from novelty would entirely be lost.

Cole quoted in Louis Legrand Noble, *The Life and Works of Thomas Cole*, ed. Elliot S. Vesell (Cambridge, Mass.: Harvard University Press, 1964), 211.

7. It is, of course, one of the stunning paradoxes of film history that the editing tactics developed in the years following the October Revolution, with the support of the new revolutionary government, as a means of assisting in the confirmation and extension of the revolutionary process, are primarily evident today in the very epitome of capitalism: the standard commercial television hour, which alternates between the formally "peaceful" editing in most television shows and the barrage editing of the commercial interruptions.

8. Larry Gottheim, interviewed in Scott MacDonald, *A Critical Cinema: Interviews with Independent Filmmakers* (Berkeley: University of California Press, 1988), 86–87.

9. This and the subsequent comment are from my interview with Gottheim in *A Critical Cinema*, 88–89.

10. Gottheim in MacDonald, *A Critical Cinema*, 87.

11. In *Landscape and Memory* (New York: Knopf, 1995), Simon Schama makes a

similar argument in connection with Albrecht Altdorfer's painting *St. George and the Dragon* (1510): "the toy-like miniaturization of the action . . . strengthens the impression that the real hero of the piece is as much the Teutonic forest as the Christian warrior" (99).

12. A good example of Cole's suppression of the realities of development in his work is *River in the Catskills* (1843). The painting does implicitly chart the history of development in the region (a man holding an ax stands near some felled trees in the foreground; the beginnings of a village are visible . . .); and yet, the overall impact of the painting is of a lovely, harmonious vista, despite the train we see entering the scene from the left in the middle ground. Indeed, the train seems to produce less smoke than a distant fire near the foot of the mountains.

13. In some paintings, Cole's central topic is the problem of development. See, for example, Angela Miller's analysis of *The Oxbow* in *The Empire of the Eye: Landscape Representation and American Cultural Politics, 1825–1875* (Ithaca: Cornell University Press, 1993), chap. 1.

14. Gottheim discusses his fascination with landscape in "Sticking in/to the Landscape," *Millennium Film Journal*, nos. 4–5 (Summer–Fall 1979): 84–92.

15. Of course, in retrospect we can see that even the conservative Cole was hardly detached from the practical processes of industrial development. As Albert Boime makes clear in *The Magisterial Gaze: Manifest Destiny and American Landscape Painting c. 1830–1865* (Washington, D.C.: Smithsonian Institution Press, 1991), those who made landscape paintings profitable for the painters (including Cole) and influential in American society at large were precisely the movers and shakers of American industrial development. In fact, Boime argues that, as the "undeveloped land is subjugated to development and speculation, landscape assumes a pregnant role in masking the commercialized objectives of those who promote it (88–89)—a process epitomized, for example, by Cole's *River in the Catskills*, discussed in note 12.

Chapter 3. Avant-Gardens

Epigraph: Celia Thaxter, *An Island Garden* (Boston: Houghton Mifflin, 1894), 27–28, with pictures and illuminations by Childe Hassam. The original Thaxter text, including the Hassam imagery, was published in a facsimile edition in 1998.

1. John Dixon Hunt, *Gardens and the Picturesque: Studies in the History of Landscape Architecture* (Cambridge, Mass.: MIT Press, 1992).

2. In Firbank's novel *Valmouth*, "Niki-Esther, at the time of her marriage went into the garden in pursuit of a butterfly, dressed in her wedding gown and carrying her bouquet." P. Adams Sitney, *Visionary Film* (New York: Oxford University Press, 1974), 103.

3. My source of information about the Villa d'Este is David R. Coffin's *The Villa*

in the Life of Renaissance Rome (Princeton: Princeton University Press, 1979), 311–40. The refashioning of the gardens and palace of Tivoli took twelve years (1560–72) and involved a group of architects, of whom Ligorio seems to have been the principal (317).

4. Anger provided this information for a catalog note reprinted by Sitney in *Visionary Film* (102–3). Sitney's brief discussion of *Eaux d'artifice* is still the most elaborate discussion of the film in English.

5. See Sitney, *Visionary Film*, 102.

6. Coffin describes Tivoli's three-part thematic design on pp. 327–29.

7. Conceivably, this conflation of eras could account for Anger's decision to present the imagery in a monochrome blue tint. The "Claude glass," popular among landscape enthusiasts during the late eighteenth century, allowed viewers to create their own picturesque compositions from within nature itself and, by the choice of a particular tinted glass ("glass" in "Claude glass" means mirror), color the scene with "one, coordinating tint" (Hunt, *Gardens and the Picturesque*, 178).

8. Sitney uses the term "the psychodramatic trance film" in *Visionary Film*, which remains the most thorough discussion of the genre to date. For his analysis of Anger, see chapter 4, "The Magus."

9. Sitney quotes the prologue in *Visionary Film*, 97.

10. Letter from Kenneth Anger to Amos Vogel, from Rome, January 31, 1953.

11. Sitney suggests a further indication in the films that Anger meant for viewers to see this connection: "For the special program of his complete works at the Spring Equinox of 1966, he hand-tinted the candle atop the Christmas tree in *Fireworks* and the scratched-out face of the man in bed beside the dreamer to underline the relationship with *Eaux d'Artifice*, which ends soon after the appearance of a hand-tinted fan." *Visionary Film*, 102.

12. In his catalog essay for New York State's Katonah Museum of Art's show "Pavel Tchelitchew: The Landscape of the Body" (June 14–September 6, 1998), Michael Duncan claims that the artist's "occasionally melodramatic and flamboyantly gay personality must be considered a factor in his art historical marginalization today. Critical detractors up to the present have bridled at the homoeroticism of his works and his 'effete' associations with the ballet, theater, and high society" (10); and reminds us that Tchelitchew's works "have often been referred to by critics as being 'morbid,' 'inverted,' 'hypersensitive,' 'neurotic,' 'narcissistic,' or 'inward.' These terms today read as euphemistic descriptions of an effeminacy and homosexuality that critics such as [Clement] Greenberg hoped would be expunged from the art world" (14) by the abstract expressionists.

13. Bill Landis, *Anger: The Unauthorized Biography of Kenneth Anger* (New York: Harper Collins, 1996), 63.

14. The Mekas obituary is available in Mekas, *Movie Journal* (New York: Collier, 1972), 413–15.

15. Brakhage uses "Yet" because, while Maas and Menken slept in the same bed, theirs was hardly a conventional heterosexual union. Maas was involved with a long series of gay lovers, some of whom became short-term living partners in the Menken-Maas apartment in Brooklyn Heights—and long-term friends with Menken. Menken and Maas are discussed in *Film at Wit's End* (Kingston, N.Y.: Documentext/McPherson & Co., 1989), 33–47; and in "On Marie Menken," in *Brakhage Scrapbook,* ed. Robert A. Haller (New Paltz, N.Y.: Documentext, 1982), 91–93.

16. In the preface to the second edition of *Visionary Film* (1979), Sitney admits that "Marie Menken's work deserves a chapter," not the passing reference he gave it in "The Lyrical Film" (Sitney's chapter 5). "But," he says, "five years ago I did not understand how crucial her teasingly simple films were in their dialogue of camera eye and nature" (xi).

17. I am using the dates assembled by Robert A. Haller for Brakhage's *Film at Wit's End* and for *First Light,* a catalog, edited by Haller, for a film series sponsored by Anthology Film Archives in 1998. Menken's records are currently unavailable to scholars, and may never become available; and as a result, dating her films, some of which she showed in multiple versions over a period of years, is not as easy as it should be. The same appears to be true of the lengths of Menken's films, which seem to vary with each listing. Either the various listings are sloppy or several of Menken's films were in multiple versions.

18. Brakhage, *Film at Wit's End,* 44. In his reminiscence of 1963, "The Gryphon Yaks," published in *Film Culture,* no. 29 (1963), Maas explains, "Marie's last real contact with Dwight . . . was when Dwight was getting over the DTs. . . . Dwight recovered and was never fun again. Marie says she did not and has been fun ever since" (53). Menken's *Dwightiana* (1957) was made during this moment.

19. When I last counted shots, I came up with sixty-two (plus two opening credits and "The End"), though a passage of sporadically lit close-ups near the end makes distinguishing separate shots difficult.

20. Leslie Mandell, "Interview with Marie Menken," *Wagner Literary Magazine,* no. 4 (1963–64): 47. A subtitle indicates that Mandell was assisted by Paul (P. Adams) Sitney, of *Filmwise.*

21. Roger Jacoby, "Willard Maas and Marie Menken: The Last Years," *Film Culture,* nos. 63–64 (1976–77): 122.

22. Mandell, "Interview with Marie Menken," 48.

23. Patricia R. Zimmermann, *Reel Families: A Social History of Amateur Film* (Bloomington: Indiana University Press, 1995), 146.

24. A 1967 *Time* review of the new avant-garde cinema described Menken's camera work in *Lights* (1964–66): "She slashes at her subject with a camera as an action painter slashes at his canvas." *Time* 89, no. 7 (February 17, 1967): 99.

25. Sitney compares *Eaux d'artifice* and *Arabesque for Kenneth Anger* in "Marie Menken: Body and Light," in Haller, ed., *First Light,* 48–53.

26. Menken was born (in 1910) in New York City to Lithuanian immigrant parents. According to Mekas, he and Menken "used to sing some old Lithuanian songs together, some of which she still remembered from her mother." Mekas, *Movie Journal*, 414.

27. Brakhage, in Haller, ed., *Brakhage Scrapbook*, 92–93.

28. When I asked Mekas about Menken's influence, Mekas responded, "Oh, yes. I liked what she did and I thought it worked. She helped me make up my mind about how to structure my films." Scott MacDonald, *A Critical Cinema 2: Interviews with Independent Filmmakers* (Berkeley: University of California Press, 1992), 91.

29. Brakhage, *Film at Wit's End*, 38.

30. Mekas, *Movie Journal*, 46–47. Marjorie Keller discusses some of the specifics of Menken's influence on Mekas in "The Apron Strings of Jonas Mekas," in David E. James, ed., *To Free the Cinema: Jonas Mekas and the New York Underground* (Princeton: Princeton University Press, 1992), 86–88.

31. Brakhage discusses this incident in an unpublished interview with the author, recorded in November 1996. The arrival of Mekas and the New American Cinema—with its commitment to the particular vision of specific filmmakers, rather than the "potpourri" approach to cinema exhibition evident at Cinema 16—changed, for better and/or worse, the nature of avant-garde exhibition, distribution, and production and was one of the factors that led to the demise of Cinema 16, the most successful film society in American history.

32. *The Garden of Eden* is about a young widow whose car stalls in the country: she is rescued by inhabitants of a local nudist camp, whose wholesome way of life transforms her (and her father-in-law who follows her to the camp). It sounds like a hard-core porn plot from fifteen years later, but my empty memory suggests it was pretty tame.

33. Schneemann discusses the evolution of audience reception of *Fuses*, at least insofar as she's experienced it on tour, in Scott MacDonald, *A Critical Cinema: Interviews with Independent Filmmakers* (Berkeley: University of California Press, 1988), 140–42, and in Kate Haug's interview with Schneemann in *Wide Angle* 20, no. 1 (January 1998): 26–29.

34. Schneemann, in the Haug interview, p. 47.

35. See David James's elegant discussion of "the touch of her [Schneemann's] hand on the film's flesh," in *Allegories of Cinema: American Film in the Sixties* (Princeton: Princeton University Press, 1989), 320; and Bruce Elder's exploration of Schneemann's work in *A Body of Vision: Representations of the Body in Recent Film and Poetry* (Waterloo, Ont.: Wilfred Laurier Press, 1997), 233–76.

36. The use of a window as metaphor for the camera has been pervasive in American avant-garde film: distinguished instances include *Meshes of the After-*

noon, Stan Brakhage's *Window Water Baby Moving* (1959), and Michael Snow's *Wavelength* (1966), as well as *Fuses*.

37. Schneemann, in the Haug interview, p. 45.

38. Schneemann, in MacDonald, *A Critical Cinema*, 138–39.

39. Annette Kolodny, *The Lay of the Land: Metaphor as Experience and History in American Life and Letters* (Chapel Hill: University of North Carolina Press, 1975), 5.

40. Schneemann, in the Haug interview, p. 30.

41. I am alluding, of course, to Laura Mulvey's "Visual Pleasure and Narrative Cinema" (see Mulvey, *Visual and Other Pleasures* [Bloomington: Indiana University Press, 1989], 14–26) and the substantial literature it has inspired. According to Schneemann, "Mulvey talked to me about the rupture *Fuses* made in pornography—how important *Fuses* was in an erotic vision. It was going to change the whole argument and discussion of filmic representation of sexuality and . . . then she couldn't touch it! Mulvey has never mentioned my films." Schneemann, in the Haug interview, p. 28.

42. Recently, Schneemann (in the Haug interview) has also expressed reservations about the way Brakhage's camera usurps the female birth function: "the male eye replicated or possessed the vagina's primacy of giving birth. The camera lens became the Os [mouth] out of which the birth was 'expressed.' "

43. I am using the *Oxford Annotated Bible*, the Revised Standard Version (New York: Oxford University Press, 1962), Gen. 1:27.

44. Stan Brakhage grew mold on the filmstrip for several films, including *Dog Star Man* (1962–64) and *Song 14* (1966, 1980).

45. R. Bruce Elder argues, correctly, that *Fuses* avoids the usual orgasmic rise-to-climax and denouement structure of narrative; but the pulsation built into the overall structure of the film—periods of energetic sexuality are followed by moments of calm—suggests a sexual as well as a daily rhythm, whether one wants to imagine the rhythm as emblematic of multiple orgasm in a single sexual moment or as a series of orgasms during a longer sexual interchange. See Elder, *A Body of Vision*, 235–36.

46. *Metaphors on Vision* was published as a special issue of *Film Culture*, no. 30 (Fall 1963); it was edited by P. Adams Sitney. Sitney included a portion of Brakhage's essay, "Metaphors on Vision," in P. Adams Sitney, ed., *The Avant-Garde Film: A Reader of Theory and Criticism* (New York: New York University Press, 1978), 120–29.

47. Brakhage's work has instigated a considerable body of commentary. Some key discussions include chapters 6 and 7 of Sitney's *Visionary Film* and Sitney's "Autobiography in Avant-Garde Film," in *The Avant-Garde Film*, 199–246; Marjorie Keller's analysis of Brakhage's depiction of childhood in part 3 of her *The Untutored Eye: Childhood in the Films of Cocteau, Cornell, and Brakhage* (New Brunswick, N.J.: Fairleigh Dickinson University Press, 1986), 179–299; David James's

"Stan Brakhage: The Filmmaker as Poet," chapter 6 of *Allegories of Cinema*, 29–57; chapters 3 and 4 of William C. Wees, *Light Moving in Time* (Berkeley: University of California Press, 1992), 55–105; and Marie Nesthus's "A Crucible of Document: The Sequence Films of Stan Brakhage, 1968–1984," a Ph.D. dissertation completed at New York University in 1999.

48. Brakhage's commitment to silence has usually been understood as a function of his commitment to cinema as a visual art and to the development of his viewer's visual sophistication. I argue for a different sense of Brakhage's silence in chapter 13.

49. Brakhage, *Metaphors on Vision*, letter to Robert Kelly, August 22, 1963. Emphasis Brakhage's.

While the particular collage technique Brakhage developed for *Mothlight* may have been original, *Mothlight* and *The Garden of Earthly Delights* are instances of a more general tradition of working directly on the filmstrip that dates back at least as far as the 1920s, e.g., when Man Ray used the "rayogram" technique for his *Retour à la raison* (1923): he laid objects such as nails or tiny springs onto film stock and exposed it to light, creating on-film imagery without the use of a camera. In the 1930s Len Lye developed a sophisticated technique for painting directly onto strips of clear celluloid in conjunction with music; and a wide variety of other filmmakers, including Norman McLaren, Carolee Schneemann, Kurt Kren, Walter Ungerer, and more recently Donna Cameron and Jennifer Reeves have made complete films without the mediation of a camera. Even the rayogram technique is alive and well, e.g., in Greta Snider's *Flight* (1997).

50. The *Canyon Cinema Film/Video Catalogue 7* (1992) notes that *The Garden of Earthly Delights* should be screened at 18 frames per second, which is not a possibility for a good many recent 16mm projectors.

51. Malcolm LeGrice, *Abstract Film and Beyond* (Cambridge, Mass.: MIT Press, 1977), 90.

52. The implicit change in metaphor from *Mothlight* to *The Garden of Earthly Delights* may signal a change in the way in which Brakhage has seen his connection to natural process: as a young man revealing a new form of cinematic vision/Vision, Brakhage could see himself as a moth fluttering around the light/ Light. As he has grown older, the cyclic nature of gardening may have come to seem more appropriate for his continuing productivity.

53. Robert Breer is often identified with this procedure, which is used in many of his early films: e.g., *Eyewash* (1959), *Blazes* (1961), *Fist Fight* (1964).

54. See William C. Wees's discussion of the elements of sight in *Light Moving in Time*, chap. 1.

55. In his catalog note for *The Garden of Earthly Delights*, Brakhage also credits Emil Nolde as an inspiration, especially Nolde's "flower paintings." This connection resonates on several levels: first, Nolde's expressionist impasto creates—in,

e.g., *Zinnias* (1929) and *Large Sunflowers II* (1940)—an extremely shallow sense of space in which the flowers' vivid color seems to rest on the surface of the canvas; and second, the flowers are often seen, as Peter Selz puts it, "removed from all environmental relationships. Like the waves seen without coastlines, they are painted without soil or vase. Nolde presents us only with petals, stamens, pistils and perhaps a few leaves." Selz, *Emil Nolde* (New York: Museum of Modern Art, 1963), 49. Of course, the most fundamental connection here is Nolde's sense of the spiritual power and importance of nature.

Another important inspiration, according to Brakhage, for this and other films, is *The Tangled Garden* (1916) by the Canadian J. E. H. MacDonald. Indeed, the Group of Seven—and especially MacDonald and Tom Thomson—could provide an interesting context for thinking about Brakhage's work.

56. Brakhage, in conversation with the author, October 15, 1998.

57. Keller, in James, *To Free the Cinema*, 87.

58. A different, but related, "furrow" is suggested by Keller's presentation of her title at the bottom of the frame: the line of verbal text is imaged as a furrow— and of course adequate verbal "plantings" do constitute a "field."

59. The child "reads" as Keller's daughter and the "old man's" granddaughter, though, according to P. Adams Sitney, Keller's widower, the girl cannot be one of Keller's daughters (who were born after the film was shot) and is more likely to be one of Mr. Keller's many great-granddaughters.

60. Donald Jay Grout, *A History of Western Music,* rev. ed. (New York: Norton, 1973), 644.

61. For useful attempts to see the interconnections of European and American avant-garde film history, see David Curtis's *Experimental Cinema* (New York: Delta, 1971); LeGrice's *Abstract Film and Beyond;* and the recent work by A. L. Rees, *A History of Experimental Film and Video* (London: BFI, 1999).

62. Keller founded and edited *Motion Picture* and taught at the University of Rhode Island.

63. See David E. James's "Film Diary/Diary Film: Practice and Product in *Walden,*" in James, ed., *To Free the Cinema: Jonas Mekas and the New York Underground* (Princeton: Princeton University Press, 1992), 145–79. James distinguishes between Jonas Mekas's ongoing diaristic record of the sights and sounds of his life and his decision to transform this record into individual "diary films" that can stand on their own as works of art (see chap. 7). In recent years Mekas has become a supporter of Robertson's work; in several telephone conversations with me, Robertson has mentioned that Mekas has told her that her films are the real diary films.

Another crucial influence for Robertson is Carolee Schneemann's diary of her domestic life with Anthony McCall, *Kitch's Last Meal* (1973–78). Robertson talks about the impact of Schneemann's work on hers in our interview: see MacDonald, *A Critical Cinema 2*, 215–16.

64. Among the reels available on VHS are Reel 22—August 23–September 1, 1982 (24 minutes): *A Short Affair (and) Going Crazy*; Reel 23—September 1–December 13, 1982 (26 minutes, 4 seconds): *A Breakdown (and) After the Mental Hospital*; Reel 31—August 19–28, 1983 (24 minutes, 36 seconds): *Niagara Falls*; Reel 71—February 3–May 6, 1990 (27 minutes, 2 seconds): *On Probation*; Reel 76—October 30, 1991–March 28, 1992 (28 minutes, 10 seconds): *Fall to Spring*; Reel 80—May 14–September 26, 1994 (26 minutes, 49 seconds): *Emily Died*; Reel 81—September 27, 1994–January 29, 1995 (25 minutes, 3 seconds): *Mourning Emily*.

65. The optimum screening situation for *Five Year Diary* is probably the one arranged by David Schwartz at the American Museum of the Moving Image in 1988: Robertson presented her domestic epic in a small gallery space decorated with objects from her apartment. Robertson lived in the gallery space during museum hours for eight successive days, projecting the film and providing in-person commentary for interested spectators. However, since few exhibitors are willing to make this level of commitment to an independent film, and since most potential viewers are likely to see *Five Year Diary* on VHS, I am confining my references to those reels that are currently available.

66. The narrating track on the VHS reels of *Five Year Diary* is one version of what is, in live presentations of the film, Robertson's in-person commentary. From Robertson's point of view, this represents an unfortunate compromise, since ideally, the commentary should be different each time the particular reel is presented—a way of reflecting how her own ongoing experiences and events around her continually recontextualize the earlier visual and auditory material of each diary reel. From a telephone conversation with Robertson, August 11, 1999.

67. There is no way for viewers to know whether they are hearing one child at various ages or several children. In fact, four children's voices are heard on the track: Robertson's nephew, Michael, in the first passage; her niece, Emily, above the traffic; another niece, Renata, talking with her mother; and finally niece Elena singing "Teddy Bear Picnic."

68. I am quoting Patricia Zimmermann's paraphrase of Marty Jezer's *The Dark Ages: Life in the United States, 1945–1960* (Boston: South End, 1982), 223–25, in *Reel Families*, 133.

69. Peter Kubelka's well-known essay "The Theory of Metrical Film" is included in P. Adams Sitney, *The Avant-Garde Film*, 139–59. Kubelka uses his early films as examples of "metrical structure" based on the assumption that the essential "articulation of cinema" takes place *"not between shots but between frames"* (141). Kubelka's emphasis. Lowder's researches became her Ph.D. dissertation at the University of Paris and Nanterre: "Le film expérimental en tant qu'instrument de

recherche visuelle: Contribution des cinéastes expérimentaux à une démarché exploratoire" (1987).

70. Lowder, in Scott MacDonald, *A Critical Cinema 3: Interviews with Independent Filmmakers* (Berkeley: University of California Press, 1998), 219.

71. Lowder has lived in France since 1973, though she was born to British parents in Lima, Peru (in 1941), and worked for some years in London (at the BBC). She has an extensive knowledge of independent cinema from many parts of the world, in part because of her work as an archivist and programmer at the Archives du film experimental d'Avignon, which she (and her partner, Alain-Alcide Sudre) established in 1982.

72. In the case of *Retour d'un repère,* this expansion was itself extended, first, in *Rapprochements* (1979), a two-projector film in which two prints of *Retour d'un repère* are projected one on top of the other (Lowder: "to see if I could make a brighter film," in MacDonald, *A Critical Cinema 3,* 234), and in 1981, in *Retour d'un repère composé,* a fifty-nine-minute reworking of the same material.

73. Lowder, in MacDonald, *A Critical Cinema 3,* 236.

74. The title of *Impromptu* refers to the fact that Lowder had been asked to screen the film before she considered it finished, and also to a series of accidents that occurred during and after the shooting. See MacDonald, *A Critical Cinema 3,* 237.

75. MacDonald and Lowder, in MacDonald, *A Critical Cinema 3,* 238–39.

76. The flowers are those that "happened to be on our balcony when I decided to introduce a pause of black in between each *Bouquet* with a single flower as punctuation" (Lowder, letter to the author, September 8, 1998): a red pourpier (portulaca or purslane); a white snapdragon; a small sunflower; a magenta portulaca; a yellow-orange marigold; a white arum lily (of the araceae family); a black-centered, yellow-petaled rudbeckia; a yellow-orange portulaca; a white arum lily.

Chapter 4. Re-envisioning the American West

1. Wayne Franklin, *Discoverers, Explorers, Settlers: The Diligent Writers of Early America* (Chicago: University of Chicago Press, 1979), 23, 24.

2. Franklin, *Discoverers, Explorers, Settlers,* 69, 70.

3. Franklin, *Discoverers, Explorers, Settlers,* 132, 131.

4. *Camera Obscura* was one journal that supported Mangolte's early films. See "Camera Obscura Interview with Babette Mangolte," *Camera Obscura,* nos. 3–4 (Summer 1979): 98–110; and Constance Penley's "*What Maisie Knew* by Babette Mangolte: Childhood as Point of View" and "*The Camera: Je/La Camera: Eye* (Babette Mangolte)," *Camera Obscura,* no. 2 (Fall 1977) and nos. 3–4 (Summer 1979): 130–36; 195–97. See also my interview with Mangolte in Scott MacDonald, *A Critical Cinema: Interviews with Independent Filmmakers* (Berkeley: University of

California Press, 1988), 279–96 (a more complete version of this interview was published in *Afterimage* 12, nos. 1–2 [Summer 1984]: 8–13).

5. MacDonald, *A Critical Cinema,* 295.

6. With few exceptions, Mangolte's visuals chart a series of journeys through particular, always rural locales. We never see Mangolte herself, her assistant, or their automobile. We are given almost no indication of their accommodations (in a single instance, reference is made to her and her assistant camping along the road, and from time to time Mangolte toys with her own decision to keep her process outside the film's visuals, by throwing pebbles into a lake from off-screen, in one instance, and by throwing snow into the frame from just beyond our field of vision, in another). Indeed, we see people only three times during the film (in two, brief, successive shots in Yosemite, first one person, then two are walking in a field; in another instance, a person is climbing down a snow-covered hillside; and near the end, a Navajo shepherd is at work in Canyon de Chelly—altogether, these shots last less than half a minute) and other vehicles in only a few instances.

7. Trinh T. Minh-ha was to use a sound track structured in virtually the same way in *Naked Spaces—Living Is Round* (1985), as a means of suggesting the hybridity of human identity.

8. MacDonald, *A Critical Cinema,* 295.

9. See Joni Louise Kinsey, *Thomas Moran and the Surveying of the American West* (Washington, D.C.: Smithsonian Institution Press, 1992), for an overview of the role of Moran (and Jackson) in the Western expeditions and in the governmental decisions to protect these and other scenic regions.

10. Mangolte makes clear her particular admiration for Ford in *A Critical Cinema:* "What I think has been missing in film recently is what you found in classical cinema, what you find above all in Renoir and John Ford, who are the two classical filmmakers I like the best: I'm talking about a trust, a belief. It's not there anymore in a lot of independent cinema" (287).

11. Barbara Novak, *Nature and Culture: American Landscape Painting, 1825–1875* (New York: Oxford University Press, 1980).

12. See Franklin's discussion of the rhetoric of the discovery narrative in his *Discoverers, Explorers, Settlers,* chap. 1.

13. That Mangolte is aware she cannot escape a cultural history that tends to diminish our awe of the sublime landscapes of the New World is evident in her abrasive sound track.

Mangolte's own *Visible Cities* (1991) is a follow-up to *The Sky on Location.* Using a strategy reminiscent of the earlier film, Mangolte contemplates the expansion of San Diego (where she lives and teaches) and the distance of the new suburban man-made environment from the landscape it is transforming. See also Mangolte's earlier short, *There? Where?* (1979), a European's view of Los Angeles.

Mangolte's reputation has continued to rest on her distinctive cinematography;

and the clear, authoritative visuality of her camera work continues to have a positive impact on the reputations of those she works for. She was director of photography on Jean-Pierre Gorin's *Routine Pleasures* (1986) and *My Crazy Life* (1982) and Ludovic Segarra's *The Road to Damascus* (*The Life of Saint Paul of Tarse*) (1988).

14. In his evocation of American place, James Benning often reminds me of Alfred Hitchcock. While many of Hitchcock's films do not seem deeply or precisely involved with place (*Psycho* could have been located virtually anywhere; indeed Ed Gein—the inspiration for Norman Bates—lived in rural Wisconsin, not in California), many of Hitchcock's most memorable films *are* memorable, in large measure, because of the way they are embedded in American landscape, townscape, and cityscape. I'm thinking in particular of *North by Northwest* (1959), which takes us from the Plaza Hotel in New York to the suburb of Glen Cove, Long Island (located somewhere on the California coast!), to the UN Building, to Penn Station and the Twentieth Century Limited—the scenes out the window during the dinner conversation between Roger Thornhill (Cary Grant) and Eve Kendall (Eva Marie Saint) are a reasonably accurate depiction of what is now the Amtrak route through the Hudson Valley highlands—to Chicago's Union Station, to a midwestern cornfield, and finally to Mount Rushmore; and of *Vertigo* (1958) and *The Birds* (1963), both of which exploit the Bay Area and nearby California locations with considerable effectiveness.

Benning's films have nearly always been deeply involved with American geography, and in many cases are interesting in large measure because, like the Hitchcock films I've mentioned, they offer viewers a tour of places that are familiar to us, either because we've been there or because these places are central to America's sense of itself: *11 × 14* (1976), the film that established Benning's reputation, begins in Chicago with a real-time ride on the El; and when the film's protagonists go their separate ways (*11 × 14* critiques the conventional convergence of narrative line by creating characters whose paths *diverge* during the remainder of the film), Benning records them on location along typical midwestern roadscapes and, near the conclusion of *11 × 14*, at Mount Rushmore.

15. Though less central to *North on Evers* than race, references to small- and large-scale violence also punctuate the film, from the mentions of a military installation near Albuquerque that takes up an entire mountainside and Trinity Site in southern New Mexico, to the University of Texas tower from which Charles Whitman killed twelve and wounded thirty-three, to the Texas Schoolbook Depository Building in Dallas, to the Vietnam Memorial in Washington where Benning finds the name of a friend, to the young woman he meets in a bar in central New York State who asks him to burn her breast with a cigarette, to his visit to Laurencia Bembenek at a prison in Taycheedah, Wisconsin (Bembenek, jailed for supposedly murdering her husband, is the subject of Benning's 1988 film, *Used Innocence*), and to the domestic violence he remembers from 1968, when he was

working in a poor white neighborhood in Springfield, Missouri. Violence, past and present, remains, as does race, a psychic frontier for Benning.

16. Franklin, *Discoverers, Explorers, Settlers*, 104.

17. Frampton, in MacDonald, *A Critical Cinema*, 49.

18. Benning provides various "curve balls" within the conceptual trajectory of his overall narrative, just as he provides extra perceptual difficulties. From time to time, he varies the order of events in the photographed visuals from what we might predict from the rolling text, and from time to time an image seems to synchronize with what we're reading, until we recognize that the connection is a fabricated (and sometimes metaphoric) coincidence.

19. Smithson, who made his own film about *The Spiral Jetty* (*Spiral Jetty*, 1979), was much involved with the concept of entropy. For a discussion of the relation of the concept to *Spiral Jetty* and to Smithson's film and photo works, see Robert A. Sobieszek, *Robert Smithson Photo Works* (Los Angeles and Albuquerque: Los Angeles County Museum of Art/University of New Mexico Press, 1993).

20. See Frampton's "For a Metahistory of Film: Commonplace Notes and Hypotheses," in *Circles of Confusion* (Rochester: Visual Studies Workshop Press, 1983), 107–16.

21. Franklin, *Discoverers, Explorers, Settlers*, 123.

22. Actually, Cadillac's ironic response to the failure of Dauphine Island to live up to what has been said about it is a means to an end: the reestablishment of higher standards and long-term success for the Louisiana colony. Franklin, *Discoverers, Explorers, Settlers*, 123, 133.

Franklin's definition of the "true settler's account" is part of his discussion of Bernard Diron d'Araguiette (younger brother of one of the men Cadillac quotes), whose journal quotes at length from the memoirs of Sieur Feaucon Dumanoir. It is Dumanoir's text that Franklin sees as typical of the settler.

23. Hamsher is interviewed in the Director's Cut video of *Natural Born Killers* (ISBN 1–57362–167–6), written, directed, and produced by Charles Kiselyak.

24. The choice of the Joliet prison may well have been motivated by the fact that in its design this prison structure is a version of Jeremy Bentham's Panopticon, that model prison that Michel Foucault discusses with such ingenuity in *Discipline and Punish* (New York: Random House, 1979 [trans. Alan Sheridan], 195–228). Foucault's discussion has been widely discussed in film circles, as offering a means for understanding the institutions of media: like the Panopticon, which allowed a relatively few prison guards to see into the lives of a great many prisoners, modern cinema and especially modern television paparazzi, like the Wayne Gayle character in *Natural Born Killers*, have become forms of panopticon that market the invasion of privacy as a means of confirming ever more rigid social control.

25. My conversations with Michael Singer, who worked as a unit publicist on *Heaven and Earth* (1993), *Natural Born Killers,* and *Nixon* (1996) and has interviewed Stone extensively, made clear to me Stone's particular admiration of Godard and *Breathless.*

26. When I asked Singer (see note 25) how familiar Stone is with American independent filmmakers and film, he told me, "Oliver is familiar with all the filmmakers you mention in your piece—and many others as well."

27. In the interview included on the *Natural Born Killers* Director's Cut video, Stone is explicit about this: "Once they [Mickey and Mallory] kill, they've entered into this world of breaking all the rules; it's fitting that the filmmaker is also breaking all the rules with them."

28. Stone shot an alternative ending for *Natural Born Killers:* in this version, Mickey and Mallory are themselves murdered by a psycho-killer, during their getaway from the scene of their murder of Wayne Gayle. The alternative ending is included on the Director's Cut video.

29. Spiro's earlier tape, *Greetings from Out Here* (1993), is a personal travel documentary during which Spiro reveals her lesbianism and travels the American Southeast, visiting gay men and women who have chosen to live in their native region.

30. The state of California attempted to have Knight's painting adjudged a danger to the environment, an event he commemorated in his song (sung entirely off-key and outside of any beat), "Toxic Nightmare": "I contaminated the bombing range/Killed most of the fish in the Salton Sea/And California's bulldozing this paintbrush from me."

31. Sam the dog died before all of *Roam Sweet Home* was shot. In some shots a handmade puppet of Sam was used. Even the sense Spiro gives us of her traveling alone with Sam is sometimes a fabrication. At times, Spiro was accompanied by Emily Mode.

Chapter 5. From the Sublime to the Vernacular

Epigraph: John Brinckerhoff Jackson, *Discovering the Vernacular Landscape* (New Haven: Yale University Press, 1984), xii.

1. Bill's "genius" is for predicting weather; he can feel and smell, *knows* what a tornado will do (early in *Twister* he is framed, next to an American flag, outdoors, alone, receiving communications directly from the atmosphere). He is the modern version of Natty Bumppo, James Fenimore Cooper's individualistic guide into the American frontier wilderness.

2. The classic overview of nineteenth-century landscape painting is Barbara Novak's *Nature and Culture: American Landscape Painting, 1825–1875* (New York: Oxford University Press, 1980), though Angela Miller's *The Empire of the Eye:*

Landscape Representation and American Cultural Politics, 1825–1875 (Ithaca: Cornell University Press, 1993), should also be consulted. While Thomas Cole and Frederic Church were the most influential nineteenth-century landscape painters; and while Church, more than anyone else, was responsible for establishing the Great Picture—the large canvas depicting the immensity of American landscape—the two painters most consistently devoted to painting Great Pictures of the American West are Albert Bierstadt and Thomas Moran, both of whom have been the subject of major retrospectives in recent years. See Nancy K. Anderson and Linda S. Ferber, *Albert Bierstadt: Art and Enterprise,* the catalog for the Bierstadt retrospective at the Brooklyn Museum in 1991; and Nancy K. Anderson, *Thomas Moran,* the catalog for the Moran retrospective at the National Gallery of Art in Washington, D.C., in 1997–98.

3. Simon Schama, *Landscape and Memory* (New York: Knopf, 1995). Schama focuses on the myth of original nature so crucial in Polish, German, British, French, and American history—especially in its deployment in wars of cultural resistance.

4. Albert Boime, *The Magisterial Gaze: Manifest Destiny and American Landscape Painting c. 1830–1865* (Washington, D.C.: Smithsonian Institution Press, 1991), 8.

5. In *Twister,* "F-5" is identified as a number 5 tornado on the Fujita scale, which measures the power of tornadoes.

6. Edmund Burke's distinction between "the sublime" and "the beautiful" (in his *A Philosophical Enquiry into the Origin of Our Ideas of the Sublime and Beautiful,* first published in 1757) has been much discussed during the past two centuries. As Barbara Novak explains it, "The late-eighteenth-century sublime . . . was associated with fear, gloom, and majesty (*Nature and Culture,* 34), while the "beautiful" represented the more balanced, controlled forms of aesthetic experience emblematized by classic Greek architecture.

7. For a contemporary review of early Kuchar screenings, see Jonas Mekas, *Movie Journal* (New York: Collier, 1972), 122–26, 166–67. J. Hoberman and Jonathan Rosenbaum discuss the Kuchars' importance to the sixties underground scene and their influence, in *Midnight Movies* (New York: Harper & Row, 1983), 51–55.

That the early Kuchar films had an impact is clear in John Waters's introduction to the Kuchar brothers' new book, *Reflections from a Cinematic Cesspool* (Berkeley: Zanja Press, 1997), edited by Mary Pacios. Waters begins, "George and Mike Kuchar's films were my first inspiration. George's *Hold Me While I'm Naked* [1996], Mike's *Sins of the Fleshapoids* [1966]—these were the pivotal films of my youth, bigger influences than Warhol, Kenneth Anger, even *The Wizard of Oz*" (i).

8. Kuchar talked with me about the early, 8mm melodramas in *A Critical Cinema: Interview with Independent Filmmakers* (Berkeley: University of California Press, 1988), 297–316. In a more recent interview, Kuchar indicates that he has

been interested in weather since he was very young; that artist Eric Sloane was important to him: see Sloane's *Look at the Sky and Tell the Weather* (New York: Funk and Wagnalls, 1961); and that his first job was doing graphics for New York City television weatherman Frank Field. Scott MacDonald, "Storm Chaser," an interview with George Kuchar, *The Independent* (July 1997): 40.

I was alerted to this early fascination with weather by Margaret Morse's discussion, "Cyclones from Oz: On George Kuchar's *Weather Diary 1*," included in *The Essayistic in Film and Video*, a catalog for a 1989 San Francisco exhibition of film and video.

9. *Hold Me While I'm Naked* seems to owe a good deal to Hitchcock's *Psycho*, one of the pivotal films for a good many young people in 1960 (Kuchar was 18). If, in retrospect, we see Norman Bates as suggesting Hitchcock's conflicts about women, conflicts that sometimes led to the director's sexually harassing actresses (see, for example, Donald Spoto's comments on Hitchcock and Vera Miles in *The Dark Side of Genius: The Life of Alfred Hitchcock* [New York: Ballantine, 1983], 408–9), the director in Kuchar's film—who lives with his mother, dresses up in women's clothing, and is obsessed with shower scenes—reflects Kuchar's self-awareness (and his utter openness about it) that part of the lure of becoming a film director is the opportunity to work with voluptuous women and, at times, to see them undressed and have power over them.

10. Though *Wild Night in El Reno* is the most obvious formal predecessor of the Weather Diaries, several earlier melodramas, including *A Reason to Live* and *Back to Nature* (both made the year before *Wild Night in El Reno*), are relevant. In both films nature becomes a curative for distress and dislocation. In *A Reason to Live,* for example, the protagonist (played by the late Curt McDowell, a frequent Kuchar collaborator) reads the book *Oklahoma Weather* and leaves San Francisco to go to Oklahoma, where he is apparently killed in a tornado.

11. This listing and an accompanying press kit are available at the Video Data Bank at the school of the Art Institute of Chicago, 112 S. Michigan Ave., Suite 312, Chicago, IL 60603; (312) 345–3550; fax: (312) 541–8073.

12. Since 1990 the Weather Diaries have tended to be considerably shorter: *Weather Watch* (*Weather Diary 7*, 1991) is 16 minutes; *Interior Vacuum* (*Weather Diary 8*, 1992), 19 minutes; *Sunbelt Serenade* (*Weather Diary 9*, 1993), 17 minutes; *Route 666* (*Weather Diary 10*, 1994), 7¾ minutes; *George, Pepe, and Pancho* (*Weather Diary 11*, 1995), 13¼ minutes; *Season of Sorrow* (*Weather Diary 12*, 1996), 12¼ minutes.

13. Thoreau in *Walden*, ed. J. Lyndon Shanley (Princeton: Princeton University Press, 1971), 36.

14. Thoreau's famous statement "I have travelled a good deal in Concord" is one of the more obvious of the many indications that he was reacting against the assumption that "real" exploration can only be achieved in remote regions.

Another is from *The Maine Woods* (New York: Penguin, 1988), 111: "We have advanced by leaps to the Pacific, and left many a lesser Oregon and California unexplored behind us."

15. Thoreau in *Walden*, 36.

16. For Kuchar's versions of this Flaherty experience, see the video *Vermin of the Vortex* (1966), in which Kuchar is captured by aliens and taken to the Flaherty to be experimented on; "The Big Stink" in *Reflections from a Cinematic Cesspool* (108–20), in which Kuchar details the experience in his own inimitable prose; and MacDonald, "Storm Chaser," 38–42.

17. Kuchar's awareness of the history of the El Reno area has developed over the years. During the Oklahoma land rush of 1889, El Reno was one of the taking-off locations. In fact, part of Ron Howard's *Far and Away* (1992) was filmed in El Reno.

18. "The Yosemite Valley and the Mariposa Big Trees: A Preliminary Report" (1865) by Frederick Law Olmsted, reconstructed and published for the first time by Laura Wood Roper, *Landscape Architecture*, no. 43 (October 1952): 17, 22.

19. Indeed, the development of ever-larger industrial enterprises during the nineteenth and twentieth centuries has resulted in the use of "sublime" in an entirely new way, as David E. Nye makes clear in his *American Technological Sublime* (Cambridge, Mass.: MIT Press, 1996), which describes instances of industrial sublimity beginning with nineteenth-century canal building. And recent years have seen the establishment of national parks to honor the industrial sublime: e.g., the Lowell National Historical Park in Lowell, Massachusetts, which boasts the industrially sublime din of the "weave room" at Boott Mills.

20. I wonder if the recent shitting sequences in *Dumb and Dumber* (1995, directed by Peter Farrelly) and *Henry Fool* (1998, directed by Hal Hartley) owe something to the Kuchar films and videos. Both create humor by emphasizing the sound of shitting, though neither director actually reveals the feces or faked feces.

21. Thoreau, *Walden*, 90, 3. H. Daniel Peck explores the relationship between Thoreau's monumental *Journal*, which he regularly kept during his stay at Walden Pond, and *Walden*, in *Thoreau's Morning Work* (New Haven: Yale University Press, 1990).

22. Olmsted, "The Yosemite Valley and the Mariposa Big Trees," 20.

23. Kuchar's video camera allows him a flexibility that 16mm filmmaking (or even 8mm or Super-8mm) does not. He can do basic intercutting and sound-image arrangement and see the results immediately. Subsequent video diaries were substantially complete when Kuchar left Oklahoma, though he fine-tuned them later, sometimes adding special effects. Paul Arthur explores some of the differences between Kuchar as filmmaker and Kuchar as videomaker, in "History and Cross Consciousness: George Kuchar's Fantasies of Un-power," *Millennium Film Journal*, nos. 20–21 (Fall–Winter 1988–89): 151–58.

Chapter 6. The City as Motion Picture

1. For a recent overview of the nineteenth century's fascination with photographic documentation of "exotic" peoples, see Ellen Strain, "Exotic Bodies, Distant Landscapes: Touristic Viewing and Popularized Anthropology in the Nineteenth Century," *Wide Angle* 18, no. 2 (April 1996): 70–100.

2. Tom Gunning discusses the formal inventiveness of some of these early films and their relationship to more recent, avant-garde film in "An Unseen Energy Swallows Space: The Space in Early Film and Its Relation to American Avant-Garde Film," in John L. Fell, ed., *Film before Griffith* (Berkeley: University of California Press, 1983), 355–66.

This fascination with imagery of the modern city is also evident before the advent of cinema. When Robert Barker built the first large-scale panorama, instigating a mode of popular entertainment that has a good many relationships to cinema, his subject was the city of London as seen from the roof of the Albion sugar mills, the highest spot in the city between Westminster Abbey and St. Paul's Cathedral. See Richard B. Altick, *The Shows of London* (Cambridge, Mass.: Harvard University Press, 1978), chap. 10.

3. Jan-Christopher Horak's discussion of *Manhatta*—"Paul Strand and Charles Sheeler's *Manhatta*"—is included in Horak, ed., *Lovers of Cinema: The First American Film Avant-Garde (1919–1945)* (Madison: University of Wisconsin Press, 1995), 267–86. A longer version of this discussion, including a shot-by-shot breakdown of the film, appeared as "Modernist Perspectives and Romantic Desire: *Manhatta*," in *Afterimage* 15, no. 4 (November 1987): 8–15. See also chapter 4, "Paul Strand: Romantic Modernist," in Horak's *Making Images Move: Photographers and Avant-Garde Cinema* (Washington, D.C.: Smithsonian Institution Press, 1997), 79–108.

A crucial and underrecognized figure in this development would appear to be Mikhail Kaufman, a colleague of Vertov's in the Council of Three, Vertov's principal editor on numbers of *Kinopravda* after no. 6, and the director of *Moscow,* a 1926 film that reviews a day in the life of the Russian metropolis. See Annette Michelson's introduction to *Kino-Eye: The Writings of Dziga Vertov* (Berkeley: University of California Press, 1984). Vlada Petric argues against the possibility of *Moscow* being an influence, at least on Vertov: "Even a superficial comparison of the two films reveals that the structure of Vertov's film is light-years ahead of the the conventional manner in which Kaufman depicts a city." See *Constructivism in Film* (Cambridge: Cambridge University Press, 1987), 71. I have not seen *Moscow.*

4. Certainly, *Manhatta* provides a premonition of the city symphony. The Sheeler-Strand film begins with the arrival of crowded ferries bringing workers into Lower Manhattan at the beginning of the workday and ends with a shot of sunset over New York harbor. A representative day is hinted at, though the body of *Manhatta* is more fully involved with new forms of imaging a metropolis than with representing typical New York activities during a composite day.

Though *Berlin* is now credited to Ruttmann, he instigated neither the project nor the term "city symphony." According to Paul Rotha, Carl Mayer "conceived the idea of a City Symphony" while standing "amid the whirling traffic of the Ufa Palast am Zoo" in 1925: "He saw 'a melody of pictures' and began to write the treatment of *Berlin*." Rotha, "It's the Script," *World Film News* 3, no. 5 (September 1938): 205. And Ruttmann was not responsible for recording the footage itself— *Berlin* was shot by Karl Freund and several other cinematographers (Reimer Kuntze, Robert Baberske, Lászlo Schäfer)—though he did provide the film's final structure and attitude. See Siegfried Kracauer, *From Caligary to Hitler* (Princeton: Princeton University Press, 1947), 182–89.

In "Two Aspects of the City: Cavalcanti and Ruttmann," Jay Chapman distinguishes between Ruttmann's *Berlin: Symphony of a Big City* and Calvalcanti's *Nothing but the Hours*—the former "a formal exercise, a reflection of the rhythm of the city"; the latter, "an homage to the lower class people of the city"—in a manner with which I almost entirely agree and which informs some of what follows. In Lewis Jacobs, ed., *The Documentary Tradition* (New York: Hopkinson and Blake, 1971), 37–42.

5. In his slide presentation for the premiere of *Berlin: Symphony of a Big City* on September 27, 1927, Ruttmann explained, "When I edited, the difficulty of rendering visible the symphonic curve before my eyes became apparent to me. Many of the most beautiful photographs had to be eliminated because the end result was not supposed to be a picture book but something like the structure of a complex machine which can be put into operation only when every part, even the smallest, is geared to the other part with exact precision." Quoted in Angelika Leitner and Uwe Nitschke, *The German Avant-Garde Film of the 1920s/Der Deutsche Avant-Garde Film der 20er Jahre* (Frankfurt: Deutsches Filmmuseum, 1989), 81.

Ruttmann's *Berlin: Symphony of a Big City* was the first German feature to have a complete orchestral score written for it, by Edmund Meisel, though for legal reasons the sound track is rarely heard now.

6. Perhaps the most fundamental loss that surfaces in a comparison between the films of "exotic" peoples and of the modern city is the ability of early societies to roam the Earth, or a substantial sector of it, in maintaining their traditional ways of life. The modern world is, increasingly, a place of precise and rigid boundaries between territories of all kinds, a kind of machine that produces a life of security and contentment (or the illusion of it) through the rigorous compartmentalization of experience. And the film frame is an index of this compartmentalization. If the Inuit, the Samoans, and the Bakhtiari seem to live without a consciousness of national borders, the people filmed by Strand-Sheeler, Cavalcanti, Ruttmann, and Vertov seem (for the most part) contented cogs in the machine of the city, which energizes the larger network of the nation. If the 1920s cinematic excursions to northern Canada, the South Seas, and the Middle East take us away

from national political boundaries, contemporaneous explorations of the great cities locate us in the heart of national territory and identity.

7. Implicit in Ruttmann's overall structure is what appears to be a commitment to a unified, thoroughly organized, and controlled society. Indeed, in retrospect, Ruttmann's rigorously orchestrated composition and editing are prescient, in general, of what we have come to think of as Nazi organization and, in particular, of Leni Riefenstahl's aesthetic embodiment of and homage to Nazi principles in *Triumph of the Will* (1935), a film that echoes the city symphony form. This may be unfair to Ruttmann and *Berlin*—and to the complexity of his intentions for the film. Nevertheless, from today's perspective, the relationship seems obvious. In *From Caligary to Hitler,* Siegfried Kracauer compares *Berlin* with Vertov's *Man with a Movie Camera:* while Vertov's film exudes revolutionary ardor, Ruttmann's is a "product of the paralysis" of authority, "a withdrawal from basic decisions into ambiguous neutrality," into what Carl Mayer complained was merely a "surface approach," or, as Kracauer puts it, a devotion to the formal qualities of objects rather than to meaning. See Kracauer, 187, 184. This tendency to see individual human beings and the particulars of their lives as design elements is precisely what has come to seem so compelling and so frightening in *Triumph of the Will.*

8. William Uricchio, "The City Viewed: The Films of Leyda, Browning and Weinberg," in Horak, *Lovers of Cinema,* 287–314.

9. Uricchio, "The City Viewed," 309. I would argue that Uricchio is a bit over-generous with all three of these films, particularly with *City of Contrasts.*

10. In general, as a filmmaker, Steiner was more interested in depicting the natural world than in documenting city life. Indeed, his H_2O was one of the first American films to explore natural scenery in a complex manner (see chap. 8), and he returned to the subject of nature in a series of films, called "The Joy of Seeing," made at the close of his filmmaking career. See my chapter, "Ralph Steiner: A Reintroduction," in Horak, *Lovers of the Cinema,* 205–33.

Copland credits working with Steiner with his involvement with film. See Aaron Copland and Vivian Perlis, *Copland 1900 through 1942* (New York: St. Martin's/Marek Press, 1984), 288–91.

11. The best source of information about Burckhardt, who after sixty years of making films remained relatively obscure even in independent film circles, is Rudy Burckhardt and Simon Pettet, *Talking Pictures: The Photography of Rudy Burckhardt* (Cambridge, Mass.: Zoland Books, 1994). Pettet's interview with Burckhardt combined with Burckhardt's own commentary provides something like a biography.

12. Burckhardt's imagery of New York City, especially of monuments like the Flatiron Building and the Brooklyn Bridge, was, no doubt, indebted to the many distinguished photographs of such landmarks by a host of photographers, including Paul Strand, Charles Sheeler, Ralph Steiner, and Alfred Stieglitz. Indeed, Burck-

hardt himself was a photographer, as well as a cinematographer, of New York City. Burckhardt and Pettet, *Talking Pictures,* provides a retrospective of the photography.

13. Hutton in Scott MacDonald, *A Critical Cinema 3: Interviews with Independent Filmmakers* (Berkeley: University of California Press, 1998), 249.

14. Other Burckhardt films that include substantial observation of New York City are *The Pursuit of Happiness* (1940), *What Mozart Saw on Mulberry Street* (1956), *Eastside Summer* (1959), *Square Times* (1967), *City Pasture* (1974), *Cerveza Bud* (1981), *All Major Credit Cards* (1982), *Around the World in Thirty Years* (1983), and *Central Park in the Dark* (1985).

15. I do not discuss *In the Street,* the 1952 collaboration of Helen Levitt, Janice Loeb, and James Agee, because its focus is not New York City in general—or even in particular: *In the Street* is a candid document of city street life and especially of children playing. It was filmed on Manhattan's Upper East Side with unobtrusive cameras, but as the film's opening text makes clear, the city spaces documented in the film are, for the filmmakers, representative of the economically disadvantaged areas of all big cities: "The streets of the poor quarters of great cities are, above all, a theater and a battleground. There, unaware and unnoticed, every human being is a poet, a masker, a warrior, a dancer: and in his innocent artistry he projects, against the turmoil of the street, an image of human existence. The attempt of this short film is to capture this image." In my view, the somber passion of this introduction is not in harmony with the imagery of the film: the children seem to be enjoying themselves like children anywhere, in any neighborhood; and what is perhaps most striking is what appears to be the easy interplay of various ethnic groups.

The concluding shot of two old women walking in the dimming light of evening does evoke the city symphony form, and it suggests that by the 1950s, the city symphony form was so well known that vestiges of it had come to be virtually inevitable in any film about city life.

16. For an overview of Cinema 16, see Scott MacDonald, *Cinema 16: Documents toward a History of the Film Society,* published by *Wide Angle* as a mega-issue in 1997. The development of the New American Cinema, and Mekas's role in it, has been widely documented. See, for example, Gregory Battcock, ed., *The New American Cinema* (New York: Dutton, 1967); and David E. James, ed., *To Free the Cinema: Jonas Mekas and the New York Underground* (Princeton: Princeton University Press, 1992).

17. I spoke with Vogel about Weegee and *Weegee's New York* in April 1996. Vogel had not spoken about his role in the film earlier because "Weegee didn't want it talked about." Vogel remembers an earlier, longer film being presented to an audience: "It was at least two hours; I remember two 1600-foot reels." Vogel edited what became *Weegee's New York,* "at a very basic level," on the Cinema 16 film splicer, and showed the result to Weegee: "He said he was delighted."

Weegee did make other films, including *Camera Magic,* a demonstration of various camera tricks. Weegee's career as cinematographer-filmmaker is in need of revaluation, as Jesse Lerner and David Serlin suggest in "Weegee and the Jewish Question," *Wide Angle* 19, no. 4 (Winter 1998): 95–108.

18. Vogel doesn't remember how this sound track got added to Weegee's film, though he may have done that as well. He thinks William Kenly, who sometimes provided music for Cinema 16 from his extensive record collection, may have been involved (Kenly has no memory of this—letter from Kenly to the author, April 18, 1996). In any case, Vogel is sure "it did not come from Weegee."

19. In "The Use of Sound in Francis Thompson's *N.Y., N.Y.*," Martin F. Norden describes Gene Farrell's score (and the additional sound effects), concluding that while *N.Y., N.Y.* is visually innovative, the sound track is thoroughly conventional, both in the types of music used and in their relationship to the visuals. In *Millennium,* nos. 10–11 (Fall–Winter 1981–82): 219–22.

20. Mylar has been widely used for (inexpensive) special effects in avant-garde films. Jim Davis had used it in *Analogies* (1953); Gunvor Nelson used it in *Moon's Pool* (1972); and Robert Huot used it in several diary films. Now that Thompson's effects are more easily recognized for what they are, some of the original impact of *N.Y., N.Y.* has been lost—at least on this viewer.

21. Thompson's awareness of New York's architectural history is evident in his *Evolution of a Skyscraper* (1939), a silent, forty-minute documentary on the history of the skyscraper up through the 1930s, produced by the Museum of Modern Art's Department of Architecture and Design. The film is generally informative—and unusually inventive in its use of visual texts.

22. Marie Menken, in *Film-makers' Cooperative Catalogue No. 7* (New York: New American Cinema Group, 1989), 370.

23. Robert Breer became well known for the "retinal collages" produced by such films as *Recreation* (1956), *Jamestown Baloos* (1957), *Blazes* (1961), and *Fist Fight* (1964). Unlike Menken, Breer was not using time-lapse excursions into the world for these effects; he animated his films so that each successive frame in a series of frames presents the eye with an entirely different image. The images "pile up" on viewers' retinas at a rate of twenty-four per second.

The use of time-lapse for a walk through Manhattan has both predecessors (e.g., Oskar Fischinger's *München-Berlin Wandering* [1927] for which Fischinger walked from Munich to Berlin, single-framing people and landscapes all the way—see William Moritz's discussion of the film in "The Films of Oskar Fischinger," *Film Culture,* nos. 58–60 [1974]: 129–30) and successors (e.g., the middle section of Hollis Frampton's *Surface Tension* [1968], which also begins with a walk across Brooklyn Bridge, and Andrew Noren's *The Lighted Field* [1987]).

The ability of time-lapsing to condense experience leads Stan Brakhage to call *Go! Go! Go!* Menken's "epic masterpiece." Brakhage sees Menken as a master of poetic rhythm: in the little " 'city symphony' that is *'Go! Go! Go!'* " she manages "to show the entire trappings of the metropolis without the consequent despair of either Ruttmann's 'Berlin' or that which prevails in the more recent 'Koyaanisqatsi.' " See *Film at Wit's End* (Kingston: McPherson, 1989), 40–41.

24. Mekas's *Walden* could easily be interpreted as a city film (indeed, I discuss it this way in chapter 7). Mekas uses Central Park as his central metaphor for finding in the modern American city the rural (Lithuanian) homeland he left behind when he fled the Nazis during World War II. Few filmmakers have been as devoted to recording the New York area as Mekas.

25. Peter von Ziegesar's *Concern for the City* (1986) is a frequently stunning film that, like *Koyaanisqatsi, Go! Go! Go!* and *Organism,* uses time-lapse in very inventive ways (by controlling the rate and regularity with which frames are exposed and by carefully choosing compositions *for* time-lapse imagery) that virtually obscure whatever urges toward moralizing the filmmaker may have. Von Ziegesar may have "a concern for the city"—one that relates in particular to the convoy of (I assume) National Guard vehicles entering a neighborhood near the end of his film—but the impact of *Concern for the City,* despite its title, is in the time-lapse imagery's virtually inevitable celebration of urban movement.

26. Hilary Harris shot some of the New York City traffic shots used in *Koyaanisqatsi,* though apparently Reggio didn't see *Organism* until after his film was well under way. See Reggio's comments on Harris in Scott MacDonald, *A Critical Cinema 2: Interviews with Independent Filmmakers* (Berkeley: University of California Press, 1992), 387.

27. See my interviews with Peter Hutton and Ken Jacobs in *A Critical Cinema 3.*

Jacobs's "Nervous System" is a projection device/process composed of two interlocked projectors (which can project a filmstrip at a variety of speeds) and various propellers of his own design. With the Nervous System, Jacobs can superimpose images and tease from the original images new (sometimes 3-D) experiences.

28. In the use of a wide range of distinctive characters, Lee is much closer to Rudy Burckhardt and Weegee than to any of the Europeans—though, of course, Burckhardt and Weegee don't use individual characters as motifs.

29. *In the Street* (1952), the widely seen (at Cinema 16 and elsewhere) documentation of New York City street life, may have been a source for Lee.

30. See Vlada Petric's *Constructivism in Film* for a detailed analysis of *The Man with a Movie Camera;* and Michelson, *Kino-Eye,* for Vertov's own comments on the film.

31. Spike Lee in the book, *Do the Right Thing: A Spike Lee Joint* (New York: Simon and Schuster, 1989), 26, written with Lisa Jones.

32. Lee, *Do the Right Thing,* 51. Radio Raheem's "love" and "hate" jewelry is an allusion to Charles Laughton's *Night of the Hunter* (1955), another American

expressionist film, in which the psychotic minister (Robert Mitchum) has "love" and "hate" tattooed on his hands.

33. Lee, *Do the Right Thing*, 103.

34. The collaborators on *Do the Right Thing* include the people from the neighborhood depicted *and* the varied group of actors and technicians who gathered in the neighborhood to shoot the film.

35. That Lee's production process was meant to model an answer to the problem his characters and plot dramatize was evident in a variety of specific ways during Lee's conceptualization of *Do the Right Thing* and remains evident, at least implicitly, in the finished film. In his "Production Notes," Lee mentions that he "wanted to cast white actors who feel comfortable around Black people. A white actor nervous about setting foot in Bed-Stuy wasn't gonna work for this film. The fact that Danny Aiello grew up in the South Bronx, and John Turturro in a Black neighborhood in Queens, made them ideal choices" (109). Lee's interest in using performers who had experienced complex interethnic connections firsthand, however, went even further. The character most incensed by Sal's refusal to include any African Americans on his "wall of fame" is Buggin' Out. More than anyone else in the film, Buggin' feels he represents "blackness," and he consistently demonstrates the distance between African Americans and European Americans in this neighborhood. Buggin' Out is played by Giancarlo Esposito, who—as Lee indicates early in his journal, just as *Do the Right Thing* is beginning to take shape—"is half Black and half Italian. He could play a character called Spaghetti Chitlins (I don't know about the name, it's the first thing that came into my mind)" (38).

On the level of audience reception, the complexity of Lee's thinking about ethnicity is also evident. For years, whenever I showed *Do the Right Thing* to my college classes, I handed out a form (immediately following the screening) asking the students to anonymously evaluate the extent of their sympathy or empathy with particular characters. In every instance, and regardless of the ethnic makeup of the class, two characters found to be sympathetic were Vito (Sal's nonracist son, played by Richard Edson) and Sal. The students recognized that Sal is abrasive and overly violent, but his commitment to his business and his affection for the neighborhood make him sympathetic for black students and white students alike (the most empathetic black characters in the film are usually Da Mayor and Jade). It is easy to underestimate the meaning of this response, as its consistency is only evident when all viewers in a given audience are polled. But what Lee has accomplished is remarkable. While his alter ego, Mookie, in the end takes sides with his race, just as Sal does in not condemning the police for killing Radio Raheem, Lee demonstrates that, *as director*, he can empathize across ethnic lines and that even as a "black filmmaker," he can create a powerful work that allows audience members to empathize across ethnic lines. There's an implicit challenge in this stance: it's as if Lee is saying, Even after centuries of European-American racism toward African

Americans, and even after all my personal experiences with this history, I can empathize with European Americans and make a film that causes you to do so as well. Now it's your turn, viewer: can *you* overcome *your* history and empathize with the Others?

36. As a result of his explorations of the American underclass, the Danish artist Jacob Holdt concluded that the fear of African-American neighborhoods that seems so natural to European Americans *is* racism, because it is virtually never based on any firsthand experiences in such neighborhoods, but merely on stereotype. See Holdt's *American Pictures* (Copenhagen: American Pictures Foundation, 1985), the book version of Holdt's epic slide show recounting his travels across America.

37. Lee, *Do the Right Thing*, 108–9.

38. For a history of early American urban photography, see Peter B. Hales, *Silver Cities: The Photography of American Urbanization, 1839–1915* (Philadelphia: Temple University Press, 1984). Hales discusses San Francisco daguerreotypy on pp. 24–39; the above quote is from p. 25.

39. Hales reprints both these early panoramas.

40. See Hales, *Silver Cities*, 47–57.

41. Hales, *Silver Cities*, 81. Hales discusses Muybridge's panoramas in detail on pp. 78–82, and reprints the 1978 panorama, which is also reprinted, larger and along with a modern panorama of the city made in 1978 by Mark Klett from virtually the same location, in *One City/Two Visions* (San Francisco: Bedford Arts, 1990).

42. The web site for American Memory is http://lcweb2.loc.gov/ammem/papr/mpixhome.html.

43. See Frank Stauffacher, ed., *Art in Cinema* (New York: Arno, 1968), for more information about Art in Cinema; and MacDonald, *Cinema 16*, for information about Cinema 16.

44. Stauffacher makes clear the importance of the sound track for *Sausalito* in a letter to Amos Vogel written on August 7, 1949: "There are a lot of local films in production. . . . I, myself, have one about half finished, a kind of personal documentary of a place. I intend having it finished by the fall. It is held up by lack of money for a soundtrack. The track will be a rather important factor in the whole, and so I'm waiting till I can scrape enough together. It will be called SAUSALITO." Letter reprinted in MacDonald, *Cinema 16*, 144.

45. See letter to Amos Vogel from Frank Stauffacher, January 6, 1951, in MacDonald, *Cinema 16*, 174.

46. Walter de la Mare, *The Complete Poems of Walter de la Mare* (New York: Knopf, 1970), 135. The second stanza (of two): "But beauty vanishes; beauty passes;/ However rare—rare it be;/And when I crumble, who will remember/This

lady of the West Country?" "An Epitaph" was the penultimate poem in the 1912 collection, *The Listeners and Other Poems.*

47. I do not know whether Stauffacher had seen *City of Contrasts,* the New York city symphony by Irving Browning. See the introduction to this chapter.

48. Stevenson's "San Francisco" is collected in Robert Louis Stevenson, *From Scotland to Silverado,* ed. James D. Hart (Cambridge, Mass.: Harvard University Press, 1966), 179–87.

49. Like Stauffacher's, Angerame's contributions to independent filmmaking go beyond the production of his own films: he is director of Canyon Cinema in San Francisco, which is the most dependable distributor of avant-garde film in the United States. In a telephone conversation (on April 9, 1997), Angerame indicated his admiration of Frank Stauffacher and his familiarity with *Notes on the Port of St. Francis.* At the time of our conversation, Angerame had not seen *Sausalito.* At screenings Anger identifies his five films as a city symphony, using the term more loosely than I do.

50. The Harbor Freeway interrupted the famous view down Market Street of the Ferry Building.

51. For a detailed discussion of *To Parsifal,* see Alan Williams, "The Structure of Lyric: Baillie's *To Parsifal,*" *Film Quarterly* 29, no. 3 (Spring 1976): 22–30.

52. See Baillie's comments on *Castro Street* in MacDonald, *A Critical Cinema 2,* 128–31.

53. Baillie, in MacDonald, *A Critical Cinema 2,* 128–29.

54. Baillie created a sound montage that provides an auditory parallel to his visuals: it is made up of various industrial sounds, including at times the sound of songs on the radio: the sounds are sometimes superimposed and sometimes dissolve into one another—like Baillie's images.

55. Lucy Fisher, "*Castro Street:* The Sensibility of Style," *Film Quarterly* 29, no. 3 (Spring 1976): 21.

56. Hales, *Silver Cities,* 78.

57. In a telephone conversation with the author, January 20, 1999.

58. Rudnick made a companion piece to *Panorama: Non Legato* (1984), a nine-minute, two-image film—the two projected images are arranged vertically: the bottom edge of the upper image is contiguous with the upper edge of the lower image—that includes time-lapse imagery filmed from his apartment, arranged so that at times the two images are quite distinct, while at others they seem to form a single, somewhat surreal larger image (though as the title suggests the two images never form a smooth continuity). As a vision of San Francisco, or even of urbanity in general, *Non Legato* is less engaging and evocative than its predecessor. My reaction may be in part a function of the fact that I've only seen a version of the film in which Rudnick printed the two images, one above the other, in a single 16mm print, thus greatly reducing the visual size of the experience.

59. Beginning with the Russian Esther Shub and *The Fall of the Romanov Dynasty* (1929) and in the United States with Joseph Cornell, Bruce Conner, and Raphael Montañez Ortiz, the practice of using earlier films as raw material for new films became by the 1980s and 1990s one of the most pervasive avant-garde strategies, if not *the* most pervasive.

60. A friend owned a print of the film, which is also in the Library of Congress collection, and gave Gehr access to it. *A Trip down Market Street before the Fire* leads off the American Memory program of San Francisco films: see note 42.

61. I have heard conjectures that *A Trip down Market Street before the Fire* was originally a Hales' Tours film. See Raymond Fielding's essay, "Hales' Tours: Ultra-realism in the Pre-1910 Motion Picture," in Fell, *Film before Griffith,* 116–30.

62. See Hales, *Silver Cities,* 25–26, including Hales's illustrations of Shaw and Johnson's "Smith and Porter's Coffeehouse" (1850) and Robert H. Vance's "The Rix Family and Residence" (1855).

63. Hales, *Silver Cities,* 57–58; Hales's emphasis. In "An Unseen Energy Swallows Space," Tom Gunning explores the way that the early, unseen camera transformed space and the relationship of such transformations to modern avant-garde film. See Fell, *Film before Griffith,* 355–66.

64. See chapter 4, "Panoramic Travel," of Wolfgang Schivelbusch, *The Railway Journey: The Industrialization of Time and Space in the 19th Century* (Berkeley: University of California Press, 1986), 52, 69.

65. Hales, *Silver Cities,* 78–79.

66. Gunning's term distinguishes "actualities," films that document the actual, or pretend to, from storytelling films and trickfilms (films that focus on cine-magic tricks).

67. While the up/down alternation is quite regular, there are moments when Gehr's composition disguises the direction of the elevator/camera. Further, shots 17/18 are filmed as a virtually continuous shot, beginning with upward motion of the camera/elevator and continuing, after a slight flare, with downward motion. Also, the film concludes with two shots in both of which the camera/elevator is moving up.

68. The sound track is reminiscent of Gehr's Berlin film, *Signal—Germany on the Air* (1985), in which imagery of a Berlin intersection is accompanied by a complex, evocative sound track.

69. Canyon Cinema Film/Video Supplement 1995, 9.

70. Gehr described the sound track during a telephone conversation on January 26, 1999.

71. Unless one counts Gehr's *Shift* (1974), for which Gehr filmed cars and trucks on a New York street, from several stories above the street, using compositional ingenuity to continually surprise us about the positioning of these cars with relation to street and camera.

72. Since completing *Water and Power*, O'Neill has completed *Trouble in the Image* (1996), which is at least as complex as the earlier film.

73. I spoke with O'Neill on June 19, 1996. According to O'Neill, the Owens Valley was the inspiration for Roman Polanski's *Chinatown* (1974) with which *Water and Power* shares a general visual tonality. O'Neill's "Notes for *Water and Power*" is included in *Millennium*, no. 25 (1991): 42–49.

74. *The Work of Atget* was published in 1982. The hands turn the pages, in reverse order, in four installments, each shorter than the previous one: specifically, the first installment reveals the Atget photographs from plates 104, 105 to plates 76, 77 (in a single shot; 1 minute, 14 seconds long); the second installment, plates 74, 75 to plates 52, 53 (in a 58-second shot); installment three, plates 48, 49 to 42, 43 (18 seconds); and the final installment, plates 40, 41 to 38, 39 (18 seconds).

75. In other instances, the suitcases are arranged in other ways: sometimes they're piled out of the way; in one sequence, they are used as a projection screen; and at the end of the film, they're open and spread around the apartment, and once again, the filmmaker steps through them. The obviousness of the use of the suitcases as evolving metaphor seems a distracting, perhaps youthful indulgence on Martin's part—though as a device, the use of the suitcases may mitigate against our reading the filmmaker-protagonist as Martin himself and to empha-size the performative level of the filmmaker's activities.

76. I spoke on the telephone with Martin about his working methods on March 15, 1999.

77. In fact, the second, yellower sequence of shots was made first, and was con-sidered a mistake—though later Martin decided to accept the results and use them to his advantage.

78. Martin, in my telephone conversation with him. Martin's interest in invisi-bility was inspired, at least in part, by his admiration of Chris Marker's *Sans Soleil* (1982) which was shot by an anonymous cameraman: "I was very enthralled by that notion."

79. The most notable skyscraper visible in *Invisible Cities* is One Liberty Place, which Philadelphians would recognize as the first building to break Philadelphia's long-held building code restricting the height of skyscrapers to less than the height of City Hall.

80. Martin also records the Bridge of Sighs in his imagery of Venice, as well as St. Mark's Cathedral.

Chapter 7. The Country in the City

1. Frederick Law Olmsted and Calbert Vaux, "Designers Report as to Proposed Modifications in the Plan," dated May 31, 1858; reprinted in Frederick Law

Olmsted, Sr., *Forty Years of Landscape Architecture*, ed. Theodora Kimball and Frederick Law Olmsted, Jr. (Cambridge, Mass.: MIT Press, 1973), 239.

2. Bruce Kelly, "Art of the Olmsted Landscape," in *Art of the Olmsted Landscape*, ed. Gail Travis Giullet, Mary Ellen W. Hern, and Bruce Kelly (New York: New York City Landmarks Preservation Commission/Arts Publisher, 1981), 28–33.

3. From Olmsted's January 1859 "Description of the Park," included in *The Papers of Frederick Law Olmsted*, vol. 3: *Creating Central Park 1857–1861*, ed. Charles E. Beveridge and David Schuyler (Baltimore: Johns Hopkins University Press, 1983), 212–13.

4. See chapter 3 of Blackmar and Rosenzweig's *The Park and the People: A History of Central Park* (Ithaca: Cornell University Press, 1992).

5. Blackmar and Rosenzweig quote Vaux from a letter to Olmsted, dated June 3, 1865, in *The Papers of Frederick Law Olmsted*, vol. 5: *The California Frontier 1863–1865*, ed. Victoria Post Ranney (Baltimore: Johns Hopkins University Press, 1990), 385.

6. The best source of information on Mekas's life and career as a filmmaker is David E. James, ed., *To Free the Cinema: Jonas Mekas and the New York Underground* (Princeton: Princeton University Press, 1992); and James's own discussion of Mekas's *Walden* in that volume, "Film Diary/Diary Film: Practice and Product in *Walden*" (145–79), is the most extensive and useful discussion of the film to date. James provides various film- and art-historical contexts for *Walden*, including a discussion of the film's relationship to Thoreau's *Walden;* and then develops a distinction between Mekas's many years of recording diary footage, seemingly without a concern for transforming this material into discrete works, and his subsequent decision—beginning with *Walden*—to transform, in James's terms, his "film diary" into a series of "diary films."

James's conclusion that the final reel of *Walden* clarifies Mekas's own practice "as one of personal perception defined not against Hollywood, but against the avant-garde, which is now revealed to be debased, commercialized, and sensational" is, however, unconvincing. The broad variety of independent cinema included in the "entries" of "Reel Four" of *Walden* simply extends Mekas's ongoing excitement about the world of alternative cinema he was so instrumental in developing. Indeed, in his *Lost Lost Lost* (1976), Mekas was to see his experiences in the United Stated as a rebirth into the extended family of art and alternative cinema he documents throughout *Walden*. See my "Lost Lost Lost over *Lost Lost Lost*," *Cinema Journal* 25, no. 2 (Winter 1986): 20–34.

7. In Mekas's *Walden* the apparent informality of the Lumières' *L'Arrivée d'un train en gare de la Ciotat* (1895), *Feeding the Baby* (1895), and *Boys Sailing Boats, Tuileries Garden, Paris* (1896) is emulated in images of friends, train trips, events in Central Park, and so on, though, paradoxically, Mekas's attempt to emulate this apparent informality led him to a filmmaking procedure quite different from the

Lumières' formally controlled films (each of which was always a single, carefully composed, unedited, fifty-second shot, filmed by a Cinématographe mounted on a tripod). Not only did Mekas film with a hand-held camera handled quite loosely (an influence of Marie Menken and Stan Brakhage whose work had become important enough to Mekas by the late 1950s to transform Mekas's own way of recording imagery), but he single-framed rather erratically so that the resulting imagery sometimes hovers between stillness and motion and at other times creates a kaleidoscope of color and shape. If Mekas's informality was, on one level, an emulation of the Lumières, it was also simultaneously an instance of visual overload with a good deal in common with the fast-accelerating pace of TV advertising—indeed, in some passages Mekas's single-framing and his in-camera superimpositions challenged viewers with considerably more images per minute than even the fastest TV ad montage.

8. Mekas, in a telephone interview with the author, August 24, 1995.

9. Thoreau, in *Walden,* ed. J. Lyndon Shanley (Princeton: Princeton University Press, 1971), 3–4.

10. The broadside is available from Mekas at Anthology Film Archives, 32 Second St., New York, NY 10003.

11. *Walden's* serial organization encodes Mekas's defiance of standard film-consumption patterns. Because any particular passage can represent, at least roughly, the vision of the entire film, viewers of the individual "reels" of the film can leave a screening with a feeling of completion. Of course, while the overall serial organization is consistent, individual viewers will find one or another passage of the film more or less interesting. For sheer pleasure in filmmaking energy and ingenuity, and for emotional engagement, I prefer "Reel One" of *Walden,* though each of the subsequent reels has passages to recommend it, both in terms of Mekas's dexterity with the camera and with editing and for the window it opens on the period of 1964–68. In "Reel Two," "KREEPING KREPLACHS," Allen Ginsberg, Peter Orlovsky, Andy Warhol, and others "MEET TO DISCUSS WORLD PROBLEMS" and the Velvet Underground makes its first public appearance; in "Reel Three," Mekas pays an extended visit to filmmaker Stan Brakhage and his family in Colorado; and in "Reel Four," John Lennon and Yoko Ono stage their Bed-In in Toronto.

12. See Patricia R. Zimmermann's *Reel Families: A Social History of Amateur Film* (Bloomington: Indiana University Press, 1995) for an overview of the history of home-movie making in the United States. Zimmermann mentions Mekas in her chapter "Reinventing Amateurism," 146.

13. According to Patricia Zimmermann, this emulation of Hollywood standards was at least partly a result of the fact that "by the 1950s photography and family magazine writers inscribed technical manipulation and a slavish conformity to Hollywood narrative visual logic as the goal of amateur production." Zimmermann, *Reel Families,* 122.

14. Thoreau, *Walden*, 6.

15. Mekas, in Scott MacDonald, *A Critical Cinema 2: Interviews with Independent Filmmakers* (Berkeley: University of California Press, 1992), 101.

16. Thoreau, *Walden*, 303.

17. In a sense, Mekas's filmmaking is merely a technological extension of his earlier career as a poet. Vyt Bakaitis discusses the relationship of Mekas's poetry and his diary filmmaking in James, *To Free the Cinema*, 121–37.

18. Greaves discusses the production process used in the Symbiopsychotaxiplasm project in Scott MacDonald, *A Critical Cinema 3: Interviews with Independent Filmmakers* (Berkeley: University of California Press, 1998), 42–63.

19. See Arthur F. Bentley, *Inquiry into Inquiries: Essays in Social Theory*, ed. Sidney Ratner (Boston: Beacon Press, 1954). In his first chapter Bentley defines terms:

> My friend Mr. M. A. Lane . . . has suggested a sort of terminology [more useful than "the individual" and "society"] derived throughout from Greek roots which will have sufficient elasticity to meet the needs of future investigations. . . . The initial term that of course suggests itself is *symbios*, life in common. (The fact that symbiosis is already a biological term is not a deterrent, because of the limited nature of the phenomenon the biologist uses it to designate.) Combine with this *taxis*, arrangement, and the final *osis*, and we get symbiotaxiosis, which may be used as a general term for the totality of the ordering or arrangement of social life. A symbiotaxium would be any society. Symbiotaxiplasm, or more simply taxioplasm, would be the mass of men (or, alternatively, any associated animals) and assimilated things which forms the society, regarded as matter. Symbiotaxis would be the social process or function regarded as such. (11–12)

20. Greaves, "Sunday in the Park with Bill," *The Independent* 15, no. 4 (May 1992): 26.

21. After my interview was published in *The Independent* (see note 20), the film's production manager, Bob Rosen, wrote to argue that while Greaves had made the most of the footage after the shooting was complete, he had not "deliberately adopted 'a flawed, vulnerable persona' in order to provoke the crew and the cast to rebel on camera." Rosen contends the film was made by a "flawed, vulnerable director, who was struggling to do something new and different without perhaps knowing what he was really doing." Greaves himself responded,

> [H]aving worked on scores of films before *Symbiopsychotaxiplasm*, I was consciously violating many of the basic conventions of filmmaking. These violations in scripting, shooting strategy, and directing of the two actors were often new and disturbing to the crew. They provoked discussion behind my back and, eventually, the crew's open rebellion. No doubt my "flawed, vulnerable persona" also helped trigger the crew's reactions, as did my periodic inscrutability . . . However, I did not "deliberately adopt a vulnerable persona to provoke the crew's on camera revolt." Rather than "pretending" vulnerabil-

ity, I was consciously allowing myself to be vulnerable in order to increase my credibility as a person on the screen. For a director to allow him—or herself—to be vulnerable on camera in this competitive world of filmmaking takes some courage, I think.

See Rosen's letter to the editor and Greaves's response in *The Independent* 15, no. 6 (July 1992): 2.

22. Greaves, "Sunday in the Park with Bill," 27.

23. Even Mekas's comparatively low-budget process was expensive enough that Mekas needed to wait until the 1970s and the institution of public grant support for film through such organizations as the National Endowment for the Arts and the New York State Council on the Arts to make completed films from footage shot in the 1950s and 1960s.

24. I have not been able to learn the name of Greaves's benefactor, who, according to Greaves, contributed $35,000 to the project. Greaves approximates the total cost of *Symbiopsychotaxiplasm: Take One* as somewhere between $100,000 and $150,000 (including the cost of the recent revision) and claims to have put $70,000 into the project. Greaves, in an unpublished interview with the author, July 8, 1995.

25. See Blackmar and Rosenzweig, *The Park and the People*, 214 ff.

26. When *Symbiopsychotaxiplasm: Take One* did not find a distributor in the 1970s, Greaves moved on to other projects. The film was revived by the Brooklyn Museum of Art as part of a 1991 retrospective of Greaves's career. It was presented at the Robert Flaherty Seminar in summer 1991. In May 1994 Greaves modified the version of *Symbiopsychotaxiplasm: Take One* that had been touring this country and Europe, adding 4 ½ minutes of material previously left out, to make clearer that *Take One* focuses on one couple of five and that one member of one of these couples was Susan Anspach, a well-known actress at the time.

27. For Greaves, who lives and maintains an office near Central Park, the contrast between the park and its commercial surround is a daily fact of life.

28. If Blackmar and Rosezweig's *The Park and the People* has a flaw, it is the authors' seemingly calculated refusal to admit the obvious: that Central Park—for all the less-than-savory social realities reflected in its development and history—is a work of genius.

29. Even this one reference to the "horsey set" is undercut by Greaves's yelling to the camerapeople, "Here's that woman with the tits! Get her! Get her! She's coming!" Though Greaves turns to the camera immediately after this and says, "I'm just kidding. Don't take me seriously!" whatever dignity might otherwise accrue to the horsewoman has been abrasively undercut.

30. Greaves, in MacDonald, *A Critical Cinema 3*, 28.

31. Greaves, in MacDonald, *A Critical Cinema 3*, 57.

32. The issue of ethnicity and the Olmsted park is also explored in Austin

Allen's feature documentary, *Claiming Open Spaces* (1995): Allen's film focuses on the controversy surrounding the use of Columbus's Franklin Park, an Olmsted-style park that had become a central dimension of African-American community life in Central Columbus, for Ameriflora, an international flower exposition that monopolized the park for years until the exposition failed and the black community reclaimed the park on Malcolm X Day in 1971. Allen uses the Franklin Park controversy as a catalyst for an exploration of five city parks, in five American cities, where the issues of open space and African-American community development, and in some cases rebellion, have been interwoven. The five parks Allen visits are Belle Isle (Detroit), an Olmsted park designed and built (though not completed according to Olmsted's design) in the 1880s and a crucial facet of black Detroit life; Congo Square (New Orleans), a gathering place for African diasporian culture (and a sometime flashpoint for slave rebellion) that in recent years has been replaced by a monument to Louis Armstrong; DeFremery Park (Oakland, California), a recreational space much used by the Oakland black community for a variety of youth activities—dances, clubs—until the city (seemingly as a result of the refusal of the black-run recreation program to buckle under to police excesses) redefined this and other Oakland parks as "natural" spaces and defunded the recreation program (DeFremery Park later became a center of Black Panther activities); and Kelly Ingram Park (Birmingham, Alabama), the space across from the state capitol building where rebellious blacks gathered (and were fire-hosed by police) during the height of civil rights activities in the early 1960s: the park is now a memorial to the struggle for civil rights.

Chapter 8. Rural (and Urban) Hours

Epigraph: Raymond Williams, *The Country and the City* (New York: Oxford University Press, 1973), 46.

1. In *The Magisterial Gaze: Manifest Destiny and American Landscape Painting c. 1830–1865* (Washington, D.C.: Smithsonian Institution Press, 1991), Albert Boime explores the paradox of this pattern: it was often precisely those who were profiting either directly or indirectly (as artists, for example) from industrialization who had the means to escape the city, experience the pleasure of living more fully in contact with nature, and bemoan its desecration (in which, of course, their very presence played a significant part). See, for example, Boime's discussion of Cyrus W. Field and Frederic Edwin Church, pp. 61–65.

2. Frampton, in Scott MacDonald, *A Critical Cinema: Interviews with Independent Filmmakers* (Berkeley: University of California Press, 1988), 49.

3. In *Push Comes to Shove* (New York: Bantam, 1992), Tharp's autobiography, p. 70.

4. The term "structural film," coined by P. Adams Sitney—see chapter 12 of

his *Visionary Film* (New York: Oxford University Press, 1974)—while useful, has always been problematic. Sitney's term focuses on the films of Frampton, Michael Snow, George Landow (a.k.a. Owen Land), Paul Sharits, Tony Conrad, Ernie Gehr, and Joyce Wieland, as "a cinema of structure in which the shape of the whole film is predetermined and simplified, and it is that shape which is the primal impression of the film" (407): "The structural film insists on its shape, and what content it has is minimal and subsidiary to the outline" (407–8). One difficulty with Sitney's definition is that nearly all forms of film—especially popular, mass market films—have easily identifiable shapes. Indeed, genre terminology—"horror film," "suspense thriller," "cartoon," and others—generally signifies the different "shapes" of popular films so that audiences can conveniently choose among them. Of course, to be fair to Sitney, he was defining one set of avant-garde films in a context of other forms of avant-garde cinema.

5. For the complete verses, see volume 1 of the *Heath Anthology of American Literature* (Lexington, Mass.: D. C. Heath, 1990), 308; or Scott MacDonald, *Screen Writings* (Berkeley: University of California Press, 1994), 54. *Screen Writings* also includes Frampton's original notes for *Zorns Lemma* and the text of the narration of the film's third section.

6. We *do* see the framed space within which there "should be" imagery; we are confronted with a *potential* for imagery.

7. Frampton's title is a reference to the eleventh axiom of set theory, the "existential axiom," originally conceptualized by the mathematician Max Zorn. It proposes, to use the simplest, least mathematical description, that within any set of sets there is a further set composed of a representative instance from each of the other sets. Zorn's lemma has sustained a variety of mathematical expressions. In their *Mathematics Dictionary*, 4th ed. (New York: Van Nostrand, 1976), for example, Glenn James and Robert C. James provide the following entry:

> *Zorn's Lemma.* The maximal principle: If *T is partially ordered* and each *linearly ordered* subset has an upper bound in *T,* then *T* contains at least one *maximal element* (and element $x<y$). Other alternative forms of this principle are: (1) (*Kuratowski's lemma*) Each simple ordered subset is contained in a maximal linearly ordered subset. (2) If a collection *A* of sets has the property that for each *nest* in *A* there is a member of *A* which contains each member of the nest, then there is a maximal member of *A*. (3) (*Hausdorff maximal principle*) If *A* is a collection of sets and *N* is a nest in *A*, then there is a nest *N* that contains *N* and is not contained in any larger nest. (4) (*Tukey's lemma*) A collection of sets which is of *finite character* has a *maximal member*. (5) Any set can be well ordered (see ORDERED—ordered set). (6) The axiom of choice (see CHOICE). If the finite axiom of choice is assumed, all of the above principles are logically equivalent.

8. After the schoolmarmy voice completes the verses from *The New England*

Primer, Frampton provides one run-through of the alphabet, using the letters alone, seen in relief.

9. Frampton, in MacDonald, *A Critical Cinema,* 54.

10. Frampton's inclusion of end-of-roll flares in the final section of *Zorns Lemma* has a good many precedents. Indeed, by the early 1970s flares and end-of-roll perforations had become a modernist signature in a body of work that aligned itself against the illusionism of the popular cinema. Early instances of flares and perforations can be found in Ken Jacobs's and Andy Warhol's first films and in George Kuchar's *Hold Me While I'm Naked* (1966).

11. For the complete text of Frampton's quotation of Grosseteste, see MacDonald, *Screen Writings,* 68–69.

12. Huot is also present in *Zorns Lemma* in at least two other places. He paints a wall as the replacement image for K, and his hand bounces a ball in the replacement image for O. The replacement image for K is an allusion to a conceptual-minimal painting by Huot, done at Paula Cooper Gallery in March 1969: *Two Blue Walls (Pratt & Lambert #5020 Alkyd): Sanded Floor Coated with Polyurethane: Shadows Cast by Architectural Details and Fixtures Using Available Light.* See Lucy Lippard, *Six Years* (New York: Praeger, 1973), 92, for a description and contextualization of Huot's contribution to early conceptual art.

13. Don McDonagh, *The Rise and Fall and Rise of Modern Dance* (New York: Outerbridge and Dienstfrey, 1970), 310.

14. Tharp, *Push Comes to Shove,* 72–73. Tharp seems to indicate that this painting used a new color of pink Huot had invented (71), but while Huot does remember the moment Tharp describes, he believes Tharp has combined two different paintings: *Goosthalf* (ca. 1965; the title is a pun on "goose" and "Gustav"), for which Huot mixed a new fluorescent pink (incidentally, this painting hung in Frampton's New York loft for several years); and *Chriss* (1964), the painting Huot believes Tharp pulled the tape off of (Huot in conversation with the author, December 11, 1998).

15. Huot and Frampton were for a time, in Huot's words, "as close as brothers" and had collaborated on several films, including Huot's *Black and White Film* (1969) and *Nude Descending the Stairs* (1970), for both of which Frampton was cameraperson. Frampton includes a portrait of Huot in *Manual of Arms* (1966), and Huot appears in *Artificial Light* (1969), Frampton's last completed film before *Zorns Lemma.* Frampton's *Lemon* (1969) includes the dedication "for Robert Huot."

In *Manual of Arms,* the Huot portrait can be read as a premonition of Huot's final appearance in *Zorns Lemma. Manual of Arms* is an homage to fourteen "friends and lovers," including several artists: Carl Andre, Rose Marie Castoro, Lucinda Childs, Lee Lozano, Larry Poons, Michael Snow, Twyla Tharp, Joyce Wieland—and Huot. While all the other artists sit until Frampton's portrait of them is complete, Huot's portrait ends with Huot standing up and walking out of the image: whether Frampton scripted this action, or merely accepted Huot's action, the implication is that Huot is a man of action who sits still for no one.

16. Throughout the 1970s, Huot made both diary films and "diary paintings." For the diary paintings Huot bought partial rolls of canvas from a canvas goods company. He would roll out a segment of canvas, paint it and let it dry, then roll that segment up, revealing the next segment of unpainted canvas, paint *that*, let it dry and roll it up, revealing the *next* segment, and so on. He would not see the entire painting until all segments were painted and he unrolled the entire painting on the lawn (he and Twyla Tharp do this in *Rolls: 1971*). Often the diary paintings were very long (the specific length was determined arbitrarily by the length of the rolls of canvas he bought)—sometimes as long as ninety feet (usually the diaries were eight feet high). In some diaries, individual segments are dated, and as one walks along the finished painting, one proceeds through the year.

In some ways, Huot's diary paintings are reminiscent of the moving panoramas of the nineteenth century, which were unrolled during exhibition (see chap. 1), though the movement in the moving panoramas was more spatial than temporal.

17. Frampton's description of replacement image K, "Painting a wall. Another simile = starting something + finishing it through human work. The space ends up white; the wall is the film frame" (in MacDonald, *Screen Writings,* 63), suggests that it may be a subtle in-joke that refers to Huot's *Black and White Film* (which Frampton shot), where a nude (white) actress, standing in a dark room in front of a black wall, paints herself black.

18. Susan Fenimore Cooper, *Rural Hours* (Athens: University of Georgia Press, 1998), "Tuesday, [May] 16th," 45, 46. I am quoting from the new, complete edition, edited by Rochelle Johnson and Daniel Patterson.

19. Aldo Leopold, "Wilderness," in *A Sand County Almanac* (New York: Oxford University Press, 1949), 188.

20. In chapter 2, "Arktitos," Lopez recontextualizes the four seasons of the Temperate Zone, seeing them from the perspective of the biseasonal winter/summer above the Arctic Circle.

21. A seasonally organized film that fits the first of the three options I've listed is Norman Bloom's ingeniously structured *Beaver Mountain Meditations* (1974), a fifty-minute film for which Bloom used the walk from his mailbox to his cabin in the woods (in Vermont) as one axis and the seasonal cycle as the other: having divided the walk into 365 segments, Bloom shot a few seconds a day from successive positions on the walk, so that as we travel from the mailbox to the cabin, we also travel through the seasons.

22. Dorsky, in an unpublished interview with the author, July 1998.

23. Dorsky's ability as cinematographer and editor has provided him a modest living since the 1960s. He has worked on a variety of films by other filmmakers.

24. For an accessible and beautifully illustrated introduction to the *The Book of Hours*, see Roger S. Wieck, *Painted Prayers: The Book of Hours in Medieval and Renaissance Art*, a catalog published on the occasion of the exhibition "Medieval Bestseller: *The Book of Hours*" at the Pierpoint Morgan Library (which houses one of two great collections of illuminated manuscripts in the United States; the Waters Art Gallery in Baltimore is the other), September 17 to January 4, 1997–98.

25. There were, of course, the traditional biblical stories: Adam and Eve, Cain and Abel, the Nativity, the Crucifixion, etc.; but also appeals to a fascination with the horrific not so different from the contemporary horror film—see, e.g., the following illustrations in Weick, *Painted Prayers:* p. 82 ("Isaiah Sawn Asunder," Rouen); pp. 96–97 ("Last Judgment," Bruges)—and to the erotic: see p. 95 ("Bathsheba at Her Bath").

26. The lives of the saints, including Saint Jerome, were frequently illustrated in *The Book of Hours*. For an illustration of Saint Jerome, see John Harthan, *The Book of Hours* (New York: Thomas Y. Crowell, 1977), 46, 48. Jerome Hiler is Dorsky's saint, not only because of their personal intimacy, but also because *this* Jerome, like Dorsky, is a filmmaker who has made filmmaking a spiritual quest. Dorsky claims Hiler as one of his primary cinematic inspirations, and believes his partner has been an inspiration to other filmmakers as well, though he rarely completes a film. According to Dorsky, Hiler sees filmmaking as a practice, rather than a means for producing products (Dorsky in conversation with author, July 1998). Hiler's working on film is a motif in *Hours for Jerome*.

27. After the long first shot, the passage speeds up: shot 2 (3 ½ seconds) reveals golden buds, filmed as the camera zooms in; shot 3 (13 seconds) is a long shot of woods that echoes the opening shot; shot 4 is a four-second shot of thin branches with green buds in close-up; shot 5, a four-second zoom-*out* (and fade out) of the golden buds, which is followed by a four-second close-up of the green buds from shot 4; then by a mini-montage of golden buds (this 79-frame mini-montage suggests the powerful energy at work in this apparently quiet spring woods); then by a nine-second shot of a stream; by a four-second shot of the green buds in close, this time in fuzzy focus; and finally, by a fourteen-second shot of a hillside woods. Even this breakdown of Dorsky's timing doesn't entirely convey the complexity of the sequence, since it is punctuated by tiny fades-in, fades-out, and moments of darkness.

28. See Eisenstein's influential discussion of collision montage in "The Cinematographic Principle and the Ideogram," in *Film Form: Essays in Film Theory*, ed. and trans. Jay Leyda (New York: Harcourt, Brace and World, 1949), 28–44.

29. Dorsky in conversation with the author, November 4, 1998.

30. *Hours for Jerome* is peppered with imagery that refers to meditation: in section 7 of Part Two, Dorsky concentrates on a man meditating: his inner vision is referenced by the gorgeous light periodically thrown onto him by a nearby win-

dow; in section 16 of Part Two, Dorsky zooms in on and away from beautiful autumn leaves—red, yellow, yellow-green—against a blue sky; the zooming transforms the leaves into high-energy mandalas . . .

31. In the 1920s it was found that 24 frames per second was technologically preferable for sound-on-film.

32. This constriction of options has proceeded by degrees. In the 1970s many 16mm projectors had a switch that allowed one to choose between 18 fps and 24 fps. Later, the switch disappeared and other, more complex adjustments were necessary: e.g., on the popular Eiki model RM1, the back of the projector could be removed, and an adjustment made, to slow the projector down to 18 fps. But in more recent models—the widely used Eiki SSL/ESL series, for example—sound speed is the only option. Of course, the original Lumière Cinématographes could show film at virtually any speed, and early projectionists had leeway in interpreting the filmed action with their projectors.

33. Dorsky in conversation with the author, November 4, 1998.

34. Angela Miller, *The Empire of the Eye: Landscape Representation and American Cultural Politics* (Ithaca: Cornell University Press, 1993), 243–44. Miller includes a useful review of the term "Luminism," which she replaces with "atmospheric luminism," which she borrows from Rodriquez Roque in *American Paradise: The World of the Hudson River School* (New York: Metropolitan Museum of Art, 1987), 47.

35. See Barbara Novak, *Nature and Culture: American Landscape Painting, 1825–1875* (New York: Oxford University Press, 1984), chaps. 2 and 3.

36. Film scholars are in the process of reconstructing early American film history, and while landscape has, so far, played little role in this process, a new generation of scholars has begun to recognize that even during the dawn of cinema history the depiction of landscape, or at least "landscape," was of significant importance, at least in American cinema. While landscape is not a central issue in the early actualities and protonarratives included on the reels of Edison and Lumière films that are in wide circulation in colleges and universities across the country, the "landscape film" was an early genre of American filmmaking. The Library of Congress lists dozens of titles that claim as their central focus not only American landscapes but also, in a good many instances, precisely those landscapes made so popular by the Hudson River and Rocky Mountain painters of the mid-nineteenth century: the Catskill Mountains, Niagara Falls, Yosemite Valley, Yellowstone. For a listing of these films, see Iris Cahn, "The Changing Landscape of Modernity: Early Film and America's 'Great Picture' Tradition," *Wide Angle* 18, no. 3 (July 1996): 85–100. However, while the titles of many of these early films identify landscape as their subject, it must be said that many of the films are really about railroad travel through landscape and are more fully focused on the railroad tracks *into* the landscapes than on the landscapes themselves.

37. In *Westerns: Making the Man in Fiction and Film* (Chicago: University of Chicago Press, 1996), Lee Clark Mitchell sees Albert Bierstadt's Western landscapes as formative in the development of the American Western. See chap. 3.

38. Baur apparently coined and explored "Luminism" in John I. H. Baur, "American Luminism, a Neglected Aspect of the Realist Movement in Nineteenth-Century American Painting," *Perspective USA*, no. 9 (Autumn 1954): 90–98. Ila Weiss reviews discussion of the topic in chapter 1 of *Poetic Landscape: The Art and Experience of Sanford R. Gifford* (Newark: University of Delaware Press/Associated University Presses, 1987); and the term is debated throughout *American Light: The Luminist Movement, 1850–1875*, a collection of overviews edited by John Wilmerding and published in 1980 by the National Gallery of Art in Washington, D.C., on the occasion of a major exhibition. See also note 34.

39. Novak, *Nature and Culture*, 32.

40. Miller, *The Empire of the Eye*, 243.

41. Steiner and Leo Hurwitz, "A New Approach to Film Making," *New Theatre* (September 1935): 22.

42. Steiner had begun one earlier film, the focus of which was amusing road signs, but he gave up on the project when he "realized that . . . if you're making a film, what you were filming should move. Revelation!" Steiner, quoted in Joel Zukor, "Ralph Steiner: Filmmaker and Still Photographer," a Ph.D. dissertation completed at New York University in 1976, pp. 120–21.

43. During research for my chapter on Steiner for Jan-Christopher Horak's *Lovers of Cinema: The First American Film Avant-Garde (1919–1945)* (Madison: University of Wisconsin Press, 1995), I divided H_2O into sections based on the particulars of Steiner's focus on water at various points in the film. During the first 3 minutes, 13 seconds, there are 39 shots (4.9 seconds/shot on the average); during the next 4 minutes, 53 seconds, 30 shots (9.7 seconds/shot); and during the final 4 minutes, 5 seconds, 22 shots (11 seconds/shot).

44. See Miller, *The Empire of the Eye*, chap. 7.

45. Exceptions result from Steiner's decision in a few, brief shots to turn his camera upside down; the result, for those perceptive enough to see it, is that in the finished film, these shots are in reverse. Of course, this "trick" too is solely a function of composing with the camera; it involves no other technology—though the impact is very different, "trickier," than right-side-up shooting.

46. In a superimposed text, in fact, Steiner argues that visually "bigness" is not necessarily better than "smallness"—a theme of several of his later works. In *Beyond Niagara*, however, the remarkable beauty of the images of Niagara Falls that Steiner includes to contextualize his investigation of the smaller rapids upstream undercuts his argument.

47. *Hooray for Light!* and the other landscape films he made in the late 1960s and early 1970s—he called the series "The Joy of Seeing"—are marred by music

sound tracks that not only do not enhance the visuals, but in general overdetermine our responses to them in unproductive ways. Indeed, it is my view that when seen silent, the "Joy of Seeing" films seem a good bit more impressive than seen as Steiner released them. Steiner's later films have received little attention, in part because they've long been out of distribution. *Hooray for Light!* and *One Man's Island* (1969) include Steiner's most impressive landscape work. Incidentally, Nathaniel Dorsky edited three of Steiner's "Joy of Seeing" films: *A Look at Laundry* (1971), *Beyond Niagara,* and *Look Park* (1974).

48. Hutton, in Scott MacDonald, *A Critical Cinema 3: Interviews with Independent Filmmakers* (Berkeley: University of California Press, 1998), 243–44. Hutton's earliest films, especially *July 1971 in San Francisco Living at Beach St. Working at Canyon Cinema, Swimming in the Valley of the Moon* (1971), and *Images of Asian Music* (1974) are visual diaries that have much in common with Huot's *One Year (1970)* and *Rolls: 1971.*

49. See Powell's overview of Luminism, "Luminism and the American Sublime," in Wilmerding, *American Light,* 80, 81.

50. Of course, commercial cinema was never truly silent: audiences have always made themselves heard, and musical accompaniment was a nearly automatic dimension of the film experience until sound-on-film made sound entirely automatic. Even those silent films produced by American independent filmmakers of the 1960s—Stan Brakhage is the most prominent example—for whom sound seemed an expensive, and, for a visual artist, an aesthetically unnecessary extra, were generally characterized by heavy editing (and sometimes shocking imagery), causing the films to seem visually "noisy," even without sound tracks.

51. The relationship between Hutton's film and Cole's bizarre painting is implicit. Much of Hutton's *In Titan's Goblet* focuses on a rubber fire that men on bulldozers are attempting to extinguish. The bulldozers are filmed from a considerable distance and the result is that they look like toys. This distortion in size echoes the even more obvious distortion of scale evident in Cole's painting.

52. Like Cole, however (and unlike the Luminists), Hutton is, at least from time to time, overtly moralistic about the dangers to the natural environment he records. This moralism is also evident in his imagery of New York City in *New York Portrait, Part II,* when he cuts from the imagery of the Statue of Liberty and a celebration in New York Harbor to a series of shots of homeless people. Cole generally moralizes by focusing on the passage of time; Hutton, by juxtaposing spaces that reveal the paradoxes of contemporary life.

53. The variation in the lengths of these moments of darkness seems a function of intuitive timing that has to do with allowing the viewer to "digest" one image and to prepare for the next.

54. The two shots that conclude *New York Portrait, Part I,* are particularly reminiscent of Fitz Hugh Lane, not only by virtue of their unusual composition—the

images are both deep and flat like Lane's and composed horizontally—but because they form a dyad: the second image reveals a space directly to the right of the first. Hutton simply panned his camera slightly rightward, just as Lane sometimes made discrete paintings of successive sections of his panoramic drawings. See Barbara Novak's illustration of Lane's panoramic drawings in *American Painting of the Nineteenth Century* (New York: Praeger, 1969), 118–19.

55. Also, the fact that Hutton's urban images are frequently reminiscent of the Luminists doesn't mean that the Luminists were a conscious reference. In fact, the particular images in the *New York Portrait* films suggest not just nineteenth-century painting, but twentieth-century photography. Shot 7 in *New York Portrait, Part II*, seems an obvious homage to Charles Sheeler, whose painting and photography Hutton admires, and who—in collaboration with Paul Strand—made *Manhatta* (1921), which intercuts between poetic texts and imagery of Lower Manhattan—a forerunner to Hutton's depictions of New York. See Jan-Christopher Horak's "Paul Strand and Charles Sheeler's *Manhatta*," in *Lovers of Cinema*, 267–86. And several images in *New York Portrait, Part I*, are reminiscent of Alfred Stieglitz. Indeed, the history of photography clearly plays an important role in Hutton's thinking: it's a relationship that could sustain a considerable discussion.

56. While the foregoing discussion argues for a connection between Hutton's work and Luminism, a different choice of films might lead to other kinds of connections. For example, despite its titular reference to Cole, Hutton's focus in *In Titan's Goblet* on the night sky could easily lead to a discussion of Hutton as a Tonalist, whose work is related to such painters as Albert Pinkham Ryder. Wanda M. Corn's description of the Tonalists—as painters who "confronted Nature as a private and extremely personal experience. They sought out its most gentle and intimate themes. . . . They were not interested in the grandiose drama of nature, but were attracted to its most suggestive moments—when burnt with the hues of autumn, at the break of dawn, in a clearing mist after rain and snow had bleached out sharp contrasts, or under the magic pall of night illumined by gaslamp or moonlight"—could easily refer to Hutton. See Corn's *The Color of Mood: American Tonalism, 1880–1910* (San Francisco: M. H. DeYoung Memorial Museum/California Palace of the Legion of Honor, 1972), 1.

Chapter 9. Expulsion from the Garden

Epigraph: This is the first haiku in Wright's collection, *Haiku: This Other World* (New York: Arcade, 1998), edited by Yoshinobu Hakutani and Robert L. Tener.

1. Cole's essay was originally published in *American Monthly Magazine* 1, n.s. (January 1836); and is included in John McCoubrey, ed., *American Art, 1700–1960*, Sources and Documents in the History of Art Series (Englewood Cliffs, N.J.: Prentice Hall, 1965), 98–109.

2. Cole, "Essay on American Scenery," 109.

3. The most distinguished version of the *Expulsion* is probably Masaccio's in the Capilla Brancacci of the Iglesia del Carmine, Florence, Italy.

4. I've quoted from Cole's letter to his patron, Daniel Wadsworth, of April 11, 1828, included in J. Bard McNulty, ed., *The Correspondence of Thomas Cole and Daniel Wadsworth* (Hartford: Connecticut Historical Society, 1983), 37. See Ellwood C. Parry III, *The Art of Thomas Cole: Ambition and Imagination* (Newark: Associated University Presses, 1988), 70–73, for a discussion of the two paintings as companion pieces. Until 1990, *The Garden of Eden* had been lost from public view for 160 years—and had not been seen with *Expulsion from the Garden of Eden* since 1828—until the Amon Carter Museum acquired it in 1990. The Amon Carter's exhibition of the two paintings together in 1994 was accompanied by the catalog, *Thomas Cole's Paintings of Eden* (Fort Worth: Amon Carter Museum, 1994), which includes " 'A Higher Style of Landscape': Thomas Cole's Paintings of Eden," by Franklin Kelly, and technical notes on the restoration of the painting by Claire M. Barry.

As Cole scholars have pointed out, Cole's paintings may have been indebted to the English landscape artist John Martin: specifically, to his series of mezzotints illustrating Milton's *Paradise Lost,* especially *Paphian Bower* (1826), *Adam and Eve—The Morning Hymn* (1825), and *Adam and Eve—Driven Out of Paradise* (1827). See Parry, *The Art of Thomas Cole,* 68–80; and " 'A Higher Style of Landscape': Thomas Cole's Paintings of Eden," 21–24, 36–40, for overviews of the controversy over Cole's use of Martin's imagery.

5. Cole to Daniel Wadsworth, April 23, 1918. McNulty, *The Correspondence of Thomas Cole and Daniel Wadsworth,* 38.

6. In terms of the way in which *The Garden of Eden* seems to guide my eye, these components seem articulated in much the same order as Cole elaborates them in his essay: my eye is drawn to the mountain and waterfall (and the lake or river it drops into), then explores the variety of foliage in the foreground and middle distance, then notices the sky.

7. Both Franklin Kelly and Bryan Jay Wolf discuss the relationships of Cole's paintings and Milton, in " 'A Higher Style of Landscape,' " 21–24; and in *Romantic Re-Visions: Culture and Consciousness in Nineteenth-Century American Painting and Literature* (Chicago: University of Chicago Press, 1982), 82–91.

8. See Bryan Jay Wolf's discussion in chapter 3 of *Romantic Re-Visions.*

9. Richard B. Altick discusses a variety of eighteenth-century entertainments that incorporated volcanic interruptions in chapter 7 of *The Shows of London* (Cambridge, Mass.: Harvard University Press, 1978); in his discussion of Philippe Jacques de Loutherbourg's elaboration of the magic lantern show—the Eidophusikon—which during its second season presented a vision of Pandemonium based on *Paradise Lost,* which included "mountains, ignited from their bases to

their lofty summits, with many colored flame" (chap. 9); and as part of Diorama shows (chap. 12).

10. See Parry, *The Art of Thomas Cole*, 89–90, 76–77.

11. Cole, "Essay on American Scenery," 109.

12. "Big Boy Leaves Home" is the opening story in Richard Wright's *Uncle Tom's Children*, a collection of five stories—"Big Boy Leaves Home," "Down by the Riverside," "Long Black Song," "Fire and Cloud," and "Bright and Morning Star"—preceded by the autobiographical essay "The Ethics of Living Jim Crow." Each story reenacts a particular biblical moment: "Big Boy Leaves Home," the Fall; "Down by the Riverside," the Flood; "Bright and Morning Star," the Crucifixion. In its original publication in 1937, *Uncle Tom's Children* included only the essay and the first four stories; "Bright and Morning Star" was added later.

13. For a review and analysis of the depiction of the swamp in nineteenth-century American literature and visual arts, see David C. Miller, *Dark Eden: The Swamp in Nineteenth-Century American Culture* (Cambridge: Cambridge University Press, 1989). Miller focuses on the swamp as a hideout for runaway slaves in his chapter 3.

14. The use of African-American actors to play people of other "races" has been widespread in American film history. *King Kong* is merely a noteworthy instance—one that includes at least one poignant irony: Noble Johnson, the actor who plays the tribal chief so memorably, worked in many Hollywood films, playing an Arab or a Mexican *and* was cofounder, with his brother, of Lincoln Pictures, one of the first Black Underground production organizations, in the wake of the success of D. W. Griffith's *The Birth of the Nation* (1915). See Thomas Cripps, *Slow Fade to Black* (London: Oxford University Press, 1977), chaps. 3 and 5, for further information on Johnson.

15. For a detailed discussion of the complex racial hierarchy developed in *King Kong*, see Fatimah Tobing Rony's *The Third Eye: Race, Cinema, and Ethnographic Spectacle* (Durham: Duke University Press, 1996), chap. 6.

16. The screenplay of *Daughters of the Dust* is available in Dash's *Daughters of the Dust: The Making of an African-American Woman's Film* (New York: New Press, 1992).

17. In her research, Dash discovered that "almost every Sea Island has a little inlet, or a little area where the people say, 'This is Ibo Landing. This is where it happened.'" The reason for the pervasiveness of the idea of Ibo Landing was crucial in Dash's thinking about the film: "[T]hat message is so strong, so powerful, so sustaining to the tradition of resistance, by any means possible, that every Gullah community embraces this myth. So I learned that myth is very important in the struggle to maintain a sense of self and to move forward into the future." Dash, *Daughters of the Dust*, 30.

18. Dash, *Daughters of the Dust*, 4.

19. Dash, in "Dialogue between bell hooks and Julie Dash, April 26, 1992," in Dash, *Daughters of the Dust,* 65–66.

20. *One False Move* was shot on location in the area of Cotton Plant, Brinkley, and Claridon, Arkansas, about halfway between Little Rock and Memphis. Cotton Plant is also a location in James Benning's *North on Evers* (1991), which is also about the issue of race and American nature: see chapter 10.

21. That this kind of relationship—and its abuse of power—isn't uncommon is suggested when the Texas Ranger Fantasia later shoots is talking with the countergirl at a little rest stop where Fantasia and Ray have just bought supplies. As the cop gazes after Fantasia, the countergirl says, "She's too young for you, Bill"; and Bill responds, "I like 'em young."

22. See Wright's analysis of Bigger Thomas in "How Bigger Was Born," in most modern editions of *Native Son.*

23. From the foreword to *A Sand County Almanac* (New York: Oxford University Press, 1949), ix.

24. For information about the Flaherty Film Seminars, see Erik Barnouw and Patricia Zimmermann, *The Flaherty: Four Decades in the Cause of Independent Cinema,* a special mega-issue of *Wide Angle* 17, nos. 1–4 (1995). The two films Mekas and the others were "fighting for" represent an early assault on conventional definitions of gender (Smith, who directed *Flaming Creatures* and is the protagonist of *Blonde Cobra,* was one of the first openly gay American filmmakers) and a defiance of the ideological and formal complacency of American commercial moviemaking, exemplified in the Hollywood Code. Indeed, the legal case that was generated by *Flaming Creatures* helped to topple the New York State censorship laws. See my discussion with Ken and Flo Jacobs about this incident in *A Critical Cinema 3: Interviews with Independent Filmmakers* (Berkeley: University of California Press, 1998), 374–75.

25. The sense of avant-garde cinema production/exhibition as a spiritual practice had a variety of implications for filmgoers. For example, much attention was given to screening conditions: devotees expected perfect exhibition and total silence in the theater, an expectation embodied most perfectly, perhaps, in Peter Kubelka's design for "The Invisible Cinema," a theater built for Anthology Film Archives, when it was housed in what is now the Public Theater in Manhattan: The Invisible Cinema was entirely black, so that nothing in the room was visible during projection except the image; and baffles were built between individual seats to prevent talking or other distractions. See P. Adams Sitney's introduction to *The Essential Cinema* (New York: Anthology Film Archives/New York University Press, 1975), vii–viii.

26. See Murphy's comments on his early involvement with alternative cinema in Scott MacDonald, *A Critical Cinema: Interviews with Independent Filmmakers* (Berkeley: University of California Press, 1988), 177–78.

27. The basic procedure used by Murphy and Small—mounting a camera to observe a carefully composed scene over time—has been widely used in film and in video. Among the most interesting instances are the Canadian David Rimmer's *Real Italian Pizza* (1971), which records a New York City street scene, including a pizza stand, from September 1970 until May 1971; Larry Gottheim's *Barn Rushes* (1972)—for which Gottheim mounted a camera in a car and drove past an upstate New York barn, filming eight, continuous, 100-foot-roll-long shots (approximately 3 minutes per shot), at various times of day; and Bill Viola's imagery of the Washington Monument, in the video *Ancient of Days* (1979–81). Of course, time-lapse is an intensification of this technique, and has been widely used not only by independent film- and videomakers but also in recent TV advertising (see chap. 6).

28. See Murphy's discussion of *In Progress* in MacDonald, *A Critical Cinema*, 182–83. Ed Small has remained involved in independent film and video, as a teacher and as a writer: his *Direct Theory: Experimental Film/Video as Major Genre* was published by Southern Illinois University Press in 1994.

29. Norman Bloom's film *House Painting* (1973)—an approximately seven-minute record of Bloom's cabin in the Vermont woods, during an autumn day, filmed at regular intervals (approximately eight seconds per interval) from dawn until dusk—is a perfect companion piece for *In Progress*.

30. For example, one image was made by shooting into a store window: in the "completed" image (the one closest to the original) we can see the store window display *and* the reflection of Murphy and his camera in the window. In another image, of a bird hopping in a backyard, we can only tell that it is raining during the one or two prints closest to the original.

31. British commercial director John Boorman has explored the parallel between the precariousness of green on modern film stocks and of the green surface layer of the Earth, in *The Emerald Forest* (1985), his film about the destruction of the Amazon jungle and of indigenous ways of life by a power company building a dam. Like other Boorman films—*Deliverance* (1972) and *Excaliber* (1981)—the *Emerald Forest* privileges green both as a film color and in the ecological sense.

32. I've discussed the film further in Scott MacDonald, *Avant-Garde Film/Motion Studies* (Cambridge: Cambridge University Press, 1993), chap. 4. See also James Peterson's *Dreams of Chaos, Visions of Order: Understanding the American Avant-Garde Film* (Detroit: Wayne State University Press, 1994), chap. 6.

33. Murphy's films of the late 1970s included three forays into what has come to be called "recycled cinema" (films that are made by "recycling" other films; see chap. 6, note 59). In *Ice* (1972), Murphy projected Franklin Miller's abstract film, *Whose Circumference Is Nowhere* (1970), on one side of a block of ice and rephotographed it from the opposite side, allowing the "lens" of the ice to transform the original imagery; in *Movie Stills* (1977) we watch a series of 300-foot-roll-long shots of Polaroid photographs developing; the photographs are of imagery shot by

Chuck Hudina; and for *Science Fiction* (1979), Murphy reedited an old science film, eliminating the science-lecture segments and thereby decontextualizing the bits of drama used originally to demonstrate the scientific ideas: the result is a funny, surreal travel film.

34. Avant-garde filmmaking has never received anything like adequate critical response either from reviewers or from academics. I am aware of no written comments that attack Murphy for his choice to "go commercial"; but I did hear such comments when I attended avant-garde screenings during the late 1970s and early 1980s—indeed, I have heard them recently.

35. Murphy, in MacDonald, *A Critical Cinema*, 185.

36. These figures are at best rough approximations, since it is often difficult to decide what production costs on independent films actually are. If the filmmaker, actors, and crew are not paid during the production, the production "cost" may seem quite small, despite contributions of time and energy that, in a more fully commercial production, would be worth considerable amounts of money.

37. Loseth auditioned for Carl Franklin's *Devil in a Blue Dress* (1995) and was called back several times before the female lead was awarded to Jennifer Beals.

Chapter 10. Satan's National Park

Epigraph: Anne Carson, "God's Justice," in *Glass, Irony and God* (New York: New Directions, 1995), 49.

1. While many states boast impressive systems of state parks, New York was "the first state not merely to preserve the environment but also to restore it and, moreover, to pay to do so." National Heritage Trust, *Fifty Years—State Parks* (Albany: National Heritage Trust, 1975), 4.

2. Ernest Hemingway, *Green Hills of Africa* (New York: Scribner's, 1935), 148–50.

3. As Hemingway explains, "A continent ages quickly once we come. The natives live in harmony with it. But the foreigner destroys, cuts down trees, drains the water, so that the water supply is altered and in a short time the soil, once the sod is turned over, is cropped out and, next, it starts to blow away as it has blown away in every old country and as I had seen start to blow away in Canada. . . . I suppose they all end up like Mongolia (*Green Hills of Africa*, 284–85).

4. David E. Nye traces the early stages of the development of the "technological sublime" in *American Technological Sublime* (Cambridge, Mass.: MIT Press, 1996).

5. In an interview, I asked Watkins if he planned to dramatize atomic/nuclear war as he had done so powerfully in *The War Game* (1965); he responded, "Absolutely no. What we must move away from now is the feeling that a nuclear war is inevitable. To continue to dramatize the effects of nuclear holocaust can only serve a negative purpose now." *The Independent* 7, no. 9 (October 1984): 24.

6. In February 1999 Conner wrote me, in response to several questions I had sent to him, that "the original material from the National Archives is exactly what you see. I own the splices and the use of the music and titles. I used about 20% of what I bought. I was careful about what I purchased. . . . I did not change any speed on the footage."

7. The German titles of the sections are: 1. "Ein Hauptstadt"; 2. "Der Krieg"; 3. "Nach der Schlacht"; 4. "Fundstücke aus Folterkammern"; 5. "Satan's Nationalpark"; 6. "Kindheit"; 7. "Es stieg ein Rach auf, wie ein Rach vom ofen"; 8. "Eine Wallfahrt"; 9. "Saurier unterwegs"; 10. "Protuberanzen"; 11. "Das Versiegne der Quellen"; 12. "Leben ohne Feuer"; 13. "Ich bin so müde vom Seufzen"; 14. "Herr, laß es abend werden."

8. In "Satan's National Park" the narrator quotes Revelations 16:18–20: "And there were flashes of lightning, loud noises, peals of thunder, and a great earthquake such as had never been since men were on the earth, so great was that earthquake. The great city was split into three parts, and the cities of the nations fell. . . . And every island fled away, and no mountains were to be found"; in "And Smoke Arose Like a Smoke from a Furnace," the narrator quotes Revelations 9:1–2, 6: "And the fifth angel blew his trumpet, and I saw a star fallen from heaven to earth, and he was given the key of the shaft of the bottomless pit, and from the shaft rose smoke like the smoke of a great furnace, and the sun and the air were darkened with the smoke from the shaft"; "And in those days men will seek death and will not find it; they will long to die, and death will fly from them." I'm quoting from the *Oxford Annotated Bible,* the 1962 Revised Standard Version (New York: Oxford University Press, 1962).

9. John F. Sears, *Sacred Places: American Tourist Attractions in the Nineteenth Century* (New York: Oxford University Press, 1989), 169–70. Among those who saw Yellowstone as unappealing, at least in part, was Rudyard Kipling. In *From Sea to Sea: Letters of Travel* (1910), Kipling, too, saw Yellowstone as suggestive of Hell but—like many tourists then and now—was amused by the connection. In No. 30, Kipling describes "the uplands of Hell. They call it the Norris Geyser Basin on Earth. . . . Not ten yards from the road a blast of steam shot up roaring every few seconds, a mud volcano spat filth to Heaven, streams of hot water rumbled under foot, plunged though the dead pines in steaming cataracts and died on a waste of white where green-gray, black-yellow, and pink pools roared, shouted, bubbled, or hissed as their wicked fancies prompted." In No. 31: "I think they call it the Riverside Geyser. Its spout was torn and ragged like the mouth of a gun. . . . It grumbled madly for a moment or two and then was still. I crept over the steaming lime—it was the burning marl on which Satan lay." I've quoted from the Mandalay Edition of Kipling's works (Garden City: Doubleday, Page, 1925), 1:125–26, 135.

10. Langford, "The Wonders of Yellowstone," *Scribner's Monthly* 2 (May–June 1871): 10.

11. Wolfgang Schivelbusch, *The Railway Journey: The Industrialization of Time and Space in the 19th Century* (Berkeley: University of California Press, 1986), 1–2.

12. *Shoah: The Complete Text* (New York: DaCapo Press, 1995), iii.

13. I am using Sandy Flitterman-Lewis's translation, included in her fine analysis of *Night and Fog* in "Documenting the Ineffable: Terror and Memory in Alain Resnais's *Night and Fog*," chapter 12 of Barry Keith Grant and Jeannette Sloniowski, eds., *Documenting the Documentary* (Detroit: Wayne State University Press, 1998), 207.

14. Annette Insdorf's *Indelible Shadows: Film and the Holocaust* (Cambridge: Cambridge University Press, 1989), now in its second edition, remains the authoritative text on cinematic depictions of the Holocaust. Some would argue, with considerable justification, that Marcel Ophuls's *The Sorrow and the Pity* (1971) and *Hotel Terminus* (1988) are equal to *Night and Fog* and *Shoah;* but my sense is that, as remarkable as these films are, their influence, at least in the United States, is not comparable to the Resnais and Lanzmann films.

15. I am simplifying, but only slightly. Survivors' stories are presented primarily by Abraham Bomba, Richard Glazar, Filip Müller, Simon Srebnik, and Rudolf Vrba, with contributions of varying lengths from a dozen or so other interviewees, plus information from Adam Czerniakow's diary of life in the Warsaw ghetto that is presented by Holocaust historian Raul Hilberg. Lanzmann talks briefly with perhaps two dozen Polish villagers, and at greater length with a few of what he calls (in the booklet distributed with the VHS version of *Shoah*) "bystanders": Czestaw Borowi, Henrick Gawkowski, and Jan Piwonski, plus, near the end, the scholar Jan Karski, who visited the Warsaw ghetto in 1942. Two Nazis (first, Franz Suchomel, SS Unterstürmführer; and later, Walter Stier, former head of Reich Railways) are filmed with hidden cameras; two others—Mrs. Michelson, wife of a Nazi schoolteacher in Chelmno; and Dr. Franz Grassier, deputy to the Nazi commissioner of the Warsaw ghetto—agreed to talk on-camera. Lanzmann also confronts Joseph Oberhauser in a Munich beer hall about his involvement at Belzec, but Oberhauser refuses to speak with him. Clearly, for a 9 ½-hour film, the number of interviewees is quite small.

16. Here, and throughout this discussion, I'm using the English translations in *Shoah: The Complete Text*.

17. Simon Schama explores the history of the sacred wood and the holy confluence, specifically in relation to the Holocaust, in *Landscape and Memory* (New York: Knopf, 1995).

18. Much research has been done on the moving panorama and on the panoramic tendency of much mid-nineteenth-century American painting. See chap. 1, notes 15, 17.

19. Eisenstein, in "The Cinematographic Principle and the Ideogram," in *Film Form*, ed. and trans. Jay Leyda (New York: Harcourt, Brace and World, 1949), 38.

20. Obviously, much of this volume is devoted to key instances of this counter-cinema, though the movement may be said to begin with Andy Warhol's defiantly slow films of the mid-1960s.

21. To put this within a more particular cinematic trajectory: Lanzmann's exploration of the city that was Auschwitz-Birkenau is cinema's most potent critique of the city symphony form that took its name from that (remarkable) visual paean to modern German industrialization: Ruttmann's *Berlin: Symphony of a Big City*. See chap. 6.

22. "Especially restoration" because the decision *not* to fully restore Native American ruins (which would necessitate the return of artifacts that fill American museums of natural history) suggests that the ruination of certain ways of life was essential for the evolution of "ours."

23. Formally, the city symphony form is a composite day in the life of a nation's preeminent city. Lanzmann does not create a composite day; nevertheless, the kinds of imagery of Warsaw included in *Shoah* are reminiscent of the great European city symphonies of the 1920s—and especially of Ruttmann's *Berlin*—and of more recent American instances of the form.

24. The Lodz ghetto confined 165,000 people to 1.6 square miles. By comparison, the population density of New York City is about 25,000 people per square mile.

25. The pace of *Shoah*'s visuals is consistently slow, throughout the film, so consistently in fact that the single instance of more conventional pacing I am aware of—a moment during Jan Karski's narrative of his visit to the Warsaw ghetto where we see three brief shots (2.9, 2.7, and 2.6 seconds long) of items, now overgrown and almost invisible, taken from the Jews on their arrival at one of the extermination camps—is clearly the exception that proves the rule.

26. The Land Ordinance of 1785 went into effect on May 20; substantial excerpts are reprinted in Henry Steele Commager, ed., *Documents of American History*, 4th ed. (New York: Appleton-Century-Crofts, 1948), 123–24.

27. See chap. 8, note 5. Sitney's category and the assumption of some critics, historians, and filmmakers of the 1970s that structural film was *the* legitimate new cinematic avenue became the subject of considerable contestation.

28. I have argued elsewhere that the new feminist cinema of the 1970s and 1980s *used* structural concerns as a means of responding to conventional cinema's usual ways of gendering narrative. See part 2 of my *Avant-Garde/Motion Studies* (Cambridge: Cambridge University Press, 1993).

29. Benning's imagery is accompanied by sound, but nearly all the shots are relatively quiet, except for the narration; the sound track feels minimal. All the sound was recorded separately from the imagery, and was postsynched. While in

general the sound seems ambient and is virtually "invisible," at times Benning uses sound more suggestively.

30. The network of sound-image interconnections Benning develops in *Deseret* is reminiscent of the sound-image structuring of Larry Gottheim's *Mouches Volantes* (1976) and *Four Shadows* (1978), and of the complex visual rhymes in Gottheim's *Horizons* (1973; see chap. 2).

31. The racial bigotry institutionalized in Topaz is a pervasive theme in *Deseret*, from the racism of Mormons and others toward Indians, which remains an issue throughout the film, to the refusal of the Mormon Church to treat even Hawaiian converts equally, to the decision by the Mormon Church on June 10, 1978, that— as a result of a divine revelation—blacks could be ordained into the Mormon priesthood. Despite various responses to bigotry, Benning makes clear that racism remains alive and well in Utah, as it is virtually everywhere in America.

32. Use of Utah as a mock battlefield began in 1914: the "April 26, 1914," *Times* story announces that "President Wilson . . . withdrew today 18,700 acres of public land in Utah for use of the Utah National Guard as a target range and manoeuvre grounds."

33. During the first half of the film, Benning's black-and-white shots are composed in a manner that evokes the imaging of the West by the generation of American photographers that included Timothy O'Sullivan, William H. Jackson, A. J. Russell, Carleton Watkins, and Eadweard Muybridge. In conversation with me (in November 1998), Benning indicated that he was not particularly aware of the photographic history of the West—except for Ansel Adams. What this suggests to me is the power of Western landscape to demand respectful, often classic, symmetrical photographic compositions.

34. A more sophisticated history of the concept of entropy, including its development by the German physicist Rudolf Clausius in 1865 and subsequent explorations of the idea, is available in any encyclopedia.

35. Benning's admiration of *The Spiral Jetty* is also obvious in *North on Evers* (see chap. 4): Benning visits *The Spiral Jetty*, films, provides background, and conjectures that, in a sense, his journey around the United States "ended there at the end of the spiral."

36. The four artworks are Monet's *Poppy Field in a Hollow near Giverny* (1885), which is composed so that a rectangular, i.e, "four-cornered," bed of poppies is in the center of the painting: the nearer two corners coincide with the corners of the film frame; Tolliver's *George Washington* (1989), painted while looking at a dollar bill; "Yukuwa's" pictograph, which Benning imagines was painted around A.D. 100; and Johns's *Flag* (1955), a pencil sketch of an American flag.

37. As in *Deseret*, all the imagery was recorded first and the sound added later. The forty-second length is not entirely adhered to: Benning allows himself a bit of leeway, to accommodate his sense of timing.

38. Benning is aware that, despite his counter-Hollywood aesthetic, he is, in some ways, complicit with the industry. Benning: "I'm also somebody who's demanding a service that's polluting the earth: filmmaking isn't a clean industry, so one can question my righteous view. We're *all* the enemy in this story. To make *Deseret,* I drove to Utah from California nine times." Benning in an unpublished interview with the author, March 23, 1996.

39. Benning has continued to explore the West in two recent features: *Utopia* (1999) and *El Valley Centro* (1999). *Utopia* is a visual exploration of desert terrain from Death Valley south into northern Mexico, accompanied by a stolen sound track (Benning explains at the beginning of *Utopia,* "Except for some additional ambience, the entire soundtrack of this film has been taken [without permission] from *Ernesto Che Guevara, the Bolivian Journal* by Richard Dindo"). Benning's combination of landscape imagery and recycled sound creates a complex viewing experience involving a variety of forms of intersection between image and sound, including an awareness of how Che Guevara's activities in Bolivia were and are relevant to the Mexican-American border territory.

For those familiar with Cormac McCarthy's Border Trilogy (*All the Pretty Horses, The Crossing, Cities of the Plain*), the image of Benning traveling the desert, as part of a quest to use his filmmaking, not simply to honor the remarkable look of the land, but to confront its complex history, may suggest McCarthy's John Grady Cole and Billy Parham.

El Valley Centro, just completed as I write this, focuses on California's Central Valley as an American paradigm of agricultural exploitation.

Chapter 11. Benedictions/New Frontiers

Epigraph: From two letters by William James to Pauline Goldmark, excerpted in Josephine Goldmark, "An Adirondack Friendship: Letters of William James," *Atlantic* 154, no. 3 (October 1934): 268, 265.

1. There are exceptions to this pattern, the most obvious of which is Zen Buddhism, which has developed a high level of respect in certain sectors of academe—and has been a major influence on American art for half a century.

2. I've used the figures Claude Lanzmann supplies in the pamphlet distributed with the VHS of *Shoah* (1985).

3. Strand is not clear where she found this haiku.

4. According to Strand, the women are actually swimming in a pool, but the natural sounds create a sense of an Edenic natural space. This sequence is invisibly edited so that we seem to be seeing a continuous shot.

5. The rippling water was shot at Tomales Bay on the Pacific, just north of Marin County, California.

6. Douglas Burton-Christie, *The Word in the Desert: Scripture and the Quest for Holiness in Early Christian Monasticism* (New York: Oxford University Press, 1993), 146.

7. Noren, in Scott MacDonald, *A Critical Cinema 2: Interviews with Independent Filmmakers* (Berkeley: University of California Press, 1992), 178.

8. The most useful exposition of Brakhage's vision/Vision remains his own *Metaphors on Vision*, special issue of *Film Culture*, no. 30 (Fall 1963). See chap. 3, note 46.

9. All of us remain indebted to P. Adams Sitney's yeoman work on early Brakhage, work that culminated in his *Visionary Film* (New York: Oxford University Press, 1974). See chap. 3, note 47, for information on other Brakhage sources.

10. In the *Ithaca Times* (October 2–8, 1997, 15), Brakhage told Kenny Berkowitz, "For me, painting on film has always been my favorite activity as a filmmaker—I had been painting for years, and had no thought that I would be doing anything but painting for the rest of my life."

11. Brakhage, in an unpublished interview with the author, October 28, 1998. As of 2001, Brakhage seems to have recovered from the surgery; no sign of the cancer remains. As late as October 1997, nearly a year after the surgery, however, Brakhage would tell Kenny Berkowitz, "I have a fifty-fifty chance to survive the next two years." See note 10.

12. Brakhage, in conversation with the author, October 28, 1998.

13. Noren, in MacDonald, *A Critical Cinema 2*, 176–77.

14. Noren was a prolific filmmaker in the 1960s, though most of his early films were lost in a fire; indeed, his presence in the underground film scene of that era resulted in Jim McBride's modeling his David Holzman—in *David Holzman's Diary* (1967)—on Noren. Of course, anyone who has met Noren, or who knows Noren's *Huge Pupils* (1968), will recognize that David Holzman is a far less complex figure than the real Noren. For information on the relationship of Noren and David Holzman, see L. M. Carson, introduction to the screenplay of *David Holzman's Diary* (New York: Farrar, Straus & Giroux, 1970), viii–ix.

15. Noren's slowing the sound also lowers the tone of the gong; and the lower and slower the striking is, the more evident the sound reverberations. It should be noted that, while *Imaginary Light* is clearly and definitely structured, Noren's structure is flexible and intuitive, rather than rigorously formal: e.g., the framing passages are not of equal length (the opening passage lasts fifty-nine seconds, the concluding passage only fifty seconds; and the slowing of the pace of the clock striking is generally, but not specifically, consistent: during one passage, I timed every other interval for several minutes; the results, in seconds, 13/11/14/14/12/12/14/15.

16. E-mail to author, December 13, 1998.

17. Noren, in MacDonald, *A Critical Cinema 2*, 199.

18. In my experience using *Riddles of the Sphinx* at Utica College and at Hamilton College, I discovered that *no* topic seems as terrifying to upper-middle-class young people as domestic labor, especially child care: it is, for them, the essence of boredom. In fact, I have begun to use a postscreening ritual as a segue into a discussion of the film. I ask students to write "Riddles of the Sphinx" on a piece of paper, then crumple the paper up into a hard little ball, stand, and at a pre-arranged signal throw the paper balls at me with as much energy as they can. This ritual "stoning" seems essential in venting the frustration created by the film, so that the implications of this frustration and of the film's revolutionary approach can be explored.

I discuss *Riddles* in more detail in *Avant-Garde Film/Motion Studies* (Cambridge: Cambridge University Press, 1993), 79–92.

19. One obvious exception may seem to be that prolific strand of documentary (and avant-garde) film history where filmmakers use their personal relationships and family life as subject matter—well-known instances include Martha Coolidge's *David: Off and On* (1973), Amalie Rothschild's *Nana, Mom and Me* (1974), Ed Pincus's *Diaries* (1976), Mitchell Citron's *Daughter Rite* (1978), Ross McElwee's *Backyard* (1982) and *Time Indefinite* (1993), Su Friedrich's *Sink or Swim* (1990), and Alan Berliner's *Nobody's Business* (1997)—but the focus of these films is the melodrama of family life, not domestic space and domestic labor.

20. See Hutton's comments in Scott MacDonald, *A Critical Cinema 3: Interviews with Independent Filmmakers* (Berkeley: University of California Press, 1998), 244, quoted more fully in chapter 8.

21. Unpublished interview with Pierce, October 21, 1998. Pierce is referring, of course, to Stan Brakhage's famous attempts to return to a form of vision "under childhood," before language, and to use film as a way of creating metaphors for innocent, untrained, child vision. Brakhage's films and Pierce's films and videos provide a useful context for each other.

22. It is a convention of avant-garde film exhibition that filmmakers are present at screenings of their films. Pierce's experience of seeing the long version of *50 Feet of String* with audience after audience (and often with audiences relatively new to avant-garde cinema in general and serenely paced films in particular) caused him to have second thoughts about the extent of the original version. While the shorter version of *50 Feet of String* is certainly impressive, I prefer the challenge of the original duration.

23. Only two shots in *50 Feet of String* break this rule: the long continuous shot from "pickup truck" discussed later, and the shot of rippling water (recorded in the Adirondacks) that immediately precedes that shot.

24. Because the option of inexpensive synchronized sound came later to low-budget, avant-garde filmmaking, avant-garde filmmaking has tended to deal with

sound in one of two ways: some filmmakers have defined cinema as essentially a visual art and have refused sound altogether; others privilege the visuals but assume viewers need sound *accompaniment* in order to make watching the visuals comfortable.

25. In an e-mail on December 21, 1998, Pierce described three aspects of his subtle, complex technique, focusing at times on a particular moment in *50 Feet of String* during the "50 feet of string" section:

> #1. Depth of field and flatness.
> I want to get the shallowest depth of field possible (shortest amount of Z-axis in sharp focus). To do this I open up the iris all the way (shooting usually an f-2 or 2.8). Since I'm usually out in bright sun I need to cut the light with neutral density filters and usually a polarizing filter as well. Shooting at a high frame rate also cuts the light down significantly. To reduce depth of field even more, I also use the telephoto end of the 10–100mm zoom lens (usually a Zeiss 10–100 but sometimes a 50 or 75mm prime lens—*Red Shovel* [1991] was a Bolex with a 150mm lens). This also has the effect of reducing the perceived depth of the image—flattening it somewhat. Interestingly, since the frame seems flatter from the telephoto effect, lateral movement in different planes creates surprising figure ground relationships.
>
> #2. Diffraction (light getting bent around edges of solid objects).
> In a lot of shots in *50 Feet*—for example, the toy tractor moving toward the camera in a field of shimmery grass [see plate 24], also in *Red Shovel* and *Glass* [1998]—I use diffraction to color the depth. Edges of solid objects close to the lens are out of focus but they bend the light coming into the lens from more distant objects. . . . With a telephoto lens and shallow depth of field, that effect can be concentrated. If there are many objects all out of focus and waving around (like grass or weeds) you can really start messing with those distant light rays.
>
> #3. Camera position.
> This is obvious I suppose, but small changes in camera position create extremely different perceptions of the activity in the frame. The toy tractor shots (and many others too, I'll just keep to this example) took most of the morning to set up and shoot. I changed elevation, tilt, angle, location, etc., in very small increments. Since I was on the ground, a few inches in elevation drastically changed the horizon and the effect of the out of focus but diffracting grass. This might explain partly why I shoot from the ground so much, I like the effect of grass. It also causes me to keep my grass longer than the socially accepted norm!

26. There are precedents for Pierce's use of refocusing within a single shot. It is a figure of style in Nathaniel Dorsky's *Summerwind* (1965) and is *the* structuring device in Barry Gerson's *Metamorphosis* (1970). Indeed, the relationships between Gerson's work and Pierce's are worth exploring at length.

27. Unpublished interview with Pierce, October 21, 1998. Pierce has continued to work on sound pieces, not *musique concrète,* but what he calls "imageless movies."

28. Unpublished interview, October 21 1998.

29. E-mail to author, February 6, 1999. See also Ernie Gehr's similar use of sound in *Side/Walk/Shuttle* (see chap. 6).

30. One notable precedent for Pierce's creation of sound events that "move past us" without actually becoming part of the visual image is the early films of James Benning, especially *11 × 14* (1976) and *One Way Boogie Woogie* (1977), in which such moments are a central figure of style.

31. Leighton Pierce, in Scott MacDonald, "Transcendental Domesticity: An Interview with Leighton Pierce," *The Independent* 22, no. 6 (July 1999): 34.

32. Unpublished interview, October 21, 1998. The nature writer Terry Tempest Williams is best known for *Refuge* (New York: Random House, 1991).

33. Emerson's comments are found in the numbered sections of the universally anthologized "Self-Reliance": in the third paragraph of no. 2 and in the first paragraph of no. 3.

34. Henry David Thoreau, *Cape Cod* (New York: Penguin, 1987), 76, 133.

35. The 1980s saw a variety of such statements; the most widely discussed was probably Fred Camper's "The End of Avant-Garde Film," published in the twentieth anniversary issue of *Millennium Film Journal,* nos. 16–18 (1986–87): 99–124. Camper's essay was a primary instigation of the International Experimental Film Congress, held in Toronto in 1989.

36. Gatten in an e-mail to the author, December 10, 1998. Subsequent comments by Gatten are from the same e-mail.

37. Gatten's title is a variation on the title of part five of T. S. Eliot's *The Waste Land* (1922), "What the Thunder Said," which follows the short fourth section, "Death by Water," from which Gatten got one of the two texts with which he opens the film: "A current under sea/Picked his bones in whispers. As he [Phlebas the Phoenician] rose and fell/He passed the stages of his age and youth/Entering the whirlpool." The other introductory quotation is from an unpublished Nathaniel Hawthorne story, "The Devil in Manuscript." Gatten found the passage in Susan Howe's *The Birth-mark* (Hanover, N.H.: Wesleyan University Press, 1993), 8: "The papers were indeed reduced to a heap of black cinders, with a multitude of sparks hurrying confusedly among them, the traces of the pen being now represented by white lines, and the whole mass fluttering to and fro, in the draughts of air."

38. The length of the three sections of *no. 2:* 30 seconds; 3 minutes, 35 seconds; and 1 minute, 50 seconds; the lengths of *no. 3:* 1 minute, 10 seconds; 55 seconds; 30 seconds.

Index

Designer: Nola Burger   **Compositor:** BookMatters   **Text type:** 9.5/14.25 Scala
Display type: Franklin Gothic Book and Demi   **Printer and binder:** Friesens